The Gifted Passage

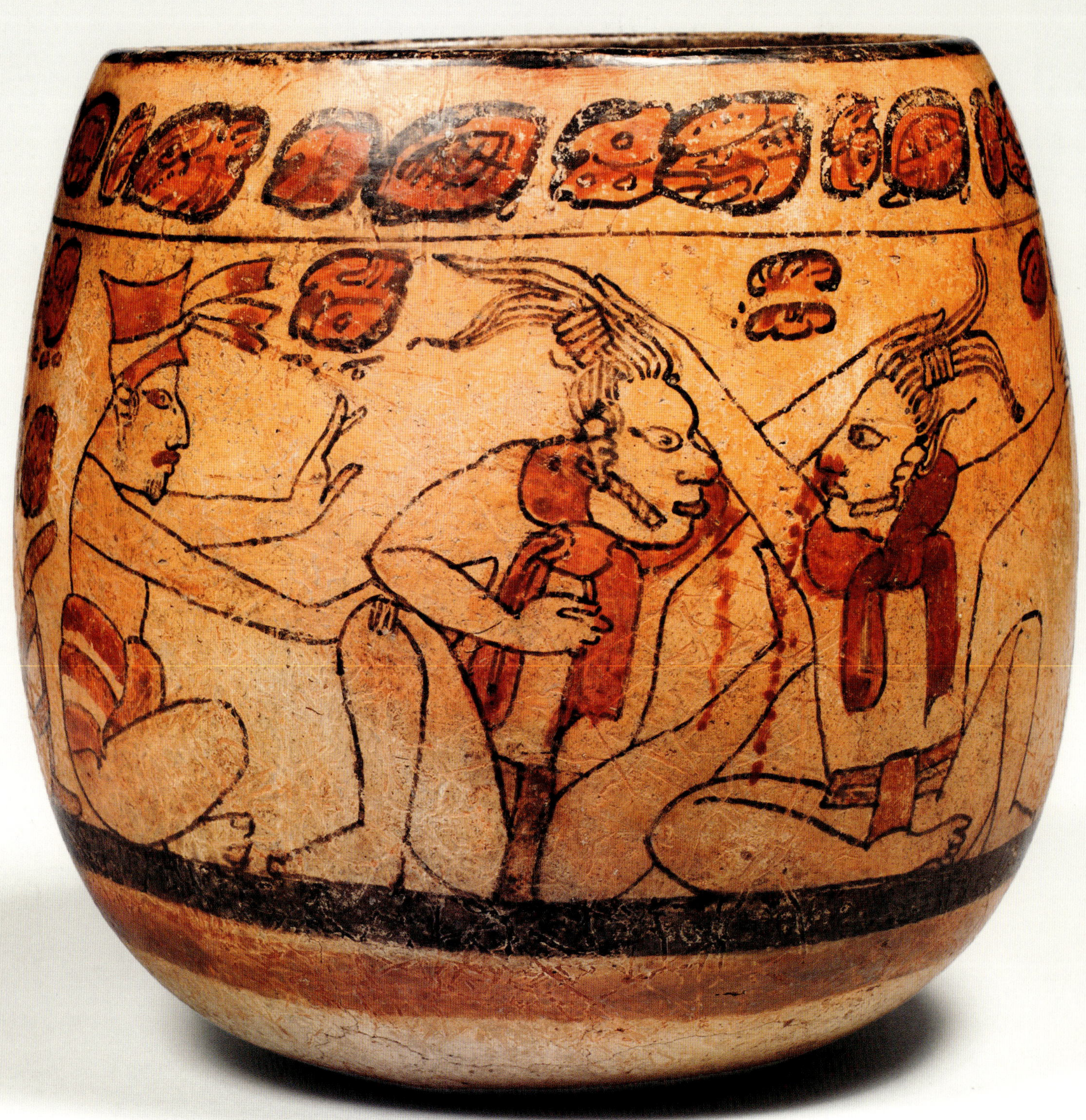

The Gifted Passage

Young Men in Classic Maya Art and Text

Stephen Houston

Yale University Press   New Haven and London

Designed by Leslie Fitch
Set in Crimson and Source Sans Pro type by Leslie Fitch
Printed in China through Oceanic Graphic International, Inc.

Library of Congress Control Number: 2017938184
ISBN 978-0-300-22896-0
A catalogue record for this book is available from the British Library.
This paper meets the requirements of ANSI/NISO Z 39.48-1992 (Permanence of Paper).

10 9 8 7 6 5 4 3 2 1

Jacket illustrations: (front) Mirror back with youths (detail of fig. 27); (back) Shield Jaguar III and young noble (fig. 86).

Frontispiece: Maya chocolate or maize porridge bowl (fig. 3).

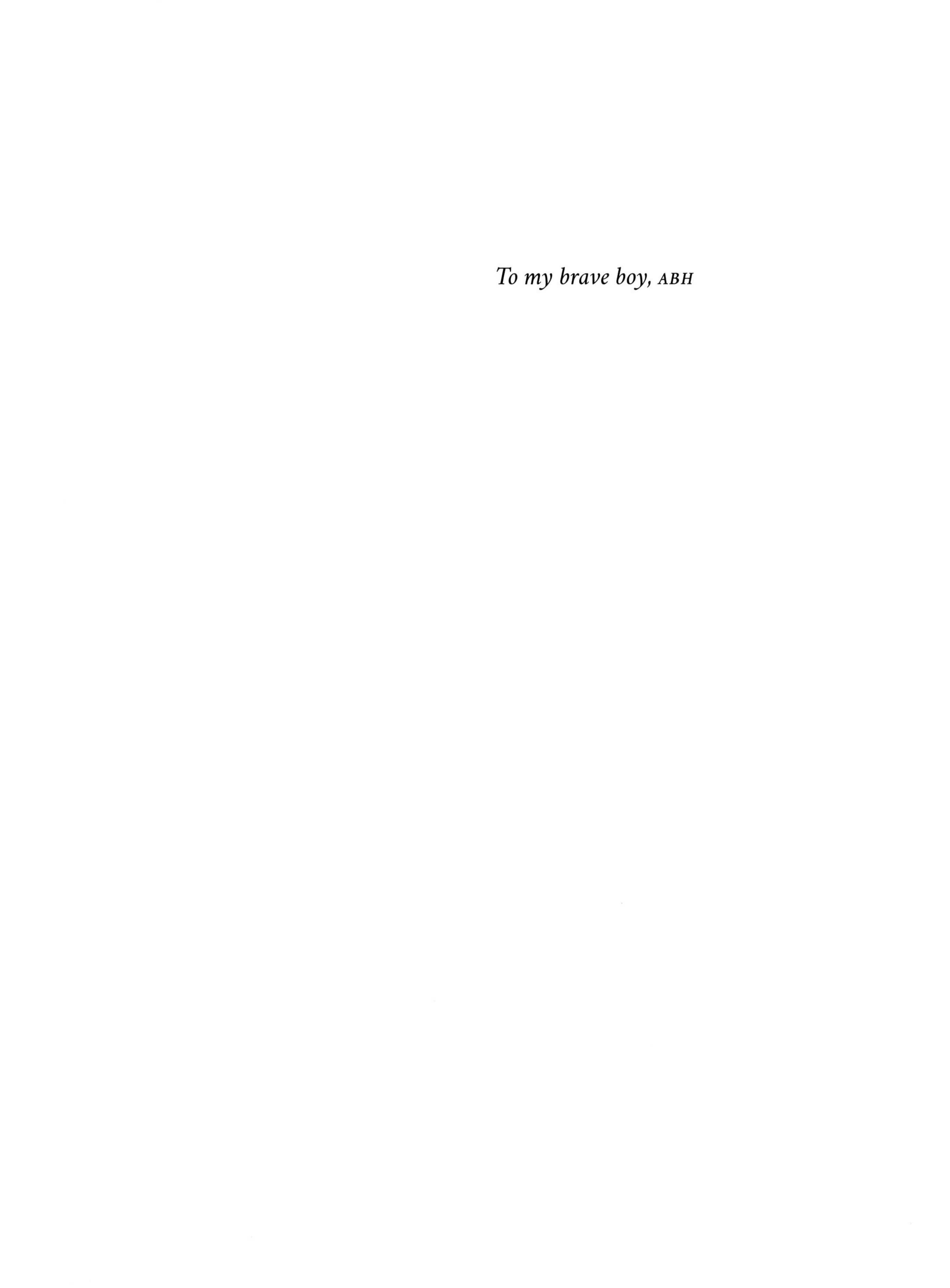

To my brave boy, ABH

CONTENTS

This is not a book about the power and influence of young men. It looks instead at their domination by others, at how they were shaped and "grown" in elite Maya society during the first millennium AD. The vegetal allusion is at once metaphoric and literal. "Growth" refers to the tender, sprouting nature of young men and their cultivation by older men and women. In the mythic past, too, all humans came from maize. Gods crafted them from processed dough, a tasty meal for divine appetites. But here is the surprise, highlighted in this book: in and around the Yucatan peninsula, concerted and sustained energy went into texts, pots, buildings, and carvings that expressed the ideals of male youth. A large cultural investment went into depicting, recording, and housing boys and young men. They were not marginal figures, moping or brawling to the side, but a gathering point of loving attention and, at times, anxiety.

Few scholars talk about them. If they do, it is only about the early years of childhood or in terms of masculinity and its many forms of oppression. Less inclined to judge, I wish mostly to understand, and from the vantage of a specialist in ancient images and texts, some recently decoded. I cannot hold my own background at bay, of course, nor the clamor of present-day ideas. The first chapter explores the seemingly limitless literature on "emergent adults" and adolescence. I am mindful of playing tourist in this complexity. A man writing about men also prompts some doubts about bias. The wrong word or an unintended tone tends to quash dialogue, and a suspicion of ulterior motive crowds around the work. Then there is our ragged and selective evidence. What painters and sculptors showed is not an unguarded glimpse of their world. They gravitated toward the norms and expectations they found appealing, whatever our current views on those beliefs.

With the young, much is at stake, past and present. Society must reproduce itself, and the passage through adolescence needs to be handled and studied with care. According to a report from the World Bank, there will be, by 2035, some 1.5 billion people in the world between 12 and 24 years of age. As of 2006, "the current cohort of young people in developing countries [was] the largest the world [had] ever seen" (Fares et al., *Development*, 33). More unsettling changes are taking place, too. As I write, teenagers, once treated as "minors" in the United States—thus avoiding severe punishment for certain transgressions—are being treated as adults and jailed as adults (Ripley, "Outlawed

Adolescence"). The country itself is said, with some overstatement, to have "outlawed adolescence." All ages present a predicament, of course, a wide array of possibility, hope, or despair. But being a young male may top them all. It is natural, even pressing, to think back in the long term on how others dealt with these transitions. Some, like the Classic Maya, even gloried in the vibrant passage to manhood.

❖ ❖ ❖

This book was written with much help. Key insights by David Stuart triggered our entrée into the world of youths among the Classic Maya, and I must credit him here for his friendship and collegiality over the years. I knew Dave when he was a mere *ch'ok* (youth or sprout) himself. Others, such as Simon Martin and Karl Taube, always provide inspiration and insight. At a busy time, Simon read the manuscript carefully as a reader for the Yale press. Former students including James Doyle and Sarah Newman, sedulous readers of earlier drafts, give me reason to continue as a university professor. Nor can I forget colleagues Charles Golden and Andrew Scherer, who also have been plagued with a swarm of chapters. The speed of their responses is exceeded only by their acuity. Mary Miller involved me years ago, to my great benefit, in her expansive, technically sophisticated, and energetic project with the Bonampak murals. Mary was also a formal reader of this manuscript, a wise counselor in shaping the manuscript into more finished form. The Bonampak work was supported, again through Mary, by the Getty Grants Program, Yale University, and also Brigham Young University (my former university, which I remember with great affection), and with overall permission from the Instituto Nacional de Antropología e Historia of Mexico. Dr. Gene Ware, a genie of an engineer, Lord of the Vidicon Camera—a label that would embarrass him—helped by sweating out difficult weeks with me in the mural building at Bonampak. It was a misery, and it was a joy. Later, Claudia Brittenham showed saintly patience in sorting through images from Bonampak. With her usual perception, she commented on several chapters to my lasting gain. Scott Hutson did so too, along with Gary Urton and David Webster. I thank them warmly.

Few people truly deserve a MacArthur Fellowship, that random lottery of good fortune, but somehow I received one. It made possible much of the initial work on this project, as did leaves authorized by Brown University, its respective deans, and the chairs of my own department. In succession, those deans were Rajiv Vohra and Kevin McLaughlin, my chairs Williams Simmons, Catherine Lutz, and Daniel Smith. Two fellowships made me think and work harder. One was at the Sterling and Francine Clark Institute, which awarded me a fellowship in 2011–2012. Michael Ann Holly, Keith Moxey, and the other fellows made that year memorable and, in retrospect, one of the most productive. Thank you, too, Ashley Lazevnick, now at Princeton: she was my peerless research assistant at the Clark. My other fellowship, where the bulk of this book came into being, was at the Center for Advanced Study in the Visual Arts at the National Gallery of Art, where Elizabeth Cropper is its dean. Associate deans Therese O'Malley and Peter Lukehart offered gracious hospitality and encouragement. I was fortunate to spend time among the fellows of that year. They all contributed in many ways, not always known to them. I must single out Rob Bork (go, Lemmy!), Kate Cowcher, Nikolas Drosos, Kathy Foster, Chris Heuer, Adam Jasienski, Miri Kim, Lihong Liu, Sarah McHam, Rob Nelson, David Pullins (and Basile), Mary Roberts, Rachel Saunders, and Susan Siegfried. They were (and are) formidably smart and much admired by a certain trespassing anthropologist. Parts of this book, especially sections on Bonampak, appeared in somewhat different form within the pages of the *Cambridge Archaeological Journal.* Its editor, John Robb, kindly authorized their reworking here. For images, I give heartfelt thanks to Laura Amrhein, Giannina Bardales Aranibar, Dmitri Beliaev, James Brady, Claudia Brittenham, Christopher Campbell, Arlen Chase, Oswaldo Chinchilla, Mike Coe, Roger Colten, James Doyle, Barbara Fash, Maria Gaida, Simone Giorgi, Judith Strupp Green, Nikolai Grube, Ulla Holmquist, Heather Hurst, Despina Ignatiadou, Takeshi Inomata, David Joralemon, Bryan Just, Justin Kerr (who was especially generous with his incomparable photos), James Kohler, Guido Krempel, Simon Martin, Karl Herbert Mayer, Leonardo Meoni, Mary Miller, Juan Antonio Murro, Katherine Myers, Megan O'Neil, Jorge Pérez de Lara, Alex Pezzati, Jeffrey Quilter, Kim Richter, Andrew Scherer, Piper Severance, Robbi Siegal, Paul Tarver, Alex Tokovinine, Alicia Vallina, Ben Watkins, and, among institutions, the Bodleian Libraries, Cleveland Museum of Art, Dumbarton Oaks Research Library and Collection,

Museo de América, Museo Popol Vuh, the National Gallery of Art, Washington, D.C., the National Museum of Athens, Palace of the Governors, Peabody Museum of Archaeology and Ethnology at Harvard University, the University of Pennsylvania Museum, and the Yale University Art Gallery. My editor at Yale University Press, Katherine Boller, was always supportive and sensible in her counsel. I am grateful for her guidance and that of my meticulous copy editor, Elma Sanders.

A few notes to the reader: Mayan glyphs are rendered according to a system used by most specialists, including the boldface for word signs and syllabic glyphs. For some, this convention lunges out from the page, but it conforms to standard practice and sets signs' values apart from what readers made of them when transliterating actual words. I also avoid the more standard *b'* in favor of *b;* in my opinion, the apostrophe conveys no useful information—it simply clutters text. Drawings not otherwise attributed in the captions are by the author.

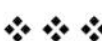

A book about young men brings to mind one in particular, my son Anders Bliss. Beset by challenges, he always moves ahead, step by step. He lives with a courage I cannot begin to understand. I send him my abiding love and this book from a proud and grateful father.

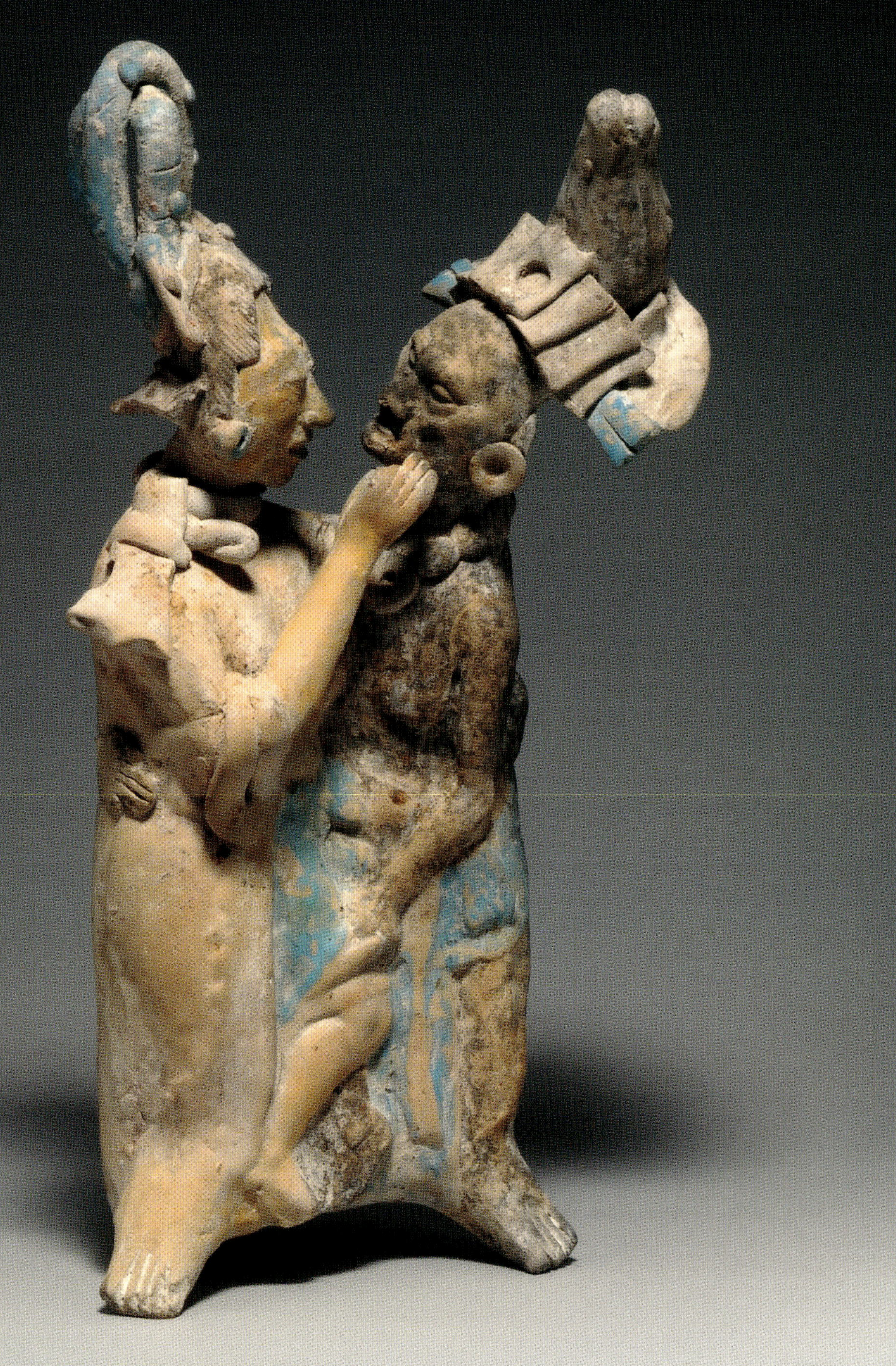

1   A Splendid Predicament

Picture this: a boat glides along a river. It carries a child who, in the next frame, transforms into a youth (fig. 1). Gesturing toward an ethereal castle of hope, the young man will never reach that goal—soon, the river rushes on to darker places.[1] In the worst of it, fully grown, the traveler wrings his hands. Rapids toss the boat, storms gather, the tiller breaks. All control is gone. Somehow, though, the trip ends well. Old and bowed, the passenger sits in heavenly light. He can expect unending life to come, with one further comfort. He has never really been alone. An angel steered the infant's boat, stepping ashore during the boy's teenage years. In harsh adulthood, the guide floated away, although still visible above. At trip's end, he drew close again, almost touchable. The lessons are clear. The very young and old attract the divine; in between, as hearty, boisterous males, they repel it. Yet the teenager seems the real anomaly. Imaginative and yearning, surrounded by promise, he is, more than his other selves, adrift in self-deception. Life will soon grind away at his hopes and fantasies. Angels are needed to complete the journey.

This is one man's voyage. It also stands for every man's journey, played out on four canvases, the *Voyage of Life*, painted in 1842 by the American painter Thomas Cole. Purchased by the National Gallery of Art, Washington, D.C., the paintings exemplify one man's notions of young men and their passage in antebellum America. The heavy-handed moralizing betrays their time.[2] Over-the-top gestures, perhaps lifted from stage acting, appear against backdrops of natural drama. Each frame epitomizes an internal state. Each highlights an episode of growth, vibrancy, or decline. Dawn lights the infant, a cloudless sky stretches over the youth. Storms mark the trauma of adulthood, and beams from heaven, glimpsed through the murk, reassure the old man. There is another trait, too. In one sense, the voyage is an uninterrupted flow. Yet, in these images, Cole has staged a four-part progression through life—stop-action movement rather than a cinematic stream. There could have been more stages, according to authors that Cole knew. In *As You Like It,* Shakespeare sliced a man's life into seven periods. A "mewling and puking" infant gave way, in a final, sorry performance, six stages later, to "second childishness and mere oblivion, sans teeth, sans eyes, sans taste, sans everything."[3]

Continuous life is hard to show. Western imagery, from the fifteenth century on, dealt with this challenge by blocking out ten-year spans, up to an optimistic projection

SEE FIGURE 87

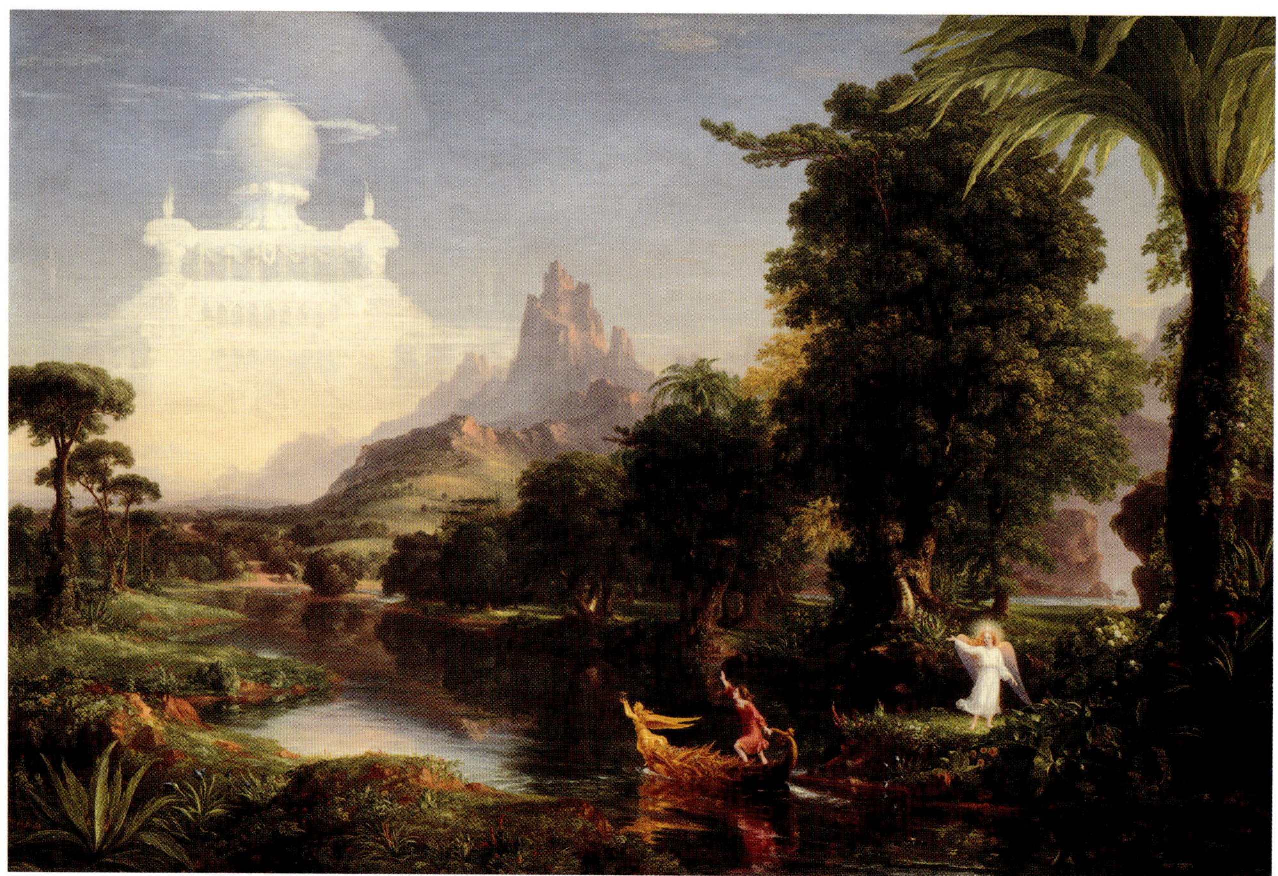

FIGURE 1

Thomas Cole, *The Voyage of Life: Youth,* 1842. Oil on canvas, 52⅞ × 76¾ in. (134.3 × 194.9 cm). National Gallery of Art, Washington, D.C., Ailsa Mellon Bruce Fund, 1971.16.2.

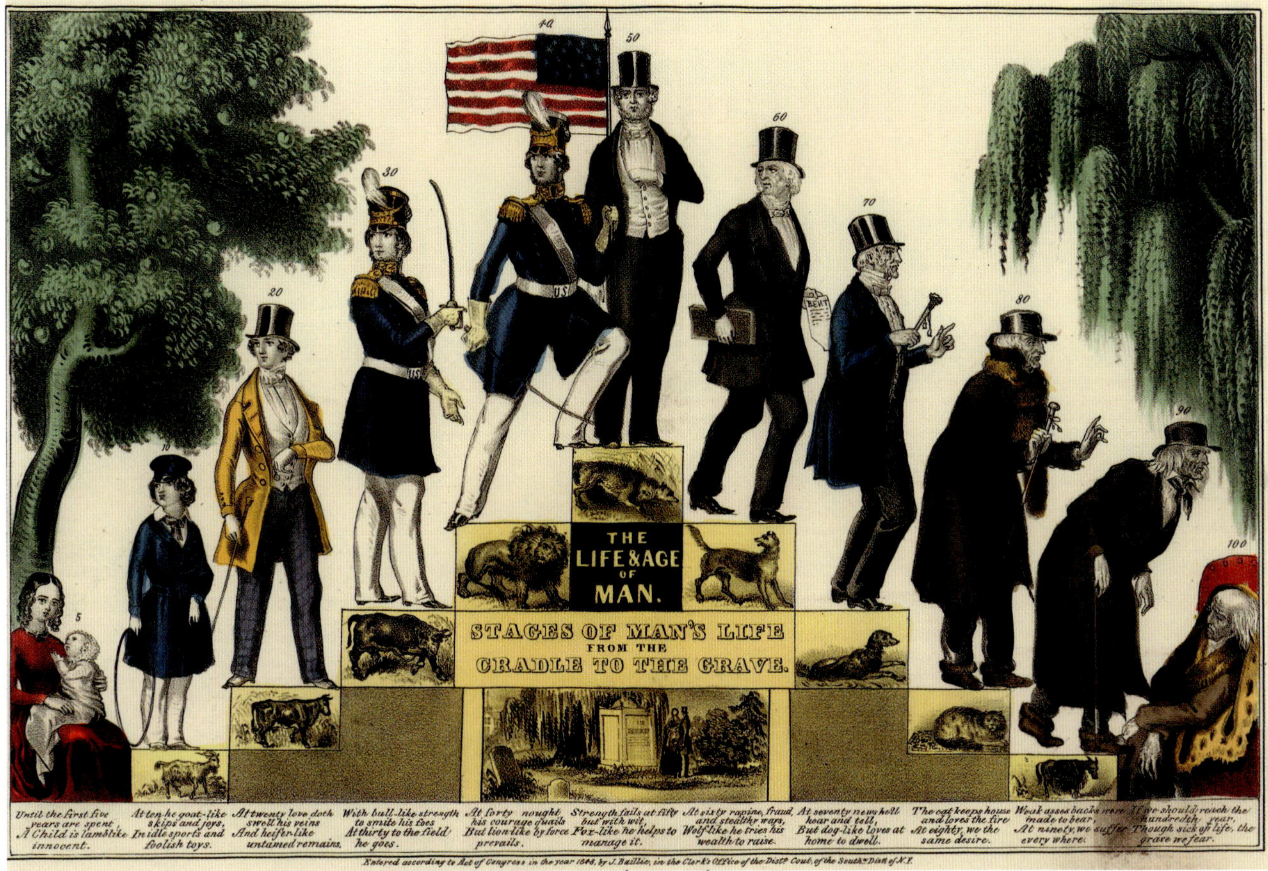

James S. Baillie, *The Life and Age of Man: Stages of Man's Life from the Cradle to the Grave,*" c. 1848. Hand-colored lithograph, 9½ × 13½ in. (24 × 34.3 cm). Library of Congress, Prints and Photographs Division, Washington, D.C.

of 80 to 100 years of age (fig. 2). Women, a logical binary to men, had their own stages and charts. Decimal tidiness allowed the blocks to be ticked off on the fingers, the first decade, say, on one pinky, all the way to the tenth on the other. The wide appeal and cadence of the segments probably derived from folk rhymes. According to one ditty, "80 years—the world's fool … 100 years—God have mercy." Humorous, easy-to-visualize subdivisions worked elsewhere, too, and with reason: in the past, few people were likely to have known their exact age. Blocked-out segments provided a shorthand for essential features and laid out the ideal duties of one generation to another. The young displaced the old by taking on a family farm or occupation. Yet that benefit carried a burden. The old had labored hard and endured much to leave that legacy. For this, they deserved all the care and respect that heirs could provide.[4]

In a sense, stages of life make expectation visible. They show not what males are but what they ought to be, for good or bad. By convention and folk understanding, qualities fasten on to each stage of life. Idiosyncrasy is unimportant. What matter are the general attributes of each stage. Nor is physical decline the only prospect. Christian doctrine, to give one example, affirms a larger hope, that spiritual development should map on to bodily age, going "from grace to grace, from good to better, from perfection to

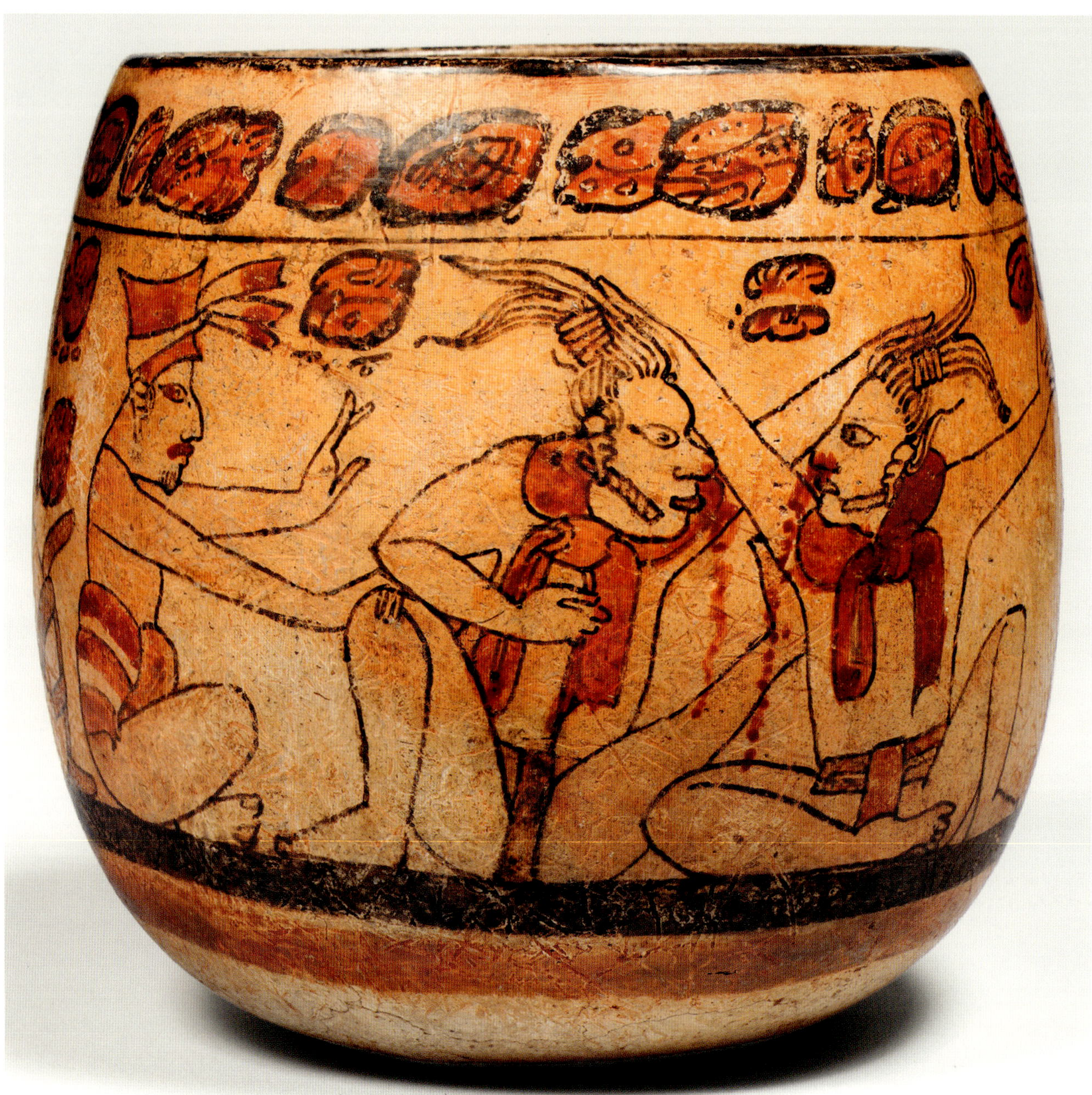

FIGURE 3

Maya chocolate or maize porridge bowl, side view and rollout, c. AD 650. Polychrome ceramic, 6½ × 6 in. (16.5 × 15.2 cm). Princeton University Art Museum, #2016-97, BAMW photography.

greater perfection." The very old are not the decrepit wrecks described by Shakespeare. They could also grow in wisdom, refinement, and authority. These correlations between time of life and intrinsic traits play out in inventive ways. A Danish source from 1594 equates youth to summer—an obvious analogy.[5] But it also links them, in less evident ways, to hot and dry, fire, the second week after the new moon, yellow bile (reflecting obsessions of the time with body fluids), choleric temperament, the east, and, finally, Eurus, god of the eastern wind. Earlier still, writing in the early eleventh century AD, the English monk Byrhtferth integrated seasonal staging with a more continuous model, that of a spoked wheel of time. God himself, the center of all things, formed its axis. Cole's *Voyage of Life* might have begun and ended, or actors left Shakespeare's stage. Yet to medieval minds the wheel of time declared a broader truth. Lives cycled through in endless repetition, a point most people would understand, anywhere, anytime. A young girl prefigured an old woman, an old man implied the boy within or the teenager he had once been. The static human was an impossibility, a contradiction in terms.

Far away, a second painter offered another view of young men (fig. 3). His world framed the subject of this book. He worked in the central part of the Yucatan Peninsula, about 1250 years before Cole started his painting cycle of the *Voyage*. This man—there is no evidence that women painted pots with legible writing—participated in Classic Maya civilization, which flourished from about AD 300 to 850. Literate in glyphic writing, he spoke at least one Mayan language, possibly more. Most likely, he belonged to a noble family. He was not a Christian like Cole (the forced conversions by Spain would come much later). On this surface, not canvas but clay, the painter presented his own take on young men. The setting was not Cole's riverine journey, with its will-o'-the-wisp longing and Edenic scenery. It was a palace, plaza, or courtyard. The participants were elites, the upper crust of society.

There are many other differences. On the pot, the action is now rough-and-tumble, with drunkenness and riotous boxing, no holds barred. An older male, bearded in a Maya convention for age, extends one hand. The other touches the thigh of a quarreling youth. "Hold on," the men seem to say. "Don't overdo it!" The accompanying texts are generic. They label types of men, not actual people. The young and middle-aged could be at any Maya site. Looking at this, Shakespeare might have huffed, as in *The Winter's Tale*: "I would there were no age between ten and three and twenty, or that youth would sleep out the rest. For there is nothing in the between but getting wenches with child, wronging the ancientry, stealing, fighting."[6] Yet, on the bowl, the Maya conceded a time and place for wild romps.

The decorous spirit of Cole's vision swerves to another view of youthful energy. Here, on the bowl, are young men who brawl—bloody, inebriated, and oblivious to limits. Older men are there to supervise or intervene. But they do not stop all this fighting, bleeding, and retching. In Cole's voyage there are no women or other companions, only angels of uncertain gender. The Maya bowl hints at a comparable "homosocial" or same-gendered setting, with behavior that can be deplored yet, to a curious extent, celebrated or seen as fun.[7] In each case, there is some prudery. Another project of Cole's, the *Course of Empire*, a series of paintings in the New York Historical Society, highlights his nineteenth-century view of primitive existence, barbarous decline, and sexual assault. Notably, not one of his figures displays an exposed breast or groin. Nudity, as he would have understood it—the meaning of naked flesh differs by time and place—disappears from view. So too on the Maya pot. Even in struggle, the loincloth stays in place, the genitalia well under wraps. No squeamishness applies, however, to the gore and vomit.

I have little doubt the pot would surprise Cole. His own paintings would probably baffle the Maya artist. But comparing the two helps in asking important questions. What was the life course of men? How might it be segmented, characterized, and interpreted, or its transitions observed, if at all? What, at the broadest level, did it mean to be a man, and a young male in particular? Depending on time and place, the answers vary. A physical fact constrains the questions, too. We all have human frames inherited from forebears. Yet, of late, asking such questions can be unsettling, perhaps a little gauche. After all, they focus on people who have long dominated the world. That unjust edge casts a certain pall. Perhaps for that reason most studies of gender—the understanding of how roles and sexual identities intersect—focus on the people marginalized by mature men. They include women, and also children or persons of alternative gender (for some reason, the elderly elicit less attention). This moral appeal cannot be denied. Raw deals need fixing, and those consigned to oblivion deserve more than they received in life. But there is an undeniable problem with such selective attention. In the past, much cultural energy went into men. Enduring works, some of genius, arose from concern about males or hopes for their future. And not just adults: lurking in the background were pimply, gawky, rowdy, and overloud teenagers. Scholarship may have shifted to other kinds of people, but the brute force of male dominance, what to make of it, and how it was crafted and sustained remain unavoidable features of the past.

Hence this book. It studies how elite men were "grown" and nurtured as youths among the Classic Maya, a set of peoples who left behind a large and revealing trove of texts and images. Some texts are recently deciphered, fresh for interpretation. When studied with images, they offer deep, often surprising views about how male gender was understood among elites. The book develops a larger claim as well, that princely and noble youths were central to the elite culture of the time. Somewhat neglected by other scholars, those younger males loom large. Or they should. Later chapters explain how and why the acts of picturing, describing, and housing them enlisted the most skilled painters, sculptors, and builders the Classic Maya could muster. The investment was lavish, notice of youths strong. Young males inspired exceptional interest, and for a simple reason. Among the Maya, they energized and reinforced courtly societies. With older male kin, they formed the chief mechanism of governance and the core of expressive culture. Without them, there would be no future for a dynasty or a kingdom. Training and shaping young men assured elites that matters important to royal families would be reproduced, that a kingdom would not dissolve, that kingship would not just endure but triumph.

NURTURED NATURE

Interpreting the Maya passage to manhood entails several steps. The first is to understand that the passage has two kinds of input. One consists of the meanings and social practices attached to these changes in boys and youths. The other comes from the physical body itself. Weighing the relative impacts of belief, society, and biology can be daunting, however. Obviously, the time from infancy to adulthood involves growth. There are new strengths and potentials, determined in part by a hypothalamic "awakening." Sex steroids suffuse the body; height increases dramatically, weight burgeons, and the jaws become prominent. Body hair erupts, cardio capacity rises. There is more nighttime activity than before. At 21, the youth grows as tall as he ever will. Across the primate order, and for humans as well, shifts occur in behavior. There is greater risk taking, sexual activity, interest in the opposite sex, and a commitment to learning social and subsistence skills. Males begin to ally with members of the same sex. Unlike other primates, however, humans spend far more time in a juvenile state. This gives them greater longevity and reproductive advantages, but it also means that older, wiser people play a necessary role in directing and pushing youths toward future responsibilities and seemly mates.[8] Yet individuals also differ biologically. There is no invariant pattern. The onset of adult physiques diverges by genetic heritage or level of nutrition, a fact known since the time of Galen, the ancient Greek physician.

Then there is the general dilemma of young men in society, in part a consequence of biology. Are they, as Shakespeare thought, a nuisance or even a bit scary? Some artists and poets believe so, as in Oskar Kokoschka's *"The Dreaming Boys"* (*"Die träumenden Knaben,"* written in 1907–8): "I am the encircling werewolf when the evening bell dies off. I stalk into your garden, into your pastures, break into your peaceful corral, my unbridled body, my body exalted with pigment and blood.... I devour you, men, women, drowsily hearkening children. The berserk loving werewolf within you."[9] According to wide belief, the energy of young men rejects any bounds. Kokoschka sees them as the wildness within us all. This is not just a poetic fancy. Many studies of adolescent males cite an appalling number of skateboard injuries or self-mutilation from fireworks. Some say worse. Teenagers behave with a "violent edge"; they enjoy killing animals large and small, delight in coarse erotica, look with abandon for "copulation opportunities," "fantasize about . . . sexual deviances," and seek "obsession rather than balance."[10]

On the whole, male youths appear reckless and impulsive. Statistically, in modern society, they stand a higher chance of being arrested than females. They are more likely to take up dangerous sports like climbing or caving. They end up in emergency rooms or, meddling with dangerous reptiles, fall victim to snakebite, as observed especially in South Africa. When attracting the attention of young females, according to another, obviously dated reference, they behave badly, pulling braids and "softly punching or hitting girls." They are, to another authority, enslaved to libido yet, in an abiding injustice, the people "most restricted in access to sex."[11] These urges and potentials are claimed to be explosive, intrinsic, and deeply rooted. Some scholars blame nature. The archaeologist Dale Guthrie perceives an ancient, "heritable component" bound, in examples of extreme risk, to "the chromosomal block known as D4DR" (other researchers dispute this conclusion). A less physically determined view, now faulting nurture, comes from Michael Kimmel, a sociologist of masculinity in the United States. He perceives a problem and gives it a name: "Guyland." This is less a place than a loutish state-of-mind. It describes young men, especially of the early twenty-first century, who lack the supervision formerly given by adults. The man-boys of Guyland, loving girls yet loathing women, seethe, according to Kimmel, with homophobia and sexism. They slouch, swagger, and affect indifference. They act aggressively, stuck in an over-long stage of life lasting from puberty to age 30. Lower ages for puberty and longer periods of adolescence, a by-product of enhanced nutrition and medicine, aggravate the bad behavior.[12]

I experienced only a little of this. When first in the jungle, years ago, I tried to avoid snakes. The open jaws of a fer-de-lance, coiled a few feet away, did not induce any great sense of fun. Nor do I recall strutting about or preying on women. Presumably, in making a man—in growing him to adulthood—there is room for free will and the influence of culture. All societies impose a set of meanings, actions, encouragements, and restrictions on their members. Which of us obeys each and every physical impulse? Do we even know where those urges come from? The idea that genetic programming determines how we act, to the minute detail, is far-fetched. Entirely too much can be made of physicality and the dictates of genes. Indignant at such views, which deny the supple responses of humans, some scholars categorize them as "essentialist." Greek philosophy bred this particular label. As used by academics, it signals a belief that the observed world is less important than the abstract attributes or "essences" behind it. In the social sciences, "essentialist" has acquired another meaning: the notion, rejected by many, that there are "hypothetically innate psychobiological structures, or cultural universals" in human nature.[13]

In essentialist views, young men possess certain traits. Otherwise, they would not be young men. These features are the kernels of their being, their package of presets. Think of all that snake handling and braid pulling. Youths take risks. They are aggressive, over-sexed, and death-dealing when it comes to animals. They cannot help it. Some of their violence targets humans, a useful attribute for leaders of gangs and armies. Young men fight and die when adults tell them to do so. Marching up Cemetery Ridge, to a grievous end at Gettysburg, they are the ones who receive orders. They seldom give them. At adult prodding, they wear the bomb vests of jihadists or wield guns for the Lord's Resistance Army in Africa. Fearful perhaps, they also yearn to fight. They do love a brawl.

What is wrong here? For starters, if only from my own experience, youths often lack such attributes, or they display them in fits and starts. Men of all ages live and act in many ways, showing "diversities of male sexualities across cultures, classes, ages, ethnicities." A vast literature proves this. Youths also have what might be called relational identities. They do not create their sense of themselves from other youths alone. Male gender, a set of ideas about how people should think, behave, and look, modulates in response to other genders. Identity does not issue solely from this or that sort of body; it arises from contrasts and comparisons with men and women, boys and girls, and the assorted identities in between. By the same token, a man's age exists in relation to other times of life. Contrasts generate these categories, comparisons lay their foundation. There is strong evidence for this view of how we look at ourselves and how we behave. In colonial Peru, as one example, gendering took place when people performed tasks and duties. Men dug, acted aggressively, and destroyed. Disposed to order, women did not so much subtract as add, by planting, gathering, and creating. One ideal category shaped the other. In Peru, gender even extended to the broader world. Unyielding rock could be seen as masculine, the soft, pliable earth as female, although the creator of both possessed an almost ambiguous sexuality.[14]

Then there are social roles and norms, subjects of long-standing interest to scholars, though not all of their work is persuasive when applied to gender. One influential figure, Judith Butler, sees these practices as a kind of rhetorical exercise. Her sources are mostly from philosophy, psychoanalysis, and comparative literature, not the enormous literature on roles and norms in the social sciences. (This oversight baffles me.) If examined more closely, Butler's vision seems to be conditioned by university life and the tools of scholarship. To her, people "cite" each other like academics inserting footnotes. They mold their own performance of being a male or female or points in between according to what they have seen before or, to press the analogy, the pages they have read and remembered. Sometimes that precedent is thought to be positive and suitable for emulation. Repetition fixes it to a person's identity. The performance can also take a different path—people may choose another gender or deviate from general expectation about which citations to follow.[15] Consciously or not, they botch their lines, misread or subvert cues, or create an entirely new persona. The social teleprompter, an inward guide to what is appropriate or not, breaks down, or the actor ignores it. He, she, or some alternative gender veers from one role to the next and back again.

That humans can be reduced to literary or academic custom appears, at best, an incomplete metaphor. But we can agree that a young man is malleable. He exists in a dynamic rather than a predetermined state. Repetitive performances, Butler's citations, instate and solidify that identity. Others of varying age and gender enforce it through comments, encouragement, or coercion. The French philosopher Michel Foucault studied the inequity that allows this browbeating to take place. Subtle or overt bullying by the people in charge helps bend others to central control. Sometimes that power will break them. Decrying essentialism or the idea of innate programming is more than clarifying. It may better humanity and liberate the self. A prominent theorist of masculinity, Raewyn Connell, insists that this is the basic goal for us all. "Understanding," she and colleagues declare, "is mainly worth having if we can do something with it."[16] The desired future, one that escapes oppressive precedent, is Connell's own castle of hope, much like the figment in Cole's canvases. It has broken free from tyrannical expectation. It has resisted power, abhorred privilege, and rejected compliance with patriarchy.

Yet there remains one point that fits less well with earnest desires for change and improvement. That is the nature being nurtured, the male body as shaped by untold millennia of evolution. I would propose again that there are two general sources of input into young men. There are meanings, practices, and relations of power, but there are also flesh-and-blood bodies. Behavior is not simply a question of mind or the search for self-determination, whatever the good intentions of Connell's plan for human betterment.[17] There are limits to a person's plasticity, to how far they can be molded and reshaped. Think of it this way. The human body operates as an unimaginably complex intersection of chemicals and evolution, and it is motivated equally by varied habits of reasoning. To theologians, looking at choice from a different perspective, the mind endows us with the possibility of free will. An elaborate choreography of body and society creates a person, and closing out one of those streams of input for the other hazards more than over-simplification, it risks the absurd. Just consider the alternatives. One view privileges mental process: an insubstantial mind is said to live outside yet to control the physical world.[18] The other is exclusively physical: it proposes that genes and chemistry regulate every last human thought, attitude, and decision.

In pure form, neither view makes much sense. This brings us back to unruly teenage males. As an exceptionless rule, they are, it should be clear, a caricature. Perhaps they have no "trans-historical core," as some scholars would put it, no meaning as a general or essential category in different times and places. But this view is inadequately grounded and an interpretive mistake. It prevents any comparison and negates the value of the social sciences and the many insights they provide.[19] It rejects, too, any observation made across cultures. By reliable evidence, from many researchers, adolescent males *do* exhibit higher rates of risk taking. Mortality increases when "teenage boys tend to do stupid things that cut their lives short," whether in present-day suburbs of North America or the jungles of South America. The Aka, a group of hunters and gatherers in the Central African Republic, have twice the mortality between 12 and 22 years of age as they have before or after that span. Adults must be there to serve, according to one scholar, as the "teens' frontal lobes," a check on their poor judgment and drive to rapid rewards. Physical competition, another study asserts, is by statistical measure an attribute of young men more than it is of young women. Some scholars peddle a stronger claim: that boys incline to higher degrees of aggression than girls. But the men are not alone, nor do they think alone. Peers goad them on, heedless of consequence. Adults, too—those people equipping youths with suicide vests and automatic weapons—come into the picture, along with local ideas about what it all means, which behaviors conform to expectation or incite disapproval, and how such transitions might be marked or softened. In texts and imagery, there is endless expressive potential for the adventure of youth. There are many decisions for artists and writers to make, about what to emphasize, what to ignore, how to broadcast certain messages, to whom, and for what purpose.[20]

The central questions of masculinity, then, are what do people make of it, and how do they interpret the physical condition of being a male? The male body, for instance, has a device, intermittently engorged for inseminating females. No surprise here: it is the penis. But treated as an object of attraction or repulsion, a proxy for the terrible things that men do, an organ of procreation, power or pleasure—that is, to the writer David Friedman, a "phallus," "an idea, not a body part." This insignificant piece of tissue has acquired shocking significance in human history. Much European claptrap, from Roman times on, connected it to the nature of Jewish identity. Intense hatred zeroed in on this one appendage. Several writers, including Gottfried Henschen, a sixteenth-century Jesuit, thought the Jewish phallus menstruated, goading their owners to the murder of Christian youth. A cure for male cramps could only be achieved by drinking baptized blood. In the United States, racists of the nineteenth and twentieth centuries feared the "immense copulatory organ" of African Americans, a menace to all white women. Nonsense, of course, and evil, too: in account after account Friedman showed how irrational claims led by short path to violence and murder.[21]

The being attached to the phallus, all the other fleshy apparatus of maleness, is equally a set of ideas. Behind seemingly erotic images are less accessible concepts about what genitalia might mean. Reflect on a Moche ceramic from Peru (was fermented maize drink an analogy to semen?) or a set of Roman talismans in southern Italy, later of prurient interest to Sir William Hamilton in eighteenth-century Naples (fig. 4). Variety is everywhere. A man can be a docile and cooperative helpmate, a hot-blooded satyr, the drunken frat boy, a muscled biker drawn by the erotic artist Tom of Finland—all of these are someone's idea of masculinity.

For the classicist Eva Keuls, much of masculinity is wholly wicked, as in ancient Athens. She sees the city as a women-hating place, worshiping the phallus and all the aggressions it implied. Moral narratives like Keuls's fit into a broader belief about "hegemonic masculinity," the use of maleness or manhood to oppress women. This could be applied to societies beyond classical Greece. Certain men may not be overtly brutal, but they benefit from that dominance. Even if not actively engaged in oppression, they still operate as accomplices. They participate in hegemony and extend it through a "lived consensus" that involves "vigilance, self-vigilance and dispute." Only the words and images consistent with hegemony are permitted, stressed or imposed by institutional authority.

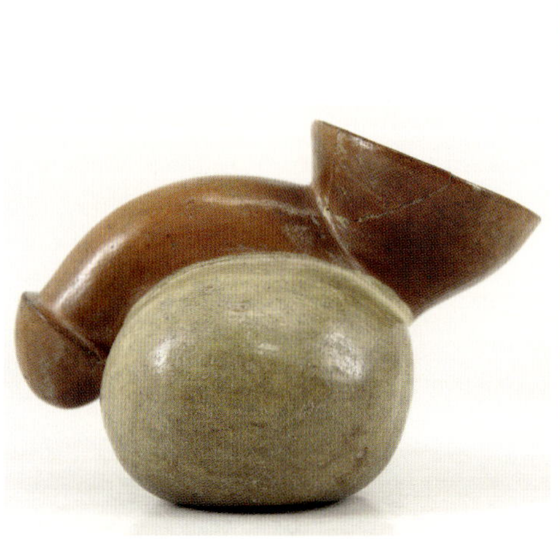

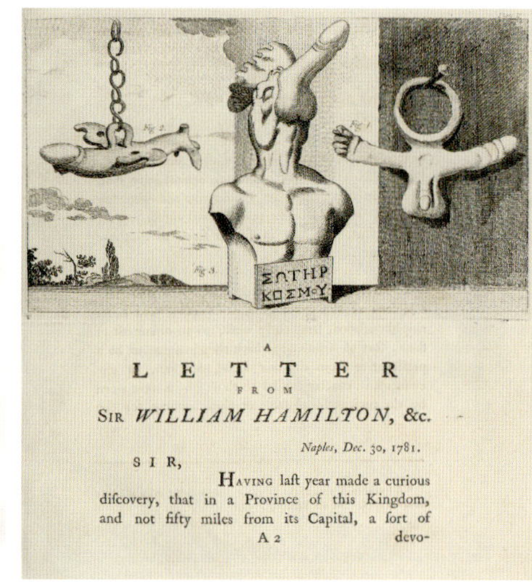

A   B

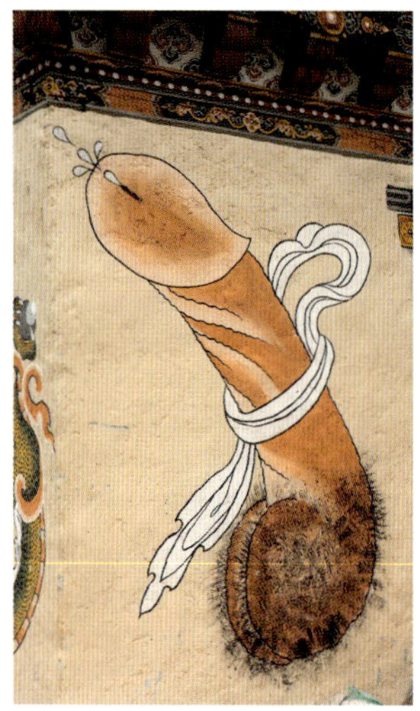

C

FIGURE 4

Phalli and local meanings: A) Moche vessel, c. AD 600. Bichrome ceramic, 4⅝ × 6½ × 4⅝ in. (11.9 × 16.6 × 11.8 cm). Museo Larco Hoyle, Lima, ML004204; B) Roman talismans, William Hamilton, *Worship of Priapus*, 1786, engraved by James Newton. Getty Research Institute; C) phallic symbols, Gaytsa, Bhutan, Alamy stock. Exterior mural.

Dominant men are held up as models for all, whatever the reality of individual practice. For their part, nondominant women are nearly as bad by upholding disempowering ideals of femininity. Playing along, they deserve just as much blame.[22]

Yet humans are endlessly creative. It stands to reason that there could be several models of masculinity, in the same place and at the same time. That they do not exist in complete harmony is what the anthropologist Gregory Bateson called a "double bind." In this uncomfortable state, one potentially damaging to the psyche, a person must carry out incompatible commands about how to behave and how to exist. There can also be different kinds of men, diverging by class, wealth, genealogy, religion, or pigmentation of skin. Ethnographers working in the Mediterranean emphasize the strong attention to manhood in peasant society, whether in Crete or Andalusia. Being male was a zone of endless striving, conflict, and jokey performance. Judith Butler would understand the process. These performances combat perceived slights to manhood that come from the emasculating wiles of women and elite or external domination. David Gilmore, another anthropologist, calls this "manplaying." Manhood is not, as many societies acknowledge, a simple matter of inheritance. It must be earned and propped up. In a sense, males make themselves, not so much physically as mentally. In masculine company, they also make each other.

A book about the ancient Maya will not resolve the relative impact of nurture or nature in human lives. It is pointless to try. One case, involving the anthropologist Margaret Mead, has a virulence that continues to amaze. Studying adolescent girls in Samoa, Mead found behavior far different from Western practice. Mead suggested that options not embraced by early twentieth-century America might lead to calmer, more contented people. Her larger point was that there was no fixity, no set patterns to attitudes about gender and sex. Much later, another anthropologist, Derek Freeman, faulted Mead's evidence, going so far as to libel her methods as a researcher.[23] Freeman aimed low . . . and missed. Most now think the debunker debunked. Yet the quarrel reminds us that, if not handled with care, arguments about adolescence can truly enrage. Hyperbole is the danger, along with an assumption of what to expect. Evidence, as among the Classic Maya, should settle at its own angle of repose.

REVIVING HAMLET

The best-selling book *Reviving Ophelia* laments the plight of adolescent females in the United States.[24] Happy when young, girls lose themselves in teenage years. Any sense of wholeness goes crashing into a "social and developmental Bermuda Triangle." Standing in for all girls is Shakespeare's Ophelia—referencing the Bard seems unavoidable in comments on humanity. Ophelia yearns for that paragon of self-absorption, Hamlet, Prince of Denmark. As we know, the affair ends badly. There is a watery death, perhaps suicide, for the young lady. But it also leads back to Hamlet himself. In the play, he is not clearly an adolescent (specialists bicker on this point). Few doubt, however, that he is an unmarried, younger prince, full of angst about things to come. Hamlet will never be happy.

Yet there is much else to ask: what was it like for young royal males in other places, as for example among the ancient Maya? What were the beliefs about their expected attributes, the duties that defined them, the terms that labeled their identity? What individual passages made them like and unlike other princes?

Maya scholarship looks mostly at adults, then children. Full-grown lords and ladies attract the greatest attention. A specialist niche looks at those just born, weaned, walking, slung in a mother's harness or astride the hip. Indeed, a ceremony for the first such placement, the *hetzmek*, is still practiced in the Yucatan peninsula. The very young are buried across the Maya world, wherever their fragile remains survive. Yet a gap emerges when boys enter their teenage years, moving on to adulthood. Obscurity awaits them, and few researchers appear to be interested. Childhood may transition to adulthood, but we are told that any stage in between, a postpubertal phase, concerns "fully formed adult humans" that come into being by age 12 or 13. Among the Maya and the Aztec of central Mexico, youths of 14, 15, or 20 are dubbed "boys," as though no different to these scholars than those at 5, 7, or 10. Adolescence is seldom mentioned if at all.[25]

Reviving the Hamlets of the past, and among the ancient Maya, involves three things. The first is to examine adolescence itself, how it might be categorized in the past and celebrated through word and image. The second is to entwine this time of life, however defined, with the matter of gender. A third targets an aesthetic of beautiful young men. Among the Maya, artists, mostly men and mostly employed by men, exulted in the male form. They gloried in its time of youthful potential. Yet the Maya had their own forms of impaired vision. To be royal or noble weighed more heavily than other attributes. After all, Hamlet was always more important than some nameless servant or drudge at Elsinore, the dynastic seat of his family. An inequity among the Classic Maya, almost a moral failing of its expressive culture, was their scant attention to low-ranking people.

Nor did they leave unguarded glimpses of past life. It was always a conventional display: not what happens but what people thought should happen in the highest strata of society.[26]

STAGING YOUTH

The rich psychological literature on adolescence is a good place to start, and the research often focuses on stages of development.[27] These imply not so much a gradient of change as marked shifts in existence. Certain traits or mentalities are felt to characterize each phase, recalling the "steps of life" in early European prints. Sigmund Freud posited a "latency stage," when youths no longer craved their mothers in churning, Oedipal lust. Instead, they began to identify with parents or other role models of the same sex. Then came Freud's "genital" stage. For such youths, interest in sex with others outside the family might actually meet with success. Whether these formulations had anything to do with young men in general—did they emanate from Freud's own experience in imperial Austria?—is less interesting than a wider proposal: how we act on sexual urges serves as one way to establish human identity.

Other psychologists have understood postpuberty, around 15 to 18 years of age, as a time of crisis. A groping for stable personalities, it can go in any direction, good or bad. It is a time of life when behaviors solidify and orderly thinking takes shape. These are said to be the achievements of adulthood, which, of course, has its own times of flux and crisis. Impressionable minds gain frameworks for larger obligations. From 11 to 14 years of age, links to family are said to weaken, those with peer groups to strengthen. Puberty has begun. In middle and late adolescence, "separation struggles between teens and parents" intensify, then abate in "a healthy sense of self-esteem," a balance of individual versus peer demands, and a more secure sense of sexual identity. After 18, perhaps up to 25, emerging adulthood takes place, a phase that is thought by some academics to be a recent, just emerging stage of life. It looks a lot like Kimmel's Guyland. There is freedom from parenthood, marriage, and steady careers, along with, on the bad side, drug use, risky sex, and binging on alcohol. Youths explore their identities. Perhaps they investigate transgenders or they settle on the gender ("cisgender") assigned at birth. They are unstable in all senses, self-focused, hopeful of fulfillment, yet falling in between, neither young nor old. Whether these features exist only in the recent past seems dubious. Moreover, a censorious view of this stage of life, that it is a mere way station to better states, does not grant the sheer delight of being young. Missing from most of this research is any acknowledgment of joie de vivre. Must youth always be seen as troubled?[28]

The worry about such statements is whether they extend beyond Western experience. Most sociologists, especially those looking at emerging adulthood, pay increasing heed to variation. It is passé to think the past is just like today, or to believe that patterns across the globe always follow similar tracks. Culture and history demand their due. To offer one example, a standard account of adolescence comes from the medievalist Philippe Ariès. He denied the existence of any modern phase of childhood or youth in the past. There was no real period of crisis. These stages were—at least in Europe, the only region he describes—rather late developments, diffusing from the upper class downward. For Ariès, the novel *Émile, or Treatise on Education* by Jean-Jacques Rousseau, which appeared in 1762, was the real "breakthrough" of the young, the first true expression of parental pride and affection. Before that, he proposed, children were there simply to live or die, and having survived, they would be indulged by wise parents and teachers and move gradually into the adult world. This view, that the teenager we know today is a relatively recent creature, received ardent support from the Romanist Marc Kleijwegt, looking at materials far earlier than Ariès had. Others contested these points, such as Emiel Eyben in his appropriately titled *Restless Youth in Ancient Rome*. Since the work of Ariès, who was not a professional historian (and clearly distasteful of coddled youth), consensus has shifted to a perspective that both rejects and accepts his postulates. It questions his interpretations but allows that "childhood and youth are no longer considered as suprahistorical givens . . . but as phenomena which are closely linked with cultural customs and change in a particular society."[29]

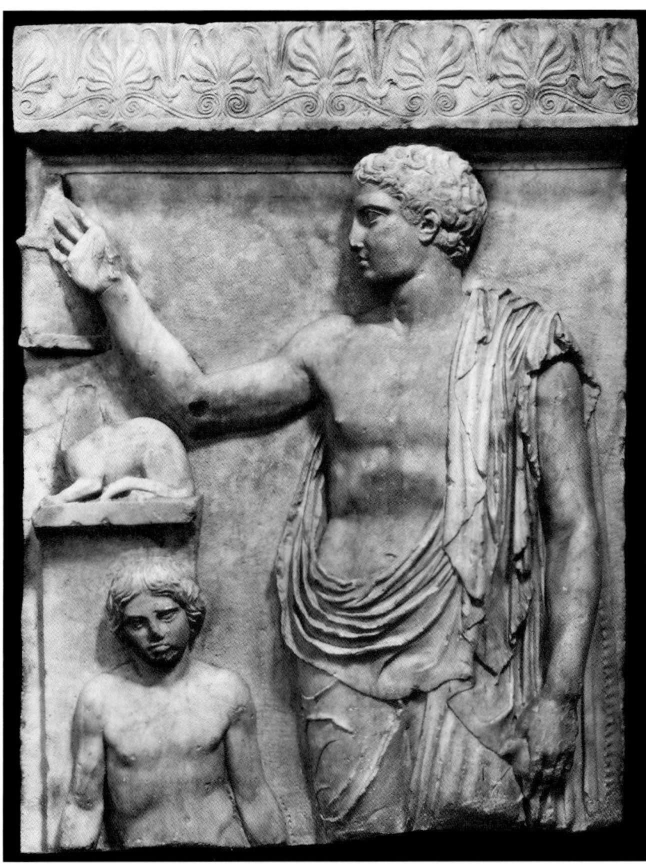

Grave stela of youth, Aegina or Salamis, c. 420 BC. Marble, 41¼ × 33½ in. (105 × 85 cm). National Museum of Athens, #715.

How life should be segmented remains a "suprahistorical" concern, however. It is of interest everywhere, whether in Cole's canvases or the "steps of life" in Europe and the United States. In the Western world, the evidence goes back very far indeed. According to one interpretation, the frescoes of Thera, an island in the Aegean Sea blasted by volcanic cataclysm over 3500 years ago, may illustrate distinct phases in the life of young men. Murals proclaim the tasks they should master, presenting a set of physical types for each phase. The youths are athletes, providers, and participants in communal rituals. Gravestones from classical Athens appear to condense this array of types, grouping them into two categories (fig. 5). There are lithe figures in their teens but also young men, stronger but not yet with beards. This set may accord with the category of *paides* (boys) and *epheboi* (youths), who continue as young men until about 20 years of age. That is when they become *neoi* at the cusp of adulthood. Romans of some centuries later also highlight youth as a stage and a state of being. After taking the toga at 15 or so, a teenager would find, as Horace asserts, "delight in horses, dogs, and the grass of the sun-drenched

Campus Martius." Then the usual lament, evocative of so many times and places: "he [the young man] is soft as wax to be seduced into vice, he is troublesome towards his educators." In general, the Romans seem disapproving of youths, both because of their own beliefs and because of Aristotle's influence, which saw them as less self-serving than adults but still "hot-tempered." Notably, the concept of problematic youth for the Romans was mostly an elite phenomenon, the behavioral luxury of a leisured class. The Byzantines, drawing on Roman precedent, recognized an extended period of preparation, too, from about 14 years of age. Boys had matured but were not yet ready for adult responsibility.[30]

In medieval Europe, lust was thought to control the teenage years. The devil became especially active. Festive rites were organized by younger unmarried males, clustered into "abbeys" exercising jurisdiction over people of the same age. Their revels gave scope for "mockery and derision," rites of inversion that helped, in fact, to ratify local order. The abbeys clarified the duties of youths in married life, defended village identity, and excoriated outside oppressors. But there could be, as court cases indicate, the occasional riot or murder. A similar ambivalence seeps into sources of early Renaissance Italy. Puberty, the time of *adolescencia,* was thought to happen at about 14. What a perilous phase it was. Youths needed to be regulated with severity and kept from contact with slightly older males of 19 to 20. In contrast, girls were married off as quickly as possible. That way they could begin to bear legitimate children. Male adulthood, at least for patrician youth, had more to do with ability to function in government and business. In Renaissance Florence, separation was an opportunity to remove or insulate young men from the "baleful influences of women." Instruction in decorous speech, even movement and gesture, occupied the time of teachers.[31] They made "harmonious the step, the act of the body, the movement of the head, of the feet, of the hands." Some men might remain bachelors, but at least they had been "weaned away from rambunctious youth into conformist adulthood."[32]

In the early years of the United States, "youth" could simply refer to people living away from home, enjoying varying degrees of dependence, between the ages of 12 and 23. Oppression and freedom characterized that state, but, as in contemporary Europe, a conventional representation of an age—steps organized into ten-year spans—differed sharply from actual lives. More than other times of life, teenage years involved spiritual peril. Too much jollity and camaraderie in Puritan New England could be viewed with suspicion, even as corrupting. Mature men needed to control such recklessness. Social clubs of the eighteenth century moderated that earlier Puritan severity, but still with an emphasis on mutual watchfulness. For teenage slaves that control was absolute: if productive, they were often sold to those moving west to new settlements (the girls being sold in turn as "fancies" or mistresses). The most vibrant accounts, from the turn of the nineteenth century, invoked such youths to embody "[the age's] own uneasiness with its heritage, its crisis of identity, and its groping for a new one."[33] Adolescents became a receptacle for all contradictory impulses, as in *The Adolescent* (1875) by Fyodor Dostoyevsky. Knowing everything, knowing nothing, they seemed sure of direction yet consistently went awry.

Stepping away from the European tradition, or digging far into its past, is a bracing move. The obvious becomes a little less so, although much remains familiar. In decades past, anthropology has probed deeply into the question of adolescence. In one sample of 186 preindustrial societies, researchers found that 173 defined this phase of life as a distinct social stage. In Highland Peru, young men danced as bears, and for good reason: both kinds of creature were barely socialized, pushy about sex, disdainful of restraint. Marquesan islanders in Polynesia had similar ideas of errant youth. Most times and places do. Whatever the hormonal reality, youths present a problem. They are flashpoints at moments of cleavage and societal conflict.[34]

But they serve also as a useful resource. The comparative sources single them out as raw labor. They are muscled beyond children but with an agility that will only diminish with age. They exist at a peak of physical ability. Consider Olympic medalists—by age 25, most are well past their prime.[35] In Ming and Qing China, adolescence was when essence and blood combined to allow reproduction, a period of flux when the *qi* force of heaven could be fully activated.[36] It came to an end when youths married and embarked on adult duties. Eventually, that *qi* would slip away and the vitalities of life diminish. If these diverse sources have anything in common it is that a very individual trajectory, a boy entering puberty becoming a male, interacts with collective practice. No one goes through it alone. The passage from boy to man often takes place in groups, either formally or informally. Cohorts help to distinguish generations, play with ideas about how they differ, determine who replaces whom, and explore how social continuity might be preserved. As cohorts, people move forward together, in sudden motion or spurts, with a veneer of equality among them. Resemblances outweigh differences.

An influential essay by the anthropologist Alfred Radcliffe-Brown—it covers but a single page in an academic journal—introduced a key distinction. This concerns age grades versus age sets.[37] *Grades* are divisions of life, a status that someone passes through, from infancy to boyhood, teenage years, and beyond, all the way to ancestorhood. Being dead is, in many places, no real separation from human society; as people, the dead still interact with the living. In contrast, a *set* represents a group of individuals of approximately similar age. It is a lifetime cohort, with a mean age and no overlap with other sets. To be sure, Radcliffe-Brown and other anthropologists often described behaviors that existed more in memory than in current practice. What they recorded was often what people remembered, or claimed to recall, not what could be seen in a fully functioning system. Yet, where they survive, associations of youths are seldom voluntary. The people in charge are older males, and the necessity of adult control and dominance receives consistent emphasis.[38] In fact, ties between young and old inform much training in specialized activities. Arrangements could be relatively informal, limited to families, or they could be formally constituted through long-lasting contracts of apprenticeship.[39]

Youths serve as a natural template for military service. They hold inherent potential as a small fighting force, loyal to each other, less inclined to weigh risk. But in few places do they enjoy executive or administrative powers. Alexander the Great and Huo Qubing, the renowned general in Han China, dead at 23, are the notable exceptions, and their careers came about because of inherited status or connections. Nor do youths act as autonomous corporate groups. In this there is a paradox. The limited rights and duties of youths encourage them, where this has been examined in East Africa, to "act wildly to the edge of delinquency." But that abandon is not an end in itself. Growing older, getting *beyond* adolescence, is the ultimate aim. In age-grade arrangements, to be senior is to be superior. Despite all the amusements of being young, the idea is to age up and out. In this way, youths exemplify the passage of time. Growing older, they affirm the continuity of humans. A youth may saunter past. By himself he is of no account. But an age grade exemplifies a segment of society, assuring that the group will move forward and reproduce itself, an anxiety doubtless present among the Classic Maya. Even in weaker, less marked form, age grades result in bonding. Lasting affinities can be promoted by means of isolation—women are mostly absent in these passages of life. Yet there is also rejoicing in new strengths, intimacies, and mutual support.[40]

Looking broadly, anthropologists have noted age grades in many settings, from Africa and New Guinea to premodern Japan. One of the most thorough studies, by Robert Lowie, examined Native Americans on the American Plains. Societies organized by age could own songs, dances, and regalia. How people were assigned to such groups undergirded society by setting the rules of transition. A boy reaching a certain age was folded in by certain ceremonies or outward signs; a young man newly married was excluded from that group and thrust into later stages of life. Often, the age grades stacked in sequence, from boyhood to dotage. How acutely or closely they were observed, celebrated, and set apart from each other varied a good deal, however, and not just in the Plains. Evidence from Africa and India suggests that some transitions and age grades might be lightly marked or flagged. This could be done by little more than a stay in a boy's hut in India—no other ages or genders are, it seems, set apart in this fashion—or a restriction of grades to youths in their teens and early twenties, as among the Nuba of Sudan. Lowie noted something else. In the Plains, some members were notionally young but, in chronological years, well beyond youth. The distinction between calendrical, biological, or social age is basic here. Hard-living alcoholics or tobacco addicts have bodies that are older biologically than their calendrical age. In some societies, an unmarried male, or someone unfit for adult duties, could be seen as socially young, whatever their number of days on earth.[41]

The evidence for age grades in deep time is controversial. Dale Guthrie, reporting on Upper Paleolithic caves and cave art in western Europe, believes these paintings and incisions were the work of youths. By measuring handprints and tracks, a miraculous survival in some grottoes, he suggests that many were made by boys or teenagers between 10 and 16 years of age (fig. 6). Dean Snow, another archaeologist, demurs, insisting the makers were women.[42] This is possible but unproven. Statistical overlap blurs the distinction between the hands of youths and grown women, and Snow's results rely on comparisons with modern Europeans, a gap of some 25,000 years. It seems probable that people were less nourished in the Paleolithic, and thus smaller than people today.

Guthrie's larger argument is that the art was intended for training: a "sheltered fooling around."[43] The goal was to instruct youths in the deadly business of hunting large game. Presiding over the whole were older males who, Guthrie believes, supervised a new form of bonding and parenting. Young men stabbed clay sculptures while training or in symbolic pursuit. The repeated animal images, dozens of aurochs or wild horses, show how much youths wanted to kill and consume their prey. Youthful eyes tuned in on animal behavior, the better to harvest meat. Engaged in "testosterone events," they also obsessed about large-breasted women or made careful renderings of female privates. Guthrie's view of cave art as a training manual or form of graphic onanism, stripped of deeper meaning, disturbs some specialists of Upper Paleolithic archaeology. Yet his larger point about the role of youths remains plausible.

Young men's organizations are better documented in later periods. Often, they could be organized for quick aggression, a theme relevant to a book about ancient Maya youth. In classical Greece, *epheboi* passed through puberty. After some years, they left that status to marry. That this was some primordial age grade in ancient Greece seems refuted by later research. In fact, as a practice, it probably came into existence rather late, at about 400 BC, and in response to a wish to train citizens in Athens.[44] When society became more diverse, it needed to re-establish bonds that crosscut the divisions of class. The historical vesting of age grades—signs that they are not one single thing but shifting in nature, responsive to local circumstances—offers a key lesson to Mayanists: even if grades are identified, their meaning and function may change over time.

In classical Greece, for example, adolescence could be a "protracted affair," with evolving duties. The state paid attention, especially in Athens. A personal journey became inflected by political needs, and central authorities intruded into young lives. For this reason, representations of young men altered over time, as did a perception of how important such youths were. The later the image, the more likely that depictions would proliferate, and with new attention to the very young. Pierre Vidal-Naquet, a specialist on ancient Greece, saw these years of development as a time when youths could be activated into military service,

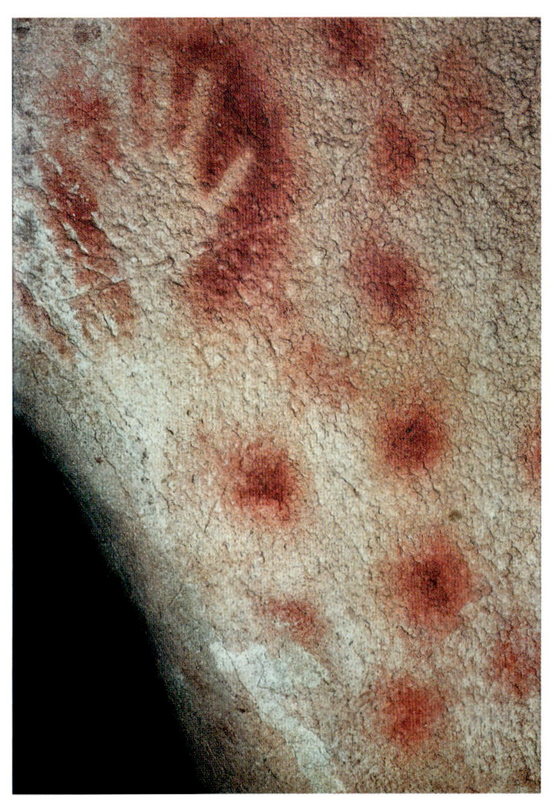

Handprints in ochre, c. 25,000 BC. Ochre on limestone. Peche-Merle, Midi-Pyrénées, France. Courtesy Peabody Museum, Yale University.

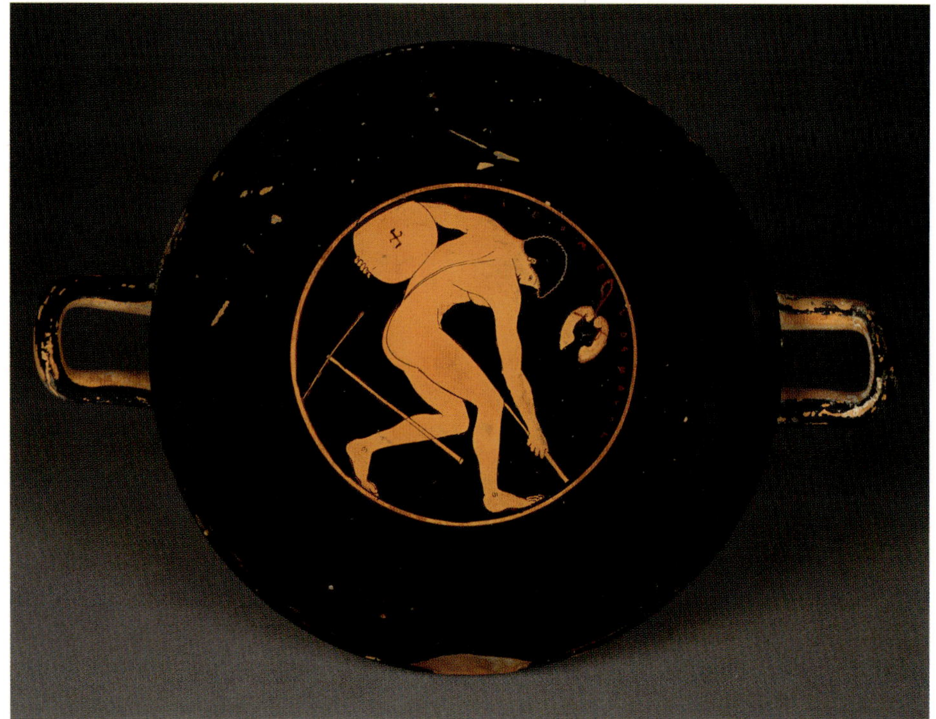

an option noted before regarding jihadists and boy soldiers. This was the case in Sparta, with its regime of legendary rigor and "herds" of youth led by "masters" or "magistrates." In much of Greece, cross-generational ties could be sexualized. Older, bearded males courted younger lovers, sponsoring them in athletic competitions. Eros, that demon who disrupted a steady life, took over and carried away any common sense. Those in love, the *erastai,* the older men, were besotted by their object of affection, the *eronemos.* When depicted, these affairs could correspond to common practices, acted on and acted out. Or they could derive from fantasies played out in exploratory ways.[45]

A stylized beauty, attentive to young males, came to dominate in a variety of media.[46] On Greek ceramics, younger lovers were shown with small genitals, buttocks or thighs rounded, their shoulders muscular. The beloved male, especially the younger ones, could be coy; boys behaving, to ancient Greek mind, more like women: rejecting, yielding. Little was furtive or concealed about these actions. *Kalos,* "beautiful"—a physical, desirable beauty—captions many such figures (fig. 7).[47] The painters evidently found it necessary to offer a superfluous comment, accenting their own delight and guiding viewers to an appropriate judgment of this or that figure, some female but most male. Sculptures known today as *kouroi* were youthful, too.[48] (The label, widespread today, was devised in 1895 by the scholar Vassilis Leonardos. Their ancient epithet is unknown.) First appearing in the seventh century BC, borrowed and reworked from Egyptian models, the *kouroi* stride forward in marmoreal perfection. Most served as grave markers, embodiments of youthful states made permanent in stone.

By some estimates, there were several thousand *kouroi* in the area of Athens. This astonishing number reveals that the imagery was ubiquitous, expressing a widespread view of an ideal male form, full of promise, face not yet bearded. Repetition reinforced that ideal. The *kouroi* also stood as signs and proxies for the idealized dead, part of a "heroic paradigm" for what young men should be and aspire to. As elite visions, they operated as luminous substitutes. Yet that doubling of the real and unreal was tragic, as such beauty would never last. Richard Neer refines this further by noting that the beauty of *kouroi* was "not just an aesthetic category but a social one." The youths extolled with *kalos* texts and shown in this manner were likely to be wealthy. Their images may have been idealized, but the inscriptions identified them as particular people. They combined the general essence of youthful beauty with the affirmation that it belonged to specific youths. Even gods such as Herakles, a figure linked to Greek athletic facilities, became models for young men. Theseus, that disruptor of iniquity and founder of a kingdom, filled the same role.[49]

The timing of these figures deserves explanation. An emphasis on youths, whether as *kouroi* or, somewhat earlier, as figures on tripods, traces a shift from spear-wielding warriors to a different idea of "golden youths" and an external appearance that coincided seamlessly with the character and soul within. Despots might not like to exalt youth, some of them fractious or rebellious, and the weight shifts away from *kouroi* by the fifth century BC. The history of how these ideal male images have been received, and thoughts projected on them, entwines the origins of art history with the visualization of longing and the sexualization of aesthetics. Johann Winckelmann, John Addington Symonds, or Sigmund Freud looked to the male form and its depiction for their own reflections on beauty and desire. Here is Winckelmann on the Apollo Belvedere: "An eternal springtime, as if in blissful Elysium, clothes the charming manliness of maturity with graceful youthfulness, and plays with soft tenderness on the proud build of his limbs." Alex Potts, an art historian, sees a delectable ambiguity in Winckelmann's prose, invoking "competing fantasies of unyielding domination and exquisite desirability." As Potts observes, later and less gushing views of this sculpture express shifting notions of ideal masculinity.[50] By the early nineteenth century, the critic William Hazlitt derided the Apollo as a "theatrical coxcomb," a far cry from Winckelmann's praise.

In behavior, however, the young men, especially the category of *epheboi*, were a conceptual anomaly to Pierre Vidal-Naquet. They inverted adult expectation. What was acceptable for youths ran counter to what mature males could do. Wild in nature, hunting by themselves, deceptive with prey, stalking the desolate mountainous areas, they stood for a disengaged life away from the center. Youths patrolled the edges of the polity, and were both socially and physically liminal to the state. In Rome, young men could be organized into such groups, with presiding "princes," the *principes juventutis.* The eminent historian Georges Duby, writing of medieval France, drew attention to similar bands of *jeunes* (youths) who lived in joyful luxury, and, in his words, "pro-longed turbulence." They served also as military formations at the blade's edge of feudalism.[51]

Ideas and practices vary greatly, as we have seen. Yet certain themes emerge in any wide-ranging survey: the mixed fear and admiration felt toward young men; the desirability of adult guidance; the grouping of youths, by others or by themselves; the homosocial or even homoerotic tinge to relations within those groups; the use of young men for labor and war; and, under specific conditions, the social and artistic prominence of adolescents or young men. There is a persistent belief, partly grounded in physical reality, that youths possess a troubling, muscular energy. In societies largely run by men, the men-to-be—those soon taking charge—command the most attention. Older people worry about how to set apart yet fold in, instruct, and improve the young. So much could go wrong. Social science jargon refers to "social reproduction," how men and women instill appropriate values and behaviors in later generations.[52] When boys grow into men a broader aim begins to form. By Marxian analysis, the continuance of male domination—elite male domination, to be exact—must renew itself, a consensus forged and enforced about "good" and "bad" masculinity. Some of this perspective of the world is overblown or, in the extreme, based on a premise of dark intrigue. How uniform or orchestrated was this urge to control, and did adults truly self-replicate in younger generations? And to the nub of it: how robotic are humans in doing what others want them to do? But there can be little doubt of one thing. Though prospects of noble youth trigger concern, it is an unease tempered with hope and pride.

In Mesoamerica, home to the ancient Maya among other cultures, regional patterns echo these features. The richest of all evidence, other than the Classic Maya, comes from Aztec or Nahuatl-language sources of central Mexico. Dating to a few decades after the Spanish conquest, they doubtless reflect older views, in that the native informants were often born prior to European rule. This is rather like the widely cited accounts from anthropologists, who, as mentioned before, often report on a memory of practices and beliefs, not actual observation of them. The Aztec documents speak of *tlācahuapāhualiztli,* the task of mastering youth. They valued a "virile heart," which might be applied to certain women as well. (Female traits, when linked to men, implied a lack of spirit or resolve.)[53] These subtleties are clarified by the lists of moral opposites so beloved of the Aztecs: a good son resembles his parents, and is "obedient, humble, gracious, grateful, reverent." A bad one is "perverse, wicked, rebellious; a vile brute . . . agitated, impetuous, fitful." Tractability, a submission to elders and betters, induces praise. So do seemly behavior, modesty, wit, storytelling ability, and fine appearance. But a smart-alecky, bad youth "goes about mocking, telling tales, being rude, repeating insults."[54]

For the Aztec, stages of life could be narrowly segmented. An infant became a toddler, then an older child, both almost nondescript in gender. It grew into a boy, youth, and mature man. Substages were recognized as well, three for youth alone. Some stages were marked by specific rites, the first piercing of ears, the insertion of labrets or lip plugs or, for girls, the scarring of breasts and hips. A page in the Codex Borbonicus, a central Mexican book dating to the first decades after the Spanish conquest, shows the ritual duties of the young in a scene of dancing around a ritual pole, the boys arranged by relative size. They differ in other ways, despite nearly identical dress. Leading the line, the two tallest (and probably the oldest) wear flowers in their hair, the next two a set of feathers. All have turquoise-blue ear ornaments. The next five do as well, but their heads are uncovered. Coming up last: two boys not yet equipped with fine ear jewelry. Eventually, according to another source, they competed to ascend the pole, pushing away their rivals, grappling and stretching, some falling from a height. The four winners seized parts of a fetish atop the pole. The strict dress codes and groupings—four in total—are evident, as is an enigmatic "god of the boys … the devil speaks in him," a figure at the bottom of a small pyramid to lower right in the image. Presumably, he is a god impersonator, the winner of the melee or a boy about to be sacrificed. For the Aztecs, both might be honored roles. The overall ritual is, however, one dedicated to the dead: youth in service of those have passed on. The author makes another point clear, "here no woman entered."[55]

Aside from such spaces, a vital demarcation had to do with taking a youth to a special place where he would live with other youths of the same gender. The Spanish fumbled for analogies, describing these places as "not unlike a boarding school," a "house of higher learning," even a "monastery" in which youths conducted lives of "chastity, poverty, and obedience."[56] Maidens aged 12 to 13 similarly went to "convents," but these are discussed with far less precision. Aztec descriptions were highly poetic: the place for noble youths, the *calmecac,* was the house of scourging, the "house of weeping, the house of tears, the house of sadness, where the sons of noblemen are cast, are perforated; where they bud, where they blossom; where [they are] like precious necklaces, like precious feathers."[57] Like perfect jewels, they were polished and displayed, their quality enhanced. Slices in their bodies let loose blood for ritual benefaction. Society, too, received direct benefit from the occupants of the *calmecac.* Evoking labor organization elsewhere, work parties made adobe bricks, built walls, hoed agricultural fields, and cut canals. On a page of the Codex Mendoza, such a building is at the top right (fig. 8). The seated father to the left has sent one 15-year-old son to that place, where the *tlamcazqui,* "head priest," receives him near his *mezquita,* "mosque" or "temple." (To the Spaniards, one abode of false religion hardly differed from another. Why not liken a Mexican temple to a place of Muslim worship?) Sculptures of sectioned conch shells, linked to the Aztec god Quetzalcoatl, a deity of esoteric learning, line its roof. Less prominent youths went to a house, the *tēlpōchcalli,* where unmarried young men arrived, sent by local social groups or city precincts.

Within this building, identities blurred and were then reconstituted. The young men were an "offering" to it, the property of the house. Tedious or demanding duties awaited them. There was sweeping, the adoption of modest clothing that did not warm very much on chilly nights, fasting, bloodletting. On the more amusing side, youths also

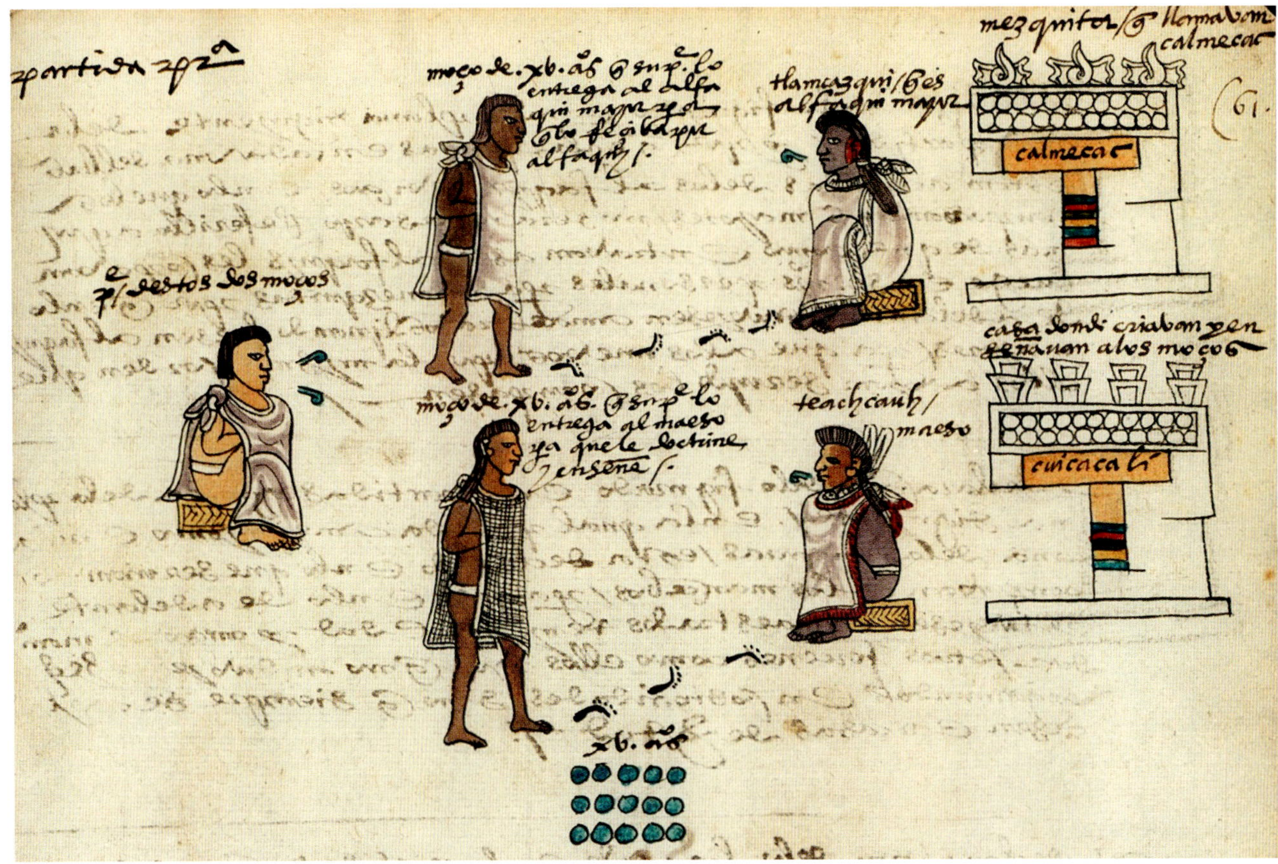

FIGURE 8

Codex Mendoza, fol. 61r, c. AD 1541.
Ink and brush on paper, 12⅞ × 9 in.
(32.7 × 22.9 cm). Bodleian
Libraries, University of Oxford, MS.
Arch. Selden A. 1.

trained in dance, song, and writing. In some feasts, youths were especially encouraged
to cut themselves for blood sacrifice. Older men presided over the labor, instruction,
and duty.[58] Singing was practiced in the *cuīcalli,* "house of song," along with the composition and recitation of poetry. In some images, that house appeared below the *calmecac,*
perhaps denoting some physical proximity or ranking. Having taken captives in battle, a
leading youth might return to "nurture and rear" his compatriots. Tasks tended to change
with age. Younger men, especially in houses preparing for the priesthood, would watch
and stoke the fires, while others took up arms at 15 and went to war at 20. Excavations
under the busy Donceles Street in Mexico City, near the Great Temple of the Aztecs, have
found what is probably a *calmecac* for young lords (fig. 9).[59] Centrally situated, it was
adorned with carvings of conch shells dedicated to the presiding god, Quetzalcoatl; the
same can be seen as roof ornaments in figure 8. An open floor plan gave access to benches
against the back wall.

Discipline was harsh in such houses. If youths drank too much or consorted
with concubines, they might find themselves in wooden cages, to be stoned or strangled.
Other sources suggest that sexual liaisons were permitted and older youths allowed privileges denied to younger ones. Young men were certainly regarded as delectable offerings

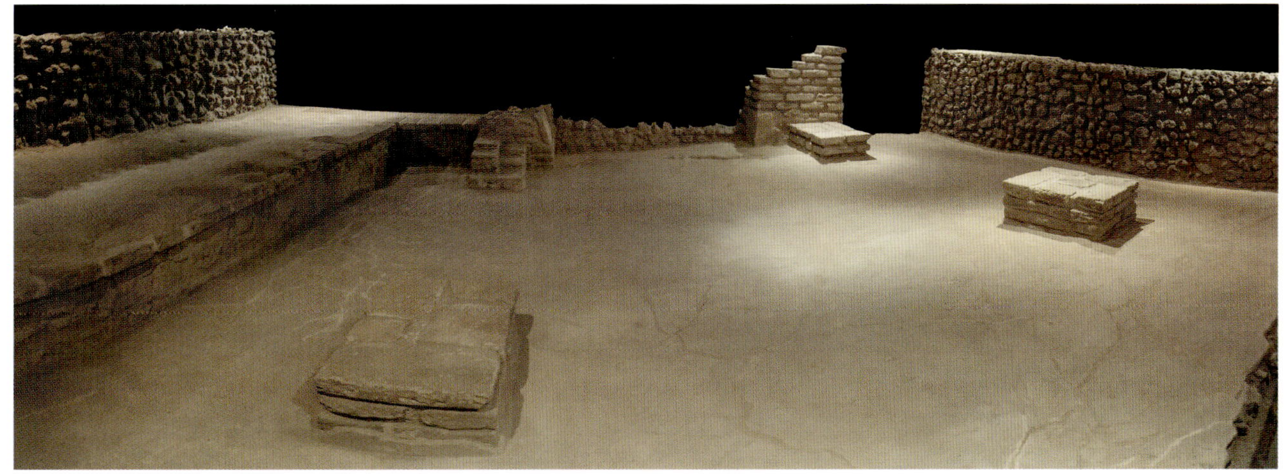

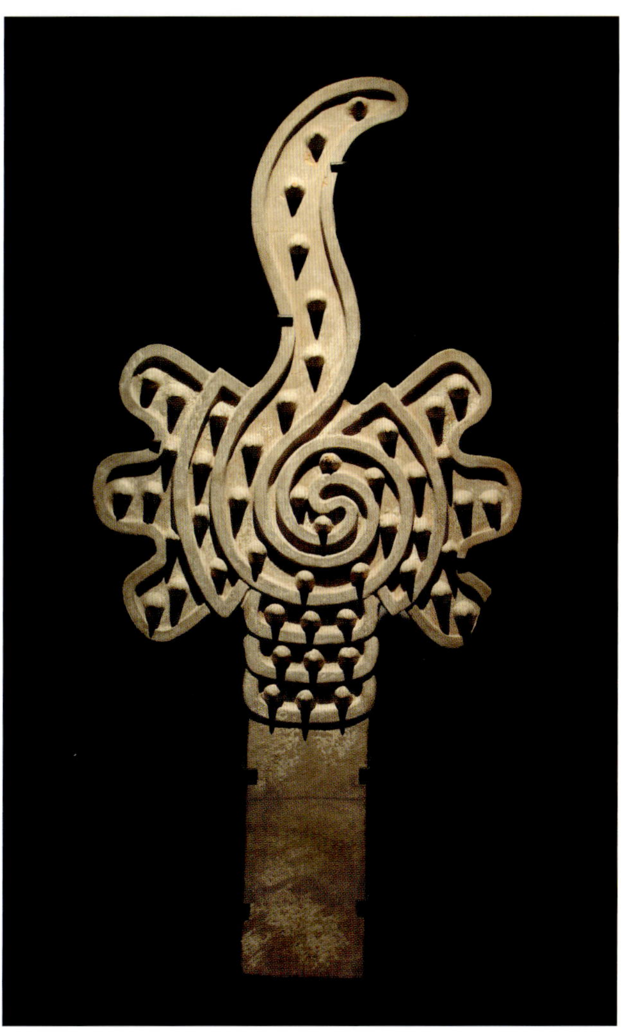

FIGURE 9

Calmecac, Mexico City, c. AD 1500:
A) Panorama; B) Roof ornament.
Fired clay. 96 in. (2.43 m). Photo-
graphs by Jorge Pérez de Lara.

to gods. In one feast, *Toxcatl,* youths were sacrificed as the images of a particular god after having carnal relations with four "comely young women."[60] Departure from the house of weeping only happened when a young man, a changed person, left to marry. Youths committed to a merchant's life had their own apprenticeship, sometimes on the road.[61] The sources are thin, but women seem to have had far shorter stays in their houses. Whether homoeroticism affected life among the young in these houses remains a matter of debate. The Aztec sources are unequivocal about punishments for such behavior. Modern authors, from a different vantage point, see it as a more common, even tolerated practice.[62] The strength of Aztec denunciations may in fact reflect Christian attitudes after the conquest, but their intensity suggests deeper origins.

❖ ❖ ❖

Thinking about human difference is, strangely enough, a refracted process. To look at others is to look at ourselves. Along the way, much takes place. For most people, life slices into notional segments, whatever the reality of continuous experience. Distinctions arise between stages and kinds of people—the privileged and the poor, male and female, or more fluid categories of gender. Means are found to mark and ease transitions, to mold, instruct, and improve. There is a strong, undeniable input from the physical body. Humans are not bees, of course, enslaved to group resolve, but they are social animals. Others have a say in how we behave. This is where looking and showing make a difference. They model how the voyage of life should take place, its stages labeled and discussed, its features depicted, and the overall trip regulated. In a sense, Thomas Cole and the unknown Maya painter were concerned with the aim of social and aesthetic modeling. They offered not reality, but how reality should be, as rendered, in general, by men who had been boys, and elite ones to boot.

There is little doubt that, around the globe, youthful maturation poses a challenge. By wide belief, and some proof, strong bodies combine with low levels of restraint or self-control. The problems can be solvable, the vexations inflated. But sometimes the whole is messy, unpredictable, worrisome, and, in the case of young men, a little unfashionable to scholars of gender. A few, such as Michael Kimmel, denounce "guys." Dale Guthrie, writing about the Paleolithic, may even overstress their importance, flattening everything to hormonal chemistry. But gender specialists in Mesoamerica seem less attentive. This is unfortunate, for the stakes could not have been higher. At center is nothing less than the continuance of society and its structures of power. The Classic Maya clearly understood the challenge for their own courtly societies. Youths mattered and were shown to matter, on pots and murals, in painted texts and inscriptions, through sacrifices and lavish interments. Boys grew into men in kingdoms that cared deeply about this troubled if gifted passage: they were splendid—beautiful to behold, active—and a very real predicament. The Maya had their own Hamlets, their treasured princes, neglected by scholarship despite a definite centrality in their society.

The many references to them are where we turn in the next chapter, in glyphic texts that identify noble youths as "Growing Men." That terminology is detailed but central to understanding these young men. The chapter just after, "A Gifted Passage," looks to the sedate features of their world, followed by a view, in "The Taming Places," of their wilder, darker side and how youths were set apart from others. It is at Bonampak, to be discussed in "The Good Prince," that a specific, exemplary career comes to the fore. This concerns a *ch'ok,* a prince of highest lineage, about whom his dynasty evinced an almost desperate interest. He lived, fought, and danced while his kingdom sank into decay. If there are young men, there must also be, as the ultimate aim, old men of wise counsel. These were the people who made it through to the other side of the unsettled, sometimes violent lives of Maya lords. They await us in the final part of the book, "Draining the Cup." For the ancient Maya, youths grow their conceptual counterparts: gray-haired, bearded men, at once wise and foolish, the decrepit who have become mighty at the end of life.

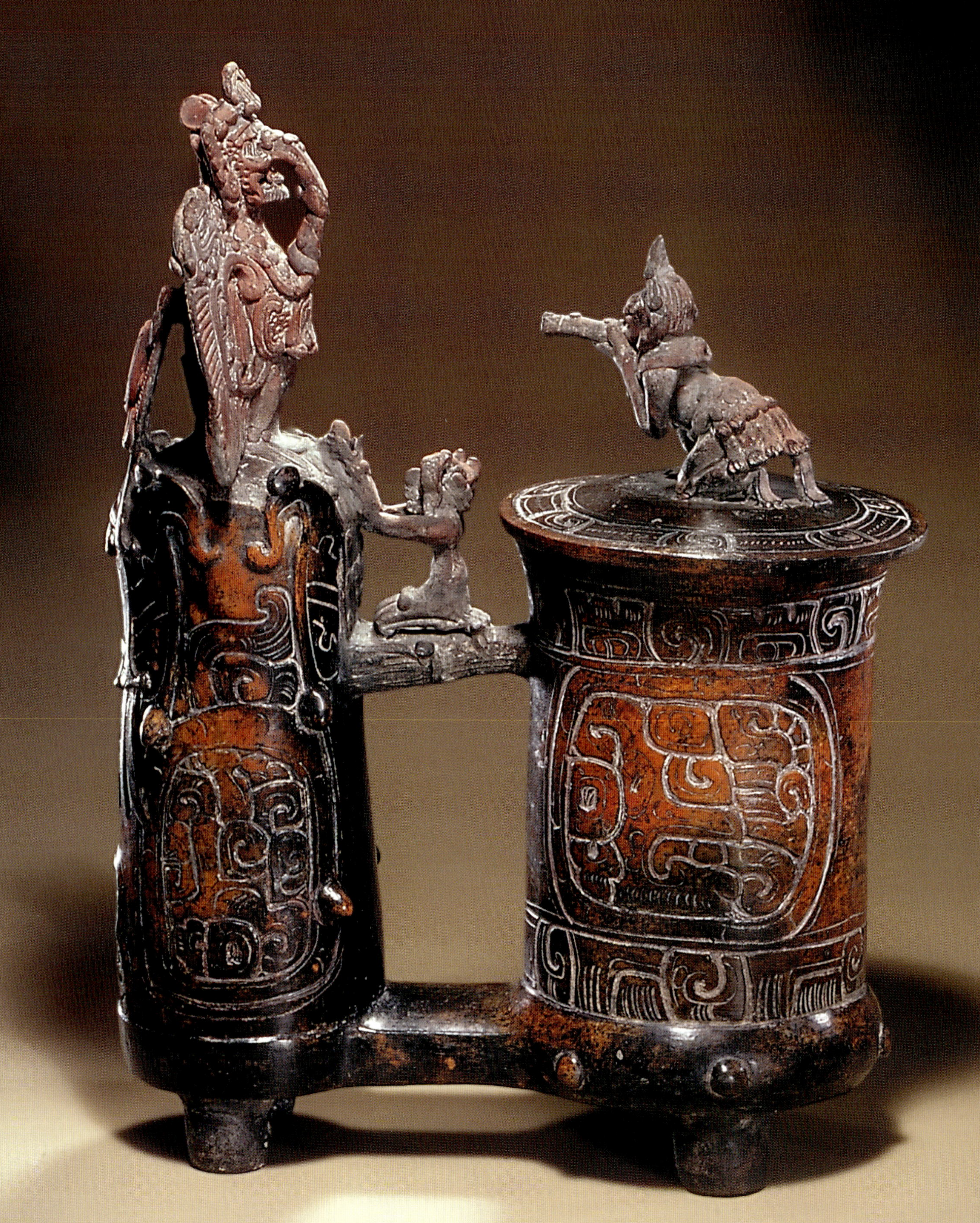

2   Growing Men Among the Maya

The Spaniards, arriving in the Maya region, took swift notice of young men. They found souls to save and future leaders to control. In the sixteenth century, Bartolomé de las Casas, Dominican "Protector of the Indians," described special houses for teenagers and unmarried males in the Alta Verapaz of Guatemala.[1] Bishop Diego de Landa, writing of Yucatan to the north, observed the same. Youths congregated in a large building "whitened with lime, open on all sides." They gambled and slept together, chastely, we are told. As with the Aztecs, they left only to marry. Las Casas observed other kinds of behavior. "The older youths in that vice [sodomy] corrupted the boys, who departed afterwards badly accustomed, making it difficult to free them from that vice."[2] Another source, probably drawn from eyewitness accounts by the conquistador Martín de Ursúa, grumbled that young men "spent most of their time in idolatry, dancing, and getting drunk at all hours and times with the strong beverages they knew how to make."[3]

At least the dances involved skill, coordination, and strength. The costumes were heavy, the performances long, and movements skilled. Other kinds of stamina were needed as well. The *Cantares de Dzitbalché*, a compilation of songs from colonial Yucatan, offered lyric poems about youthful life. Strongly erotic, even nostalgic, one canto implored females to "take off your clothes, undo your hair, remain as you were when you arrived on the earth [naked], virgins, young women."[4] Parties drew on the good things of life. There were flowers, scented copal, and tortoise shells to be struck and rasped musically with a deer antler. Calcite paste beautified the body; conch blasts energized dance. The air, we can guess, thrummed with excitement.

Why the attention to youths? Accounts from living Maya provide one explanation. At about 15 years of age, young men working in fields produce more than they consume. Among the Tojolobal Maya, a group in the mountains of Chiapas, Mexico, marriage relieves them of being *kerem*, "single," a term we will see again.[5] But it also dedicates them to grueling "whole" work. Youths exhibit new strengths for general use. Their toil ensures a good harvest, and everyone benefits from youthful service, such as digging a water hole, lifting loads, running messages, leveling a road, or reinforcing a wall. Among elites of more distant times—or so the *Cantares* affirm—young energy had other channels. It gravitated toward performance, ritual, revelry, sport, and the arts of war, writing, and carving.

SEE FIGURE 14

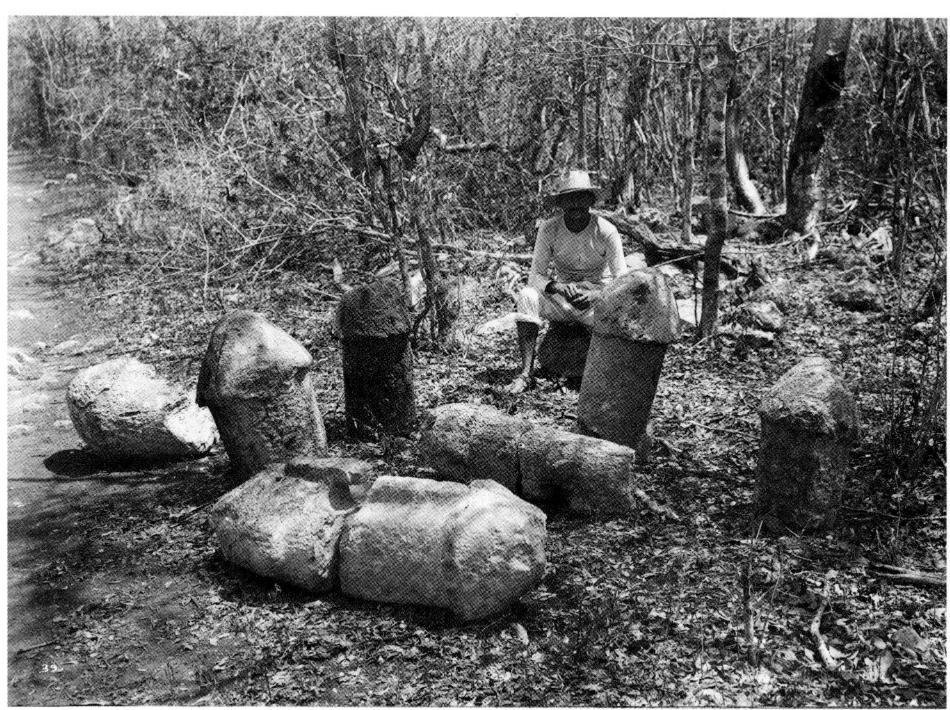

Group of stone phalli, west of the Casa de la Vieja, Uxmal, Mexico, c. AD 800. Photograph by Jesse L. Nusbaum, 1913. Courtesy Palace of the Governors Photo Archives (NMHM/DCA), Negative no. 059981.

But a point needs making: whatever the illusion of independence, young men were never in charge—a point that was emphasized in the preceding chapter. The impresarios and instructors were adults. Only with their guidance did the young learn upright behavior. Proper appearance was whipped into them or urged on them by peer pressure.

Maya evidence touches on universal themes, many raised in earlier pages of this book. Young men can be evaluated for their potential. People look at them for what they will become. But, in the here-and-now, they offer labor and liveliness. No denying it, they also induce concern. Things can go amiss in their seasoning. Society may not reproduce itself, and youthful energy could fritter away to nothing or lead to violence. The Maya, especially those of the Classic period, are telling in another respect. They display a committed interest in youths as embodiments of masculinity, even of beauty. In this detail, to eerie extent, they resemble the ancient Greeks. Disquiet was there in equal measure. Anxiety about honor and dishonor almost vibrates in surviving evidence. Here we focus on that evidence: the attributes and meaning of being male, the crystallization of those features into images, along with the labels used specifically to identify young men. Made accessible through recent study, glyphs provide an ample if at times opaque vocabulary for youths, the most common term being "sprout." How the labels appear, and in what settings, disclose how boys grew into men at the apex of Maya society. Yet not all is clear in matters of gender. Maya evidence engages the very heart of that complexity.

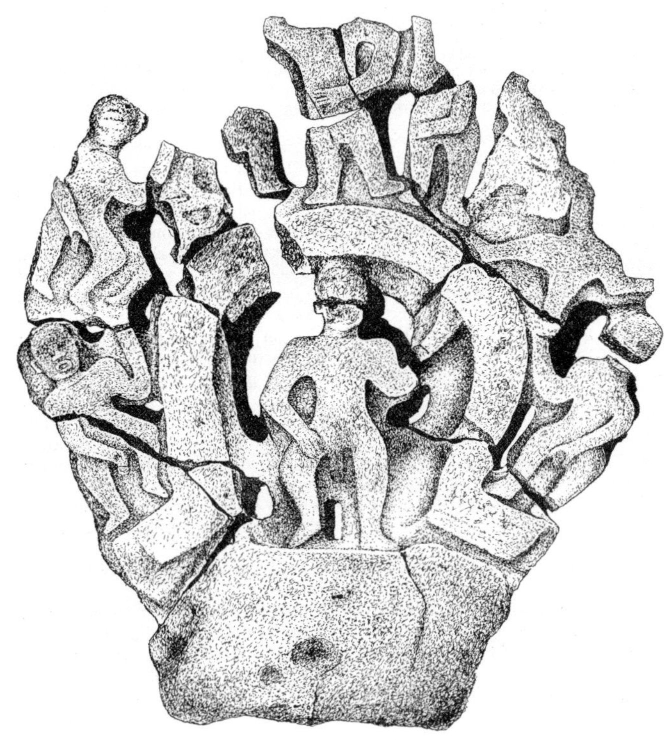

PHALLI, BEAUTY, HONOR

Physical evidence of men mortified some later visitors to Maya cities. Arriving after the Spanish conquest, they saw large stone phalli at ruins across Campeche and Yucatan in Mexico. Few carvings remain in their original context, and caretakers had often gathered them in one place. This reduced the potential for embarrassment—in the argot of the tourist industry, ruins became more "family friendly"—yet it also created a "photo-op": what better way to underscore the sheer foreignness of the ancient Maya (fig. 10)? The few phalli with context were found on the stoop or inside a temple. Priests may have dribbled blood or some other liquid over them. The carvings that survive often measure a meter or more in length. Without exception, they are columns in full "arousal," ready for action. Only a few have testicles, and all show circumcision. This may reflect a Maya version of the Jewish bris, or even a by-product of the first act of penile bloodletting (later chapters will explore the ritual in more detail). Some display sticks or thorns in erectile tissue. Genital piercing involved its own form of discipline and was perhaps the result, too, of age-related rites.[6]

In and around Telantunich, Yucatan, are relevant tableaux dating to the final years of the Late Classic period (fig. 11). Half-men or half-beasts, reeling in dance or drunken abandon, clutch their members. They look like figures from society's fringe, possibly ritual clowns—such are known for the Maya at all periods—or they are characters that lived in prehuman times. Creation stories, such as the Popol Vuh from colonial Guatemala, certainly refer to monkey men, and the faces of Telantunich veer close to the grotesque or barely human. They may illustrate stories set long before the Classic period.[7] On a few stelae, none with texts, enigmatic skeletons dance alone, in frontal pose with splayed feet. They dangle long if rather limp penises.[8]

The question is, are these tokens of the "hegemonic masculinity" described in the last chapter, the "display and performance of the idealized male," and the "sexualization" of the male body, as some studies propose? At the risk of seeming flippant, there is no question that penises belong to males—true hermaphrodites, those with both testicular and ovarian tissue, represent a small percentage of humans, numbering about one in 100,000. (This does not mean, of course, that hermaphrodites failed to intrigue people in the past: their existence disrupted easy classification of humans, leading logically to membership in sacred or monstrous categories.) Men probably commissioned the carvings. The phalli are large, beyond any human scale, and their makers doubtless wanted to impress. They may even have been uproarious. In Maya humor, the penis is cause for endless merriment. The Tzotzil, a Maya group in Chiapas, Mexico, call a boy's phallus his *mut,* "bird," and they use a bull's detached penis, waved in the face or poked, to embarrass women. Dried and stretched, it becomes a whip for clowns dressed as monkeys. Yet the meanings of these astonishing carvings are hard to pin down, in part because of an inherent range of response. A female breast elicits different sensations from a lover, a nursing baby, a prude in our society, other men and women (depending on sexual orientation), a celibate priest, an oncologist, or a very young girl. The same holds true for a phallus. Several reactions can exist at once. Think of the lingam, a phallic emblem in Hindu religion. It embodies divine energy and the god Śiva.[9] As a symbol, it descends from millennia of thought and spiritual practice. Sex or desire alone do not explain its essence or use in ritual. Indeed, any phallus in a public or ritual setting is apt to involve more complex ideas and reactions. The Maya skeletons on stelae have conspicuous if drooping members. But how erotic, really, is a carcass?

The fact is, outside of the phalli of Yucatan, the Classic Maya rarely displayed the penis. A few occur, as at Aguateca, Guatemala, in the form of what appear to be dildos, ever-erect, but of unusual material, a stalactite or stalagmite from a cave. That origin hints at nonerotic meaning. A number occur at the city of Nixtun-Ch'ich' in northern Guatemala, perhaps as sculptures inserted into walls. Most exposed phalli are in scenes of humiliated captives. One of the few visible phalli at Palenque, Mexico, sags heavily, monstrously enlarged, from what may be a captive in the east court of its palace. To exhibit genitalia was, from all accounts, to liken a person to an animal, a creature heedless of modesty. Beasts flaunt their privates or, to put this more precisely, expose them readily. With rare exceptions, people do not. Bloodletting by Classic royalty or nobles was almost coyly discreet. A penis just jabbed or ready for such cuts lay concealed behind clothing or an artfully placed thigh. Karl Taube has identified faux phalli in the Bonampak murals of Mexico. Dancers spun around and stamped, with sticks thrust through their "penises." It was all stagecraft. No penis was injured in the performance. Other images of bloodletting may show phalli, but in primordial rites by gods. Modeled figures from Santa Rita Corozal, in Postclassic Belize, feature old deities who pierce their members.[10] Turtles underfoot wallow in an ancient sea. Symbolically, the blood may have mixed with water in *ur*-oceans or the sea itself was pooled from this sacrificial liquid.

A scene in the Madrid Codex, of roughly the same date, sends shivers up the spine (fig. 12).[11] Not for the squeamish, it assembles five gods threading a single rope through the tip of their penises. Their position corresponds in all likelihood to the four directions of the cosmos, all in eternal relation to the center. The celebrants appear to be in a choreographed trance. It may have been for this dance—as performed by humans—that openings (or placeholders) were left in penises: recall the sticks or thorns in the carved phalli. Again, the incident is mythic. At the center is a building surmounted by a sea turtle and the Maya glyph for *yax,* "new, first" or the color "blue-green" (a color that, in Maya thought, corresponds to the center point of their directional symbolism). Below is a stone platform. This image of agony does not illustrate unvarnished, beefy masculinity. There is no enjoyable sex, idealization of the male body, or sense of everyday events. The concepts are deeper and penitential, the phallocracy—in Eva Keul's terms—is understated, if present at all. As bits of tissue, penises belong to males. But the effort, pain, and self-denial in piercing and bloodletting do not put sex in mind. The act itself may have been difficult to perform after such abuse. Pre-Freudians though they were, the Classic Maya seem to have transformed sites of pleasure, the mouths for eating and conversation, the penises for sex, into places of pain.

As Mary Miller points out, the Maya may have perceived some equivalence between genital sacrifice and female menstrual periods.[12] The link is plausible. After all, both flows of blood come from the groin. Yet menstrual cycles are probably best attested away from sacrificial scenes, in the so-called Moon Pages of the Dresden Codex. A nubile goddess, *Sak Ixik,* often pairs with male deities. At times, she is said to be their *atan,* "wife." Discreet coupling occurs on some pages. Delicate touches of the hand and body hint at subtle foreplay, nothing to blush about. It is probably no coincidence that her name evokes another, *sakal ixik,* "white woman," or menstruation in Yukateko Maya. On another page of the Dresden Codex, the goddess is said to *hul,* "arrive," a term close to Yukateko *hula,* "menstruation." Far earlier, in dynastic texts at Naranjo, Guatemala, a foreign princess also arrives, *huli,* to resuscitate the royal line. Was this phrasing perhaps a common expression for elite movement? Or did it allude to the fertility of a future queen? The logic resonates with modern thought. Some time ago, in describing menstrual periods, the French might have said "les anglais ont débarqué" (the English have landed), presumably considered a poor omen in that country.

Many phalli in Maya imagery and texts did not belong to humans. If there was "hegemony," it involved the dominion of gods. One of the rare sights of ejaculation or urination, from a Classic-period bowl at Cahal Pech, Belize, involves streams from a god's

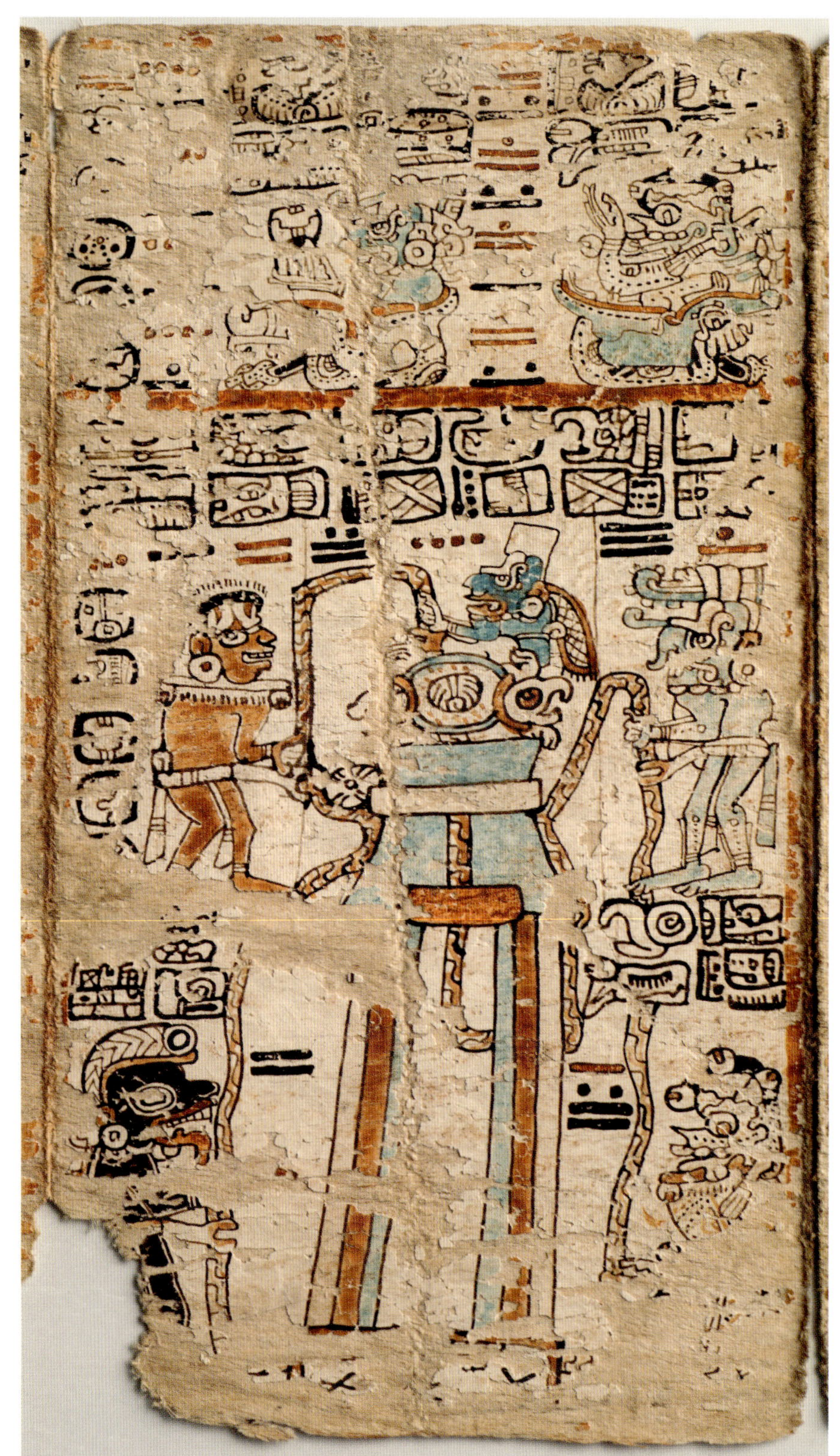

FIGURE 12
Rope dance with perforated
penises, Codex Madrid, p. 19,
Postclassic period.

FIGURE 13

Deity in ejaculation or urination, Cahal Pech, Belize, Late Classic period. Polychrome ceramic, after drawing by Andrea Stone.

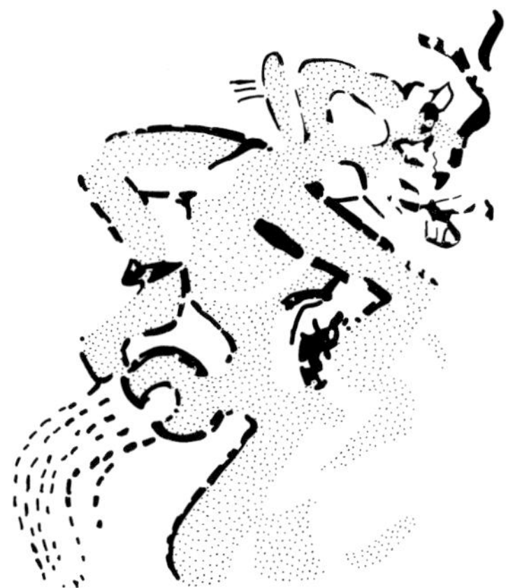

phallus (fig. 13). A penis in royal names, thought in one study to highlight human masculinity, simply labels a variant of the Maya deity of rain.[13] Rather like Thor or Zeus, he is an angry god, shooting sparks, weapon in hand. Perhaps he personified a particularly violent storm. One could go further. As hinted by their great size, the carved phalli imply nonhuman bodies. In Maya art, outsized, gigantic images of people are rare indeed, and those that exist do so because viewers were meant to see them from a distance, as in the Preclassic wall carving at San Diego or effigies of seated lords on high temple façades at Tikal, both sites in Guatemala. At Uxmal, in Yucatan, the aptly named Temple of the Phalli uses phalli as waterspouts. Other places, such as Rancho San Pedro in Campeche, Mexico, did the same, and a stucco phallus, 7.5 inches (19 cm) high, modeled on the walls of a probable cistern, was found in Xkipche, Yucatan. As noted by the archaeologist Traci Ardren, when rain fell, stony urethras gushed with generative fluid for plants. This was not a flow of human origin. The water came from clouds controlled by the Rain God. Ritual attention to liquid, conceived as divine semen, made sense in one of the driest areas of the Yucatan peninsula. Some of that fluid came from other gods, including skeletal ones of ominous import.[14]

Yet aesthetics did play a role, as did the chance that the male form could objectify beauty. In this, we remember the *kouroi* of Greece. The youthful Maize God epitomized that appeal. A quintessential male—supple, athletic, and smooth-skinned—he was sometimes accompanied by spouses or corn maidens. A few mourned his "passing" when he set off for a watery, well-irrigated death. One pot from about AD 500 has him neatly wrapped as a corpse on a bier, surrounded by weeping maidens.[15] The poetic attraction of the metaphor is that corn rises again and again from hard seed corn and a good dose of rain. In their diet and bodies, the Maya were the "people of maize." The message of renewal and rebirth, a plant rising as a sprout, must have comforted humans knowing they were sure to die. Our doughy bodies also explain why gods found us good to eat. To some scholars, head deformation of children, resulting in elongated crania, enhanced the affinity of Classic Maya to ears of corn.[16] A match was accentuated between inner essence, a flesh of "maize," and surface appearance. For living Maya, at least in traditional belief, humans do equate themselves to vegetation and to maize in particular. Among the Tzotzil, the "unripe heads" of boys and girls "mature" or "ripen" like plants. In the past, the link to maize might have been less metaphor than literal equivalence. A magical transubstantiation took place in which vegetal matter became human flesh, and flesh the "maize" food of gods.

Several specialists interpret the Maize God as a cross-dresser or a "two-spirit" person , who is neither male nor female but is something else. Such individuals are certainly found in Native North American cultures, where two-spirits discharge special ritual roles and lie outside or between conventional categories of gender.[17] There is some support for this in Maya languages. Several words suggest an elastic, changeable, or blended concept of gender. Ch'ol Maya, a tongue close to that of the Maya inscriptions, refers to ancestors by means of a collective term, *tat-na*, "father-mother," just as ancestral deities in Tzotzil went by *totilme'iltik*, "mother-father." Not all such beings are benign. Among the Tzeltal Maya, they personify the earth, lurking by paths as clods of soil, eager to steal the souls of the unwary.[18]

More puzzling—yet proof positive for dual-gender or blurred-gender theorists—is a term for priests among the K'iche' in highland Guatemala. This is *chuchkajawib*, "mother-father." The title may reflect a true fusion of genders, and there are indications in Mesoamerica that gods could embrace male and female attributes. Among the Ch'orti' Maya, a "[supernatural] is a single entity but can take on either sex at will, as the situation demands, and in some cases it has certain of the characteristics of both sexes in a single body."[19] Yet, as a title, "mother-father" could personify the collective authority behind ritual occupations. It does not so much mix gender, perhaps, as condense wisdom from parents and the men and women before them.

Proposals for blurred gender have other problems. Cisgender—gender tied to sex perceived or assigned at birth—typifies creator couples in Mesoamerica.[20] These templates for human nature are always a male and a female in necessary duality. Complementary opposites matter, not their free blending or supposed instability. I believe other clues have been misread by specialists. A single, unitary creator "goddess" at the site of Palenque, Mexico, is quite exploded by the research of David Stuart, the premier specialist in Maya writing. That deity is none other than the male Maize God. There is no intrinsic reason to see him as female or a person of fluid gender. His raiment is relevant, too. Typically, the god wears a beaded skirt that also adorns rulers and their consorts in Classic Maya imagery. For a few Mayanists, the skirt correlates with female identity.[21] If adopted by men, it signals cross-dressing or transgendering. Yet this assumes that the skirt marks gender at all. It may not. An alternative is that it links the ruler and his wives, not to transvestite conduct, but to the Maize God and his consorts. Human identities are simply mapped onto divine ones. The beaded skirt establishes a systematic bond between royalty and gods associated with the main food of Maya civilization.

There is a final obstacle to the claim for common mention of transgender in Classic-period evidence. Hieroglyphs once thought to conflate the maize deity with females, thus mixing the two, are, according to the epigrapher Marc Zender, entirely distinct signs.[22] Instead of blurring gender, the glyphs uphold a categorical difference between men and women. Of course, no interpretation escapes the conditions of its time or the biases of its framer. As mentioned in the preface, I am intensely aware of that dilemma. But perhaps too much is being asked of the Classic Maya. Have they been enlisted to reflect a worldview from the present day? Undoubtedly, the ancient Maya did

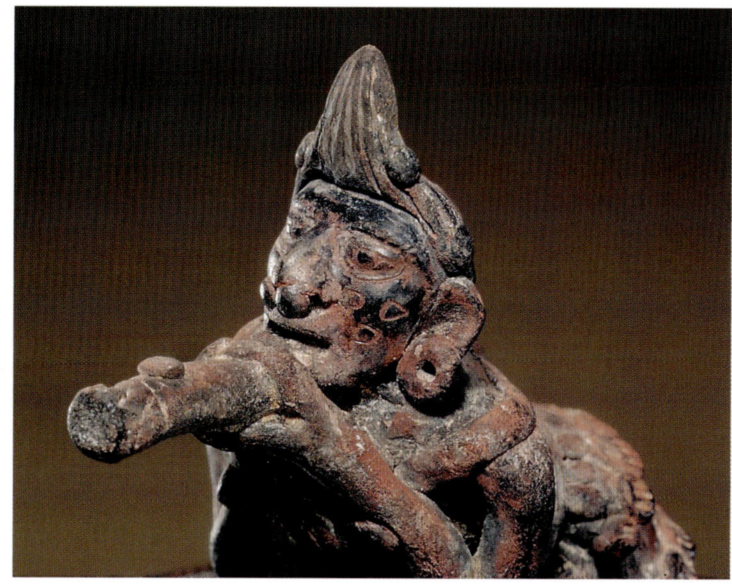

have transvestites and transgendered people. It is harder to argue that they abound in elite texts and imagery.

In one regard, the Maize God differs substantially from youthful humans. In most scenes he is already a married adult. The more likely models for young men were the so-called Hero Twins, two lords who appear together, watering the maize god while he emerges, dancing, as a new-grown plant, blowgunning mythic birds, serving kings: as Karl Taube has shown, one youth epitomizes human lordship, the other sovereignty over animals and forests (fig. 14). The Popol Vuh portrays them as mischievous, transformative, subversive of authority, not always controllable. Part trickster, mercurial and disobedient, they also make the world a better place. Upending death, they bustle with muscular energy, and, if killed, duly switch out with even more rambunctious replacements. They tend fields, go after game that destroys crops, crush upstarts who presume too much power. They are twins for a reason: their individual existence is always in relation to another male youth, the two bonded at birth, complementary in their natures but also distinct. In a sense, they embody why young men can be so distinct yet so similar. Unlike the Hero Twins, however, who were always shown in adult or near-adult form, the Maize God can also occur as a newborn. He appears as a baby on its back, arms flailing.[23] A curious fact is that some Maya gods were born in adult form, their essential nature in place, rather like Athena springing from the brow of Zeus. "All babies look like Winston Churchill," joked the journalist Edward Murrow. The Maya might have agreed. Old gods were as wrinkled and gap-toothed as infants. But, as indicated later in this book, they were anything but weak.

This does not mean that deities had little to do with youths. To the contrary, for gods youths were delectable. A report from northern Guatemala in the colonial period

tells us that the plumper the better, the more tender as "food" for gods. The *Cantares,*
so vivid in describing seduction, praise the beauty of captives, the "virile boys, unpol-
luted, virginal." Comeliness was enhanced by perfume and body paint. Beauty involved
hard work. The pain of sacrifice itself could be stretched out as its own kind of offering;
"little by little, as the Beautiful Lord God wanted it," runs an especially sinister passage of
the *Cantares.* Robust youths did this bloody work. "Men of the shield enter the middle of
the plaza in good order to test their strength in the Dance of the Kolomché. In the middle
of the plaza is a man (*xiib*) tied to the shaft of a stone column, well painted with beautiful indigo. Placed on him are many Balche flowers to perfume him, along with palms in
his hands."[24] The tone is almost soothing, to set the offering at ease. Much effort went into
making him tasty to gods.

A slight digression brings masculinity back into the picture. In moments of personal crisis—how to respond to torture, a theme in the *Cantares*—male honor was of
central concern. The Classic Maya express a consistent "timocratic" orientation. The
description derives from two words in Greek, *timē*, "honor, worth, value," and *kra-
tia*, "power." Personal dishonor affected all. Slights and slurs demanded a response, and
males were evaluated according to their compliance with this code and its expectations.
William Miller, a historian of law, detects a further subdivision in such societies. Some
focused on aggressive self-assertion or responses to insults and other jabs.[25] Fierce
conflicts in Icelandic sagas come to mind. Others, as in the Mediterranean or Near East,
attempted to control and defend the morality or sexuality of female relations. Grievances
were personally felt in both societies, but the first responded to personal slights, the second guarded the dignity of domestic groups and the purity of bloodlines. As shown in
glyphic texts, Maya lords accorded more with the Icelandic pattern, although any attempt
to characterize a whole society as agreeing with one such system is bound to fail. The
anthropologist Mary Douglas reminded us long ago that groups can never be separated
from individual maneuvers, and vice versa—lumping can be overdone, a label applied
too heavily, heedless of local evidence and the twists of history.[26]

Still, for the Maya, boasts of honor can be quantified. Lords tabulated the number
of captives taken in battle and held this as a very personal achievement. But in defeat, the
same lords lost all dignity. Enemies compelled them to grovel, to wear torn and col-
orless clothing, perhaps to show off blood. If they could, the captives endured cruelty
with stoic indifference. Here, in a test of manhood, was a sign of their worth, although
the Maya never seemed to have recorded such minor vindications. In their imagery, no
captive is ever shown to redeem himself through a good, manly death. (The Huron and
other North American tribes performed similar tortures. From them, a warrior's honor,
if not his person, could emerge intact.) Anyone looking at Maya texts perceives, without
too much imagination, the hatred seeping out from a number of them. Vengeance and
defended honor lay behind dynastic conflict, behind elite masculinity itself. The historical

record between two cities well known to me, Pomona in Mexico and Piedras Negras in Guatemala, reveal sustained antagonism, as did the barbed relations between Piedras Negras and its neighbor Yaxchilan in Mexico. Economics conditioned some politics, but emotions and grievances exercised their own sway. The beloved male body could also be reviled, a convenient focus for dynastic animosity. The most extreme examples may be those of gladiatorial conflict, including one involving a woman at the city of Tonina, Mexico. These contests targeted bodies not directly under their own control—the captives operated as marionettes of abuse, compelled to unwilling combat.[27]

SPROUTING YOUTHS: A LEXICON

The Classic Maya, living in diverse communities and kingdoms from about AD 300 to 850, left no proof that they thought of themselves as a single ethnicity.[28] But they did hold some ideas in common. One of these was *xib*, the essence of maleness and a word of great antiquity in Mayan languages.[29] In Yukateko Maya, there is a variant, *xiblal*, "the male, either a man or whichever animal." Feisty women could pulse with "manly heart," *xiblal ol* or *xiblal puççikal*, and older men might be, as in the Acalan language of colonial Tabasco, "large, or great, males."

The glyph for *xib* was deciphered long ago (fig. 15). Many occurrences are divine. In a number of texts, the word labels *Chak Xib Chahk*, a variant of the Rain God. A passage in the Postclassic Dresden Codex pairs him with Ixik Chahk, "Lady Chahk."[30] In this unique reference, the Maya indicates that the Rain God was not only a male supernatural. Much like the maize deity, he had a female counterpart. *Xib* could be brought together in collectives, as groups of four. This resonated with other parts of Mesoamerica. The Aztecs mention a rabble of vindictive young gods, the Centzonhuitznahua, 400 in total, all of whom met a bad end. The same number of divine youths, the *o' much' k'ajoläb* or "400 sons," do mischief in the Popol Vuh of the K'iche' Maya.[31] The results are just as grim. Their house, something like a *calmecac* or the buildings described by Las Casas, falls on their heads, killing them all. The sources for both stories spell out that such youths are stars. The events must have been celestial and the actors fixtures of heaven.

In Classic times, *4 te' xib*, "4 males," torment a feline deity by torching his back, the *te'* being a particle for enumerating things or people (fig. 16). On the pot, the "4 males" are reduced to a single person. This helps clarify the image, avoiding a cluttering with figures that would dissipate the narrative tension. In a Classic-era convention, the distinctive bands on the *xib* indicate that the male is *chak* or "red, great." Bound as a captive, the feline struggles and writhes. The flames draws close, the skin knows what is to come. Is this some reflection of sadistic pleasures among teenage males, an act done also by royal youths? The events may have been as celestial as those in the Popol Vuh:

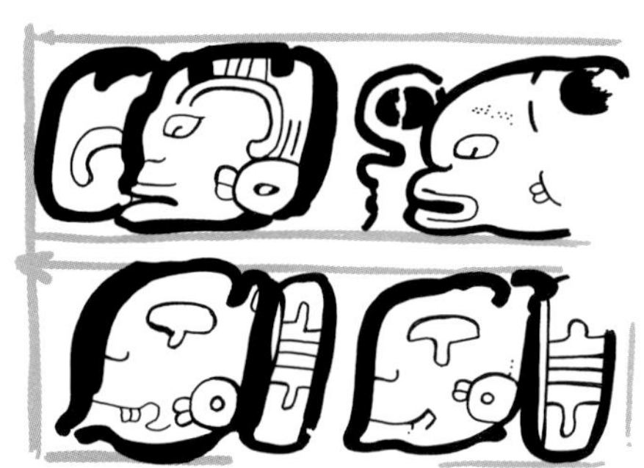

Xib in the Dresden Codex, p. 62, Late Postclassic period. Ink on fig-tree bark and lime plaster. Sächsische Landesbibliothek, Staats- und Universitätsbibliothek. Mscr. Dresd. R.310.

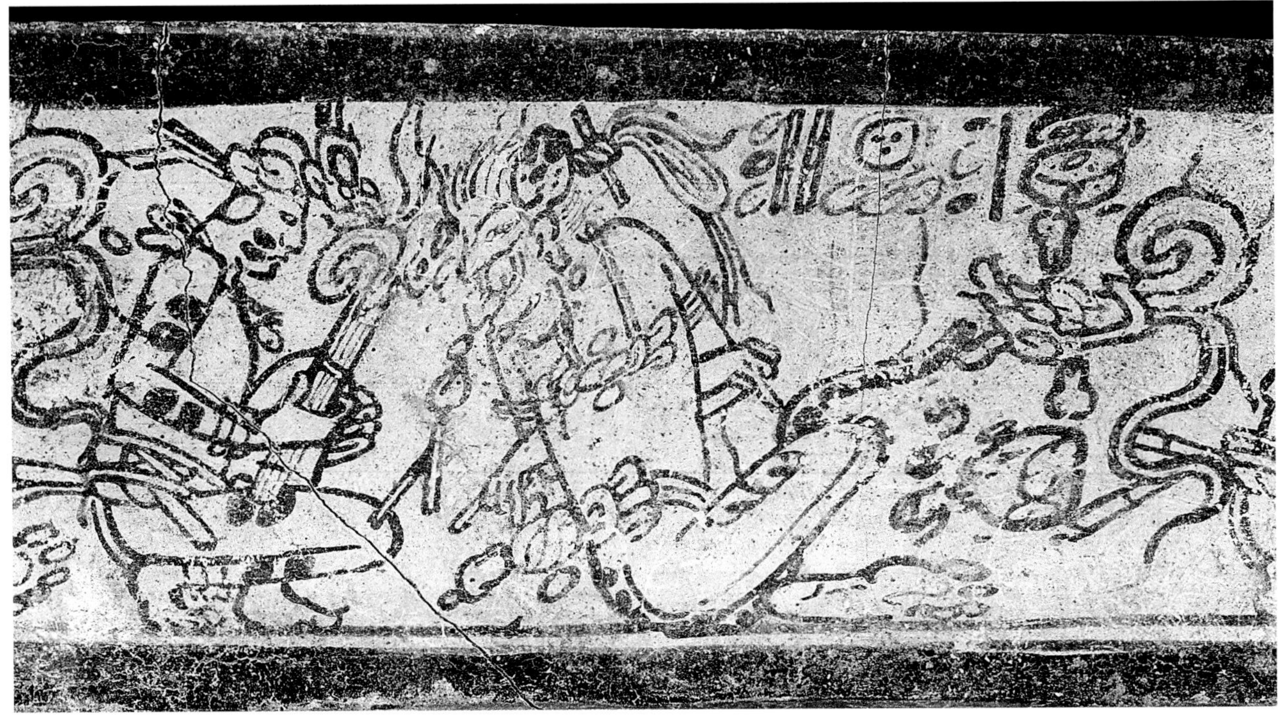

most scholars believe the bound deity represents the nighttime sun as it passes under-
ground. But final extinction is not in the future for him. He will emerge from this ordeal
in shark form, swimming in eastern waters, and then ascend as a heavenly king, the Sun
God himself. Perhaps the torching reignites his fiery nature after a dark journey. As noted
by David Stuart, the feline serves elsewhere as a patron of incense burners. Perhaps such
braziers functioned in solar rites, for ignition at darkest night.

The day of the event on the pot, *Hix,* "feline" or even "jaguar," is appropriate. It fits well
with a god who features jaguar ears, tail, and paws. The month, *Kumk'u,* is the last of the year,
a cycle roughly patterned on the solar calendar and its episodes of agricultural production.
A suspicion arises that the burning on the pot establishes some connection between mythic
sacrifice and the burning of fields at the end of the dry season in April or May. Or perhaps
it evoked the torching of vegetation after a long fallow. Such burning releases nutrients
into the soil, but it also clears and loosens the ground for planting. In studying the pot,
Simon Martin discovered a close parallel with a Late Classic stela at Naranjo, Guatemala.[32]
The same mythic events play out, not just with *4 xib* but now with *4 te' ch'ok,* a category of
youth to be discussed shortly. The titles appear to correspond to the same young men. Both
preside over the fiery agony at Naranjo, and on the same day, *Hix*—if with a different number—and in the same month, *Kumk'u.* A ruler on the front of the stela grasps a fiery torch.
Presumably, he does the work of the four youths. A later passage on the monument reveals
that the feline god belongs to an enemy dynasty. He has gotten his just deserts, and so too

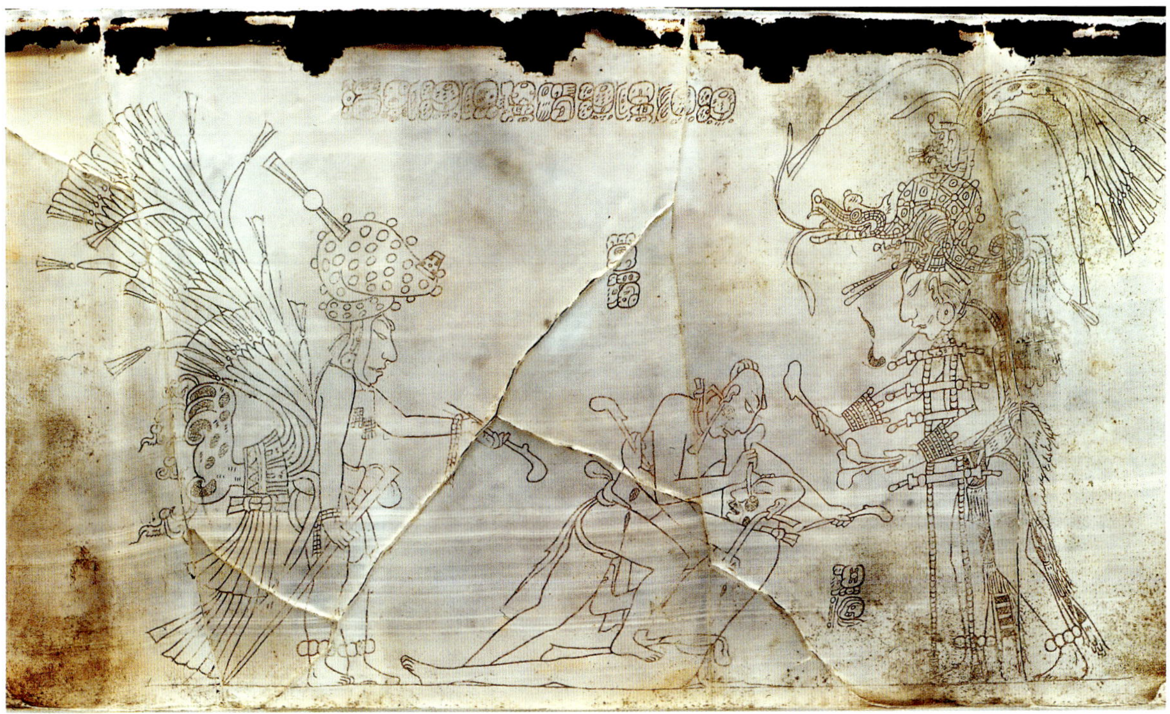

has the bound captive carved on the front of the stela. The local king equates to the torturing youth, his victim to the feline god. A dynastic present and mythic past dart back and forth in layered reference. As with the maize deity, gods and men mingle identities.

Other godly *xib* were mentioned far away, at the city of Quirigua in the Motagua River drainage of Guatemala. Organized into groups of four, they were said to be "black males." There is a geographic reason for this. To the Maya, black was connected to the west, where the sun sets and the sky darkens each night. For one phase of its existence, Quirigua was understood to be the "western" (read "black") outpost of the great dynastic capital of Copan, Honduras. Another supernatural *xib*, linked less to a direction than a task, appears as a blowgunner on a sherd excavated at Calakmul, Mexico. Hunting must have been on Maya minds: *xib* ("7 Xib," to be precise) also names what may be their god of hunting. An unfortunate fellow—he has a wanton spouse. At a certain point, she is carried off (*kuhchaj*) by an oversexed deer, perhaps in retribution for the god's hunting of his kind. Or did the abduction motivate such blood sport in the first place? Even a few supernatural dwarves are tagged as *xib*. One hops along behind a ruler in ballplay on a carving at Yaxchilan, Mexico.[33] A star rims his body, hinting that he is more figurative than literal. He may even allude to a constellation.

But many *xib* were clearly human. A spelling on an alabaster bowl captions a brutal contest between two Maya gladiators (fig. 17). An aggressor, *Aj chak xib*, "he, the great (or fierce?) male," gouges out the eye of an opponent. His weapon is a polished and sharp-

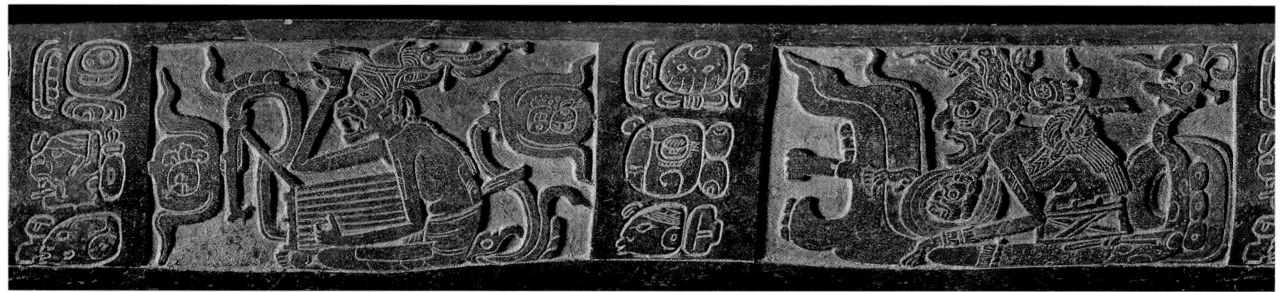

ened bone, similar to specimens recovered in many excavations of Maya cities.[34] Adult men, each with an elaborate dance costume, drive the gladiators on. They hold replacement bones should one chip in an eye socket or break off in a wound. The *xib* sign, the head of a youth, serves another purpose. Typified by a dot on its cheek, a standard marker of the glyph for "lord," the sign contains a distinct curl that curves over the head, along with an ear ornament. Maya scribes use this head as a default for "singer," the difference being that a flower or sign for "wind" or "music" emanates from the lips. No divas here: for the Maya, skilled vocalists at royal courts were men. All bands of musicians appear to have been male, too. A pot from the Puuc region of Yucatan commends this masculine accomplishment. It is the cup or *jaay* of the *itz'aat k'ayoom*, "the skilled singer," who happens to be impersonating the god of music (fig. 18).[35] Human talents stem in part, it seems, from spirit possession. A god occupied human lungs, throat, and lips and compelled them to song.

Xib is not a common sign, nor does it appear to be the only designator of maleness. Others occur in a glyph that has proved useful in understanding Maya thought. This sign, read *tz'ak*, to "order," "complete," or "make whole," fascinates scholars.[36] It expresses the concept of ordering, completion, or wholeness as a set of paired signs. The signs are always opposites and occur in what appear to be deliberate sequences. "Day" precedes "night," "green or blue"—the color of new vegetation—comes before "yellow," the color of maize ready to harvest. "Wind" or "clouds" accompany "rain" or "water," "star" paves the way for "moon," "sky" for "earth," "maize-bread" for "water." Most studies of these pairs propose that they connote a single whole: a third, more abstract concept. Thus, "day" and "night" imply a diurnal cycle. Together, they spell *tz'ak*.

What is not discussed is that they also embed theories of cause-and-effect. Their order matters. They are not reversible. Or, to frame this as logic, the pattern is not, as many have thought: element 1 plus element 2 become a single whole. Instead, the first leads to the second, so that element 1 triggers or results in element 2, resulting in a whole. Seen in this way, the signs become easier to interpret. A stingray spine, an implement of sacrifice, precedes the sign for blood first interpreted by David Stuart in the 1990s. Jabbing with one leads to gouts of the other. Green growth comes before harvestable plants. Clouds result in rain, and the wind blows before a tropical storm. A maize bread is consumed with water, and so on.

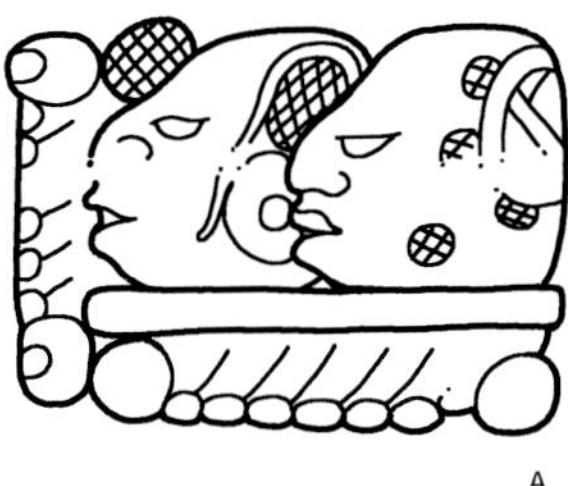

A

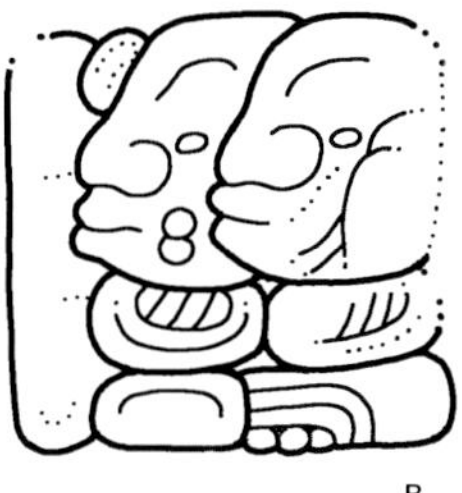

B

Not all reveal causation, however. A star sign appears before that for the moon. This may reflect naked-eye observation. The planet Venus, regarded as a star by the Maya, could rise in the evening, just before the moon dominated the sky. But the sky sign before the earth is more enigmatic—did it convey some theory about the origins of the world, the sky preceding the earth? The relevance here is that two spellings pair the heads of females and males (fig. 19). One, from Copan begins with *ixik*, "female, woman," but concludes with *ajaw*, "lord." This second figure is not just any male: he is royal. Another example at Yaxchilan, although eroded, juxtaposes what may be female and male maize gods. Again, the causation makes sense in that men of all classes come from women. But, for unknown reasons, no such pairing occurs with *xib* in a *tz'ak* sign. Its only gendered pairing is the passage from the Dresden Codex, where it appears in tandem with *ixik*, "woman" or "lady."

There are other relevant terms for youths in glyphs. One is *keleem*. It refers to males, with the added connotation in several Mayan languages of "strength," an evident attribute of youth. In what must be post-conquest usage, the word also equates to "rooster," a symbol of virility, if a late arrival to American shores. As mentioned before, Tojolobal, spoken in Chiapas, Mexico, further defines *kerem*, a related word, as a term for "single man." Texts on Maya vases sequence *keleem* with other labels for youth or person, *winik*. Possibly it identified young men, now sexually mature, who were ready for more challenging, muscular duties. Simon Martin observes that a *keleem* appears in wall paintings at Calakmul, Chiapas, at an intermediate height between adults nearby and a child. On a Late Classic vessel from the area of Río Azul, Guatemala, a courtier exclaims "*ts'akbaj keleem*," "the youths arrange themselves" or maybe "the youths are arranged" (see ch. 4).[37] In a scene nearby, four young men sit behind the throne of a ruler. The exclamation probably applies to them. Ladies nearby, one with exposed breasts, allude to past or future dalliances, although the pot may simply show a courtly scene with a ruler and his sons and royal women nearby. As with all such images, the protocols of where to sit or stand affected young men. They rarely commanded a central position but loitered in the margins, waiting, ready to serve or participate. Their time will come.

An exception—along with the spectacular Bonampak murals to be discussed in chapter 5—is an enthroned *keleem* from the city of Xcalumkin, Campeche (fig. 20).[38] Seated on a throne, he looks out from a panel on a wall near an inner doorway. The "writing," *woj* in Classic Mayan, is said to belong to him, but as an owner, not the carver or scribe. To the other side of a doorway is a second panel with an older male. Seemingly, the "strong" young man was an heir or even a co-ruler of the site. A lintel found in the same building triangulates to a third person, the wife of the more senior figure, perhaps the mother of the *keleem*. To an unusual extent, the frontal display on the panels invites direct address, and the *keleem* interacts with the viewer from a position of confident authority. Xcalumkin has, in fact, a surprising number of references to young men, and some of the buildings may have pertained to them. A final *keleem* is equally unusual, human but of abnormal shape, a dwarf dancing with a king (fig. 21).[39] Some Maya dwarves were named,

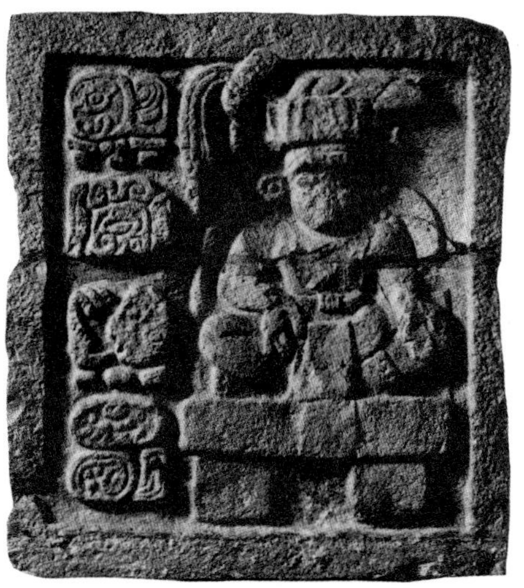

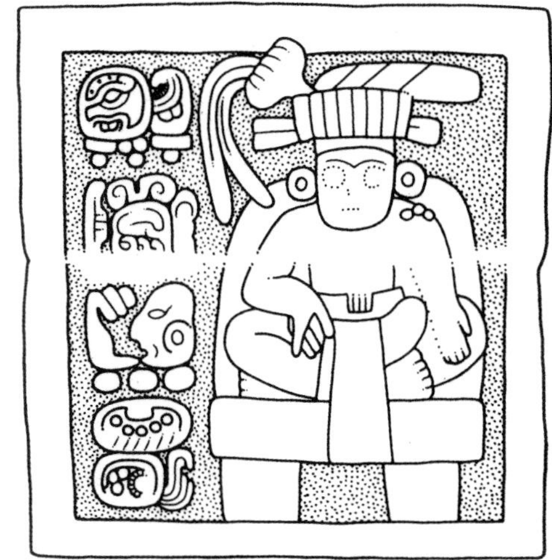

but this one is mentioned generically as *keleem ahk,* "[unmarried?] youth turtle" or "dwarf."
Keleem fits the image. A dwarf is never a tall person, but this one is smaller than usual, for
his face only reaches the knee of the king. Perhaps he was acquired and exhibited at an
early age.

But the key word for youths is *ch'ok,* which likens them to erupting, sprouting plants.
It is the linchpin for this book because it is so common. Many images are greatly clarified
when the sign appears as a caption. My teacher, Michael Coe, was the first to identify the
spelling in a pioneering study of Maya pots. Most Mayanists had overlooked glyphs on
such vessels, and no decipherment was possible at the time as syllabic breakthroughs had
just been set in motion. But Coe did offer an indelible nickname, "Rodent Bone," and noted
its widespread occurrence on sculptures and in the Maya codices. David Stuart, a central
figure in these and other breakthroughs, observed that the glyphs refer to youths before
their accession to the throne. At about that time, I had previously determined the reading
of a syllable **ch'o**. William Ringle teased *ch'ok* from the two glyphs together, relating the
term to an expression "ripe, immature, young child."[40] Others, acknowledging the decipherment, spun it in more abstract directions. "Youth" was one of its meanings, to be sure,
but less germane than "offspring" or "members of the ruling lineage other than the king."[41]
As we shall see, the glyphs should be taken at face value. No such expanded meanings
are necessary.

Mayan languages explain why. The primary meaning of *ch'ok* is "unripe." This is
a term going far back in Mayan language history, but it can be extended to all young or
immature things, including animals and plants. Some examples serve as nouns, others
as adjectives. In Chontal Maya *ch'ok* means "son or daughter, child" but also "small, young."
When the first syllable is repeated, as in *ch'o-ch'ok,* the meaning intensifies to "very young,
very small." The same language has *ch'ok ixik,* "young woman," along with *ch'ok chumli,*

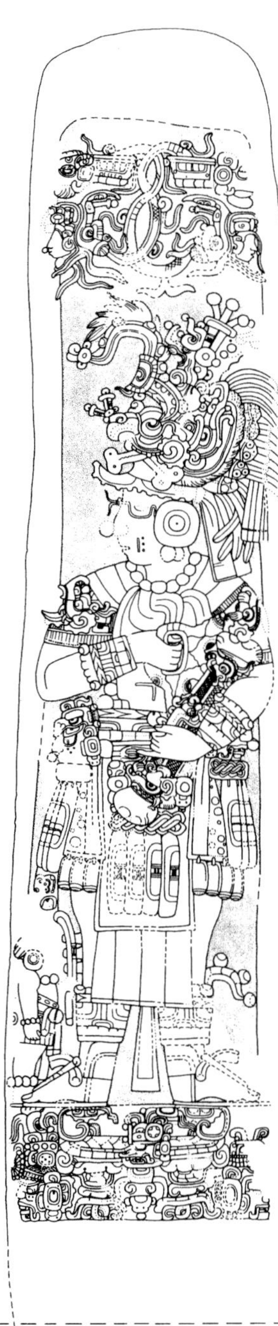

Young dwarf, *keleem ahk,* on Caracol Stela 6, Belize, c. AD 603. Limestone, 129⅛ × 29 in. (328 × 74 cm).

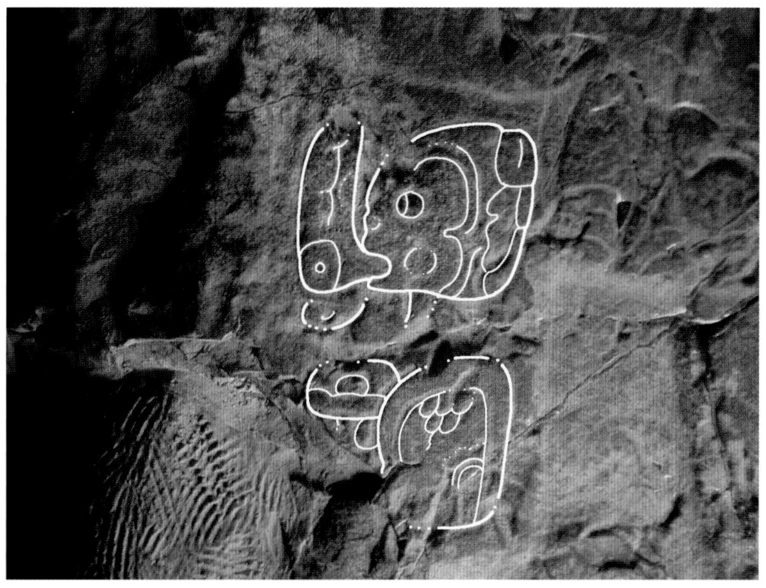

"little seat," and *ch'ok ixim,* "corn cob."[42] In Chontal, *ch'ok* defines the first segment of full adulthood, *ch'ok winik,* a young man of 25 to 40 years old. Indeed, this is one of the few pieces of evidence that links it to men so old, and, in that language, it may have more to do with marital status. Ch'orti' Maya uses the word for "tender," in an array of expressions: *ch'ok bu'u'r,* "unripe bean"; *ch'ok nar,* "unripe maize"; *ch'ok chitam,* "suckling pig"; and "new moon," *ch'ok e katu'.* In Ch'olti', the colonial-era parent of Ch'orti', some of the same words appear. *Ch'oknal* is an unripe ear of corn, just before shucking. The language also offers *ix-ch'ok ixik,* "maid." The Spanish friar who collected the term equated that expression to *donsella* in Spanish, but he probably intended "virgin" or "unmarried" rather than its other meaning, "servant." As one variant, Ch'olti' records *chak ch'ok ixik* for "maid," with *chak* for "great," *ixik* for "female." *Chak* is usually "red," but it can also convey intensification or enlargement. To this day, in colloquial Spanish of the area, youths might be described as *ischoco* or *isto.*[43]

By default, *ch'ok* is always male. The languages attach an *ix* or *ixik* to distinguish females. The close attention to plants recalls the near-vegetal nature of human flesh. And not just for the Maya: Nahuatl speakers designate adults as "earth sprouts" in order to emphasize their bonds with corn.[44] Other Mayan languages like Pokomchi use different words for "youth," yet they establish comparable links between descendants and sprouts or shoots, as well as to those who are celibate or not yet married.[45] And there is a more disturbing nuance. Yukateko Maya presents a kindred term, *ch'okteil,* "captivity," and *mun,* widespread in that and other languages, stands for both "slave" and "immature fruit," a thing not yet ripe. Trafficking of the young is an outrage of the modern world, but some clues suggest it may have existed in some form among the Maya. A stucco frieze at the

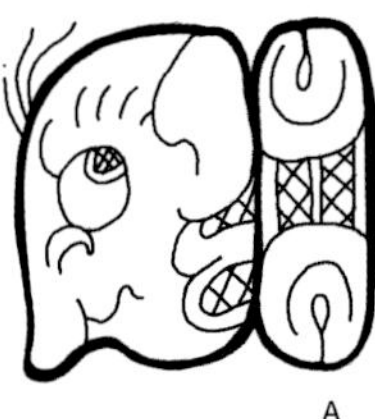
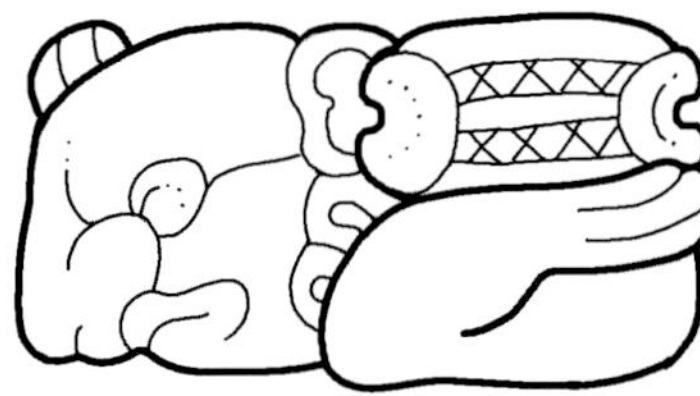
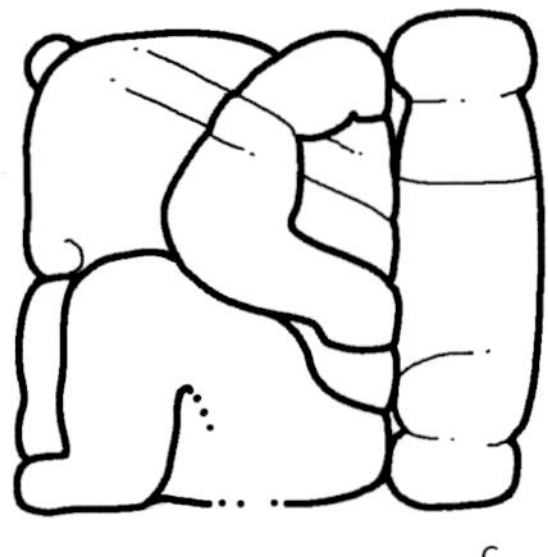

A
B
C

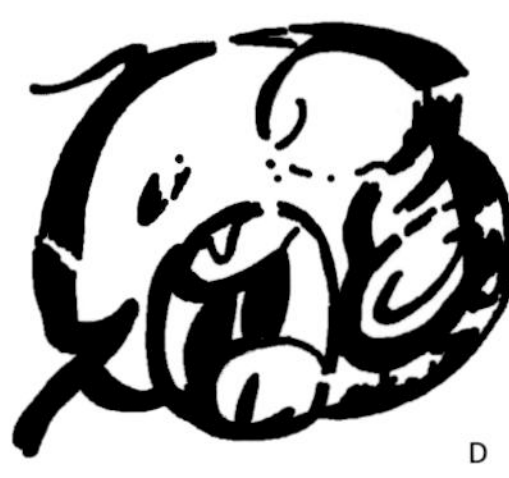
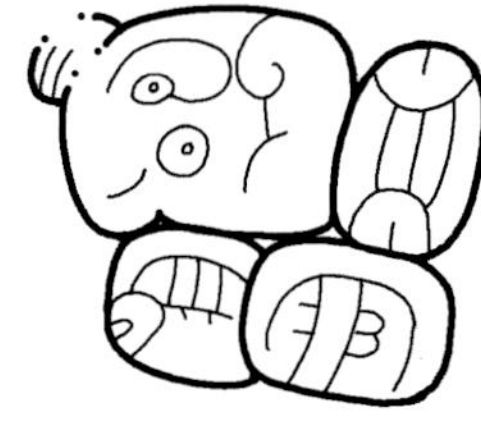
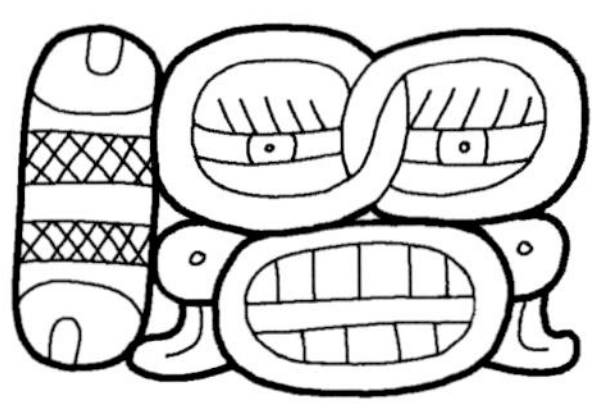

D
E
F

FIGURE 22

Ch'ok signs: A) Palenque, Mexico, Temple XIX, west face of platform, I2, AD 734; B) El Cayo Altar 4, I'2, with lifted hand, Mexico, AD 731; C) Moral-La Reforma Stela 4, K2, Mexico, AD 692; D) Bonampak murals, Room 3, Copan III-7, A3, AD 791, **ko** syllable over jaw; E) OxkintokBallcourt Ring, pR1, Late Classic period, Mexico; F) Torus-stone, H1, AD 489. Kislak Collection, Library of Congress, PC0209.

RIGHT **FIGURE 23**

Goggle-eyed warriors at Teotihuacan, c. AD 350–550. Photograph by Kim Richter.

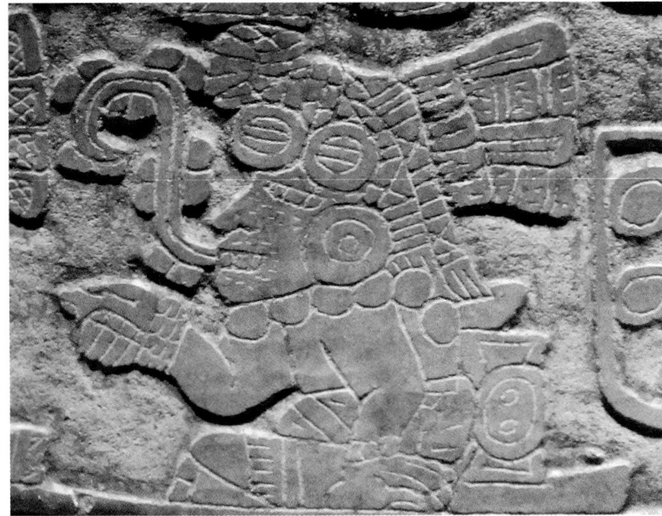

ruins of Tonina in Mexico appears to display a group of slaves, ready for servitude with sticks bound to their necks—such encumbrances, the better to manhandle them, burdened slaves among the much later Aztec. Were such men intended less for torture and sacrifice than servitude? Nor were all such youths sold or captured, although that seems to have been the main source of slaves. In Yukateko, *ch'ok* signifies a child without mother or father.[46] Indenture or servitude may have been a social mechanism for taking care of orphans. Colonial documents in Yucatan indicate that most slaves were people taken in battle, found guilty of theft (thus losing their freedom), or seized when orphaned. As in many parts of the world, parentless youths were more vulnerable than most.

Colonial or later usage provides suitable context. But it is the Classic period that displays *ch'ok* in its most informative settings (fig. 22). The word is spelled in two ways. The first draws on two syllables, a rodent or rat head, **ch'o** (Coe was correct in that identification), slotted next to a **ko** sign of uncertain origin. Perhaps it is a stylized turtle shell, but no consensus exists on that point. In fun, Maya scribes sometimes pictured the rat supporting the **ko** with his arm or they placed the **ko** syllable over his jaw, *ko* being the word for "tooth" in at least one Mayan language. The plural form, a rarity, takes a *taak* suffix.[47] The second spelling is rare but informative in its details, showing a stylized face with two ringed eyes in frontal pose.[48] Notably, this may not be a Maya sign. Faces looking out at the viewer are unusual in Maya writing, and the ringed eyes resemble those of a warrior from the great yet remote city of Teotihuacan. Even at Teotihuacan, it occurs in a hybrid form, however: a low-relief vessel on display in the site museum arrays a row of figures wearing this garb, but in typical Maya pose (fig. 23). According to Karl Taube, the central warrior enlivens the scene by speaking. His finger points in a standard Maya cue for such talk, and a flowery speech-scroll spools out of his mouth. During its heyday from about AD 100 to 500, Teotihuacan had several intense interactions with the Maya world.[49] Some involved conflict, as at the city of Tikal, Guatemala. It is probably not a coincidence that this is when the *ch'ok* title first appears, and precisely in this ringed-eye form. The full syllabic spelling arrives later.

The earliest known attestation of the ringed eyes is in now-destroyed murals at the city of Uaxactun, near Tikal (fig. 24).[50] Their exact date is uncertain, but a time between about AD 300 and 400 is likely. The glyphs accompany two figures, both slightly misshapen. One is very tall, the other short, although the latter does exhibit high status, wearing a diadem that signals royalty. Nearby is a warrior in full Teotihuacan garb. Eye coverings of the *ch'ok* title appear to correlate with foreign warriors or those connecting to Teotihuacan and its traditions of martial prowess. Age grades probably existed long before in the Maya world, but perhaps this is when their formal organization and glyphic marking took place. The warlike nature of the examples at Teotihuacan suggests that the organization had an objective. For the Maya, it might have remolded a long-standing feature of social life into a tool of state, youthful energies being harnessed to military formations.

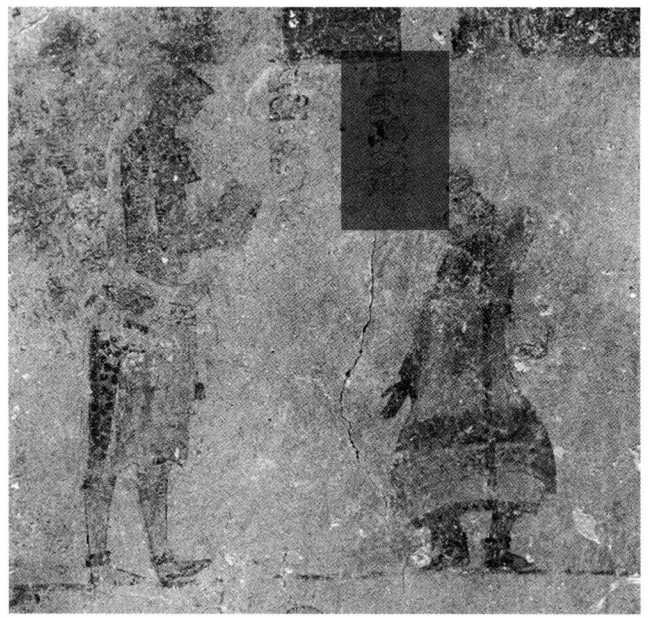

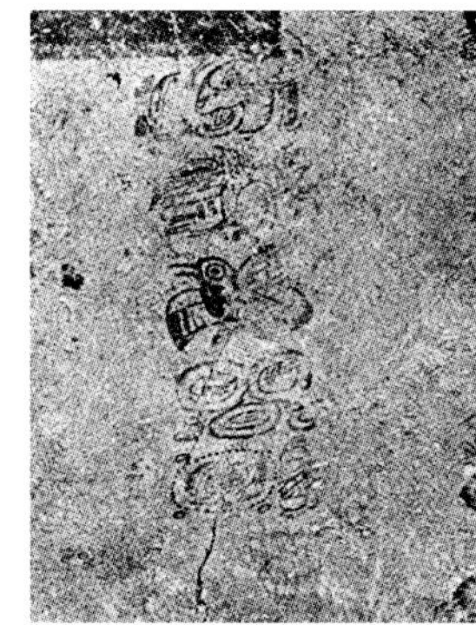

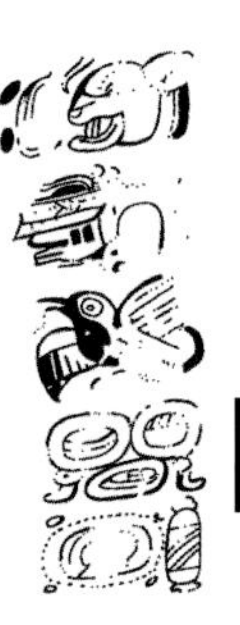

First known use of the google-eyed *ch'ok* in Maya texts, text high-lighted between standing figures, Uaxactun, Guatemala, AD 300–400.

By the Late Classic period, the ringed-eye spelling of *ch'ok* may have had an archaic quality. Most *ch'ok* were now in syllabic spellings, beginning with an alabaster bowl from Palenque in the later fifth century AD. (The image is surprising: a youth owned the pot, but the figure wears a beard, an attribute of older males.)[51] A full-figure example, with glyphs in place of a head, floats on the background of a Naranjo stela from the late sixth century AD. A priest, he holds an incense bag. The figure represents the animated name of Tikal lord Chak Tok Ich'aak II, a possible ancestor of the Naranjo ruler who dedicated the stela. It is uncertain why Chak Tok Ich'aak was identified as a youth on this monument. Perhaps, as Simon Martin suggests, it was because the king acceded when young. Piedras Negras, Guatemala, had two princely *ch'ok,* both shown in retroactive images and texts. They seem never to have ascended to rule. Panel 2 from that city features a prince as a *ch'ok* yet also depicts him with ringed eyes (fig. 25). The allusion is twofold, to his youth (a *ch'ok* sign appears in his caption, with ringed eyes and **ko** syllable), and to the Teotihuacan-style warriors in the scene. Even later images, from the ninth century AD, may use this feature on portrait sculptures. A set of polychromed stucco heads from the Governor's Palace at Uxmal celebrates similar warriors.[52] Each is slightly different. Perhaps, among other functions, the Governor's Palace extolled royal youth.

Most references to *ch'ok* tend to be situational, having to do with age at the time of reference. It is hard to imagine the stout Queen Victoria, Empress of India, as a maiden queen, but so she was at 18 when she inherited the throne. Several Maya kings could also be described as *ch'ok* when young. A stela at Piedras Negras, identifies the ruler in this way at the time of his marriage to a foreign princess, although he managed

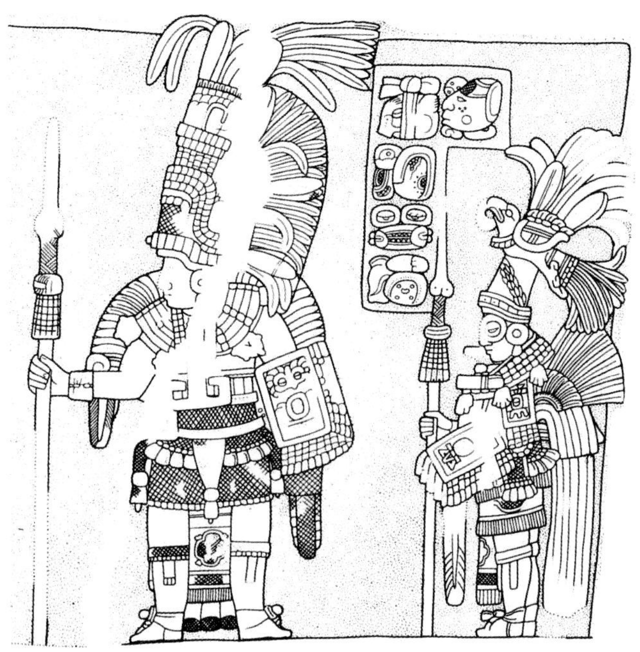

FIGURE 25

Heir with goggle eyes and Teotihuacan garb at Piedras Negras, Guatemala, Panel 2, AD 667 (but referring to event at AD 510); probable father to the left, at larger size. Drawing by David Stuart.

to live past 65. (He was then just over 21 years old; thereafter, *ch'ok* disappeared from his titles.) Some references state the obvious. Lords could be called *ch'ok* at birth, as at Piedras Negras, El Cayo, and a panel from an unknown site nearby.[53] Why? It may have emphasized long lives to come. Some were both *ch'ok* and fathers. Perhaps the title was not only about married status—although the example from Piedras Negras hints as much—and might on rare occasions apply to someone over 20 years of age, a person perceived, for social reasons, as not yet an adult. But, to an overwhelming extent, *ch'ok* seemed younger than that.[54]

Texts at Palenque exemplify the uses of *ch'ok.* David Stuart points out that this attention results from the fraternal succession that was a particular preoccupation of that dynasty (see chapter 4).[55] Several possible heirs are seen in a retroactive image that may describe an entente of orderly succession. The youths were assembled to establish a joint understanding and to avoid future bickering. Yet their later date suggests a more turbulent process. An effort was made to tidy up after the fact. Implying regency, the presence of very young rulers, as at Palenque, Naranjo, and Tonina, also hint at courtly scuffles and shifting sources of power. At Naranjo, this led to unusual prominence for the mother, a princess from another dynasty, and one king of Tonina came to the throne at 2 years of age, probably dying before he reached 20. Boy-kings were unlikely to have controlled their own courts or destinies. A bowl that has long been understood as the accession text of the final ruler of Palenque refers in fact to two youths, *2 ch'oktaak.* This suggests some volatility, even co-rule (if these are humans), at the very end of Palenque's dynasty. That two occur in the text savors of twins in Maya mythology. Caracol, in Belize, draws similar attention to *ch'ok* in its final monuments as a dynastic capital. Their prominence, as on Stela 17 at the site, which places the youth in the position of greater honor, hints at a larger role than at other cities.

The intrusive demands of brothers may account for overt markings of birth order. At times, older and younger brothers were identified with almost pedantic care. And not just kings: the courtly titles of "older-brother" and "younger-brother obsidian" could symbolize a sacrificial role, named after the substance that slices cleanly. Such figures, studied by the archaeologist Franco Rossi, highlight murals at Xultun, Guatemala, from the final years of the Late Classic period.[56] In a nice touch, several figures, painted black, appear to resemble obsidian implements, their headdresses like pointed weapons. Perhaps they were actual brothers or ordered by analogy with fraternal ties. There may have been other complexities. A mortuary text from Tonina refers to a royal youth as both a *ch'ok* and *ba'al,* "the first-born child of woman," suggesting that his importance came from a particular royal consort rather than his status as the firstborn of a king. There is also *baahch'ok,* "head, first youth." The fullest use of this title is at Palenque, where, in the case of *U Pakal K'inich,* "Shield of the Sun God," it applied to the chief heir of a sitting ruler. More than a status, it was also an office, an attribute also attested at Palenque. There, *baahch'oklel* relates to a role acquired at youth.

Like many Mayan nouns, *ch'ok* can be used as an adjective for "young." At Tonina an exalted title meaning "top of the earth," *bakab,* is often prefixed by the term. A similar order appears on two carved vases by the same hand. Each follows *chak ch'ok,* "great, or large youth," with *winik,* "person." Yet the more usual practice, especially in sites near the Usumacinta and Pasión rivers between or near the modern border of Guatemala and Mexico, is to characterize a young male as the "young" lord of a particular kingdom. The assumption is that these youths were dynastic heirs. Nonetheless, most such youths at Piedras Negras did not reach highest office. In fact, the opposite is true. They fall out of the dynastic sequence, as happened also at Dos Pilas and Aguateca. The reference at Aguateca is illuminating in other ways. It identifies the young lord as an *itz'aat* or "wise person," a rare confirmation that royal males were seen as literates or adept at esoteric knowledge.[57] A number of sculptors were not only *ch'ok,* but junior members of the royal family. Young indeed: the sculptor of the head or plinth of a foreign god at Palenque appears to have been the *younger* brother of a *ch'ok.* At Motul de San José, one such sculptor might have been a royal heir. Some of their careers can be charted. A *ch'ok* on one monument, 1 Witzil Chahk of Yaxchilan, ages out of that title on a later sculpture from his chisel. Trial pieces of indifferent quality, the by-products of apprenticeship, were found at Piedras Negras in blocks reused as masonry.[58] Perhaps these represent the work of *ch'ok* learning to carve.

A more restricted term is *tikil.* It is attested as an element used in enumeration, as in Ch'ol *tikil,* "to count animated objects." A panel from La Corona, Guatemala, refers to

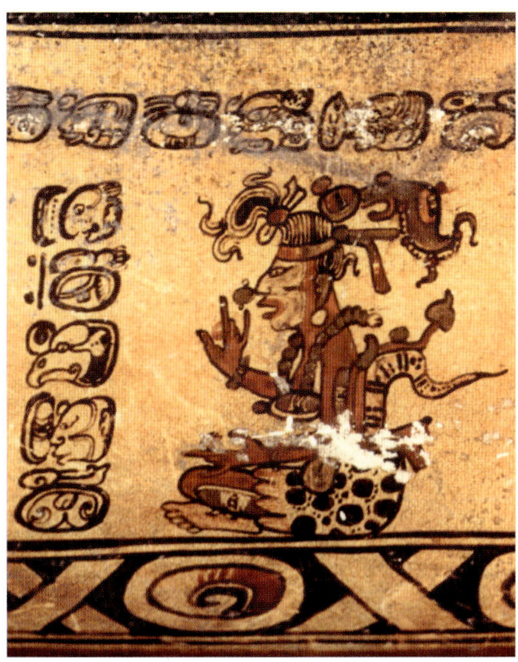

the trip of a local heir, known as the "older brother person youth" (*suku-winik ch'ok*), to the dynastic seat of Calakmul. Eighteen days later an event of uncertain nature takes place at Calakmul, involving *7 tikil ch'oktaak*, the "7 youths," the sons of the ruler of Calakmul. The lord from La Corona was already 28 years of age, a rare use of the title with a slightly older male. Perhaps his *ch'ok* alluded to unmarried status or his place as the oldest among the young men. *Tikil* also appears on the tablet of the Temple of the Sun at Palenque, where youths "fall down" (*jubuyi ?3 tikil ch'oktaak*). All were likely the sons of the ruler of Palenque. David Stuart speculates that the rite corresponds to a "pole dance" common in Mesoamerica, in which participants descend and spin from ropes attached to a central pole or *yookte'*. Such a scene appears on a vessel from the final years of the Late Classic period. A person dressed as an eagle sits atop a pole, attached by ropes to other supports and participants. Soon he will leap out in spectacular display. In an influential paper, Linda Schele demonstrated that the *yookte'* played a role in rituals involving young boys, including an eventual king who was then only 6 years of age.[59] Ritual duties were strongly present. A shattered throne at Piedras Negras—the monument was destroyed after the Maya collapse—details a ritual circuit in which a *ch'ok*, succeeding an abdicated predecessor, transports a sacred fetish to various locations.[60] Only after its final placement can the lord ascend the throne.

As with *xib*, however, many *ch'ok* or those labeled with *tikil* were supernatural. A nonhuman scribe was identified with *tikil*, and several anthropomorphic rabbits, tapir, even a drunken feline indulging in an alcoholic enema were captioned with *ch'ok* (fig. 26). A grotesque figure on another pot, now on display in the University of Pennsylvania Museum, was labeled a *ch'ok xib.*[61] His gesture of subordination, hand on one shoulder, leaves little doubt about his lower standing. The Dresden Codex also calls certain gods *ch'ok* or *keleem.* But the sets of youths, as in the gang of four mentioned at Naranjo, offer central evidence. They occur at several sites. A ritual account of the setting of stones at the beginning of a new year may also have involved multiples of gods, "youths" or *ch'oktaak.* Four such youths are mentioned at Pusilha, Belize, perhaps shown as Teotihuacan-style deities. Others occur with particular frequency in the texts of Copan, Honduras, where they served as "watchers," *koknoom,* of the city. As mentioned before, even gods are born and enter the world as squirming newborns.[62] A deity at Palenque was described as a *unen,* "baby," version of a particular deity, along with the sprawling, supine posture appropriate to babes. This expression, applied in a few areas to humans in the context of relations with parents, points to an age before adolescence.

A singular point about the *ch'ok* title is its strongly masculine nature, whatever the usage in descendant languages. Only a few females of the Classic period employed it.[63] The first was the mother of a ruler of Palenque, K'inich Ahkal Mo' Nahb. The text with this reference, the so-called Tablet of the Slaves, affirms that the woman and her husband were "youths." Yet, in an impossible anachronism, the image below the inscription presents a view of both parents with their son: K'inich Ahkal Mo' Nahb is shown at accession, long after his father's death. Probably the ruler wished to emphasize the youth of his parents at his birth, perhaps to emphasize his own difficult path to the throne as the offspring of a younger son. Another reference, on Piedras Negras Stela 8, is to the mother of Ruler 4 as a *ch'ok.* Notably, she does not employ a feminine designator, although the context assures us of her identity. At Yaxchilan, there is a very young consort of an elderly king—unlikely to be a vibrant bridegroom, he must have been into his eighties. The larger problem is why Maya texts pay so little attention to the age status of females, even at those sites where references to women are relatively abundant. To state the obvious, male youths received textual recognition because, as a group, they were important to those commissioning inscriptions and imagery. Yet they may also have drawn on social groupings or age grades that royal females did not possess.

DUTY AND MAYHEM

What is missing in these references—the detail can be overwhelming as well as reveal- ing—is an historical treatment that charts such groups and settings over time. This history is difficult to probe, in part because of patchy evidence. But the first clear occurrence of youths, at Uaxactun, was tied to Teotihuacan, the last, on a stela in a private collection, to the collapse of Classic civilization. What those young men did will be explored in later chapters. But the Spaniards and later ethnographers saw remediable worries: that young men needed transitioning to productive adulthood, that the energies of youth required harnessing or mitigation by physical separation, severe discipline or allowances for controlled transgression. From this would come habits of service, including dances, a rich store of civic or religious knowledge, and judicious obedience to older males.

Young men across the world have long been a splendid predicament, both a problem and an opportunity. Sources far and wide stress the dilemmas and what to make of this part of life's passage. Among the Maya, youth may also have sweated, recalling Aztec use of young men for civic labor. A building of about AD 600 from Dos Pilas, Guatemala, has regular, vertical segments of wall that could reflect work parties; the interior "cells" used in the fill of pyramid construction at many cities could also have come from such labor. A remarkable account from the city of La Corona, Guatemala, tells a story of what youths might also do: leave home for the court of an overlord, perhaps as a quasi-hostage, perhaps in page service or attendance at a courtly school, returning home when one's father passed away. That kind of service, attendance at court, is the context for much of what can be gathered about the activities of elite and royal *ch'ok*. Typically found in groups, youth might play ball, or be known as ballplayers, sit with the current ruler, get drunk—some with enemas of pulque drink—and perform music with conch shells. A few participated in warrior dances.[64] A finely preserved lintel from the kingdom of Yaxchilan, now in a private collection, stresses the supporting role of *ch'ok* as they accompanied warrior kings. As highlighted in chapter 4, or the Maya bowl featured in chapter 1, the carousing and drunkenness resonate with accounts of later Maya, although only older men seemed to enjoy the company of women or maidens—or so indicates the imagery. Courtesans known as *Ix Nahb*, "Ladies of the Water Lily," tended to their needs. But youths certainly preened: a mirror back from Topoxte, Guatemala, belonged to one, and it may have assisted in dressing or makeup. Young men also supported mirrors for lords. A wooden effigy in youthful form, now at the Princeton University Art Museum, holds such a mirror. Another, from the area of Xultun, focuses on a royal youth in the center of its carving (fig. 27).[65] A slate mirror back of a *ch'ok* in the Kislak Collection, Library of Congress, records its ownership by a prince from what was probably Dzibanche, Mexico.[66]

Other *ch'ok* would bring tributary items to court, bags of chocolate, heaps of cotton mantles, perhaps slung over shoulders with sticks. One is explicitly named as a *ch'ok* and "he of the tribute-cloth," *aj yubte'*. A vessel from Cerro Ecatepec in the Museo Regional de Chiapas associates a *ch'ok* with another such scene of tribute. The labors could be forced and unwelcome. A *ch'ok* on a panel at Palenque appears to record his assistance in bringing tribute to a conquering, foreign king.[67] Other *ch'ok* were probable shield bearers or warriors, among many: a title *baah-pakal*, "head shield," on a pot in the Fundación La Ruta Maya Collection in Guatemala City, suggests as much.[68] Finally, service may have continued after death. Just outside the sarcophagus chamber of Pakal the Great of Palenque, and in at least three royal tombs at Piedras Negras are the remains of

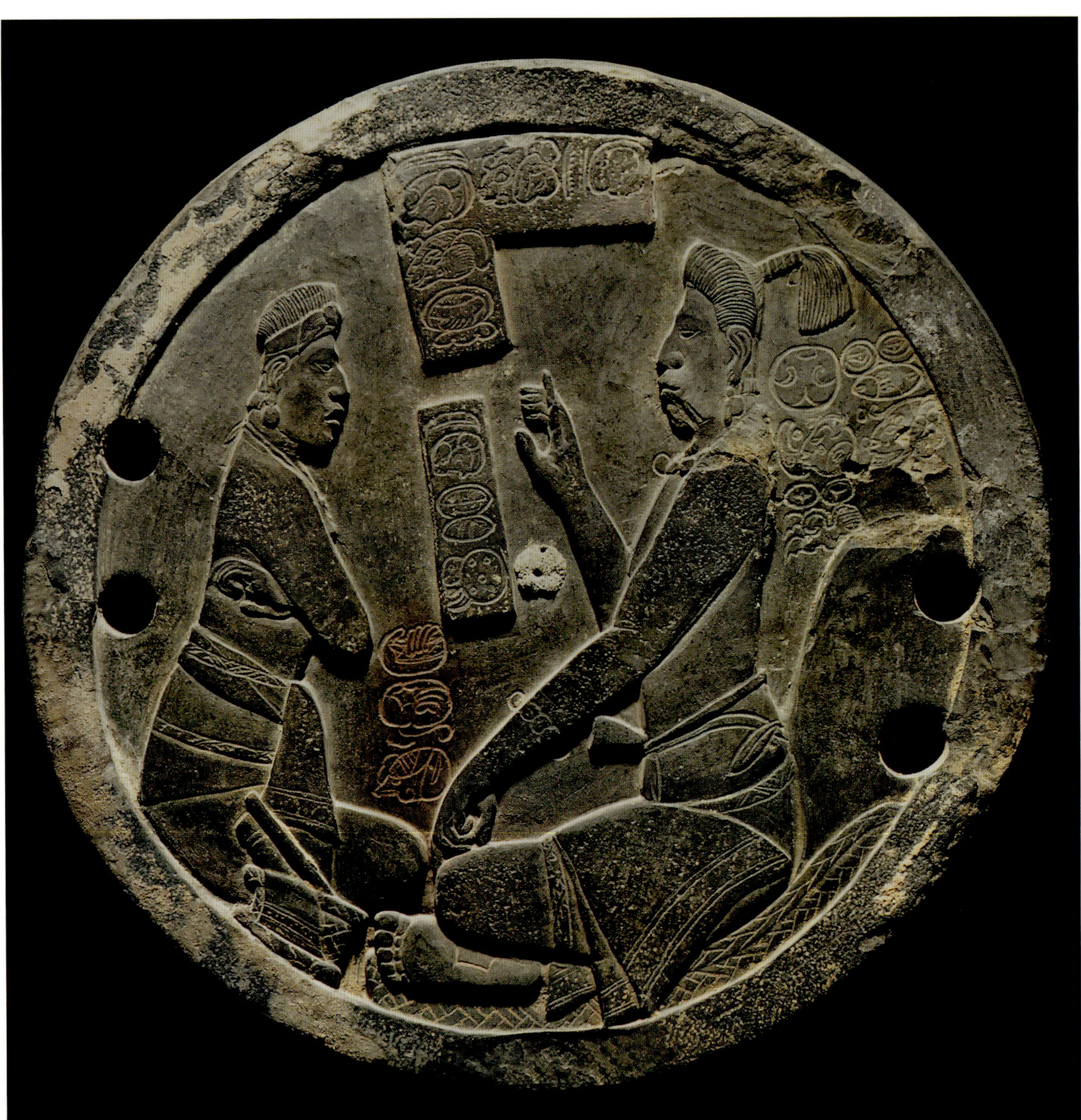

Mirror back with youths, area of
Xultun, Guatemala, Late Classic
period. Slate with red and yellow
pigment, 5½ in. (14 cm).

young men. The find of a young royal male in the Late Classic Burial 82 at Piedras Negras
had a text on a stingray spine identifying the owner as a *ch'ok* and probably a member
of the royal family.[69] Osteological evidence attests to the youth of the male. Presumably,
in death, he was supposed to continue bloodletting with his spine.

❖ ❖ ❖

Youths were not shadowy figures to the Classic Maya. They were unlike other young men
of privilege in the ancient world but resembled them, too, and powerfully so. The sweep
of their lives, and Maya attention to them, can best be understood through glyphic detail.
Their epithets carry subtleties of meaning and classification. Their identities nested within
broader, masculine ones that attended to honor and intersected with gods. Those supernaturals included deities who craved and ate them and the Maize God to whom young
men might look for a model. Gender was incisively observed and regulated, but, in my
judgment, proposals for transgendering or blurred genders founder on surviving evidence.

The glyphs assemble a vocabulary for youths, deployed according to their marital status or physical strength (*keleem*), intrinsic maleness (*xib*), and, most important, to
their status as tender shoots (*ch'ok*). Growing as single "plants," they nonetheless gathered
as collectives—no loners these, but groups brought and directed to varied service. Adults
attempted some oversight. Youths grew, but they were also grown. At the outset, in fact,
the main role of young men among elites may have been martial, in a borrowing from
practices at Teotihuacan. Mirrors belonged to them. Did they adore their faces and handsome bodies—a narcissism implicit in such objects? Or was there adolescent doubt in that
reflection? They had much to do beyond self-absorption. There was tribute to lug and
help to offer, some fun at times, monuments and lapidary treasure to carve. At Palenque
and elsewhere, they even labored beyond their time on earth, ever mindful of duty to court
and crown.

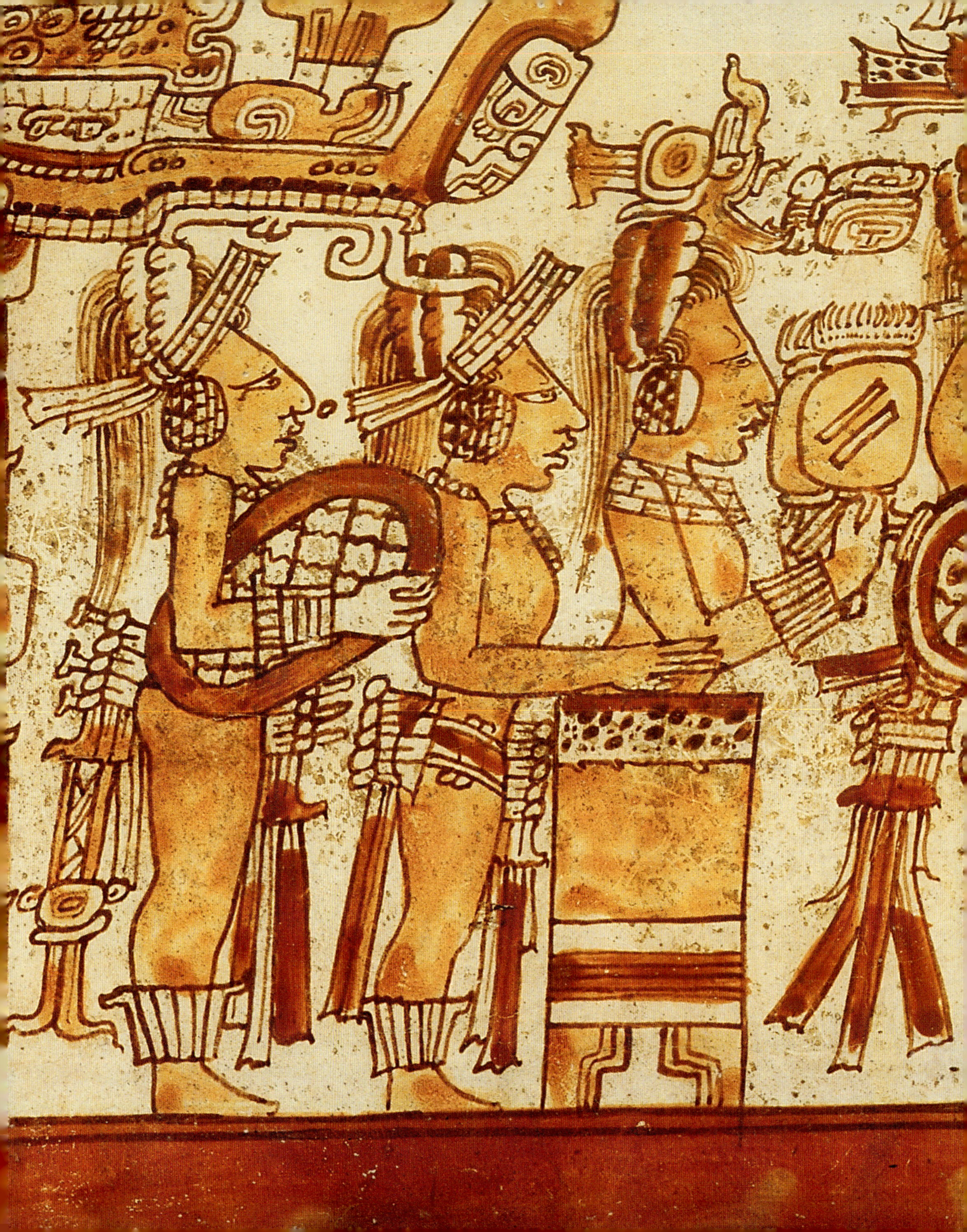

3   A Gifted Passage

Holding a Maya vase, a key possession of youths, can be a delicate or a muscular task. Some pots need only a single hand for a good grip, especially if their midsection is concave and their waist narrow, but most require two hands.[1] As the Classic period developed, cylindrical vases in particular became more fragile. If dropped, they smashed apart, permanently. The few repairs of Maya vases, and some bowls, are of single cracks near the rim. Two holes were drilled to either side, a string looped through and fastened, and the whole perhaps packed with mastic. The bottoms of broken bowls could be recut into lids.

Larger vessels, by contrast, rested on a floor or bench as quasi-furniture. Thick-walled and stable, they were harder to tip over, especially when filled with liquid. Now-vanished cups of wood or gourd ladles were dipped into them, or one pot or gourd might be used with another in the choreographed preparation of drinks. By pouring back and forth, a server created just the right amount of spume. A vessel from near Calakmul, Mexico, shows the whole process. Very much to Maya taste, bubbles frothed up in the pot below. A server then brought the vase to a figure on a throne. Earlier ceramics from the Classic period use glyphs to note the contents of pots, but they avoid depictions of them in use, or ready for use, within palaces, near thrones. By later times, a regal setting seemed to need overt reference. Such portrayals served as a visual manual for correct use and positioning of pots, hinting at ever more elaborate etiquette at royal courts.

In all such vases, serving size mattered. A small tumbler could only quench the thirst of one person. Larger vessels might be shared by many or emptied by someone with big appetites. That the ancient Maya feasted with food and drink is certain. Colonial-era accounts refer to wedding banquets and other "rejoicings and dances." Redistribution and largesse are sure to have marked these occasions, at least to judge from later evidence and dumps of smashed ceramics, possibly the residue of expansive meals. Yet most depictions of food and drink, especially those clustered near thrones, seem less about sharing than consumption by kings. To put this another way, Maya displays evoke a sense of plenty, but for one person only. The markings within most vases, just below the inner rim, may also have shown ideal capacity. If so, kingly cups ran over. Many held a liter or more of liquid, although studies of this are poorly developed in Maya archaeology. On one pot, the only consumer is a dwarf doubling as court fool (fig. 28). His insolent behavior, slurping from a bowl or gourd in the king's presence, could not have been normal—in this case, he may have been absolved by his status as a jester. Nothing like it appears on other vessels, and drinking itself may have savored of vulgarity, done of necessity but not shown. The scenes of drinking, eating, even sneezing in murals from the Chiik Nahb structure from seventh-century Calakmul accentuate the anonymity and low status of those who offer drink: *Aj ul,* "He of the *atole,*" no other names being of interest. The figures were anything but royal.[2]

Some cylindrical pots were too large for such use. Direct sipping from their rims would have been difficult. Many of these were dedicated to the spuming of chocolate, yet some probably served for extravagant drinking: their diameters lay well within the range of German steins or *Humpen* mugs, vessels designed for quaffing quantities of beer. And much like steins, vessels with large diameters allowed elaborate images to be painted on their surface. A small pot could show a complex scene but with diminished clarity and little room for multifigure narrative. Typically, the images accommodated were only a figure or two, one on either side of the vessel. In another respect, however, the Maya pots are not like steins in that they lack handles. Perhaps a firm grip with two hands controlled the liquid and prevented splashing. Later examples of chocolate pots, wide at the bottom, narrow at the top, tended, toward the end of the eighth century AD and beyond, to have restricted rim diameters. Their makers clearly wished to maintain the volume of beverage yet reduce sloshing. In any case, no one doubts that the lower, large-diameter bowls of the Classic Maya were used, as their labels indicate, for consuming *atole* gruel. Presumably, for drinking, cylinder vessels would serve just as easily as open-mouthed ceramics. Some messiness might have been the point, if not exactly suitable for display in imagery. Feasts among Native Americans in the Northwest Coast reveled in spilled excess. Chiefs competed by drinking fish oil, and spillage signaled wealth through a lavish disregard for waste.[3]

Many pots were personalized, painted, or inscribed as the possessions of certain lords and, in a few cases, ladies. Youths who were overtly identified by glyphs also owned a considerable number of these vessels.[4] The sample photographed by Justin Kerr—a peerless collection assembled over decades—has 337 texts with clear statements of ownership. Fully 99, or some 29 percent (repainted or possibly fraudulent pots were removed from this tabulation), refer to their owners as *ch'ok* (37), *chak ch'ok* (52), or *keleem* (10). Further finds not yet photographed by Kerr provide a nearly continuous accumulation of such statements. But what might such possession mean? To own something is not a self-evident proposition. Ideas about possession and property rights vary widely across the world. Each society draws on its own notion of things held in common, singly or by some subgroup in between. Even intangibles such as dances might be understood as property to be inherited or given away. More disquieting is the elusive definition of a "single person" or "individual" who might possess an object. As hard and universal entities,

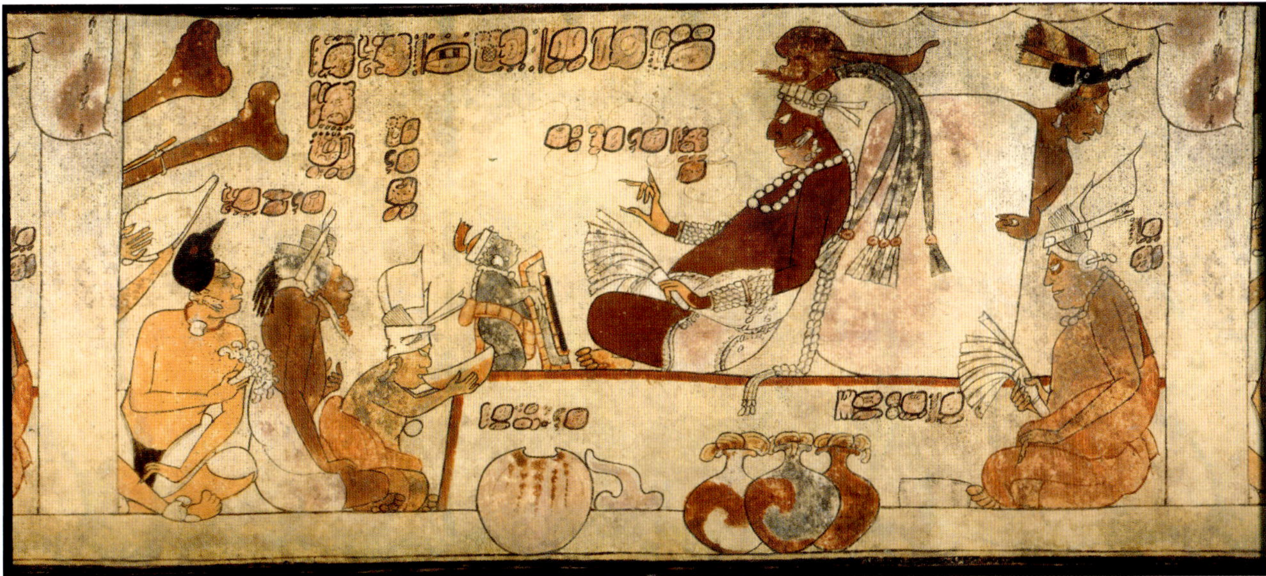

Drinking dwarf, Motul de San José area, c. AD 740–750. Polychrome ceramic, 9⅜ × 6⅞ in. (24.0 × 17.0 cm). National Gallery of Australia, #82.22.92. Photograph by Justin Kerr (K1453).

these categories of identity melt on contact with ethnographic or historical data. For the Classic Maya, personhood could infiltrate and embrace the objects owned by royalty and nobility. It might even inhabit the sculpted and painted depictions of high personages, expanding the royal "self" beyond the physical body.

This concept probably applied to certain pots. Over the course of time, some retained a sensitivity to first ownership.[5] The pots might pass into the control of others—we know this because of their appearance in other kingdoms or by finding one person's vessels in distinct tombs. Yet the initial owner continued to be present in the form of a glyphic tag. There are sensuous implications to this. For literates, close reading of tiny glyphs was unavoidable. By touching texts with their lips—many glyphs go around the rim—later drinkers would see the glyphs close up. Perhaps, as Claudia Brittenham suggests, the names recorded in those texts were even read aloud. But such usage must have jarred at times; when a vase or bowl passed out of the realm, the initial owner went with it as a presence hard-fired on the surface. At the least, the compulsion to label such owners underscored the centrality of the pots in human lives. There was a seeming urge to make that association as permanent as possible.

Colonial Tzotzil, a Mayan language with an unusually rich dictionary source, hints at related subtleties. To "possess," 'oy, concerns a state of existence, a basic quality of being. To "own," *lek*, connotes a quite different concept, a bold "occupation," even confiscation or winning of property. The first word and its derivatives look to inherent, almost unchangeable features of a thing, an office, or a person. The second describes property in competitive flux. A Maya ceramic with owner's tag could relate to both concepts. A tagged object highlights an ineradicable attribute of possession, yet, demonstrably, it also moved about, to be owned by others. A related concept suffuses ethnographic mention of spirit "owners," who corral wild animals within mountains.[6] Hunters may take beasts, eat them, flense off their skins, but the real owners are elsewhere, demanding respect or restitution. For this reason, Ch'orti', one of the languages closest to Maya inscriptions, describes an "owner," *ah yum,* as "master," "controller," and, ultimately, "deity."[7]

In legible examples, beyond the Kerr database there are at least 500 pots that pertain explicitly to kings, noblemen, and noblewomen. That may appear to be a great quantity, but, in a noteworthy twist to the idea of first owners, many are schematic or partial declarations. They record that a pot was owned, but not very clearly by whom, using only titles from a general region or age-related tags, *ch'ok,* a *chak ch'ok,* or a *keleem.* Did this provide some flexibility in passing them on to new owners? A few were painted over, on a layer of stucco, covering earlier messages in carved or painted form. Yet the most ambitious reworking, of a bowl on three pedestals from a royal burial at Tikal, Guatemala, was linked to a *single* king, the so-called Animal Skull, who ruled around AD 593 (fig. 29). Partly visible through flaked stucco, the earlier text celebrates his conclusion of an important cycle; the later, more complete text focuses on his ownership and begins with a rare and poorly understood label for this sort of bowl, *ajaljib.*[8] Grand notations of time, central to the earlier text, go by the wayside. What displace them in emphasis are the personal, the concrete, and the ownership of a portable thing.

Another trait worth mentioning is the restricted slice of time implied by such statements. The proposal here is that the vases not only celebrated a singular act, in this case of drinking and toasting, they also marked the inherently unstable status of being a young man, passing through puberty and going on to acquire new strengths and duties. The pots might endure as finished things, in use until placed in caches or royal burials, but the status they commemorated was ephemeral, and their role as gifts or commissions bound to a finite time of life. By contrast, mature men could last for decades. Making this age-related proposal for pots calls for three steps: a careful look at the ceramics, followed by a review of other cherished things that belonged to young men, and finally, attention to the social moments implied by such objects and their status as gifts to be bestowed, accepted, used, and passed on.

Yet there is a difficult matter to cover first. No Maya pots are legacies kept aboveground as stored heirlooms; all come from archaeologists or looters.[9] (A few ceramics are found by indirect means, without illegal intent, the result of road construction or digging out a well or reservoir.) By taking notes and images, and hopefully publishing those records, archaeologists leave reliable information. Looters, however, orphan the artifacts in the cruelest way—though they happen also to have found and trafficked most of the known pots linked to young men. For looted objects, find spots and parent deposits must be imagined: a tomb or cache if the vessel is whole, building fill or trash dumps if only a sherd remains. Historical glyphs, style, or chemical and mineralogical "fingerprints" in clay point to a particular phase or kingdom. But the sad reality is that our data are of compromised quality, and that this constraint demands no small measure of ingenuity in making sense of the pots.

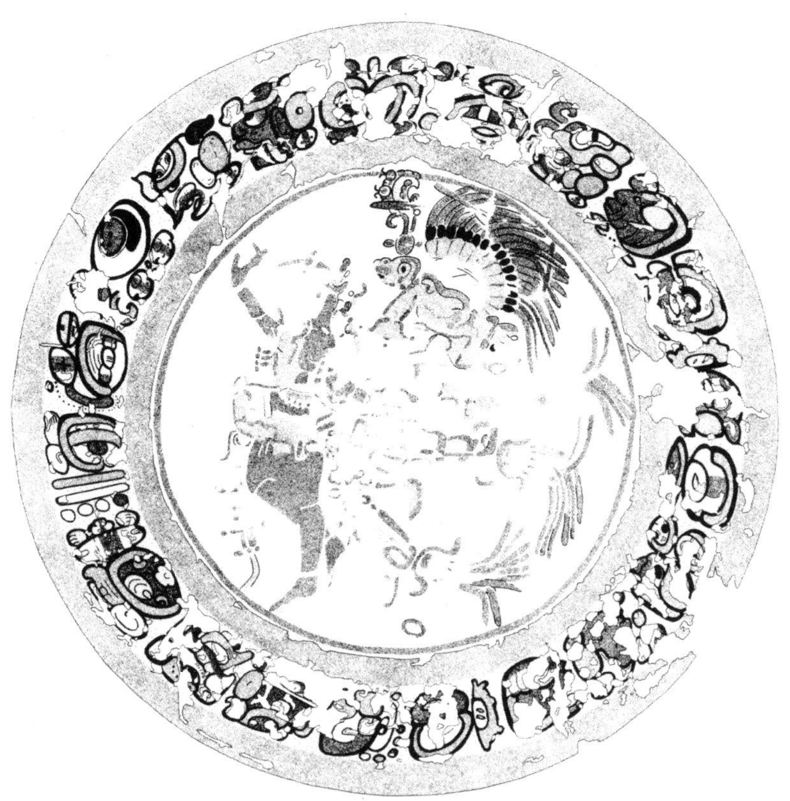

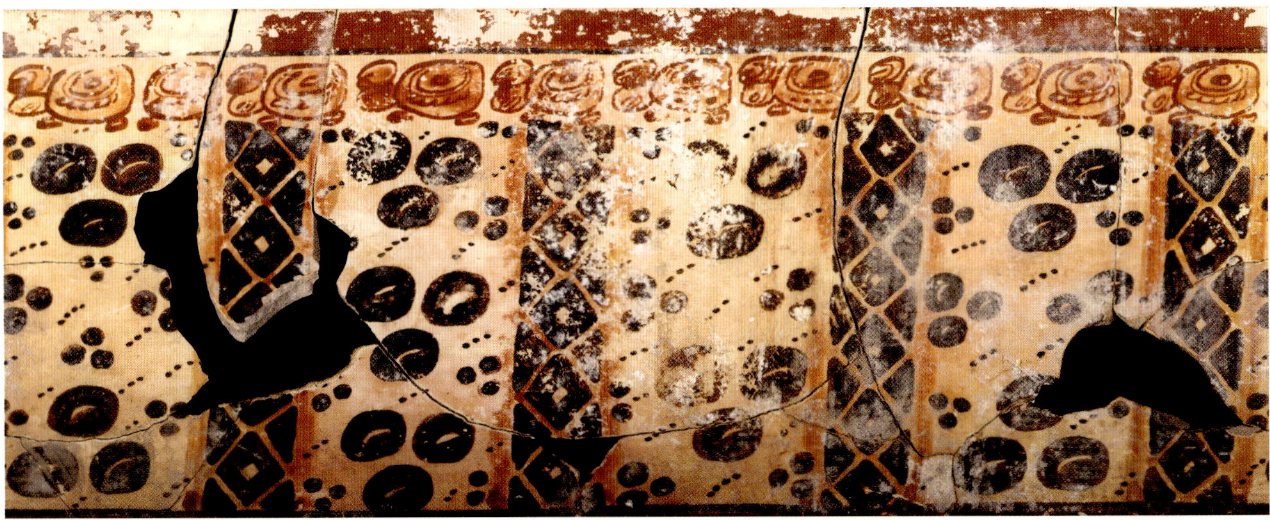

A TOAST!

Most Maya ceramics, broken into sherds or dug up in caches and burials, do not bear legible texts. Or, in several cases, they counterfeit real ones.[10] Offering an impression of written Maya words or syllables, these texts reduce signs to "pseudo-glyphs," a graphic essence of rounded outlines and thin, interior lines (fig. 30). Specific sounds and meanings seem beside the point. A still smaller sample deepens that hint of elusive meaning only to quash it after closer scrutiny. Readable signs, often a common syllable (**yi**) or easily memorized day signs (*Ajaw, Imix, K'an, Kawak*), intersperse with nonsensical ovoids, or they connect and repeat in ways that offer no meaning or sound. A visual rhythm is all that remains, along with a glimmer of how a nonreader might see a text as little more than a pattern, square glyphs alternating with smaller ones. A very few passages come close to transparency by folding in a recognizable phrase or glyphic formula. In intensity of occurrence, these practices of pseudo-writing coincide with the time of the greatest number of legible texts on pottery, from around AD 650 to 750, often in the same area, with pockets of such use in northern Guatemala, Belize, southern Campeche, and Quintana Roo, Mexico; texts also occur in the northern reaches of the Puuc hills in Yucatan. The evidence can be intriguingly variable. Around Piedras Negras, Guatemala, readable glyphs are carved, while painted ones tend to be pseudo-writing. This may express that city's social investment in sculptors. For its part, the kingdom centered on Motul de San José, Guatemala, highlighted painters.

Consider an analogy. A Roman curse tablet, equally opaque, might promise reading by revelation, a mystical penetration to a meaning beyond the obvious. In those texts, perhaps the very thwarting of meaning was a kind of inversion: an upending and twisting of letters reflected and channeled the malice behind it. For the Maya pseudo-glyphs, though, service to the occult is unlikely. The signs bow more to the dictates of good design.

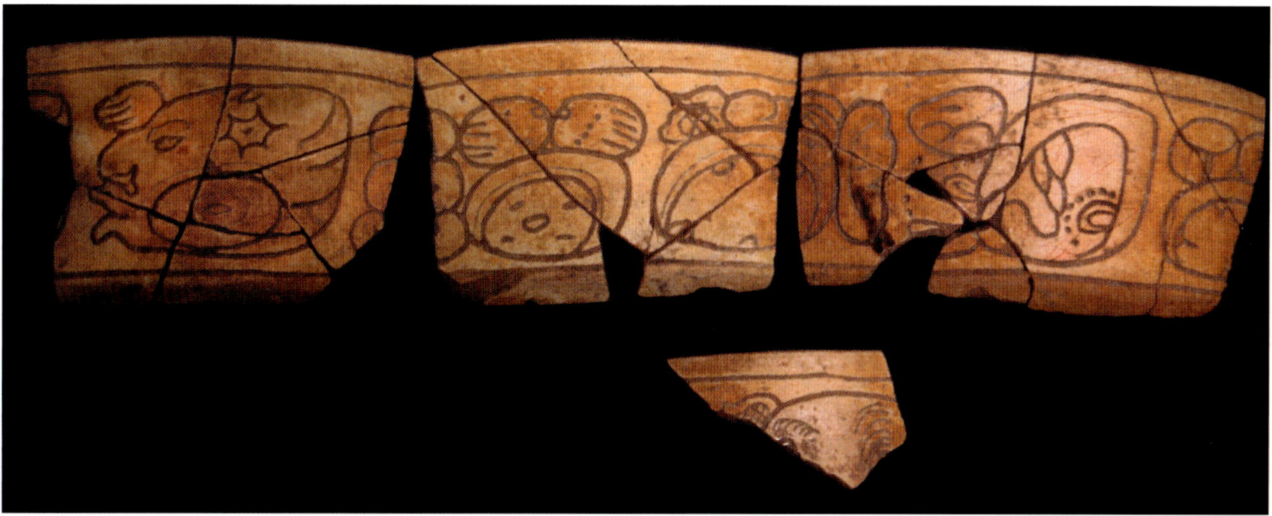

Drinking vessel, probably for *atole*, Piedras Negras, Guatemala, Operation 24B-5, c. AD 650. Incised ceramic, Paqal incised.

Put where glyphs should be, they stand in for legible rim-band texts, vertical sequences of signs, or captions positioned around human figures. However spurious, they accord with expected graphic practice and imply that written messages should conform to aesthetics and pleasing composition. Nor is there evidence of restricted use, a limiting of pseudo-glyphs to the socially unprivileged; even royal tombs have them. Such glyphs would not appear in such places if they were viewed negatively. A larger feature is that, with pseudo-glyphs, writing is present but notionally so, communicating its presence but not its substance. They offer a semantic slot, a place for sound and meaning, but not a bit of content. In part, new linguistic conditions may explain their existence. Perhaps pseudo-glyphs proliferated when general speech spoken by commoners deviated from the rarified language at royal courts. This would accentuate the disconnection between most people and elite writing. Although it sounds plausible, there is in fact little evidence for this function. In Yucatan, elites used language, Yukateko, far different from that of most people, yet pseudo-glyphs on pottery are relatively rare.[11] To the south, near the great cities of Copan, Honduras, or Naranjo, Guatemala, subtle changes in grammar signal, not a frozen or dead language, but a living one susceptible to shifts in sound. By definition, the problem of what most people spoke has no solution. Peasants left no record of their speech.

Legible texts on pottery are far more revealing (fig. 31). The earliest examples tend to be horizontal, read by turning the bowl or vase. Generally, these refer to the object and its ownership. Vertical texts, which often appear later, can be seen all at once, from one viewing angle. Smaller ones, dubbed "captions" by scholars, explain images on the vessel, labeling a person or an item of interest. In both horizontal and vertical examples, however, the texts are almost architectural in placement. Horizontal texts resemble glyphs across the front of a building façade. Vertical ones, particularly those running down the full height of the pot, pass down a column or adorn a door frame. The Maya occasionally established a link between buildings and vessels, to the extent that several pots, especially covered ones, were called "dwellings" or *otoot.* This concept operated on another level. It reminded the reader that a habitual occupant, drink or snuff in this case, could come or go.[12]

Through time, the main texts—those understood by rotating a ceramic—expand in what they have to say.[13] A third-person voice declares that a drinking vessel belongs to a particular person. By increments, other information comes into view. There is a breakdown of contents, mostly chocolate (*kakaw*) or, with certain bowls, maize gruel or *atole* (*ul*), and, latest of all, comment on the features of its surface (painted or sculpted, incised or molded), along with a few words and grammatical elements that are not yet fully understood. The kernel of the text, the owned thing, thus accretes other references. These include the written and inscribed surface and extend to the handling of the object itself. In fact, the attention to the surface betrays a subtle emphasis on the painters and carvers who made them, now elevated into view, by means of signatures or artistic autographs.[14]

The fullest versions begin with a set of signs interpreted by some specialists as "here [is]."[15] The problem is that elsewhere this cluster of introductory glyphs simply frames events in past time. Presumably readers would know that a pot was present without having to be told so. An alternative view is that the function of this sign group is the same as in other texts, that it refers to a past event. The next sign in the sequence is even more important. By wide acceptance, it reads *t'abayi,* "rises up," a reading suggested by David Stuart (fig. 32). Depicting a stylized foot going up a platform, the verb belongs to a particular class of action known to linguists as "mediopassives." These abound in Mayan languages, but in glyphs they make it hard to determine who lies behind a particular event. Something has taken place. We even know the person or object it affects. Yet the main actor eludes us. In many examples, *t'abayi* can be understood as a placement of an object or a building

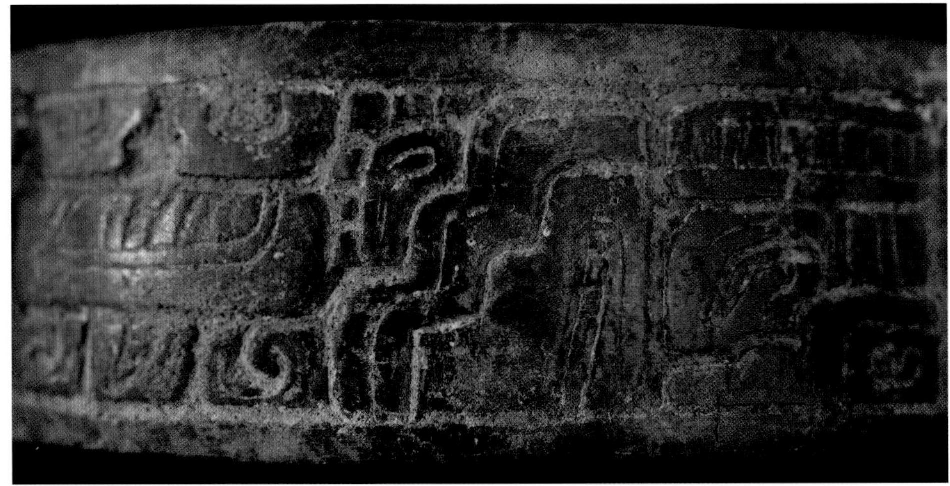

FIGURE 32

Verb for "rise," *t'abayi* (central glyph), Tikal, Guatemala, Cache 198, Early Classic period. Urita Gouged-incised ceramic, 7⅛ × 8¾ in. (18 × 22 cm).

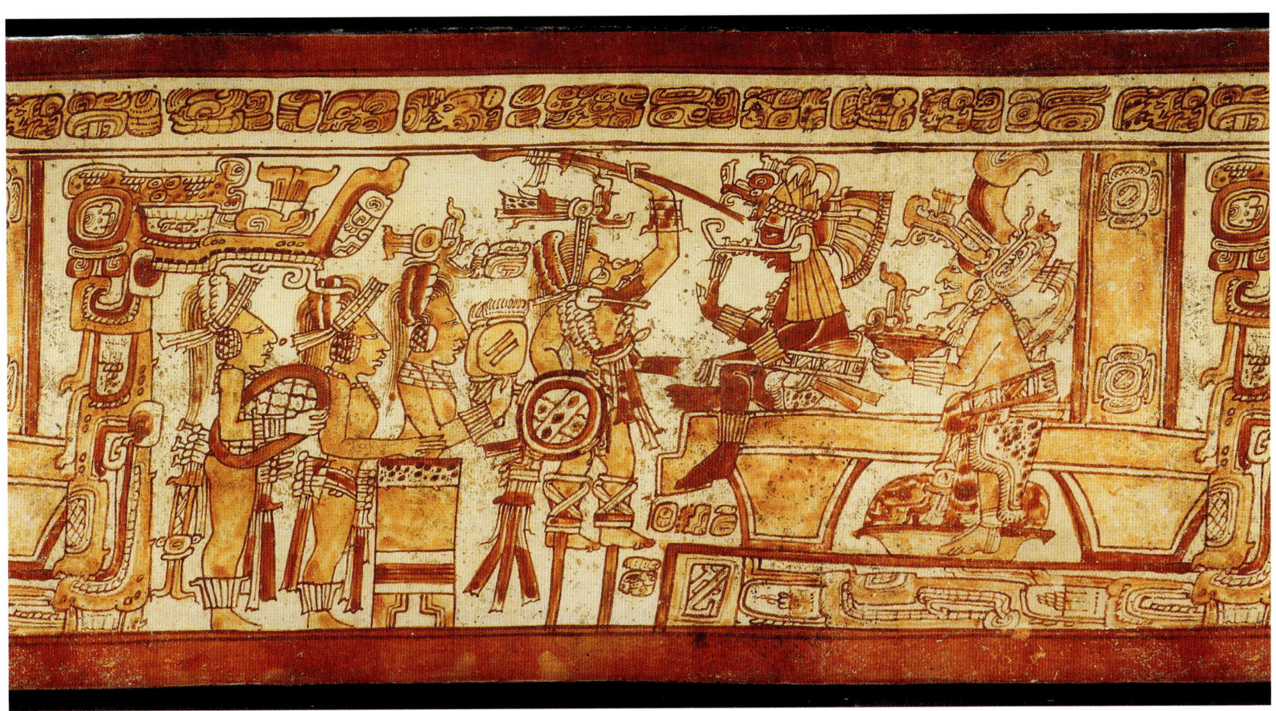

or sculpture for future use, a marker of its inception as a ritual focus, even its "dedication." In essence, however, the verb steers the reader to movement. It is about the raising up of things, lintels or stelae. Perhaps it even speaks of the lifting and wrapping of cloth around human midsections. Such *t'abayi* verbs are depicted on painted textiles at Bonampak, Mexico. It may not be a coincidence that the first room of those murals shows cloth being lifted out of a box. Youths stand above, ready to be dressed for dance.

T'abayi as "rise" or "lift up" explains one image with supernatural actors (fig. 33). Also on a pot, said to belong to a "great youth" (*chak ch'ok*) of some strength or maturity (*keleem*), it displays three young musicians coming out of a cave. One rasps a turtle shell, probably with a concealed antler, another musician pounds a standing drum, and the final youth shakes maracas. By him are glyphs that possibly read *chak ik'*, the "great wind" or "sound" (the *chak* is in a highly unusual form). But the man on stilts captures our main attention. Brandishing a staff and shield, lashed to stilts, he wears the mask of a god that reveals, in the socket, a human eye. The glyphs by his feet identify his dance and its date: *ta 5 Imix, t'abayi ik'il ook*, "on the [day] 5 Imix, they rise up, the musical [windy] feet." Percussive, stamping, the dance is greeted by an enthroned figure, also wearing a mask; an aged god looks on, too. The context confirms *t'abayi* as principally a verb of motion. The action shifts someone or something up to a place of repose or, in this performance, to a temporary perch on stilts. The vertical movement accounts for other examples, some of which occur in inscriptions from the early seventh century AD at Dos Pilas, Guatemala. Having been forced from home by a victorious rival, a lord *t'abayi*, "rises up," to various places of exile or defense.[16]

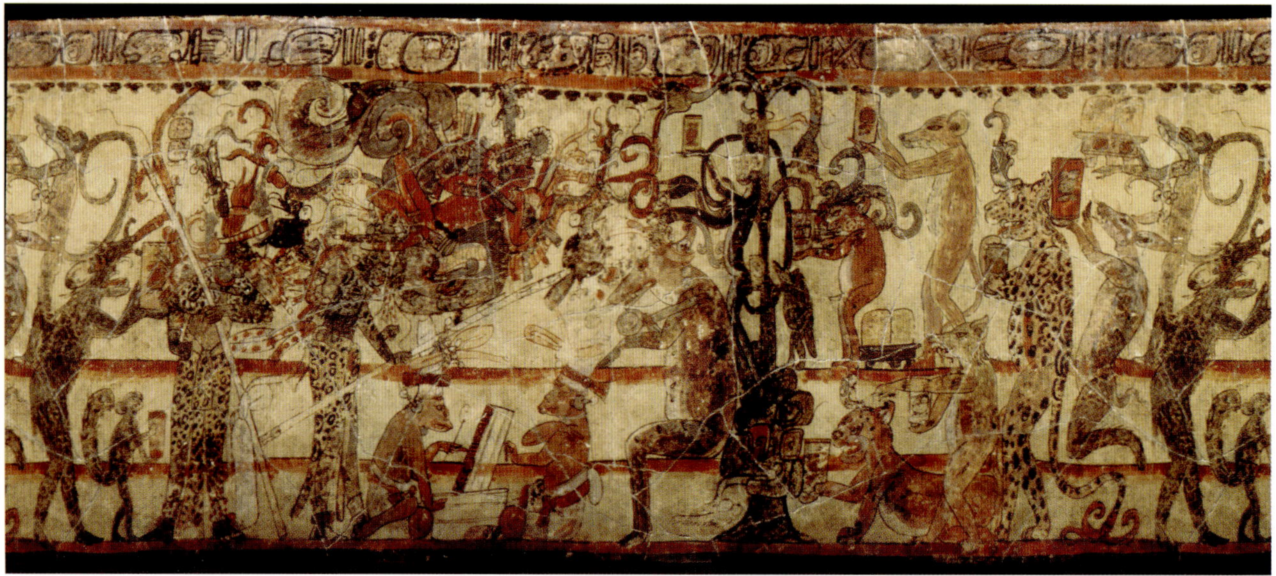

Raising up of food and drink by mythic beasts, Guatemala or Mexico, c. AD 800. Polychrome ceramic. Photograph by Justin Kerr (K3413).

An image on a vessel from the final years of the eighth century AD—the glyphs are illegible pseudo-signs, and its provenance is lost to looting—displays an uncommon sight that is likely to be mythic (fig. 34). At the same time, it may be a charter for dynastic behavior that involves a pictorial reference to *t'abayi*. A veritable zoo of bipedal animals enters a platformed palace. It is the center of all things, with a world tree in the middle, maybe a mythic ceiba thrusting high in the forest. There are two jaguars, a peccary, a pocket gopher, a smaller mammal with head straining up, deer, dogs, possibly a coyote, a squirrel, the leanest of spider monkeys—see his tail loop up and over his body. Two animals strain toward an unnatural bipedalism, struggling on knees or rising up with a paw. Of the human, or those in human guise, there are two twins outfitted with blowguns. They are the enemies of all such creatures, especially smaller flying ones. Two attentive monkey scribes, one in dutiful, subordinate posture, take note of what rolls in. Among the animal crowd, in most of their hooves, claws, or paws, are a selection of vessels and bowls marked with tiny glyphs.

The contents of the pots are unclear—they are obviously liquids—but immense, succulent tamales fill the tripod bowl resting on the palace tier. The hot or warm tamales, of maize dough, appear with cool drinks, a balance of hot and cold familiar among later Maya. The intended recipient: perhaps the lone flying creature in the scene, an avian being in partly human form, a high god whose name escapes decipherment (it might have been *kokaaj* or *itzam kokaaj*). Or are the blowgunners in charge? Strangely, in other images, the mythic bird is the victim of the hunters, and the nuances of the scene cannot be completely decoded. Gestures in the image are what count: all bowls and pots lifting up. These correspond directly to the concept of *t'abayi*, a raising up, in toast and offering, of tasty things to drink and eat. The food and drink are not being handed out, however; they arrive with subordinates. To curious extent, the combination of plates and cups resonates with later, colonial-era prophecy in the Chilam Balam of Chumayel, a book in Yukateko. Both objects appear in opaque couplets describing future units of time, twenty years in duration, and by no coincidence one dynastic plate at Tikal invokes the completion of two of these cycles.[17]

What can be inferred more broadly about human practices, beyond the offerings by mythic animals on this vase? Glyphs and images suggest one scenario, that the raising of a pot, along with its contents and painted or sculpted surface, took place at some unspecified time in the past. A few texts provide fixed dates for such events but, plausibly, most concern drink, whether of chocolate or *atole,* but in a few cases, tamales. One lone vessel specifies use for pulque.[18] That pot was hewn of wood (only its painted stucco exterior survives), hinting that certain functions or contents accorded with perishable vessels. My colleague Andrew Scherer suggests a practical motivation, based on the need to maintain or reduce the temperature of contents. Perhaps wood or gourd differed in this respect from fired clay, a suggestion that needs scientific testing. The pots also suggest, in their future use, a constant reminder of that original offering in the form of a tagged ceramic. An impermanent act—a lifting, for at some point the pot must be set down—opens the way for later drinking and eating. But those meals-to-come always relate to the first one, and to the person who owned the pot: truly, an instance of "what's past is prologue." Yet the social moment that envelops these vases, bowls, and plates is unclear. The festival of animals charts an inward flow, of inscribed or painted ceramics brought to a central point. If it has any bearing on dynastic practices of the Maya, the pots and their contents may not be self-commissions. Others, underlings, a deferential group, might have brought them to honor a special occasion.

THINGS OF YOUTH

As mentioned before, a sizeable number of pots seem to have belonged to people with the titles of youth: *ch'ok, chak ch'ok,* and *keleem.* What to make of these terms runs the gamut of scholarship. Barbara MacLeod and Dorie Reents-Budet restrict the meaning on pots to "the status of the person as closely related to, but of lesser status, than the king." Two other interpretations endorse that more expansive view. *Chak ch'ok* is said by the epigrapher Nikolai Grube to attribute "youthful power" (*jugendlicher kraft*) to men of varying age who acquire strength by imbibing drinks of invigorating chocolate. Or, to Pierre Robert Colas, the titles identify ownership or production of ceramics precisely because they appear on pots. Youthful status is immaterial. The labels merely specify the holders of the ceramics.[19]

My preferred view is literal. The glyphs can be taken at face value, identifying the pots as property of young men. Strengthening the association, not just one title of youths (*ch'ok* or *chak ch'ok*) but two (also *keleem*) occur together in the texts. One of them, *ch'ok,* is largely joined in the inscriptions to people of young age. As a key aesthetic locus of the

Classic Maya, covered with the most expert calligraphy, the pots would seem unambiguous, that they celebrate a particular age status. The pots were kingly stuff, too, in that several exhibit the royal title par excellence, the so-called Maya Emblem glyph for "holy lords." This usage accords with the evidence for youthful accessions in several dynasties, a point introduced in the last chapter.[20] Often, too, the owner's name is followed by the name of a maker or orator. Their very words equate with the writing. A few pots append, after the names of the owner, *u tz'ihb*, "[it is] the painting" of another person, a scribe; still others include *cheheen*, "says" (fig. 35).[21] The author becomes identifiable when another name follows, that of the presumed scribe. The phrase inserts speech into a written record, and the speaker appears to be someone of lower status than the owner. The blurring between writing and speech demonstrates their close intersection in Maya minds. We can infer, as well, that such ownership needed third-party testimony, a separate authority or witness "saying" it was so.

Gender is implied, but by exclusion. Only five known vases and perhaps one plate were tagged with female owners.[22] Glyphs prove the rest of those with texts belonged

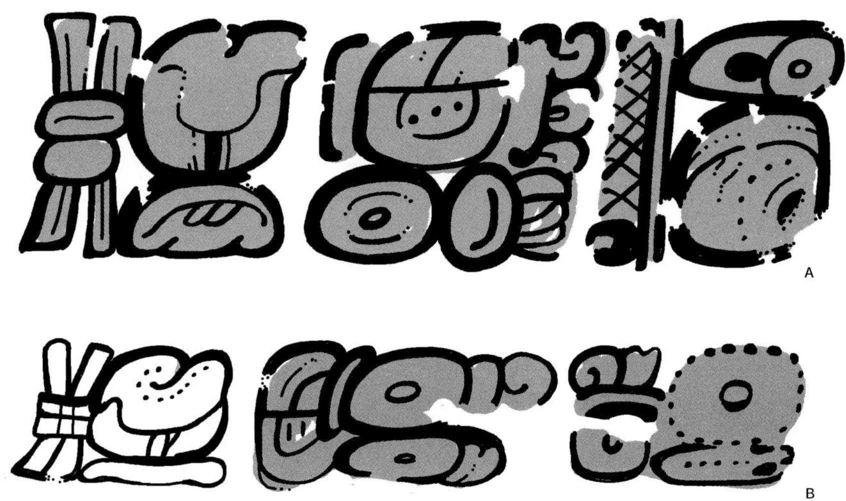

FIGURE 35

Cheheen, "says," and scribal names: A) vase, Tikal area, Guatemala, Late Classic period; B) vase, northern Guatemala, Late Classic period.

to males. The irony is that, to judge from later evidence, most pots were probably shaped by women, if painted by men—ethnography inclines strongly to this view of Maya practice, past and present, although always with a smattering of exceptions.[23] The vases that do belong to women share more than that: although painted by different hands, at least four state, either openly or by style, their link to the dynastic behemoth of Xultun, a large and heavily looted site in northeastern Guatemala. The three named princesses were offspring or close kin of Xultun's rulers. They participated in a focused practice, hedged in time—the vases can only date to a generation or two. Their size is consistent, too. One of the vases has an unusually small diameter, 2½ inches (6.5 cm), easily clutched by

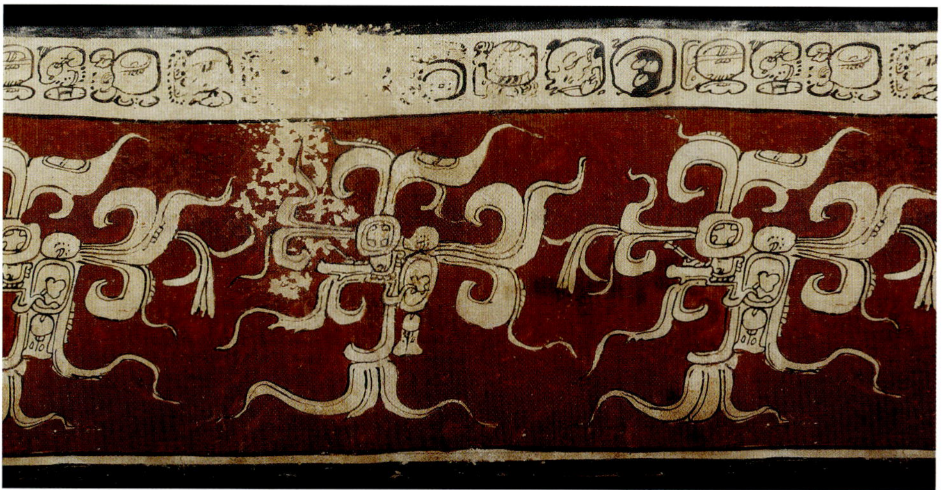

petite hands. Another, comparably slight pot, from Tayasal, Guatemala, highlights two women along with a man. Possibly it was also designed for female use, being even smaller in diameter, at 2⅜ inches (6 cm).[24]

In two vases with female owners, the texts and images double back to men. A vessel with burgundy-red background notes a woman's guardianship of a youth, *u chan ch'ok* (fig. 36). Another evidently belonged to a female who married into the royal family of Motul de San José or a place nearby and whose name accompanies a scene of tribute. A chocolate bundle, of the kind to supply the beverage designated on the rim, rests near the principal tributary. The local ruler and his spouse lean over from their throne, acknowledging the gathered treasure. That enthroned woman may have been the owner of the pot or, perhaps more likely, someone closely related to her. Otherwise, the juxtaposition of female owner and enthroned consort would be difficult to explain.

A pot excavated from Tikal was also owned by a female of high rank (fig. 37). This is one of the few women labeled as a *ch'ok,* "youth." She is also a "holy lady" (*k'uhul ixik*). The scene below features two women. The first and most elaborately dressed, her tunic filled with floral designs, offers a mask to a royal male. The bodies of these two are turned toward the viewer. A gendered symmetry pervades the image. A younger woman to the left, in profile, identified by the same enigmatic title as the main female (*Ixik sa?*), waits with a shield to complete the ruler's costume. Off to the right, a younger male, also facing into the scene, holds up a mirror for his master's approving glance. Music and dance are in the air. The king grasps a rattle, and the day of this event, 1 Ik', "wind, music," hints that song and exuberant sound are soon to come. This vessel is unusual in its secure provenience, a burial in a pyramid within the Mundo Perdido complex of Tikal. The excavators assert that the occupant of the tomb was a "sub-adult of feminine sex." A separate analysis of the bones confirms the age, 15, give or take 3 years, an estimate consistent with the *ch'ok* title in the principal text. An oxygen isotope in her molar may indicate an origin

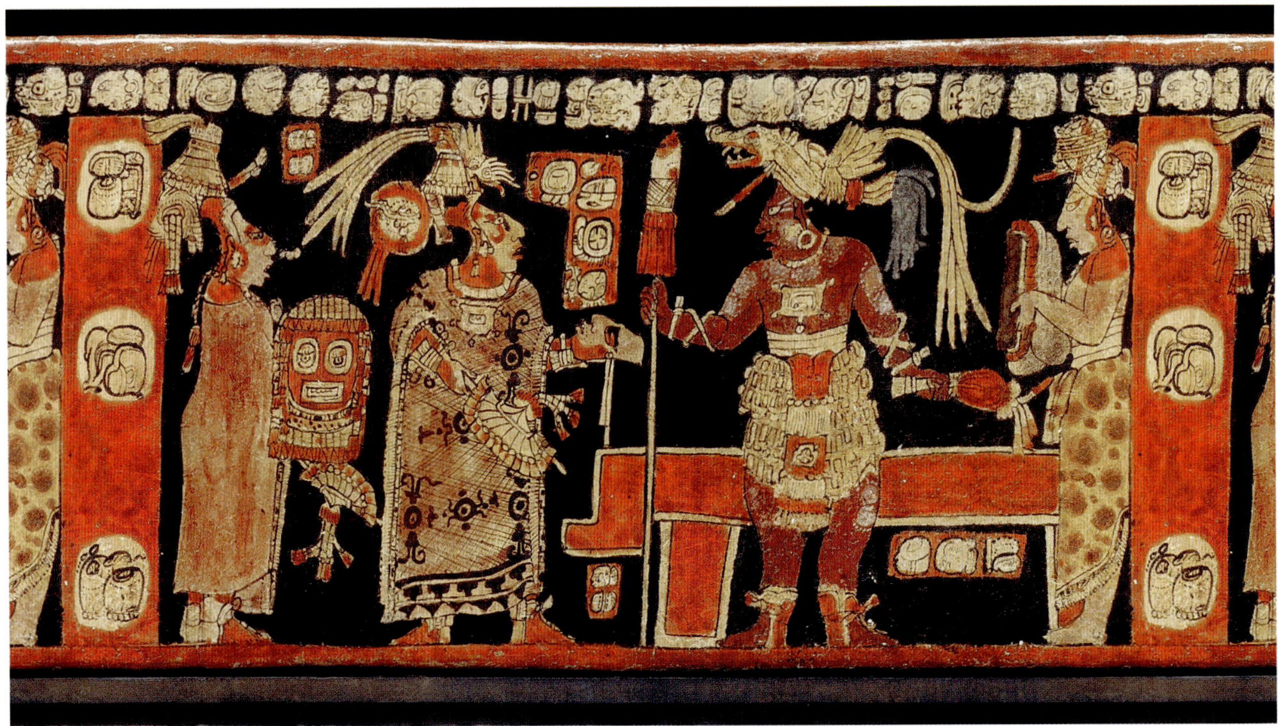

Vase belonging to a royal lady,
Tikal, Guatemala, Burial PNT-009,
c. AD 750. Polychrome ceramic.
Photograph by Justin Kerr (K2695).

in the Peten lakes some 30 km from Tikal.[25] Yet the two scenes appear less anticipatory than commemorative—a sideways glance at the actual owner. Perhaps the pots recorded the exemplary acts of other related women. In this way, the pots could dispense their contents, quenching thirst, but also offer wisdom and exhortations to good behavior.

The ceramics with youthful owners refer to a variety of food and drink. Most stored chocolate beverages, but there was *atole* too in such *uk'ib*, "drinking vessels"; a few labels even occur on plates (*lak*) for tamales and stews.[26] *Atole* could not have been expensive, but chocolate most certainly was—collected as tribute or by exchange. Gonzalo Fernández de Oviedo y Valdés, writing of early colonial Nicaragua, records that the going rate for a slave was a hundred cacao beans. More than a few of those beans would have gone into a single drink. Nevertheless, one of the most ambitious Maya bowls, the "Popol Vuh," with its troop of spirits and complex text, was for lowly *atole*.[27] Of finely ground maize, at times laborious to prepare, that drink was still commonplace, consumed by all ranks in society according to later historical and ethnographic sources. As to ownership, most tags divide into two categories. The first is generic, referring to a youth but loosely so, without personal name or dynastic epithets (we had singled out these curiosities before). The second trumpets individual possession, a point driven home by one vase in particular. After the glyph for the drinking vessel, in a position usually occupied by the name of the owner, comes a personal designation followed by *u k'aba' ch'ok*, "[it is] the name of the youth." In such texts, only one person can be the owner, not some general class of youth. In these cases, ownership was inelastic, without clear possibility of transference. The explanation for the first category may be the relative status of the owner. More exalted personages may have received a personalized statement; lower-ranking youths did not. Or, as mentioned before, the ownership of pots was deliberately left fluid, to be made for and used by a wider group of young men, on multiple occasions.

There is an expectation, given such owners, that such pots would display didactic or hortatory narratives, laying out what youths should do, be, or aspire to. Yet the images on such vessels do not show clusters of youthful themes.[28] Or to be more precise, the correlations are not clearly apparent. Instead, some scenes feature horizontal bands or flowers, evoking fragrant scent. These are of decidedly non-narrative quality and not especially common in the corpus. Pleasant, to be sure, these are features prized by elites in general. Other pots, perhaps the majority, exhibit gods. These include scenes of *Itzam,* a leering, over-sexed figure, often with maidens, but also *Chahk,* the Rain God, who spears fish or hacks at a fat beast of indeterminate identity. In several instances, *K'awiil,* probably the embodiment of lightning, peers out from smoke or fire. A dramatic story appears in one well-studied example, with the descent of the Principal Bird Deity, an emphasis on a few other pots as well. These accounts, other than those featuring the lissome Maize God, do not refer perceptibly to youthful activity or to deeds they should emulate. A few pots do stress the usual spaces of noble youths. There are vignettes at court, sometimes of gods. Others stress seated figures in a palace, or dressing or preparing for dance or display; several vessels exhibit royal diadems, the *hu'n,* based on a concept of paper headbands. But the lack of historical scenes with known or identifiable personages is striking. Of the two such scenes, the first is on a pot that belonged to a young woman, an anomaly in this set of ceramics. Interpreting these mythic images would require some training in conventions and broader allusions.

The earliest *ch'ok* vessels are anything but generic. At the outset, the first references to youthful ownership come in astonishing quantity from a single lord, a king of Naranjo, Guatemala (fig. 38).[29] Spanning sixty-nine years or more, from AD 546 to about 615, his reign is one of the longest in Maya history. Reading his name in full is not yet possible. A few elements are decipherable, others not, leaving the rough approximation of "Aj Wosal." Convenience more than confidence dictates its use by specialists. At least nine bowls belonged to the king as a youth, a *chak ch'ok keleem,* a "great youth, strong [one]." Nominally, the emphasis always rested on his age-linked titles, to be followed by his personal name, and more rarely his dynastic titles. Reinforcing this attribute, one vessel refers to him by the stripped-down designation *winikha'b,* a term cuing one unit of twenty years. This suggests his tender age, and the same combination of *ch'ok* with someone under 20 years old occurs on a vessel in a private collection.[30] A pot with a novel decorative scheme of roundels and dark background dating to later years in his reign records a more complete version of the *winikha'b* expression, but now for an Aj Wosal between 40 and 60 years of age. The titles of youth have now disappeared, and in this text his sacred lordship

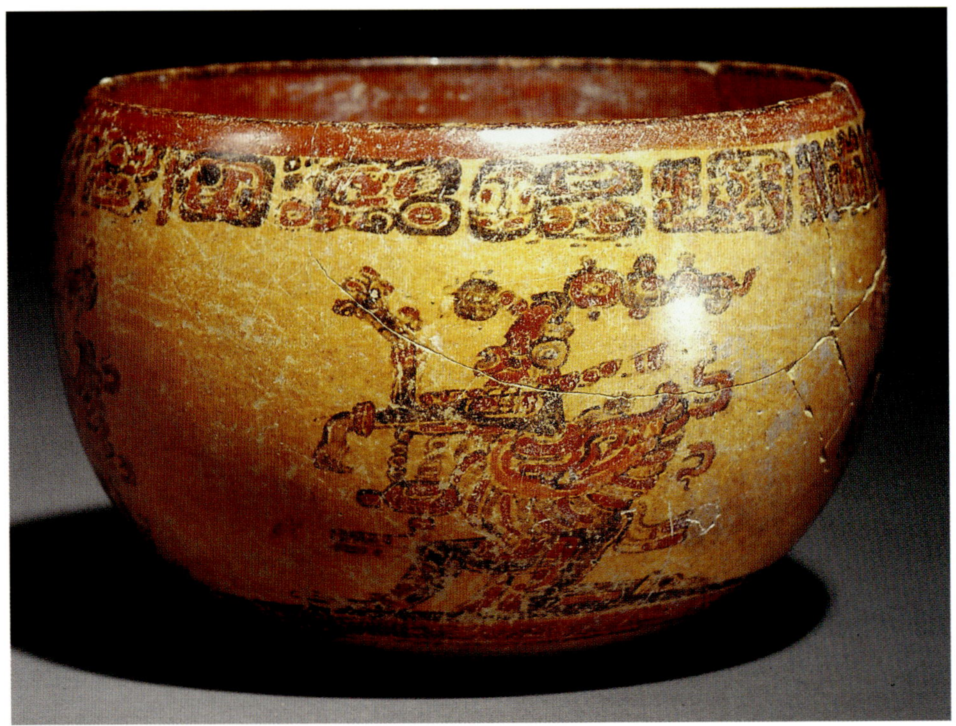

takes precedence in the string of signs. At that point, the king was heavy with experience—historical details certify that, at accession, he was no more than 12 years old. Many years lay ahead for this young client of the so-called Snake Kingdom, the foremost dynasty of the time. A lucky man, he would advance to more than 80 years of age. But unlucky too: his world surged with conflict between the Snake Kingdom and Tikal, in tensions that roiled the area for another century or more.

Rulers at twelve are not ready for the task, an observation noted in the last chapter. A gray eminence or council must hover nearby or, as at Tikal, govern in unison with an immature heir or heiress. From this period in Aj Wosal's life come the bowls with youthful titles. The images on them, which bend below sight, distorted by the convexity of the sides, range from dancing maize gods in a flowery milieu to the Principal Bird Deity as an emissary of sorts. Animals gambol. There are coati, watery serpents, and drunken animals in the midst of a rip-roaring party. On one vessel, now in the Mint Museum in Charlotte, North Carolina, the bestiary ascends to folkloric explanation. A rat or mouse paints the spots on a feline, neatly accounting for such marks. Other creatures rush to greet a high god, and spider monkeys cavort nearby. Even his late pot, done, we presume, decades later, shows insects perched on flowery forms.

The obvious question concerns the social setting that ordered up these pieces, along with their transmission and manner of use. Unusually for dynastic vessels (with few exceptions most ceramics with legible texts derive from looting) two have reliable provenience.

One came from a burial in an outlying part of Tikal, not from the sectors where kings interred their own. A second, in the collection of the Museum of Anthropology and Archaeology at Cambridge University, was discovered in a rich tomb at Caracol, Belize.[31] A selection of facts helps to navigate the murk of this surprising distribution. The pots compose the earliest but most abundant set of such service-ware owned by youths; they pertain to a king notable for his early accession to the throne; two bowls traveled by mysterious means to other kingdoms (Caracol and Tikal) for eventual deposition in a lordly but nonroyal burial; the other, comparable examples in the same style pertain to that rival kingdom; and the period of such use corresponds to the beginnings of far-reaching quarrels, expressed in war and alliance, between the powers of Tikal and Calakmul. The variance of style in the pots, among which no two derive certainly from the same hand, suggests a longer time of production. An alternative view might even see them as retrospective works, pots intended to recall a ruler's salad days.

This uncomfortable possibility brings to mind the only pot in the series with a discrepant combination. It records youthful titles (*chak ch'ok keleem*) along with a reference to the slightly more advanced age of 20 to 40 years, which is the next category of note for biographical spans among the Maya. The vessel has signs of over-restoration but not enough to throw doubt on the record. A possibility is that Aj Wosal had gone only a short way into his twenties. Perhaps he had not yet married or otherwise ascended to full adult status.[32] Still, the overall, unremitting message of the pots is their connection to Aj Wosal as a young man and, from the find at Tikal, to their movement through political networks outside the kingdom. The great number of vessels indicates the probability of many find-spots, many tombs or caches, not just one. (Looters have done irreparable damage here.) As objects of statecraft, the entire set arrives at a moment of evident regency. A princely possession, they must also have left his hands and transferred to others. Or, as Claudia Brittenham suggests, they were given to him as cherished gifts, thus accounting for their diverse hands. In any case, the creative burst represented by Aj Wosal's pots, along with the time of life they imply, suggests a motivation for their existence, and for subsequent imitations by other lords. If Aj Wosal did not start the practice, his pots establish a daring pattern for others to follow, from the sixth century AD on.

In times that proved ever less stable, with greater populations to control, more enemies to combat, and heightened complexity of diplomacy at all levels, the pots for young men entered into, and multiplied within, a particular kind of world. Coming of age, maturation, and certification of legitimate status became acutely important. Dynasties depended on it. That these matters were played out on and through drinking vessels, presumably for wide distribution, underlines another feature: a young lord was now thought ready for courtly protocols of consumption. Prepared to receive, to host, to be seen in public, he could be expected to behave properly. There would be no embarrassment in the refined milieux of royal palaces. The pots announce that progress to full socialization.

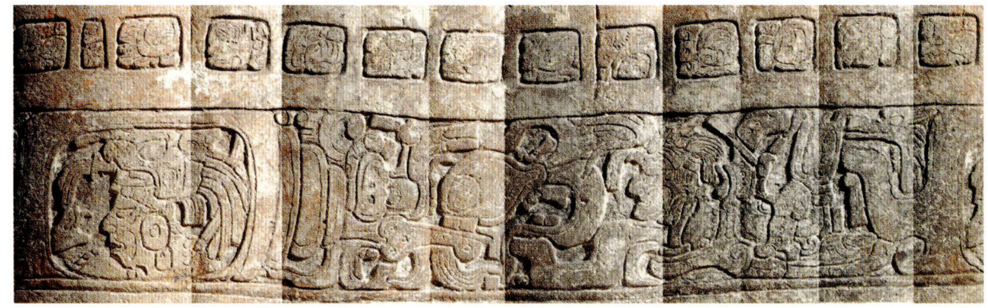

The Aj Wosal bowls have landmark status. They inaugurate ownership of multiple vessels by a single person, one of *ch'ok* status to boot. Other nonceramic objects also belonged to *ch'ok.* An alabaster drinking vessel from the area of Palenque, Mexico, identifies its owner as a young ruler of Palenque.[33] It is the earliest text from the site, as all others appear to be retrospective. Curiously, the image nearby depicts an older man with a beard—was this added later, to a finely made bowl received in younger years, now updated to reflect the owner's current appearance? In useful symmetry to Naranjo, another set of *ch'ok* vessels dates to the final years of such practice, around AD 800 or perhaps a decade or two before (fig. 39).[34] The appearance of stamped glyphs gives the impression of mass production, and such is clearly attested at this time for other ceramics, including examples discussed later in this chapter. Auguring things to come, the makers of the second set of pots wished to emphasize uniformity and the possibility of broad, replicative diffusion. The regular multiplication of texts displaced any stress on singular work. Did this express a severe reduction of scribal competence? Or an enlarged audience for high-style productions, through objects taken to foreign kingdoms? Paradoxically, in the second group of *ch'ok* pots, the dots and linework show clear signs of individual carving or finishing.

One of Aj Wosal's pots ended up at Tikal. For the second series, of late date, there is another in firm context. It was discovered in a multiple burial within a residential group at the city of Caracol, from "the late Late Classic period," around AD 775–800.[35] The other vessels, now in museum and private collections, disclose exactly the same handling of forms, assured line, and confident excision of leather-hard clay. The glyphs look identical, and surely one hand alone created these pots or the carvings on them. The inventory of images varies somewhat, however. A looted example, its original burnished brown surface intact, depicts a mythic vulture, man-eagles—four in number, a satisfying totality in Maya thought—and the acrobatic Maize God in his legs-up contortions (fig. 40). At the center of the action sits the probable Maya Sun God. The other vessels depart from that scheme. Watery and serpent-themed, they show figures emerging from snakes or fixed within the body of a conch. Repeated on both, too, is the head of a man with jaguar headdress. Yet, for all these pots, the owner is the same, a *ch'ok itz'aat,* "young skilled one," with a sequence of signs found to varying degree on each member of the set. There is nothing to link this person to Caracol. Quite the opposite: the vase with well-preserved surface refers to an *'a-ik'*, "he from the Wind [place]," a title possibly tied to the kingdom of Motul de San José and related settlements in northern Guatemala. Again, much like Aj Wosal's pots but two hundred years later, these ceramics had belonged to the same young male and were dispersed to areas away from their place of manufacture, finding themselves, before interment, in different hands. Some of these people were not clearly royal, being buried in smaller groups away from palaces or dynastic mortuary temples. The existence of the pots, recovered by chance in legitimate digs or the furtive probes of looters, leads to a wider surmise, that many *ch'ok* pots were not singletons but were parts of broader sets—certainly, groupings of like ceramics are well attested in Maya archaeology, as for example in a remarkably uniform assemblage of bowls from Holmul, Guatemala. Dating to the late seventh century AD, they can be understood less as random pots for sale than a collection with social meaning. Though we cannot know, they may well have been distributed at single events, even coming-of-age ceremonies. Such sets were certainly known in tombs with almost identical ceramics, including from Caracol, Holmul, Tikal, and many other sites.

Another assemblage of ceramics, also from Naranjo but dating to around AD 775 or even later, were all painted by the same hand (fig. 41). One names the calligrapher, a local man, perhaps a "wise orator," *itz'aat-ti*. Diagnostic details, a way of spelling the glyph for "chocolate" with an outsized **wa** syllable, leave little doubt that he painted the pots. Three belonged to "great youths," *chak ch'ok*, yet their names vary enough so that at least two, possibly three, different people were involved; these names also confirm that the owners of the pots, specified by glyphs, were not their makers or painters. The vase not marked for youthful ownership nonetheless records a full statement of parentage. This proves that the young man was the offspring of two royal lines: a father who ruled Naranjo from

FIGURE 40

Vase of four mythic eagles, eastern Peten, Guatemala, c. AD 800. Stamped, excised ceramic. Photograph by Justin Kerr (K8242).

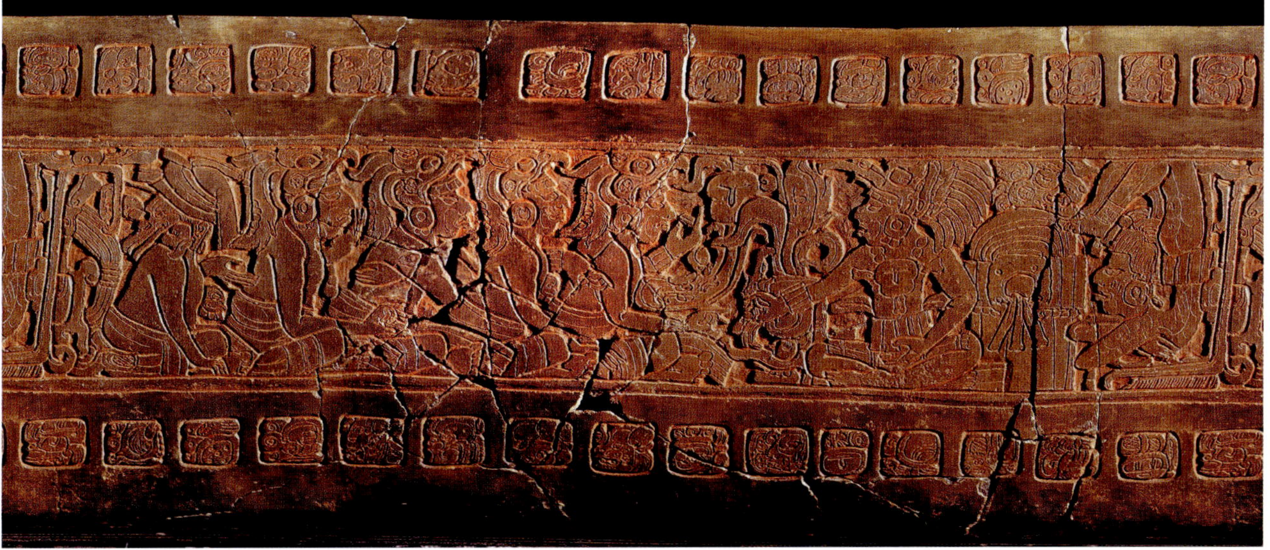

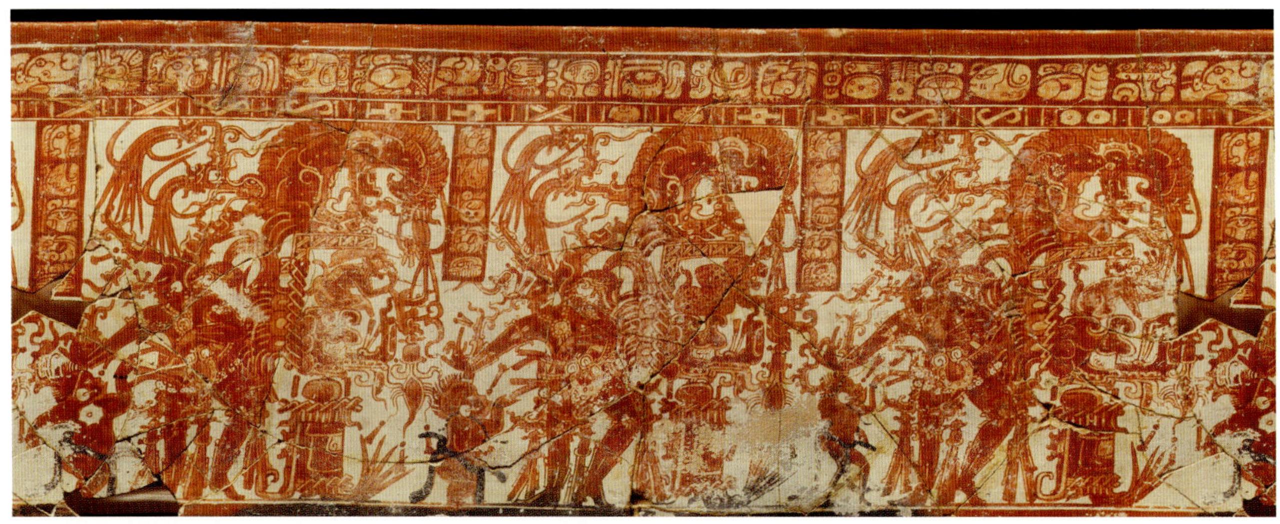

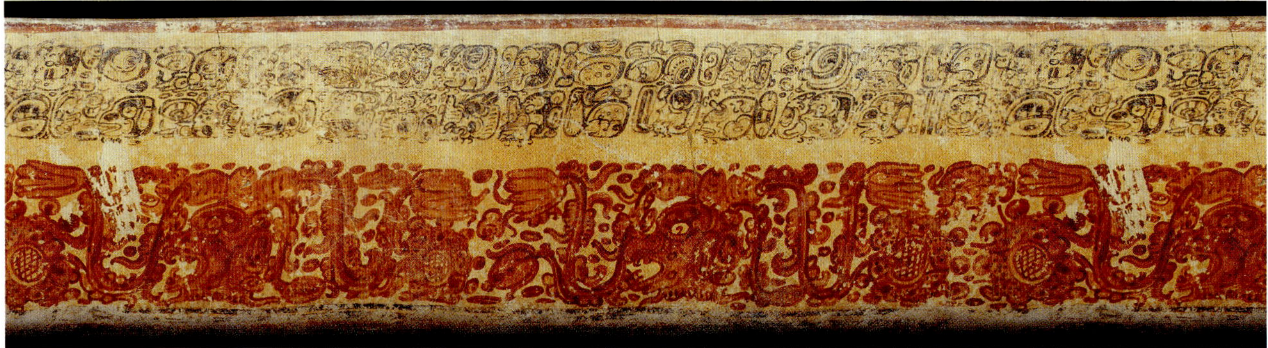

AD 755 to about 780 and a mother from the nearby dynasty of Yaxha, Guatemala. Of the set, two highlight complex scenes from primordial or mythic time, the gathering of gods in darkness and the dance of maize gods linked to distinct dynasties. The gathering may have been copied and thematically reduced or reworked from a square-sided vessel dating to an earlier reign (its roster of figures is larger, although many features remain the same). Possibly, both were copied from a local book, now lost.[36] But the dominant interest of the series is that the same artist crafted images for several youths. The earlier series from Naranjo evinced very different hands.

A third category of owner transports the reader to an unexpected level of complexity. Several texts on ceramics allude to joint possession. Against all precedent, a vessel from the area of Tikal, Guatemala, presents two rim-band texts identifying two separate owners (fig. 42). To judge from style and historical reference, the date must lie in the latter half of the sixth century AD. The top band mentions a probable ruler of Tikal, one Wak Chan K'awiil, to whom the vessel was said to belong. This king reigned from AD 537 to 562, following an anomalous period of Tikal history. The "Lady of Tikal," a queen, held office just before, along with a somewhat older, male regent, perhaps a guardian or consort.[37] (Ruling queens exist in Maya history but rarely so; their presence mostly occurs at dynastic ruptures, when no male heir appears to be viable.) On the pot, the king's high title, *kaloomte'*—an honorific of uncertain meaning—crops up after the *yuk'ib*, "his drinking vessel." A final phrase probably records the name of his mother.

Below the first rim-band text runs a second, clearly painted at the same time. But now the owner is a youth, a *chak ch'ok keleem*. As above, the first glyphs after the statement of possession, "[it is] his drinking vessel," are general titles. Only then does the scribe note a personal name. The elaborate parallel between the upper and lower glyphs and the seeming contradiction of ownership raise one possibility: the glyphs represent alternative ways of describing one person, a ruler of Tikal. The upper passage might note his regnal name and reveal his kinship to a crucial woman. The lower accentuates his youth. Yet the cumbersome repetition and unusual phrasing could be taken literally: two people possessed the vessel. The first, the older and more senior, might have passed it, by open avowal, to a young man. That youth might have been an heir, close kin, or a beloved. Painted at the same time, the two statements hint at that relationship: joint ownership of a durable object presupposes a bond that will last. The statement also implies an event in which that connection was affirmed through toasting and drinking. The second owner would touch the pot with his lips and, perhaps, hand it on to others.

Some owners are not so much two different people, each with their own mouth to drink from the chocolate pot, but rather the second owner is a god, who in Classic Maya thought can be understood to inhabit the same body. For the Classic Maya, this was not, it seems, a stable or sustainable cohabitation. A god descended to reside in a human frame, and he left that body at the conclusion of this rite. "Impersonation," a masked performance with humans taking on godly roles, is too limiting a description for this process. In such states, gods were probably seen as physically present in the world. By sacred possession, they animated the flesh, sinews, and mouth of a living person. Remarkably, they could also, in that transient state, possess drinking vessels.

An explicit example involves a thin vase—labeled *jaay* in Maya writing—from the Puuc region of Yucatan or an adjacent part of the Mexican state of Campeche (see fig. 18). Made in the eighth century AD, its text introduces the owner, identifying him with two general titles, the first of which may serve as an adjective for the second. Labeled in a vertical band, this Maya lord is both an *itz'aat*, a person of wise accomplishment, and also, in a probable reading of the glyphs, a *k'ayoom* or "singer." Or, tying the two together, as readers would likely have done, the performer displayed rare skill as an *itz'aat k'ayoom*, a master singer. In a revealing element, the glyph for "singer" highlights the head of a *xib*, a man, emitting the sign for wind. A small line extrudes from the mouth in a convention for speech or song. The second text on the pot pinpoints the source of his skill: deciphered as *u baahil a'n* (*ahn?*), the signs spell out a common phrase for deity impersonation; the being summoned to earth, coaxed to live in a human body, is the Maya god

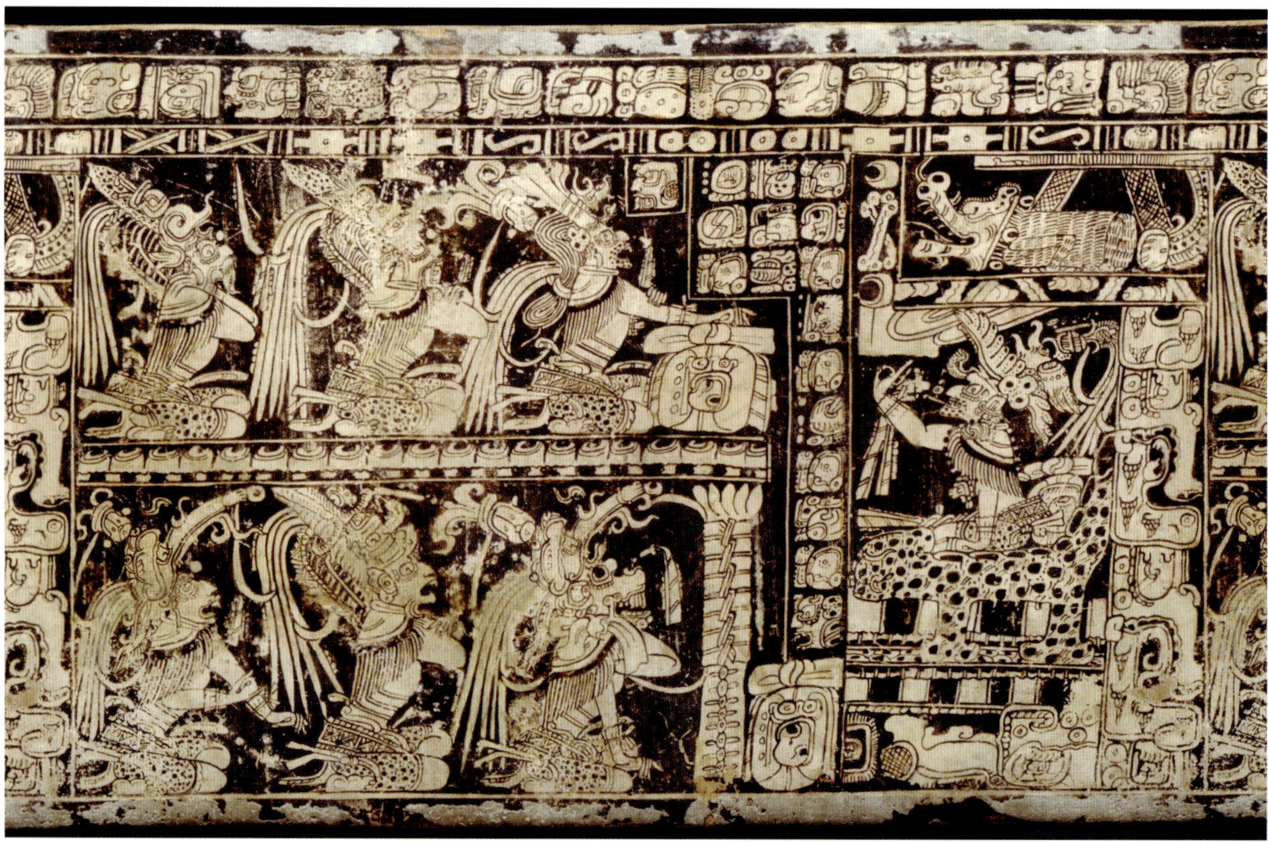

of music (*ik'*, "wind") and good times generally, a being linked to flowers, fragrance, and joyous living.[38] The two identities, one human, the other divine, could not be seen at once. Presented separately in the text, they would only become interpretable by swiveling the pot. In itself, that split presentation resonates with the very nature of impersonation among the Classic Maya. One scene on the vase features the mythic essence of a wise man, a howler-monkey scribe with an open book in full-throttle song or speech. The image on the other side of the pot, an elderly god with nocturnal, jaguar attributes, is less securely relevant to the inscription. As an unprovenanced object, the cup is socially opaque. There is no easy entrée to its circumstances of use. That it was a gift to a valued singer, even a master of such ceremonies is one possibility; impresarios are known for late Postclassic and early colonial-period dances. Another is that the pot was used in a trance or episode of twinned identity. As the glyphs assert, his skill as a singer did not result solely from human effort—a god bestowed or reinforced that ability. A vase with historically recognizable figures from the kingdom of Motul de San José states that a youthful owner, a *ch'ok*, was also impersonating the god of music, and that youth also seems to have held more than the vase. Not just song was involved—the deity is associated with obsidian, a sharp material favored in cutting flesh.

Other pot owners impersonated the Sun God, deities given to ballplay, and a variety of supernaturals active in the primordium. One is mentioned as a "Lord of the Black Hole," a place of early or mythic events; another mingles with a god summoned millennia past, at the beginning of the current era.[39] Several vessels stress the illustrious parentage of the owner. The most unusual of these, distinguished by its square shape, citation of a primordial assembly of gods, and calligrapher's signature, refracts such possession back to youths. The owner, a ruler of the city of Naranjo, was a skilled ballplayer (*itz'aat pitzil*) but also a *keleem*, the label of strong young men. That he commissioned or used the pot as a young man seems probable. Another pot from the city abbreviates the scene (fig. 43). Exhibiting equivalent skill in painting and esoteric knowledge, it wraps a similar image around a cylindrical vessel, the property of a *chak ch'ok keleem.*

There is an added subtlety. With other pots, the vase spotlights a decided paradox about ownership by impersonators. An assumption: to be one with a god was an unstable condition. No living Maya king claimed this fusion on a long-term basis. Rulers were godlike, but not, according to current evidence, gods themselves. Yet the pots recalled these miraculous (if fleeting) fusions in permanent form, and they did so with some planning. Painting and firing a pot would have involved a matter of days, not quick action on a spontaneous whim. Preparation was a mode of anticipation, of getting ready. The pots and their texts might have referred to a specific act of consumption, with a vessel gifted to or employed by humans in states of trance. Impersonation did not just involve dance or masking—a reasonable proposition in view of Maya imagery—but also, to judge from the vases, participation in meals. A shift in mode had taken place, to the time of first or intended use in formal display. Afterward, in a third temporal mode, the vases came to others in commemoration of this wonder working; or they were set aside and stored, as dinnerware or a related kit for later rites of impersonation. All but one example involved drink; that text, belonging to a *chak ch'ok keleem*, is on a plate (*lak*) whose label focused on its shape, not its contents.[40]

Consumption figured equally with a distinct set of small jars or flasks, not for display or public show but for clutching within a single fist (fig. 44). Separate glyphic evidence indicates that most held tobacco snuff, a pounded stimulant mixed with slaked limestone.[41] Swabs could be dipped in or a nostril placed over the opening. Then: a snort, some tingling, even mild vertigo, followed by, according to the ethnographer Kevin Groark, "a feeling of calm." A few are bespoke, incised or painted with the name of their contents and their owner. Later examples, all from the final years of the Classic period—eighth to early ninth century AD—are among those anomalous texts and images that were mass produced. They could not have been intended for specific people but, rather, served consumers of a general sort, unknown to their makers. The contents, tobacco snuff, may have been the real item of value, the snuff jars a means of packaging them. Several appeal visually to the common equation of containers with "houses" or dwellings. They detail doorways and, on their tops, the thatching of Maya roofs.

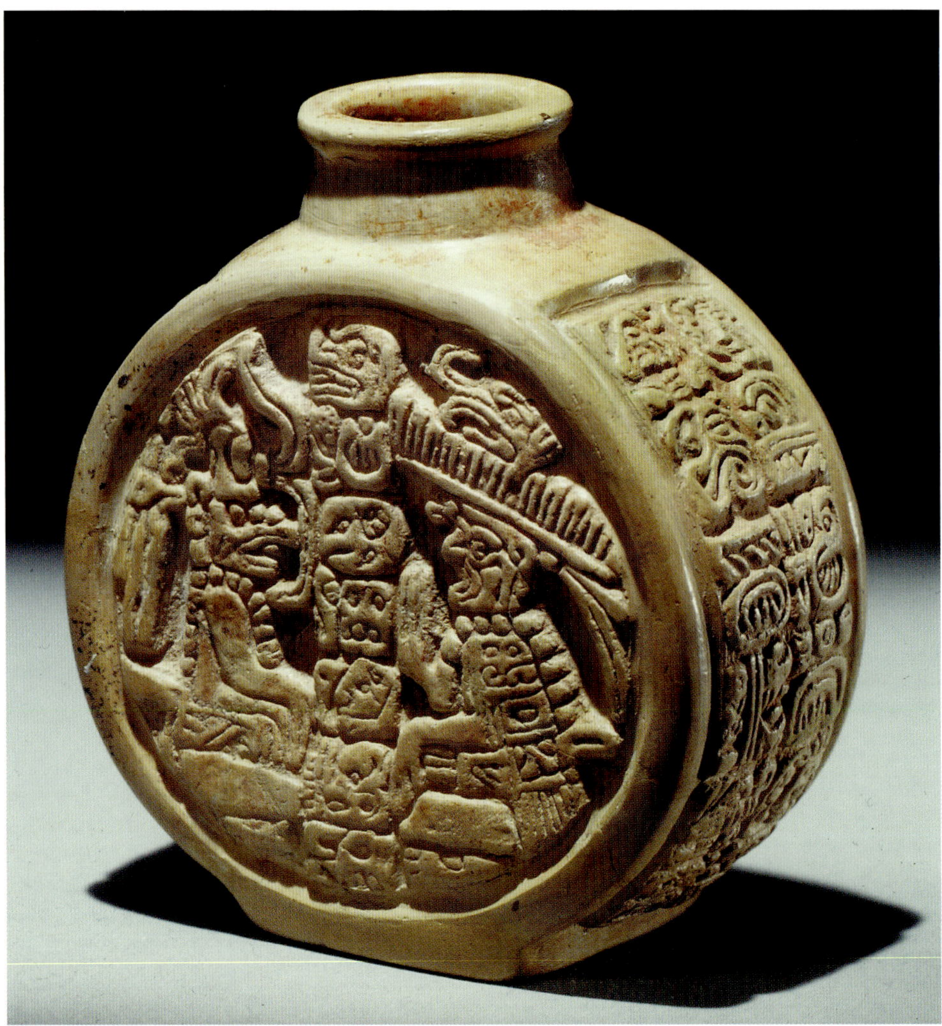

The direct bearing of such jars is that many refer to ownership by "youths" or "great youths" at the close of the Classic period. At that time, dynastic society experienced a process of reduction or transformation, an evident reordering of elite relationships. As such, the jars may represent an expansion of what had been an elite-centered tagging of youthful possessions. The last drinking vessels of *ch'ok, keleem,* or *chak ch'ok* occur in the Puuc region of Yucatan and Campeche, Mexico, again in the late eighth century AD. But ownership by the young seems to have changed. Once concerned with bespoke vessels for chocolate, painted on an individual basis, the sphere of possession extended to tobacco. This was probably a finished product, not concocted for the occasion. The jars may have been packed at the source, easily transportable, or tamped with local powder for single-person use. Some might have been shared, passed from nostril to nostril, but the most likely use was individual, as a small and private pleasure. Unlike a pot, which could be seen, held aloft, and sent around a group, consumption was more intimate. Later use of snuff suggests another feature: that it served as medicine and a protective substance, largely consumed or employed by male or female curers.[42] Introduction to snuff may also have been, as today, a sign of age and self-control; it was not for children, but for those coming into adulthood.

A scattering of other types of objects belonged to young men. There is a possible mace, a doughnut-shaped stone, now in the collection of the Library of Congress. Dating to August 7, AD 489, this was also a piece that, when placed on a stick, could be held aloft. Its function explains the presence of *t'abayi* as a verb. A final series of possessions is tied more transparently to young men. These are backs for mirrors, all relating to youths of the highest status. A slate example in the Library of Congress, from the Snake Kingdom, identifies its owner as a youth using an Emblem title; the most exalted epithet, that of "holy lord," attaches to his father, who is also named on the mirror back. The back probably comes from the late seventh century AD. Endowed with both glyphs and images, a second mirror, also of slate, originates in the city of Xultun and appears to highlight a youthful heir to the throne (see fig. 27). He is the "elder brother" (*saku[n] winik*). A youth (*ch'ok*), he nonetheless embodies an almost adult level of confidence in the scene. Gesturing authoritatively to a subordinate, the young man sits ramrod stiff on a mat, with his back to a bundle support. A third mirror, dating at least a century later, is alone in having certain provenience; the other two are looted objects, having circulated on the international art market (fig. 45). Found in Burial 49 at Topoxte, Guatemala, with a "youth [20–35 years of age] possibly of masculine sex," the excavated mirror was placed with a treasury of burial goods, mosaic shell, and an engraved bone, which belonged to another individual. The owner was a *chak ch'ok*, not simply a *ch'ok*. Such finds merit cautious appraisal. The estimated age of the deceased accords with the title, and the mirror, a carefully carved piece, was unlikely to be tossed when its owner reached 20. Yet, lacking textual consistency with the inscribed bone, we cannot be certain if the human remains correspond to the first owner of the mirror.[43]

In Classic imagery, mirrors were employed in dressing to provide assurance that all items of clothing fit correctly. The vessel owned by a young woman, discussed before, illustrates the practice. Dress that was layered, composed of many materials, and separately lashed could be impressive in its complexity. This was coordinated effort; clothing a Maya dancer involved many hands and eyes to ensure that all was fastened and tightly cinched. Most such scenes show preparation for dance about to happen—a vigorous performance, with rattling and shaking, and things always ready to come undone. Youths are not the only ones to concern themselves with their appearance. Rulers have mirrors on or near their thrones for an occasional glance. Well attested in ancient Mexico, the prophetic or augural use of mirrors is another possibility, though among the Classic Maya most such scenes concern not visions or scrying the future but hierarchical interaction. That men hold up mirrors for the ruler suggests that they were

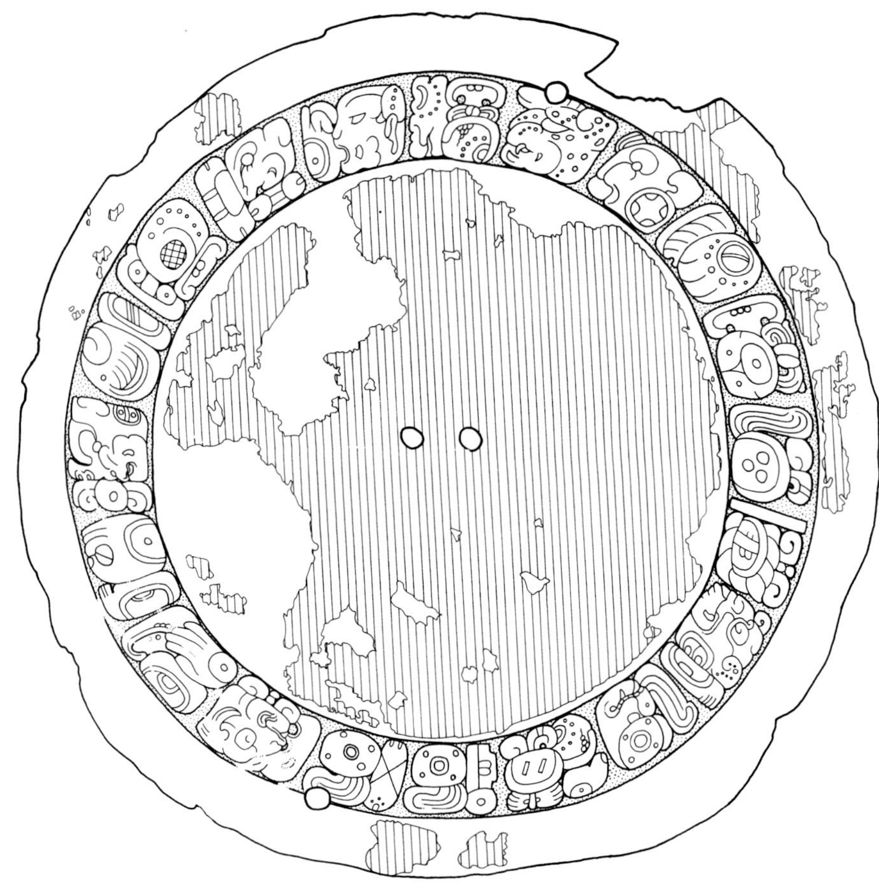

not just for callow self-regard but that mirrors may have been employed in new service
at court, a kind of page duty in kingly attendance. The verb on the Topoxte mirror, *t'abayi,*
"to rise" fits well. A youth might lift a mirror for an approving glance by the ruler. At
the least, the appearance of the *chak ch'ok* title, "great youth," an intensifier of youth, as
it did with the pots, provides a potential marker. It set apart those males at the cusp of
full adulthood. More than *ch'ok,* they may have formed a distinct class. Nor did that status hinge on birth alone: one owner of a pot was both a *ch'ok* and a "holy lord," the son of
a king.[44] Had *chak ch'ok* equated to high birth, he would have qualified on that basis, yet he
fails to use the title. The supposition here is that as a designation *chak ch'ok* segregated a
distinct set of young men. Graded by age, they were no longer mere *ch'ok,* having grown to
the status of "great youths."

TO AND FROM

The pots and other objects marked as possessions of youths existed within an expanding
frame of time and action. At first, they operated as things worth owning. They were valued enough that someone asserted possession through glyphic tags. A century later, the

scribes added further information. Possibly it was implicit before, but there seemed little need to include such detail. Now we read of vessel contents, the kind of chocolate, *atole,* or, more rarely, a combination of the two. Refined drinks became important to identify by recipe. No such information was needed for hard food. The surface began to count, its handling with paint, its chiseling or creation in a mold, its flatness or three-dimensionality. But, above all, the texts referred to acts of lifting, offering, perhaps toasting, sometimes on a specific date. Further signs under discussion seemed to position these acts in past or mythic time.

God impersonation, that hazardous, unsustainable fusion of humans with deities, underscored the fleeting nature of the events recorded on pots. It also established a sub-category of possession in two senses: ownership of a ceramic and the spiritual custody of a human body by a far stronger force. One set of hands held a pot, but two beings presumably "drank" from it. Gods may not just have come to earth to dance and speak, but also to feast. The texts were also painted or carved in advance of an act that would later become, as a record, commemorative and backward-looking. The new stress on offering or dedication (or just "bottoms up!") expressed an action known before but tacitly so. Perhaps it corresponded to a new form of activity. As much as a pot helped form and share in a person's identity, that relation both persisted and evolved with the movement of bowls, pots, plates, mirrors, and mace-heads. The ceramics from Naranjo and the area of Motul de San José show they were not always buried with the initial owner. Understanding the circulation of pots, especially of youths, suggests a range of possibilities. The owners of the pots were not the makers—the appearance of scribal signatures, documented in at least seventeen texts, and the *cheheen* statements substantiate this—but they could have commissioned them from skilled artisans.

The other option is that they came to youths as gifts. This is implicit in a unique flat-bottomed dish excavated from a Late Classic tomb at Holmul, Guatemala, and now in the Peabody Museum at Harvard (fig. 46). Tagged as a plate, *lak,* it was also said to contain chocolate drink, perhaps for ladling out to guests. Water birds preen on the interior, frisking in the liquid. (Similar fancies are seen on ceramics from classical Greece, for example calling to mind Homer's "wine-dark sea" by showing a line of ships under the inner rim of a Greek krater.) The plate must have come from Naranjo, a city in long-standing contact with Holmul. Its owner was a prince, a *chak ch'ok keleem,* but the text also mentions his father, a ruler of Naranjo from AD 755 to about 780. The mother appears nowhere. Was she someone other than the official consort, a woman of highest rank, known to come from a foreign dynasty? Or does the subtle omission stress the main donor, a father who was also a king? The flattery and exhortation are clear at least. By looking into the bowl, the owner would see, shimmering below, a Maize God in splendid dance. He would also view, superimposed, his own face—a playful conceit also used by Greek potters and painters.[45] That the Maize God was linked by a small text to the city of Tikal hints at the ultimate overlord of this young prince.

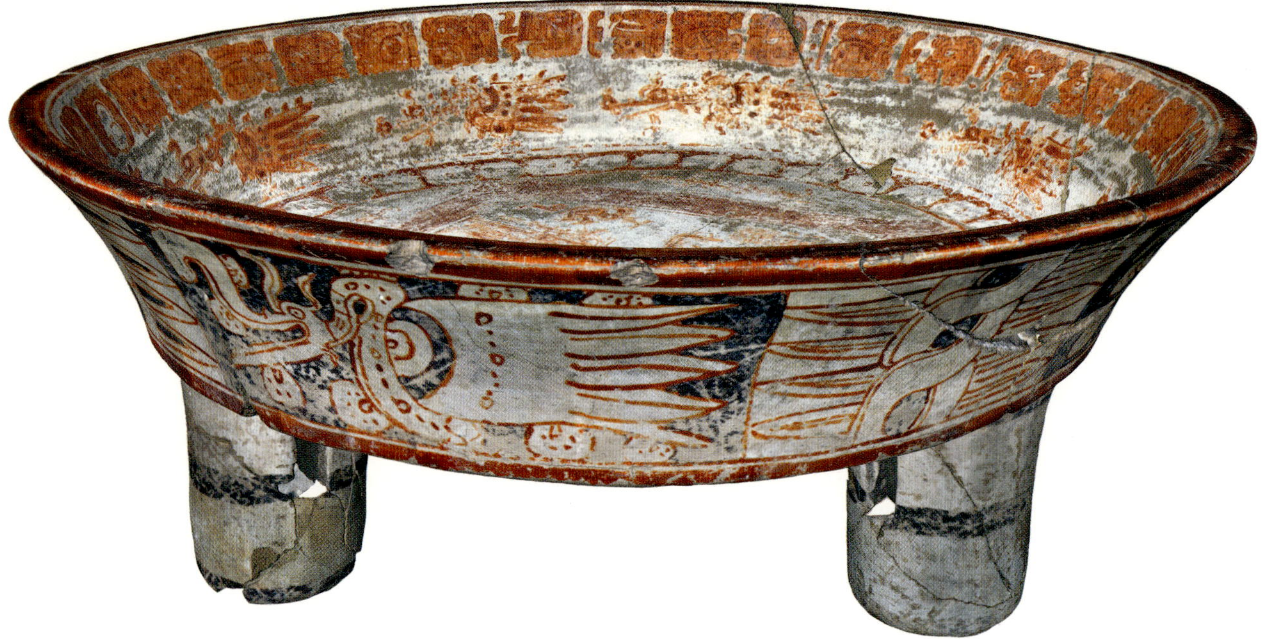

"Gift" is laden with meaning in later Mayan languages. Colonial Tzotzil, spoken in the highlands of Chiapas, Mexico, endows it with royal shadings, as the bounty coming from rulers. Yet there is also the connotation of "offering," *k'eelil,* a "gift" freely given up, also a "sacrifice." Reciprocity tinges some terms, such as linking "gift" with the idea of "double" back (*pakol*), one good thing deserving another by way of moral obligation. (Christian nuances of gratitude or early modern notions of liberality doubtless influenced the friars who compiled these sources.) The same word applies to tribute, *pak patan,* emphasizing the network of social obligations and press of noblesse oblige. Many Mayan languages, either attested or in reconstructed form, yield *matan.* This term targets the recipient and that which is received. There is also, in Ch'orti' Maya, a reference to "give away," *puhk,* as a term of hospitality. Giving that object back "returns" it (*suht*) to its original place. The same root applies to a "reply," equating a material thing—or, in local language, a returned woman—to short-lived words. The strong sense is of material "discourse." Rather than (or in addition to) metaphor, the expression signals that objects might circulate like oratory.[46]

Glyphic texts record gifts with a variety of terms. Again, the emphasis is bifurcated, split between that which was received or given away, what flowed in or streamed out. With few exceptions, however, the language is ethereal and godly in tenor. "To give," *ak',* often describes offerings to deities, as at Palenque in Mexico, or on a panel from La Corona in Guatemala, where pulque may have been served up to a god. At Palenque, during a tumultuous period of lost kingship, such gifts become impossible; with dynastic revival, back they come, in service to local deities. David Stuart even wonders whether the act of sacred dance, *ak'ta,* derives from this basic word for offering and presentation. Commenting on a passage at La Corona, he also draws attention to a green-feathered flute (*k'uk' amaay*). This may have been bestowed by a deity, Yopaat, an aspect of the Rain God. Such practice recalls the offering today of drinks to the guardian lords (*yuneiló?ob'*) of fields in Yucatan. *Atole* (*saka?*) in gourds was thrown to the four quarters, and vital moments of "measuring, burning, planting," required that one "stand(s) up drink." Giving liquid to the lords will "bring in water" for the farmer craving rain.[47]

Stuart had already shown that an expression, *mayij,* found in select inscriptions, descended to the Ch'olti' word *maii,* "give," "offering," or "disinterested gift." Care and personal cost went into this offering. *Mayij,* in the Classic-era spelling, describes the slicing or jabbing with a stingray spine. For men, the suffering body part was the penis, for women, the tongue. Bloody effusions rained on paper for eventual burning in censers. The smoke would then transmute into smells delectable to gods. The nature of smoke—seemingly solid but ever shifting, hard to pin down—accorded with the nature of deities themselves. Evidently, the tools for this bloodletting were stored in small boxes. One survives in recognizable, tagged form in the Kislak Collection at the Library of Congress. Of just the right dimensions to hold spines, it proclaims in a glyphic text that it was the "dwelling place" of a "gift."[48] A Maya metonym may have operated here in that the instrument of bloodletting and its outcome merged into one. Our next chapter reports in more detail on how youths were involved.

Another probable term for "gift," spelled *sij* or, in later texts, *sih,* appears in paternal statements. Maya relationships are often spelled out indirectly. One person is described in terms of another, much like the English-language "Stephen, the son of Craig." The focus is on "Stephen," but "Craig," the father, expands the reader's knowledge of how to place "Stephen" within a line of descent. In Maya glyphs, the relationships shift by parent. Someone is the *huun tahn,* "guarded thing"—"first of the chest" or even "first-born"—of a woman, a baby nursed, kept close to the mother's body.[49] In paired manner, the offspring is said to be the *sij,* "gift," and *ch'ahb,* "fast," of the father. "Fasting," another concept to be explored in the next chapter, insisted on the hard work of bloodletting. Perhaps there was a conceptual symmetry. The mother's body released an effusion of blood during childbirth; so did the father's by this act of self-injury. There is an added ambiguity. Was the "gift" of life accorded by the father? Or was the child, always a son in this expression, the "gift" *to* the father as a result of paternal ritual? The syntax fails to clarify the uncertainty, which may have been deliberate. A father gives but also receives.

Here is the puzzle. Not one Maya pot owned by a youth records a glyph for "gift." They are never said to come from someone else or to be intended for regifting. Quite the opposite: the texts register indelible statements of ownership. Moreover, the attested lexicon for offerings concerned gods and their appetites, with unclear evidence of what was expected from them in return. In this there is, in Classic sources, a thorough severance between social reality and rhetoric. No kingdom could survive by ignoring the need to reciprocate and redistribute; colonial authorities refer in plenty to such practices. Yet in texts and images of the Classic period, goods, tribute, offerings, sacrificial victims all surge upward or to close allies.[50] For humans, these goods are centralized, accumulating in heaps of chocolate beans, jewels, cotton mantles, and *Spondylus* shell. The ruler never deigns to take them physically; there is no hand brushed by accident against an underling's. The goods sit at the feet of his throne. A separate track offers ephemera—blood that will coagulate and harden, burning paper, pulque that will spoil—to the gods. Beings at higher states of existence receive; they do not have to return the favor, at least not in ways that are laid out in glyphic texts.

Sociologists Marcel Mauss and Henri Hubert understood that sacred offerings were done with a nod and a wink. For them, relations with gods were mediated by sacrifice but conceived as dialogue. Ritual might or might not ensure that something wondrous would happen, although this hope or petition was not always specified with clarity. What did occur was an invitation to "talk." A supplicant tapped gods on the shoulder, awakened them, made them alert to human entreaty. Useful outcomes might emerge. Mauss pushed further, arguing that the structure of traditional communities relied on a related concept, *do ut des,* a Latin expression meaning "I give so that you may give." For humans, the truly unrequited gift was liable to fester. It might undo, in Mauss's view, the social contract that bound people together. Perhaps this is why Jacques Derrida, a philosopher enamored of contradiction, called gifts "the impossible." They were an altruistic gesture mired in selfishness. Without gifts in return, resentment would pile up, and bonds of trust and esteem crumble away.[51]

The historian Natalie Davis observed that gifts vexed in other ways. Writing of early modern Europe, she stressed their essential, storm-tossed nature. The conventional view is that the transmission of gifts leads to harmony, smooth relations, and amity. The more probable effect is quite different, involving "obligation anxiety," dispute, and jealousy. In his *Essais,* written in the late sixteenth century, Michel de Montaigne groaned at the dissimulations and personal compromise that gifts induce: "I find nothing so costly as that which is given to me, for then my will is mortgaged by a title of gratitude."[52] Presents sent to kings were the most troublesome. Givers and recipients seldom felt complete satisfaction. This was especially pronounced when, in Davis's words, "monarchs were claiming more sovereign authority and subjects more rights of control." Less emphasized by Davis was the sheer emotional charge of gift exchange. As tokens of affection or esteem, they distilled how people felt or wanted to feel about each other. Cold appraisal of the gift, its relative value, the stratagems behind it, did not rule out strong sentiment. And once aroused, such emotions mixed in a volatile brew. Gratitude could swerve into dissatisfaction, friendship into enmity—or back again. Human contradictions being such, these emotions could even co-exist.

Gifting as dialogue may need stronger emphasis than is accorded by Davis. In Europe, spoken or written messages—a billet-doux, a plea for a gold ring in seventeenth-century

Holland, a groveling note to a prince—usually accompanied gifts and spelled out their meaning. Indeed, the "anonymous gift" may be the oddest innovation of modern times, meriting
its own study. One view would italicize the gifting process as the "management of meaning."
Mauss understood that gifts had a public dimension as well, as in the potlatch of the indigenous North American Northwest Coast peoples. This was the social frame of the gift: the fact
that gifts did not circulate in single line from one person to another, followed by pressure to
reciprocate, but rather they involved an audience and a process enacted over the long term.
There could be multiple participants, things large and small, brought together, perhaps of
varied meaning. People discussed what they were doing, in commentary worth noting. Then
there was collective judgment. Moving around by periodic cycles, gifts could be evaluated by
witnesses. Honor and all it implied, the timocratic orientations discussed in the last chapter,
were at stake in these "courtesies." The potlatch of the Northwest comes to mind in particular, for its main concern was often the transmission of titles and confirmation of status at
times of generational shift.[53] For this reason, the anthropologist Arjun Appadurai called them
"tournaments of value," and some are.[54] But the breathless competition, the sense of risk or
recklessness, and the tight coordination did not apply to all such incidents of small-scale
exchange. The substance of what passed around, the tales of who owned it, must surely have
been relevant, not just their status as objects in abstract episodes of gifting.

That gifts are a human universal is a fact. That their exchange was rule-governed
or guided by underlying principles seems uncontroversial. Here, Mauss thought big. The
existence of gifts was, for him, basic to all social feeling. He spoke of them with the same
nostalgia reserved for most of his anthropological observations. Personal exchange would
strengthen society, he believed, more than capitalism ever could. Mauss was not alone in
this disposition or in pining for anything other than the twentieth century and its errors
or missteps. Another early sociologist, Georg Simmel, likewise defined gifts as the "moral
memory of mankind." Yet, as a person of his time, Mauss did not comprehend the degree
to which many gift cycles arose from colonial encounters. Mauss almost never left his
figurative armchair. The gifting he studied, whose features he traced, was not the default
setting of archaic practice. Each pattern of gifts had a history, a cast of contestants, a
rhythm and range of expected or unforeseen consequences. The deferred yet undeclared
nature of gifts—there is usually no small wait for a reward, if it comes at all—loomed less
large to Mauss than for later sociologists such as Pierre Bourdieu. Attentive to oppression, Bourdieu was also more persistent than Mauss in seeing gifts as weapons of dominance and the role of honor and its disparagement in gifts.[55]

The centrality of gifts to humans has prompted other thoughts, elaborations,
and dismissals. There is no end to comment about the matter, nor will there be. One
tempting mine of information is always personal experience. Thus, for Mark Osteen, the
editor of one book on the subject, gifts must be spontaneous, disinterested, superfluous
or unnecessary to present or immediate needs, pleasing, and, above all, risky—of course,
for the unlucky, nothing may come in return.[56] Comparisons around the world indicate,

however, that these features sometimes occur but not always. Gifting is a process rather than a package of traits. One critic, the ethnographer Nicholas Thomas, doubted that Mauss understood a potential problem, that his concept of the gift was, to some extent, everything a commodity was not. The category stood less on its own than in opposition to the idea of trading by impersonal means. Mauss focused on those who were involved within a transaction, but a more stinging question might be, who was excluded and why? Further, his focus was principally on objects, less on the land, titles, labor, and other intangibles that predominate in much evidence from the Middle Ages and elsewhere.

Thinking about the Pacific, Māori capes in New Zealand and Hawaiian tapa cloth, Annette Weiner faulted Mauss and others for their inattention to the women who made and wore such garments and to the existence of gifts that were never really transmitted. Memorably, Weiner pointed to a paradox of "keeping-while-giving," an ebb and flow of objects "imbued with the intrinsic and ineffable identities of their owners which are not easy to give away." In these things, through them, decay and loss of identity transformed into a history of connected ownership. Over time, objects given to others renewed and underwrote an identity attached to others, and not just to anyone but to those thought appropriate. The object formed part of their personality; it became layered with past ownership. Buried with the dead, as with certain *taonga*, a treasured or contested thing among the Māori, it cut off that long narrative of owners and stories about them. The object had become too drenched in chiefly power, too tempting for others to manipulate, too incompatible with sustained use by humans. In fairness to Mauss, he knew of such practices: "because the thing itself possesses a soul, is of the soul. Hence it follows that to make a gift of something to someone is to make a present of some part of oneself."[57] Weiner was also insistent on the added complexities of exchange, ongoing but not constant; exchange was, as the historian Edward Thompson would also emphasize, conditioned by social contact more generally.[58]

Studies of gifts in antiquity often lead toward early Greece.[59] More evident in classical texts than among the Classic Maya, the conventions of gift giving still involved upperclass behavior and pots in particular. Many involved men, young men, in ways to be discussed in the next chapter. The setting was, as with Maya drinking vases, convivial. But the comparison remains imperfect. The blatantly erotic (and homoerotic) enters into Greek practices of the symposium or drinking party, along with affectionate praise and flattery and a rhetorical posture of equality and friendship. Boys with pleasing, muscled shoulders and meaty thighs offer wine, and their eyes meet those of older lovers. Perhaps, as suggested by classicist Kathryn Topper, such scenes reveled in the practices of earlier, "primitive" times, reflecting precedent for feasts, not their current reality. The Classic Maya may have envisioned an equality of status, but that was vested within profound attention to hierarchy. This emphasis seems violated only by limited registers, such as a procession of returning warriors, perhaps in a dance of conquest; even then, the scenes prefigure a sequence in which the warriors arrive home, to kneel before an enthroned ruler.

In Greece, and one suspects among the Classic Maya, such gifts were themselves a form of material dialogue. Giving a vase bolstered an assurance of friendship. The marking was overt: a mixing bowl made by Exekias was inscribed "Epainetos gave me to Kharopos." In similar manner, a gloss on a line in Pindar, "to toast," *propinein,* explains it as "to make a gift of the cup along with the mixture of wine." To maintain the fiction of equals and friends, who stood outside monetary transactions, courtesans became known as *hetaerae,* "companions," thus wiping away, in the classicist Richard Neer's words, "the often violent reality of Athenian sexual hierarchies."[60] (We will meet the *hetaerae* again in our final chapter.) The identity of the gift mattered as tokens of homoerotic courting, usually involving the display or offering of hares or other animals. Not all feasts were generic, of course. Michael Dietler, studying Celtic society, refers to some gatherings that were meant to accent inequalities.[61] That food and drink were controlled in such gatherings bears repeating. Someone managed the diners and drinkers, their menu, and in ways that underscored their vulnerability. The ultimate trust was that the food would be both edible and nontoxic.

Strands of this literature accord with the young men's pots among the Classic Maya. The objects seem exempted from purchase by their dynastic nature and by their curious degree of inalienability.[62] Along with drink, an implied conviviality and highlighted identity come to the fore. Mayanist discussion of the inalienable crystallizes mostly around ethnography, where an object attains that status if it appears necessary to complete a perceived whole. This applies to body parts and blood, but even to a sense of social relations between things. Writing of Q'ekchi' Maya, the linguist Paul Kockelman offers the most detailed exposition of inalienable words. All imply the necessity of possession, occurring with high frequency in the language: "mother," "head," or names, items of clothing, a spirit or shadow. Grammatical particles of such concepts in inalienability exist in glyphs of the Classic period, as in suffixes like *is* or *aj;* these see use when relevant words float without possessive pronouns and no clear (but needed) owner. No particle certifies this notion for pots, but texts of ownership imply that objects were "kept" while also being "given away."[63] In a sense, these were contact objects, known to have been grasped physically and cared for by another. With the objects reviewed in this chapter, youthful possessions were clearly designed for special acts of consumption, a lifting up in presentation, an act of joint drinking while possessed by deities, or, separately, as at Tikal, in intimate sharing between father and son; they traveled to other places, if by shadowy, unreconstructible routes, and in certain cases they shifted to hands of lower status. Flow could not always have gone up and up, for eventual consecration to gods. From explicit tags we know that skilled but lower-ranking artists made at least two of the objects. Two lords received pots created by many different hands; in contrast, several recipients owned vessels made by the same painter. Pots may have been shaped by females, though as noted before the painted surface that completed the ceramic came, by all surviving evidence, from the brushwork of men. But women were there: the lone image of chocolate

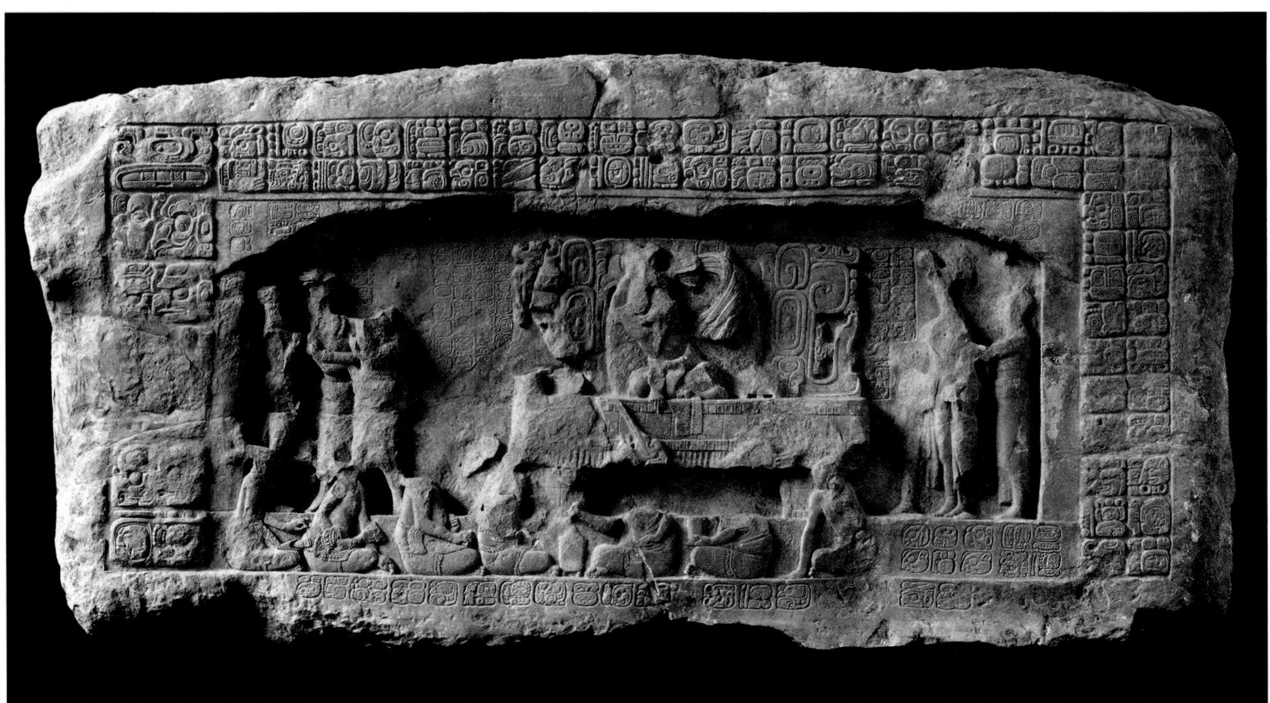

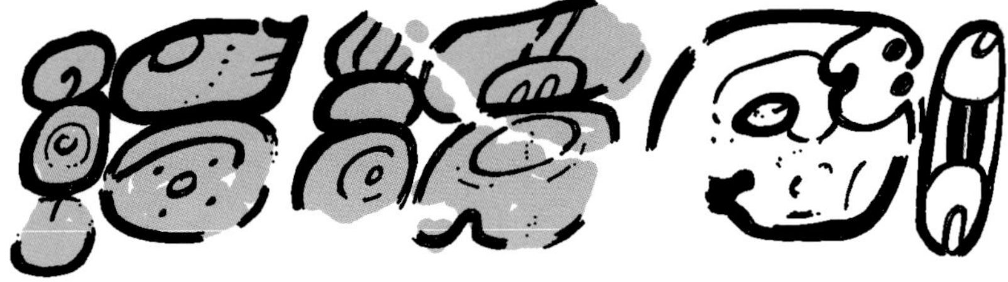

preparation involves two comely females, from a mythic scene; tamales were, in several other tableaux, patted and flavored by women.

To review: a decorous activity at court, refined dining by young men—no sloshing or brazen slurps, no drunken ribaldry—was marked by vases, bowls, plates. Some appear to have been part of larger commissions, conceived as sets. Ceramics were not merely ad hoc productions, created in response to random requests. Several seem to have been made at the same time, as vases for people in close relations. More generally, youths were now, at last, invited to the table. Their attendance may not have been taken for granted. An especially detailed scene of drinking, on Panel 3 from Piedras Negras, shows young men in the palace standing, not partaking (fig. 47). Imbibing chocolate, labeled as *uk'ni,* "he drinks," is done by the king, at least so the text tells us. His honored guests below, all members of the high nobility, alone have access to a vase. As for young men, the *ch'ok,* even the young heir and that scion of a foreign dynasty … they stand. On pots more broadly, the variety of titles employed by the young men hints at a comparable variety of objects. Did some come into youthful hands at an earlier age, for mere *ch'ok*, while others, for the *chak ch'ok*, celebrated a new threshold to fully adult status? The practice of using marked vessels for youths correlates notably with tumult and insecurity. The largest set relates to a ruler likely guided by regents, in a period when large-scale politics caused most courts to tremble. The tension, finally, is more analytical than not. The objects of the *ch'ok* did not employ the expressions for "gift" used in other texts. The lone certainties are who owned them, either in specific or loose reference, and their continued use. It did not come to an end with that first, tasty drink by the noble or royal youth.

A closing text rounds out this chapter and leads to the next, where wilder behavior becomes evident, and transitions were marked by more than the gift and reception of a delicate vase. The telltale evidence: an eroded and shattered cylindrical vessel in the Juan Antonio Valdés Museum in Uaxactun, Guatemala, also tagged for youthful possession (fig. 48).[64] The glyphs have a cadenced coloration of two red-painted glyphs followed by one left uncolored. This scheme recalls the rim-band texts of luminous vessels, as in a bowl from the area of Tikal, now in the Museo Popol Vuh in Guatemala City. The pot at Uaxactun must date from AD 682 to 734, as shown by related historical information. The vessel in Uaxactun has a sequence that identifies the owner as a *ch'ok*, its painter (one Sak Mo'), but with a key passage, an expression, *ti yax ch'ahb*, "for the first fast/penance(?)." The import of that phrase, looming large in the next chapter, is clear: the vessel at Uaxactun was intended specifically for an age-grade ritual, the first (presumably) of many sacrificial offerings from a noble youth. Did it offer a restorative draft of costly liquid after an act of penance? Was it a gift to others who might witness his ascent to adult duty? Of these matters we cannot be sure. But the likelihood is now strong that most such vessels materialized shifts of status. A gift-marked passage carried males from boyhood and adolescence to the obligations of elite men.

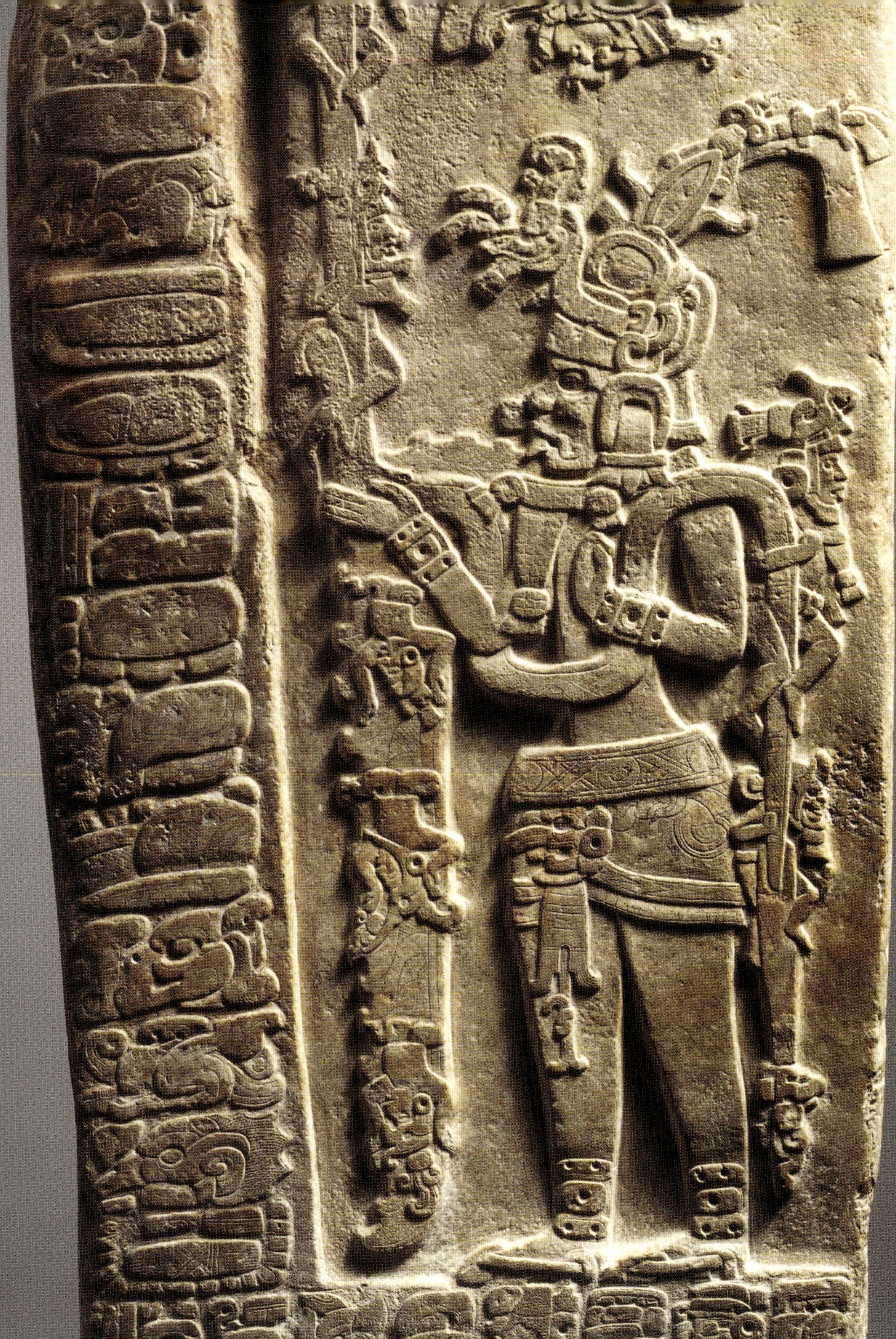

4 The Taming Places

Initiation celebrates life's passage and lays out spans within it. The goal is ritual demarcation, to make life less a flow of experience than an orderly sequence of stages. Birth leads to maturity, old age to death and beyond. Near the beginning are young men among the Maya, along with the texts and images that mark their passage. The underlying premise of initiation is that radical shifts correspond to all transitions between stages, followed by relatively static phases of existence. Physically, of course, life is more complicated than that. Changes occur rapidly or suddenly, on a daily basis, or they stretch over longer spans. What count, though, are the perceptions and formal recognition of such shifts.

Early anthropologists, principally Arnold van Gennep, publishing in 1909, focused on the drama of transformation. For van Gennep, "rites of passage," as he called them, began with a process of setting apart. A passage was unlatched, a door opened that led to a marginal or liminal state. In dynamic play, identities came unstuck, to be inverted, played with, rearranged, and augmented. Then, if all went well, reintegration took place, a figurative folding back into society.[1] A redefined person came into existence, and another stage of life and identity ensued. Yet this was not just a personal journey. External forces guided it. Both authority and tradition determined the timing, meaning, and participants of rites—in fact, the managers and overseers mentioned in earlier chapters. Formal and sacred, the process could be as miraculous as it was mysterious, an extraordinary transformation of ordinary lives. For van Gennep, all humans went through a staged reshaping of identity, if not always with the same emphasis or pronounced attention to ritual. More to the point, rites of passage not only celebrated changes but also, according to some beliefs, caused them to happen. Humans took charge of shifts that often actually lay beyond their control. Even gods appear to have had births, infancy, and decrepit old age.[2]

Anthropology is the most sprawling of academic disciplines. It compares just about anything humans do, think, and practice, with the premise that there is some interpretable order to it all. Not surprisingly, it has much to say about initiation. There are striking commonalities in such rites, regardless of area. Some transitions involve pain, leaving permanent scars and altered teeth, or, at the least, a scourged and hurting body. Along the way, in many places—mostly, at this writing, in times long past—people separate by gender, boys away from girls, men away from women. There is intense interest in how people differ and what they should become, and procedures are put into place to ensure a desired outcome. In a liminal state, when young men or women are set apart, ready for something new, obstacles need navigating by body and mind. Skills must be mastered, knowledge absorbed, novel strengths cultivated. This most difficult part of the journey is disordered. In a sense, to follow van Gennep's logic, humans occupy a sequence of "rooms" with doorways in between, the relevant word being *limin,* Latin for "threshold." Transfigured inside and out, the person only re-enters society, slipping through these portals of being, when a transformation has taken place. Marking this new status and making it visible are acts of purification, consumption, clothing, and learning. The person is, in a sense, reborn. This is why van Gennep's three-part sequence also applies to death, burial, and the afterlife. By common belief, for many people, other stages await us long after the last breath.

Some critics fault van Gennep's proposals. Max Gluckman thought the three parts merely described a pattern in which rituals begin, have a middle section, and then end. Perhaps van Gennep had found truths so widespread as to be unremarkable, even banal. Looking for nuance, others do not so much dismiss or question his scheme as see more subtle variety to the world. Cultural detail and history make all the difference. In some cases, the three-part process could be subdivided further, into a large number of such progressions, thresholds within thresholds, or they might reveal an unequal emphasis on a particular part of the sequence. Anthropologists such as Jean La Fontaine insist on fundamental contrasts that depend on the person going through the portals. There might be mere life cycle rituals, an individual passage observed in detail but of one person only, or there could be true initiations, an immersion of similar males or females, grouped by age, into a world of secret knowledge and joint action.[3] Depending on local need and time, a mix of these rituals, some emphasizing individuals, others an age grade, tends to be the norm.

For Victor Turner, a scholar of broad influence, read by social scientists and literary critics alike, van Gennep prompted a wholesale reinterpretation of ritual. Turner went far indeed along this path, expanding van Gennep's three-part sequence into a process that, from pilgrimage to revolution, was thought to galvanize and renew societies everywhere. Liminality became the explanation for most change and much human creativity. It was a "timeless condition, an eternal now." Sacred things or "sacra" operated as mnemonics, "storage bins" of knowledge about "cosmologies, values, and cultural axioms."[4] By means of such drama—Turner understood human behavior in terms of lively performance—tensions relaxed and contradictions came to resolution. People moved ahead, a crisis had been dealt with and shoved safely and comfortably behind.

Turner's ideas were daring for the time. Perhaps more than a little they reflected his own journey through life. During World War II he set himself apart as a conscientious objector and for a time lived among gypsies—hardly a privileged position in English society at mid-century. Then there were the 1960s, when he read and reworked van Gennep during a time of social and cultural upheaval. In some pages of his books, rock concerts and the "summer of love" exemplify a state of positive euphoria, the murder and mayhem of Altamont not quite registering in his mind.[5] Almost inevitably, his hunger for topicality led to a measure of irrelevance. Turner's work is no longer so widely mentioned, other than in introductory classes or histories of ritual studies. But the real problem is less a matter of what might be modish than of intellectual substance. To a critical reader, Turner's writing starts to resemble a set of doctrines. There is, to some eyes, a preachy transcendence of local detail, an explanation of the world not as it is but as it should be. Yet his accounts do accord with many rites of passage. Turner noted social leveling (if controlled by figures of authority), a perception of suspended time (if affected by acute attention to age of life), and ecstasies or strong feelings that encouraged a sense of community (if tempered by the certainty that harmony cannot last). In Turner's vision, to find personal wholeness required risk, and to pursue it, a beguiling danger.

Much research on initiation and life-cycle rites pertains to boys and young men. This is understandable. The transition from infertile to fertile states and small to large duties leads to thoughts about what it might mean. Sex and gender are also inescapable, for both men and women. After all, as formal acts, rites of passage establish, accentuate, and explain the differences between people. Anthropologists take notice as a result. Working in Madagascar, Maurice Bloch studied initiation on two levels: as practiced by villagers and as appropriated by royalty. He concentrated on the circumcision of young boys, most still infants. Cutting made them "clean" or "sweet and beautiful," with the goal of allowing them to achieve, at some point, a high level of sexual potency. But the rite also involved youths. For the circumcision rituals, they were asked to collect and, in brazen maneuvers, to steal plants conceived as "sprouts," a metaphor for the children at the heart of the ritual. (The Malagasy knew nothing of the Maya, of course, but the comparison results from similar reasoning about the budding, tender nature of the young.) Along the way, the youths crossed boundaries to collect and transport purifying water. Embodying group strength, they were likened to "wild, strong cattle," ripe for taming. Bilateral descent was crucial. Such youths had to have two living parents and thus exemplify a "continuing chain of moral life and blessing."

Cunning royalty in Madagascar took such ritual, performed for all, and tinged it with self-serving ends. In 1844, at a time of political expansion, youths were sent for sacred water but "in reality [constituted] a military platoon, who crossed the territory of several subject peoples, called upon to do homage on its passage." Seldom haphazard, royal claims found precedent in the logic of everyday life. Bloch, a committed Marxist, saw ritual as a lateral, indirect reason for royal control, lending it an air of timeless necessity or inevitability. For him, elites wish always to be seen as indispensable. A few detractors, such as Corrine Kratz, who studied women's initiation among the Okiek of Kenya and Tanzania, doubted Bloch's supposition that such rites played out by a rigid playbook. But Kratz added an observation he would endorse, that youths find friendship in their cohort by "visiting, hunting, raiding, and looking for girls."[6] Ultimately, though, adults are in control. The rites slide youths under the authority of elders, which, with luck, they will eventually become. Not just action but talk, song, and dance enliven these transitions.

In the details, comparison between the Classic Maya and cultures from Africa or beyond tends to collapse. Looking at the matter broadly disregards the local circumstances that maintain these rituals. It fails to show how they adjust to do the work at hand. Yet, for all that, certain themes are nearly universal. These include: painful transitions, in multiple stages, either group-focused or linked to individuals; a preoccupation with the definition of gender; the enabling of future procreation; a subordination—amidst riot and wildness—to adults; and, as Bloch suggests, elite or royal recasting or purloining of common practices. The Maya evidence fits these themes. It also testifies to patterns of its own, or best understood in the broader setting of Mesoamerica.

PENANCE AND PERSONAL ORDEAL

A focal glyph helps to refine discussion. The last chapter ended by mentioning the Maya sign *ch'ahb*. The decipherment is secure, reinforced by clues from syllables. But the glyph cannot be easily understood with regard to shape or meaning. Arching within a partial circle, its internal lines signal a hard, polished surface—other such cues appear on gleaming celts or the bright fruit of mythic trees. In a sense, the sign also pivots physically. Earlier examples orient to the viewer; later ones, for some unknown reason, swivel to the side. A suggestion that *ch'ahb* represents a sliver of obsidian seems reasonable.[7] Several scenes tie it to bloodletting, a rite performed with this volcanic glass. At Yaxchilan, Mexico, royal ladies pierce their tongues; the sign either tags this activity in accompanying texts or, combined with another sign, it occupies a plate of a sacrificial dish, heaped with blood-spotted paper, as on Yaxchilan Lintel 13 (fig. 49A). The queen celebrates the birth of a son with a form of bloodletting other than, or in addition to, placental delivery. Yet obsidian happens also to occur in Maya images and inscriptions. Hooked and serrated, perhaps to stress its sacrificial function, the sign looks nothing at all like *ch'ahb*.

Explaining *ch'ahb* poses a challenge. Present in many Mayan languages, the term actually conveys the idea of "fast" rather than bloodletting per se. Food deprivation or abstinence in general marked much Christian practice. Eager for analogies, the friars who collected these words noted a corresponding behavior among the Maya. Contact with deities required physical preparation, a point made repeatedly by Diego de Landa for colonial Yucatan. Calamity would result for those who broke away from expected duty. The flagellation and vigils of Christians also found an echo in Yukateko Maya "shedding their blood and afflicting themselves, with watching, and fastings and abstinences."[8] A body so scourged needed that pain to access signs from divine beings.

This is no less so in the recent past. Among traditionalists, not yet converted to Protestantism or other beliefs, abstinence can take place before vigils, feasts, ceremonies,

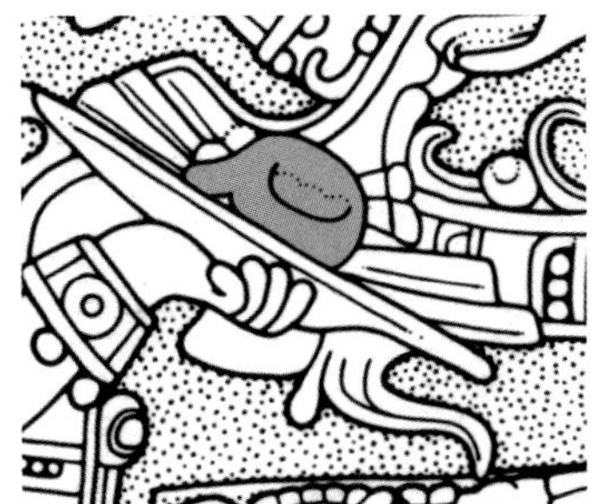

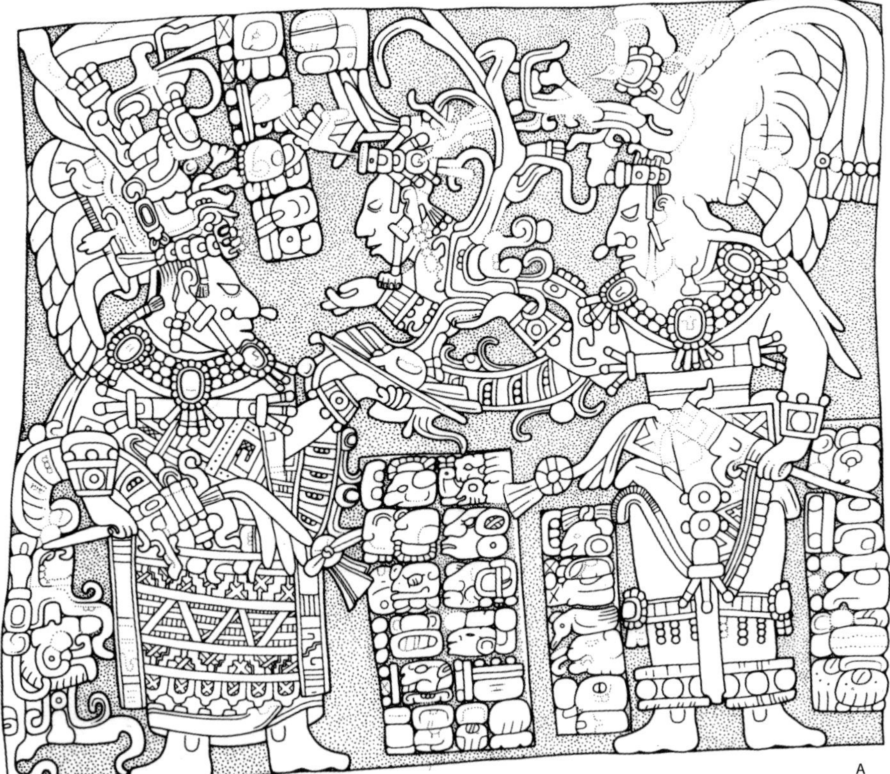

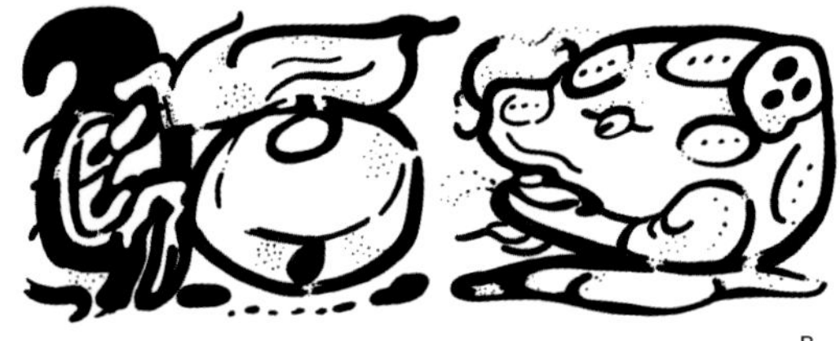

FIGURE 49

Ch'ahb-ak'ab and actual sign for obsidian: A) Yaxchilan, Mexico, Lintel 13, Feb. 15, AD 752, a retroactive date, glyph highlighted in detail above. Limestone, 29½ × 38¾ in. (75 × 99 cm); B) codex-style ceramic, with hand-holding obsidian as initial glyph in royal name, "Sacrifice (?) of the Crocodile's Heart (*Yohl Ahiin*)," c. AD 750.

supplication of gods, collection of sacred incense, even planting. For the Q'eqchi' Maya, sexual energy should be channeled into the young maize. Young men, hot with fertile essence, are best at "insemination" or sowing, provided they direct it at plants rather than women. The Tzutujil Maya, south of the Q'eqchi', highlight similar ideas. A once-annual ceremony, now less frequent, involves youths, the *aii'*, the "young men together," who go on an arduous journey to bring or, in their view, "capture" ripe fruit from the coast. On arriving home, the fruits fairly ooze with juices. Celibate at the time, withholding their semen, the young men's essence and "heat" of temptation transform into rains that nourish crops. Only then might the youths marry. Young children vie with them in not-so-subtle ways, attempting to grab the fruit brought by the *aii'*.

Locating the overall sense of *ch'ahb* could mean expanding its definition.[9] Denial, pain, self-control, and sexuality are evident in Maya practice. At Yaxchilan in Classic times, *ch'ahbil,* the abstract essence of this word, referred to women in acts in bloodletting. Yet, by all later use, the term itself relates to fasting. In colonial Kaqchikel, a language of the Guatemalan highlands, "penitence" covers the idea of abstinence, "discipline," and more, such as to avoid planting fields for corn or cacao, refrain from hot drinks or foods flavored with salt, and draw away from fire.[10] There is a simple explanation. Fasting or *ayuno* formed part of a gamut of practices, all of them necessary for ritual, encounters with the supernatural, and productive results. The Maya speaking to Landa certainly thought so, and for this reason, they also employed *ch'ab*—Yukateko drops the internal *h*—for "penance" more generally. In fact, that basic concept, of ritual abnegation leading to a desired outcome, may account for *ch'ahb.*

The procreative themes lie close at hand. In Yukateko Maya, the word *ch'ab* signifies "create," and an opaque expression, *ch'ab-ak'ab,* equates in the *Ritual of the Bacabs,* an incantatory book of the colonial period, to "creation" and "dark."[11] This same phrase, first detected by the epigrapher David Stuart, occurs as *ch'ahb-ak'abil* in Classic Maya writing. (Note that *ak'ab,* a distinct word recorded in glyphs, is not the same as the symbol for "dark" on obsidian, a cue to the cloudy and often black appearance [fig. 49B].) Some royal fathers in the Classic period described their sons as both "gift," *sij,* and as *ch'ahb.* A "penance" truly: severe disciplines of the body may have prepared for dynastic procreation or helped to express thanks for successful outcomes.

Notably, the queen of Yaxchilan in *ch'ahbil*—the state of being in penance or spiritual preparation—bore no clear heir to the kingdom. Was she barren, doing all she could to ensure a son? Where she failed, or seemed to fail, another succeeded: a stela at Yaxchilan shows a rival consort letting blood from the tongue, and the text duly records her *mayij* or sacrificial gift.[12] Now, the outcome was positive. She did have a son, a truly great one: Bird Jaguar IV. But when did her offering occur? The stela raises two possibilities. One is that she played a role at court as late as AD 741, in joint ritual with her Bird Jaguar's wife, depicted on the other, more visible side of the stela. Her own image, in studied inaccessibility, crams close to a stuccoed wall (only the front is visible in figure 50; the back is difficult to photograph). This may have been a secondary placement for the sculpture, moved from some other location. As an alternative, it could also reflect a gendered practice for what is an unusually small monument—carved stelae outside buildings are often much larger.

The second option is that the queen was already dead. Her painful offering, an act of procreative intent, lay far in the past, around the time of Bird Jaguar's birth in AD 709. This may be more than a wild guess. Her name appears with the later date, 741, but as an apparent goddess. Her *ch'ahb* expression also conflates with the head of the god *K'awiil,* a deity summoned, so the glyphs tell us, by her daughter-in-law. At a later date, on Lintel 13 at Yaxchilan, the mother of another ruler wields a bloodletter and a bowl with the *ch'ahb-ak'ab* sign at the birth of her son. The father also grasps a bloodletter, indicating that he also played a ritual role in a woman's task.

FIGURE 50
Yaxchilan Stela 35, front, June 28, AD 741, Structure 21. Limestone, 59¼ × 16 in. (150 × 41 cm). Photograph by Gustavo Jerónimo.

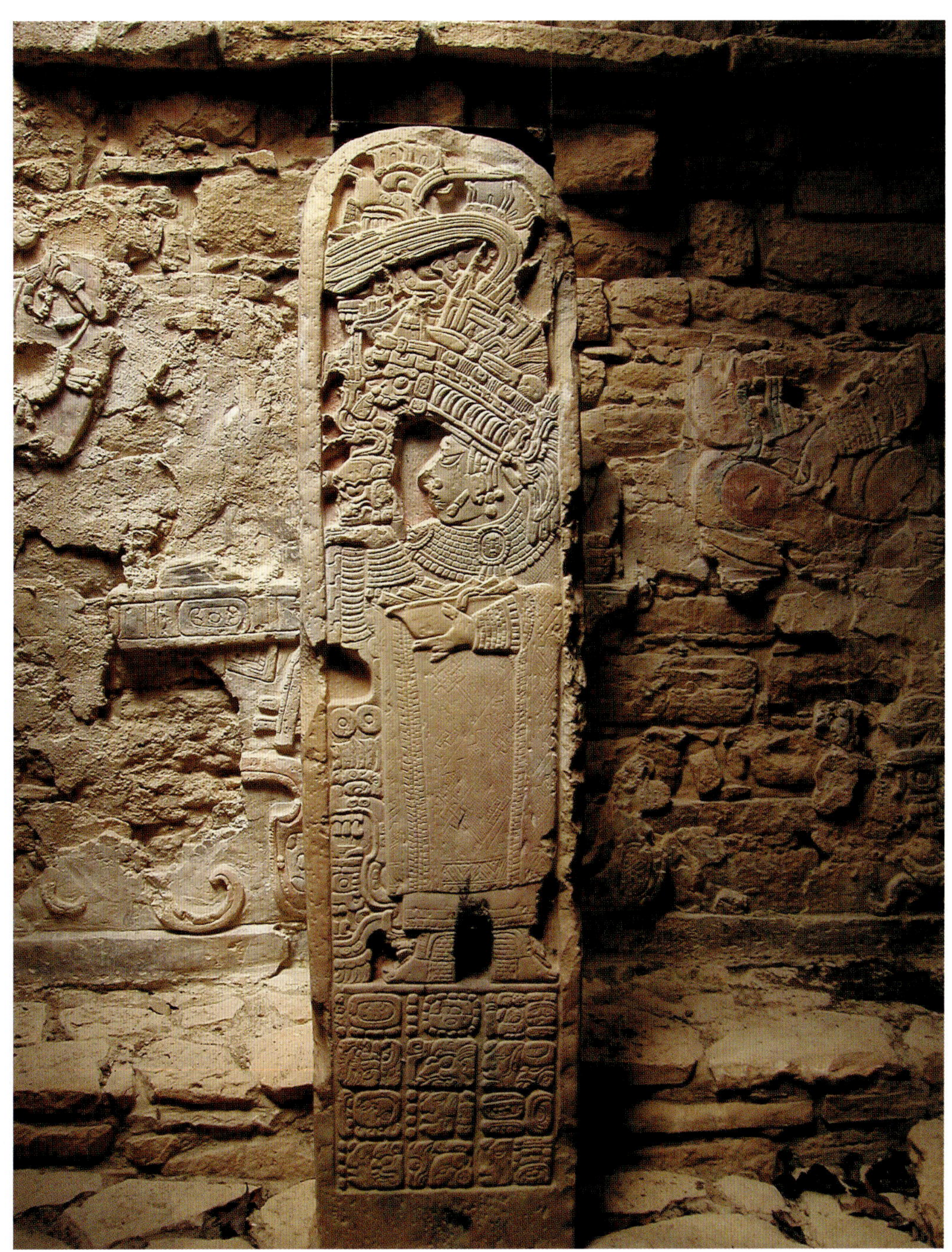

The use of *ak'abil,* here and elsewhere, is harder to explain. It too may belong to the suite of afflictive yet creative practices implied by *ch'ahb.* If there was "penance," there might also have been *ak'abil,* "darkness" or "night." Ritual sequestration, removing participants to dark places, recalls a broader idea. Among the Maya and other peoples of Mesoamerica, a predawn world existed before the current creation.[13] Did *ch'ahb-ak'abil* commemorate a related concept of human action, one that, through effort, self-denial, sacrifice, and setting apart, led to new life? Whatever the proposal, *ch'ahb* seems reliably to be understood as a ritual that disciplined the body in ways connected to reproduction. When negated, *ma-ch'ahb, ma-ak'abil,* as in labels for prisoners of war, the Classic Maya appeared to pry that attribute from the defeated.

Willful self-denial, removal from human contact, and offerings of blood imply a mature state. Letting blood would have been a serious business, risking infection and, with an arterial gush, life itself.[14] From it flowed a spirit force particular to royalty. Abstinence from sexual pleasure presumes that someone is capable of such urges. Even with help, it is the rare youngster capable of inflicting pain and privation on their own body. The beginnings of this activity would thus merit notice, especially if treated formally in surviving evidence. Now at hand: a new status, a novel capability, auguring further rites to come. For young women, the Classic Maya heralded such changes by referring, in a very few cases, to the "covering" or "enclosing" (*mak*) of a female. This rite may have covered the genitalia, the hair, or some other part of the body. As an unproven (and probably unprovable) alternative, it alluded to a kind of purdah, the removal of females from contact with unrelated males. A princess received her own establishment and servants, but in secluded state, away from inappropriate gaze.

The best-known case concerns a foreign princess at Piedras Negras, Guatemala. Her future father-in-law supervised her covering or enclosing while he lay close to death. Within a short time after his death, glyphs call her the "wife," *atan,* of his son, the next king. If the princess had not passed to puberty, her husband certainly had—he was 22 years old. The backs of the stelae depicting the queen and her daughter have an intriguing orientation. They look up to elevated, restricted parts of the royal palace, a line of sight hinting at female seclusion. The ceremony was rare but not unprecedented. Over a century before, in AD 514, a princess of Tikal, Guatemala, was covered or enclosed at 3 years and 2 months of age. Her name is missing from the shattered monument recording these events, but most likely the ritual was intended for her. Some years later, now 6 years old, she became a queen with a male co-regent. For a near-toddler, marriage, betrothal, or gendered seclusion might seem improbable, yet there are parallels in far times and places. Richard II of England, a widower, married the 6-year-old Isabella of Valois, and tribal practices in Pakistan countenance marriage for babies before birth or, for girls, while they are still infants.[15] Dowries, alliance, and the settling of feuds are at stake. The wishes of children have no bearing on these arrangements.

The princess of Tikal undertook another ritual before the final date on the sculpture. At most she was 10 years old, and probably younger than that. The rite was an authentic ordeal, a *yax ch'ahb,* her "first fast" or "first penance." Introducing adult responsibilities, it separated a prior phase of life from future duty. She was not alone in passing this marker. Her mysterious co-regent at Tikal experienced his own *yax ch'ahb,* although we have insufficient evidence to pinpoint his age at the time. The other penitents in Classic history are males, too, beginning with a small stela 33 inches (84 cm) high, now at the Art Museum of Princeton University (fig. 51). Difficult to date, in archaic style—its glyphs are later in form than the portrayal of the deity—the text is nonetheless clear: *yax ch'ahb tu k'uhil,* the "first penance" or penitential ceremony for the god (*k'uhil*) of an historical figure.[16] The recipient of that offering must have been the deity or set of deities. Three small torsos plummet from near his body, spilling their guts. Commenting on the stela, David Stuart wonders whether its small size fits with a rite of first bloodletting. A miniature stela would suit a young patron and accord with his physical stature.

When mentioned, first penance often occurs with figures of dynastic transition or troubled succession. A prince at Caracol, Belize, eventually to become an important king, underwent the ordeal after his fifth birthday on May 29, AD 593. Was this age the lower limit of responsible decision, just prior to a lifetime of ceremonial obligation? It is an age of great meaning to the Classic Maya: many sacrificed humans in tombs date to this time of life or a few years later. His elderly father was between 60 and 80 years of age, dying six years later. Yet we know that this prince, Sak Witzil Baah, had an older brother by a different mother. Patron of two large stelae, among the largest at Caracol, the brother would disappear from view, to be replaced by Sak Witzil Baah. The younger man's claim to the throne may have been tenuous, however. By stressing his first penance, the new ruler established bona fides for high office, long after the event.

The same ritual takes place at Dos Pilas, Guatemala, again in circumstances of dynastic tumult. The first local king, Bahlaj Kan K'awiil, dominates the story. A sprig of Tikal's royal family, he was planted many kilometers south of ancestral lands. Notably, he felt it necessary at a later date to emphasize his first penance, at about 9 years of age. The event differs slightly from prior examples. The penance is now "held up" or "offered" (*k'ahlaj*). As with the Princeton stela, the recipient may have been a deity—the painful duty was for a purpose, almost transactional in function. But it also opened the young lord to future expectations of productive and even reproductive ritual. Another representation of the same offering, in this case explicitly of "first blood" (*yax ch'ich'*) and a sacrificial gift (*mayij*), inaugurates the ritual role of an heir to the dynasty of Palenque, Mexico.[17] A throng of gods witnesses the ceremony of this 6-year-old boy. As at Caracol, the reference is tinged with retroactive justification, for he succeeded a brother who had no heir of his own. The Palenque text raises a submerged theme into full view: pain and penance were involved, but, more than anything, blood offering too, at ages when boys (and

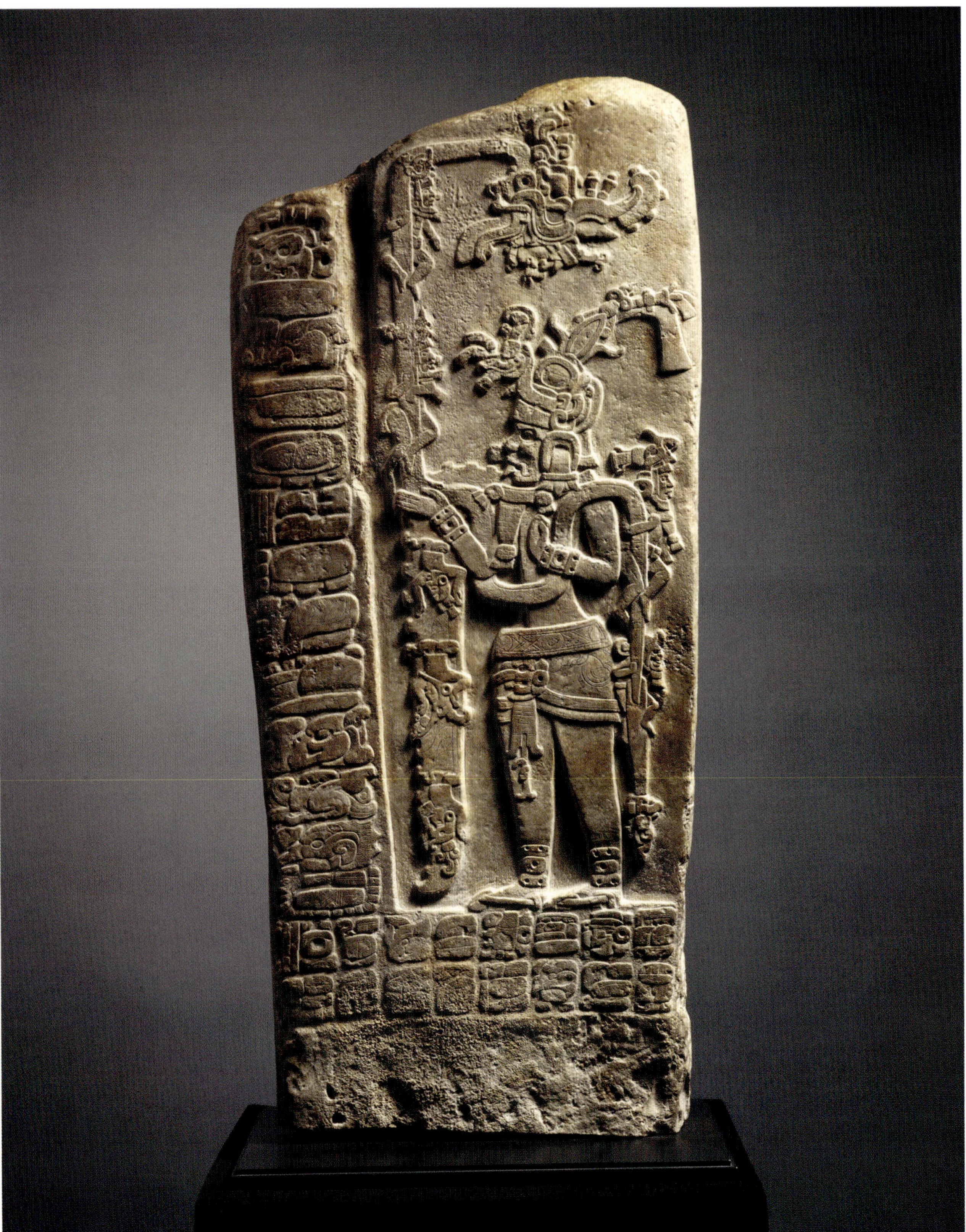

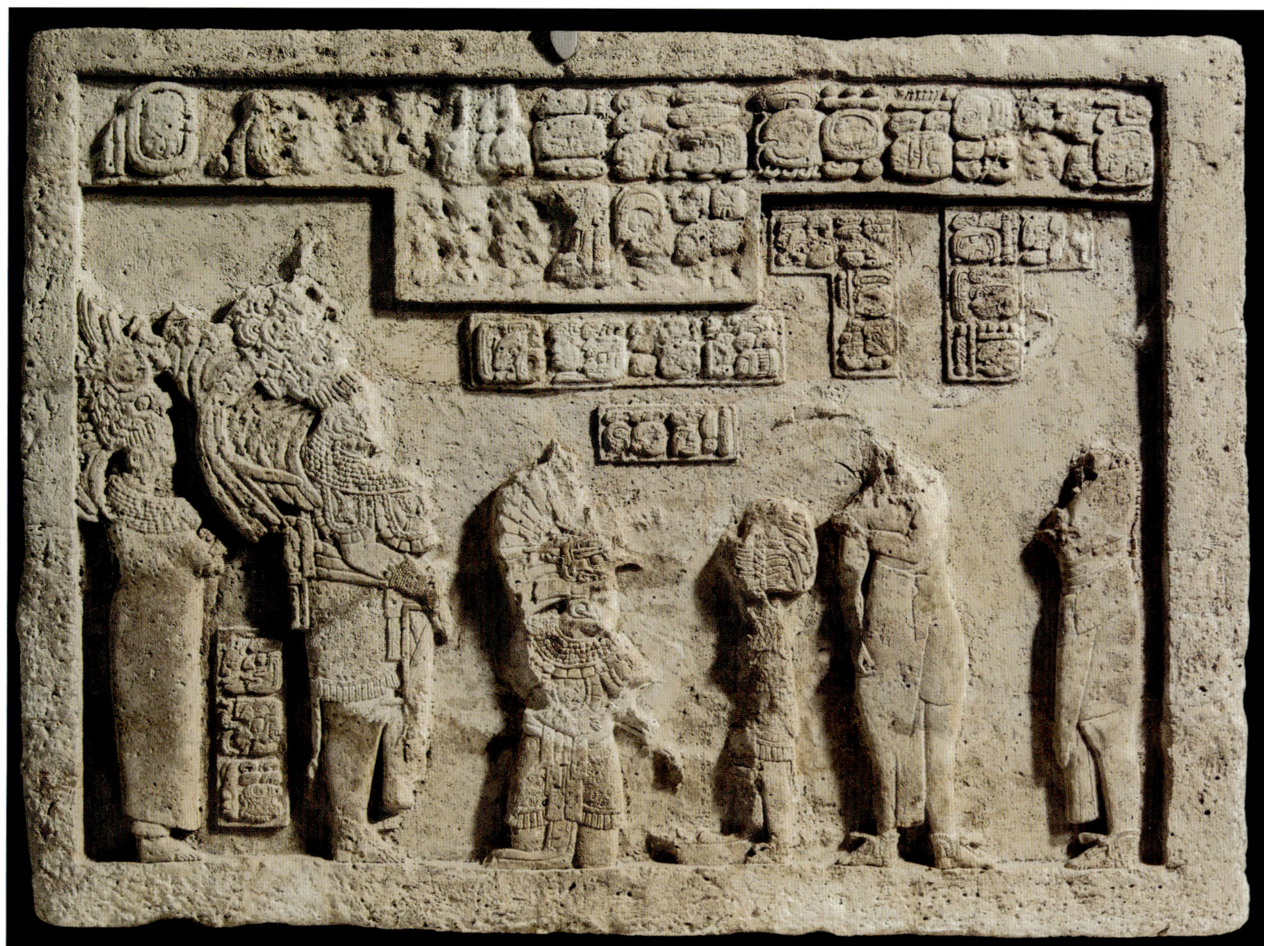

one girl) were capable of speech and the acceptance of adult responsibility. They had survived the rigors of early childhood, a time typified by high mortality. Their first penance, with a suggestion that procreation might soon become possible, needed gods in the mix. Yet there are signs of anxiety, affecting instances of fraternal accession that needed special authorization or notice. There was a princess anomalous in her inheritance, a young king ruling in a foreign land, and, with the Princeton stela, an archaizing sculpture that seemed not quite of its time. Perhaps it was commissioned to show the beginnings of a dynasty.

A mutilated image may represent *yax ch'ahb* (fig. 52). Discovered in fragments, not all recovered, it lay behind a modest residence at Dos Pilas. That is an unlikely location for an important dynastic carving. The original setting was probably as a wall panel in a true "dower house," a small palace holding the interment of a queen, just off the main plaza of the city. Buried in that house, she may well have had her own housing after the death of her husband.[18] That queen appears to the far left. She clasps her upper arm in a well-known token of respective attendance, as does a counterpart male on the far right, her name glyphs float in front of her lower body. Far more richly dressed is her husband, the second-to-last ruler known to have lived at Dos Pilas. His costume is that of a dancer, suggesting that the setting is more public, on an open platform rather the recesses of a palace, or they have left, or will soon enter, such an open space. The other instances of *yax ch'ahb* yield no such information. The *ch'ahb* events of women do appear palatial, less public, clustering in buildings associated with women. In its ambitious program of lintels, Structure 23 at Yaxchilan recounts the career of a queen, in exemplary roles that support her husband; on one of its lintels, other royal women of high birth are in attendance. Structure 21, which contains Stela 35, is unique at Yaxchilan for placing the monument within the building, not outside (the exact findspot has not been published).[19] Two of the lintels in that structure refer to important consorts, suggesting a partial dedication to queenly rites.

To the far right on the Dos Pilas panel are nobles in simpler dress. The figure in frontal view leans over a young royal, so identified by his jaguar-pelt kilt, visual centrality, and, making it plain, the large banner text above: it refers to a *ch'ok mut ajaw*, the heir or "young lord" of the Dos Pilas dynasty. Unlike the others, he needs no glyphic caption. The banner text is more than enough. Leaves (a penitential garment?) cover his back, valuable plumes erupt as a diminutive headdress.[20] Kneeling in front, also in full view, is a person of likely royal status. His dress recalls that of the king: in lavish array are a jaguar-pelt kilt, beaded collar, pendant flaps with knots, and earspool with a projecting, cylindrical bead. But his clothing is distinct from the king's: instead of plumes, sacrificial paper stands up, and his flaps and lower kilt have but one braid, not the two borne by the king. The frontal orientation could be employed to provide visual syncopation, to invigorate an otherwise dull set of bodies in profile. Yet mostly the pattern heightens emphasis. The kneeling lord is flagged as a key participant, along with the simply dressed male leaning over the boy. Looking at them from the same orientation, viewers are drawn in to inspect their respective roles. The rite is bloodletting, and is for, to judge from his size, a boy of the same age as others in the act of *yax ch'ahb*. Droplets trickle from the child's midsection. Bloodletting from the penis is likely, given its ritual prominence among the Classic Maya, or, as suggested in an earlier chapter, the foreskin had been sliced away. The effusion lands in a bowl with folded paper, to be burned at some point. Assisting, the noble grasps a stingray spine, the slicing now done. He extends his hand, as does the king, in a gesture of offering. Despite the lack of architectural features, the banner text above assures us that the setting is the eastern sector of Dos Pilas and that "28 lords" have assembled to witness the event. This group may allude to the court or to less visible authorities, a convocation of gods.

Three hieroglyphic captions deepen our reading of the scene. The kneeling ritualist—a Maya "mohel," perforating or circumcising the foreskin—has a personal name: Sakjal Hix, perhaps "The Whitening Cat." He also carries a title of great interest to specialists in Classic civilization. Written out as a glyph, it contains a headband used by various courtiers, and, in this text, the head of a bird (**be?**) and a syllabic suffix (**ta**). Reading this title has proved elusive, but a candidate comes to mind, with solid rooting in relevant languages. This is *ebeet,* a term spelled out with syllables in the Bonampak murals of Chiapas and in other texts around the Maya world. The word fits with the syllables **be**(?) and **ta**, its meaning reconstructible as "messenger" but also as "worker" or "servant."[21] As a headdress, the title goes far back into the first years of the Classic period. Courtiers in murals at Uaxactun, Guatemala, use it throughout. By the Late Classic period, a title sufficed to record that role. The very same glyph appears in the name of a noble who owned a wooden box, on which glyphs point to storage of sacrificial equipment.

Much longer captions label the simply dressed figures to the right of the panel. Closest to the prince stands a noble leaning over in attentive, perhaps protective concern. His caption labels him "guardian of the youth." In Maya writing, "guardianship" usually involves a close relationship between a captor and his war captive. It was a close but miserable bond: most captives could expect humiliating display or worse, from torture to execution. The panel at Dos Pilas enlarges the meaning of "guardian" by applying it to attendants of a royal youth. Unlike captors, they rank below their young charge. At Dos Pilas, too, high-level politics ripple through the scene. The caption attributes the guardian to Dos Pilas's most potent ally, Calakmul (Mexico). As a regional power, Calakmul thought deeply about princes from subordinate cities. The line between guest and hostage ran thin. One inscription from La Corona, Guatemala, tells us that a prince traveled to Calakmul for a lengthy stay, returning only when his father, the local ruler, passed away. Such service seems never quite to have ended. Later, still described as an "older brother" *ch'ok*—at age 28—he was summoned to Calakmul by his overlord (see chapter 2). After several days he performed ceremonies with the seven sons of the king of Calakmul. The summons may have been related to dynastic validation, maybe to confirm the heir to Calakmul in the full company of local and provincial lords.[22] The use of *ch'ok* for a mature man is curious, but an explanation may be that it seems he had yet to marry and may never have done so. He is also one of the Maya lords to accede twice to a throne, an event that only happened after this summons to Calakmul. His younger sibling, labeled as *itz' winik ch'ok,* the "younger [brother] person, youth," eventually came to power.

The carving at Dos Pilas reverses this process. If princes could not go to Calakmul, Calakmul might come to them. A tutor or "governor" shipped out to a subordinate kingdom, for central billing on an innovative panel—the sculpture, unusual in the region, could almost be a rollout from a Maya vase. The other figure indicates what such guardians do. His youthful charge, the prince, is *aj bolon ti',* "he of the nine [many] mouths" or "tongues"— *ti',* "mouth" and its cognates are common Mayan expressions for "languages."[23] Perhaps the guardian was a tutor, skilled in languages—no empty task. The likelihood of Maya multilingualism is high given the number of distinct tongues in the Maya lowlands today. Historical study of grammar and words confirms long-standing contact between those languages; someone was needed to train the diplomats and messengers who might cross such boundaries. Control of foreign languages often set royalty apart, as in the German spoken between Queen Victoria and Prince Albert of the United Kingdom, or the French shared by intimates of the Prussian king Frederick the Great. The central point is that, in the Late Classic period, special figures tended or taught the royal young. At Dos Pilas, at least one of these tutors or supervisors came from the courts of overlords.

The panel is of overriding importance for another reason. The youth so commemorated, whose panel was eventually smashed into fragments, may not have come to the throne. His name, detectable in the main text, is found in no other sculpture, and the next ruler of the city had an entirely different set of epithets. If Panel 15 is showing a *yax ch'ahb* event—remember, the shattered inscription makes this conjectural, if reasonably so—it would coincide with other examples. The rite looms in significance at moments of dynastic turbulence, contested or dubious inheritance, or unstable claims to thrones. The panel at Dos Pilas was positioned upright in a wall, perhaps close to where the act took place. Its destruction obliterated that narrative, and the sculpture ended up as a tumble of small stones at the margins of the city. The image, with references to witnesses and open display of parents, a ritualist, and guardians, implied a kind of contrived consensus. The youth was up to his duty, all agreed to his role and certified his performance, with hints toward his fertile potential; he was a worthy heir. But the consensus did not last, and events overtook the young prince.

Guardians of youths deserve more attention, since they occur in texts and scenes outside Dos Pilas. A late polychrome vessel, assembled from fragments in the destroyed palace of Aguateca, Guatemala, features a palace scene (fig. 53).[24] Darkness wraps around the palace, relieved by stars or constellations above. To the side, in jaunty stance, a figure smokes a cigarillo—this signals night, and the effect can be imagined, of embers pulsing bright at every inhalation. Just above, a text refers to the "guardian of a youth," a role the courtier might have filled when not pausing for a smoke. He stands behind the seated king, showing high status, but not high enough to be seated in his presence: worth depicting, a named person of confidence, yet not quite royal. An unprovenanced pot (perhaps, as Simon Martin suggests, from the city of El Palmar, Mexico), shows a variant image of the courtly guardian. He sits in front of an enthroned king, who converses with another seated figure, both spooling out speech scrolls from their mouths. Mute, without scrolls, the guardian is described as "he, the youth-guardian," a role that displaces any more personal reference (fig. 54).

Parents also could extol their guardianship. A central title for a king from the area of Bonampak, Mexico, was "guardian of the youth." Found in his son's statement of parentage, the description has two explanations: it might be martial, the father having taken a nameless youth into battle, or it may refer to parenting and an unusually close connection—of training?—between father and his son. At about this period, on a sherd dug up at Buenavista del Cayo, Belize, a king of the far larger site of Naranjo, Guatemala, describes his guardianship of a youth as part of his name.[25] A set of three vases from the area of Xultun, Guatemala, from approximately the same time, mid-eighth century AD, extends

FIGURE 53
Reference to guardian of youths on polychrome vessel, with figure smoking cigarillo below, Structure M7–35, Aguateca, Guatemala, c. AD 800.

FIGURE 54
Guardian of youth attending ruler on throne, on polychrome vase, Guatemala or southern Mexico, c. AD 750. Photograph by Justin Kerr (K0625).

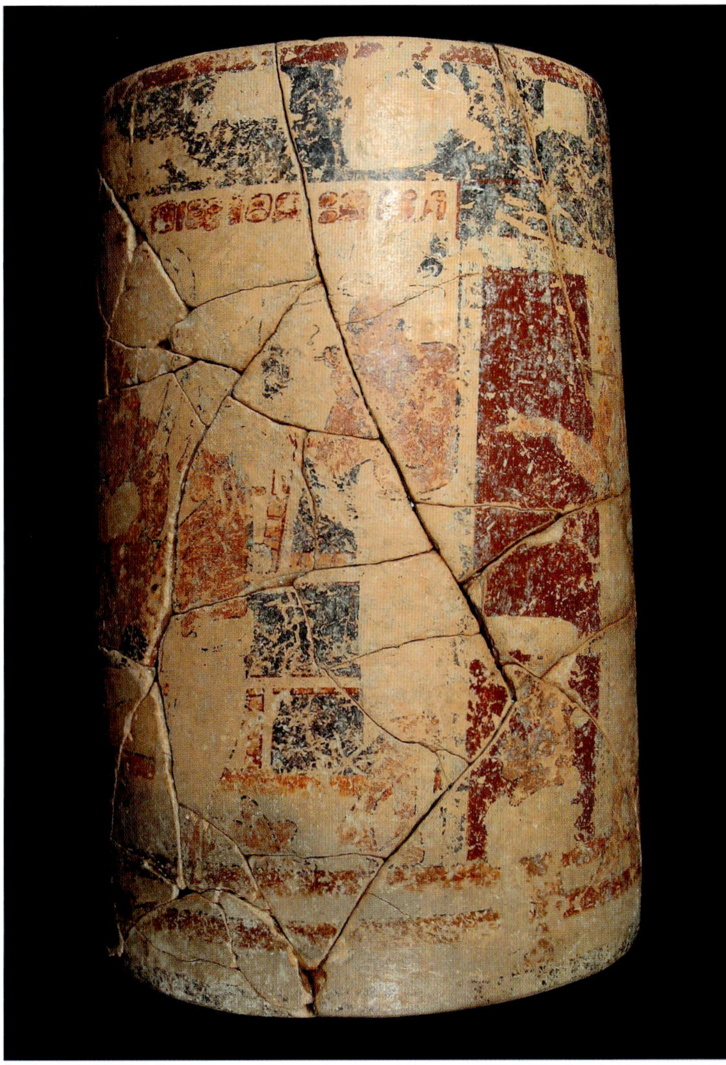

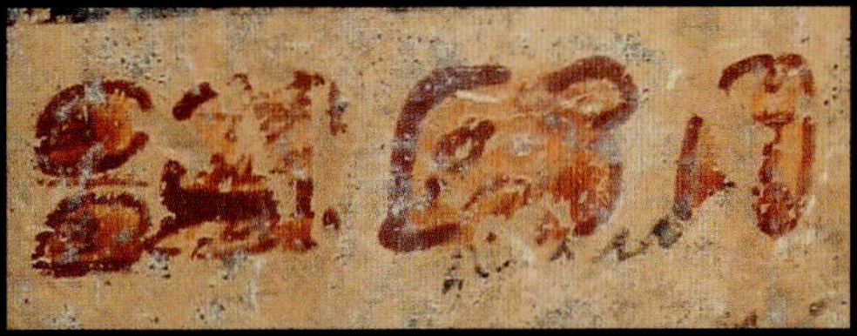

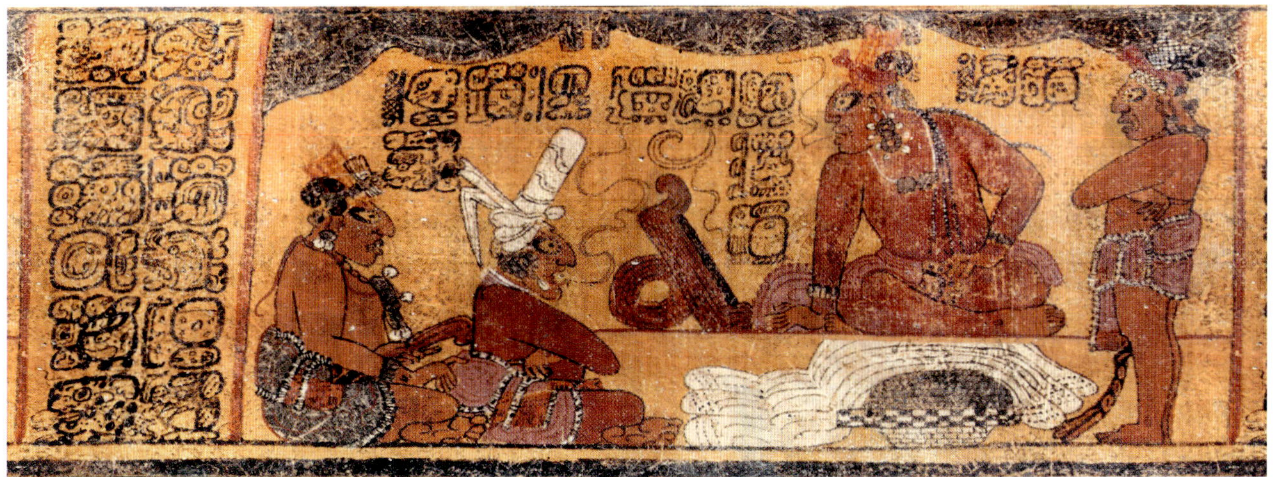

that role to a royal lady (fig. 55, see also fig. 36).[26] Among the few females said to own
a vessel, this one is the "guardian of a youth." The relation here is, especially for a woman,
improbable as a reference to a war captive.

The two other vases are all by the same hand, with identifiable details in the handling of suffixes, and one carries almost precisely the same color scheme as the lady's. The
embodiment of paper for royal headbands appears twice on the surface of the vessels.
The female's pot shows a similar set of heads, but with the sign for *k'an*, "yellow," "precious," or "ready for harvest." The male glories in high rank—note the *bakab*, "head of
the earth," among his titles (at position J1 in the rim band, fig. 55A). The third pot presents
similar attributes, including the living embodiment of royal headbands, yet with far bolder
painting and more subtle touches: the burgundy background of the male-female set give
way to an inky black, while glyphic and figural outlines are no longer dark but light red,
and inner areas modulate with pockets of pink (fig. 55B). The glyphs at the top stretch
across a red rather than the cream-colored background on the first two pots. In a sense,
the third chocolate pot both responds aesthetically to the others and contrasts with them.
The owner is neither woman nor adult man but a "great youth," a *chak ch'ok*. Looting has
robbed these pieces from Guatemala along with their context, yet they appear to form
a coherent set, clearly by the same painter. An intriguing suggestion would be that they
were created at one time, for use on the same occasion. The lady's pot could thus cross-
reference the youth.

Several ceramics fold the ritual of "first penance" into their texts. The vessel mentioned at the end of chapter 2, probably from the area of Uaxactun, Guatemala, makes
this explicit: a chocolate pot was dedicated to use by a youth in the course of *yax ch'ahb*,
as preparation for, or as relief after, the rite. A fast may have been broken by a long, satisfying drink. Other vessels belonging to young men are less overt in making this link, and
their use may have varied, as tokens of participation in formal repasts and signs of socialization. Still, the vase from near Uaxactun suggests a more precise function, not generic
in use but targeted as a marker of new status. The owner of an *atole* bowl in the collection
of the San Diego Museum of Man, first pointed out to me by Judith Green, is a prince
from the kingdom of Hix Witz, "Cat Hill," in northern Guatemala, perhaps in the area of
Zapote Bobal.

The bowl forms part of a larger assemblage of vessels. There is a plate, too, on
loan to the New Orleans Museum of Art (fig. 56A). All date to the first years of the Late
Classic period, at about AD 600. Each belonged to a *yax ch'ahb winkil*, "a first-penance"
person or, on the plate, to a *ch'ahb winkil*, an abbreviated version of the same phrase (*winkil*,
"person," a near-supernatural expression in Ch'orti' Maya for "supernatural protector," is
a decipherment by David Stuart).[27] As with the set from Xultun, the calligrapher appears
to one individual, except for an outlier example with especially rough, nearly illegible
glyphs (fig. 56C). All texts were created with a heavily charged brush. Rubbery in movement, the human bodies are loosely but vigorously delineated. And all had the same owner,

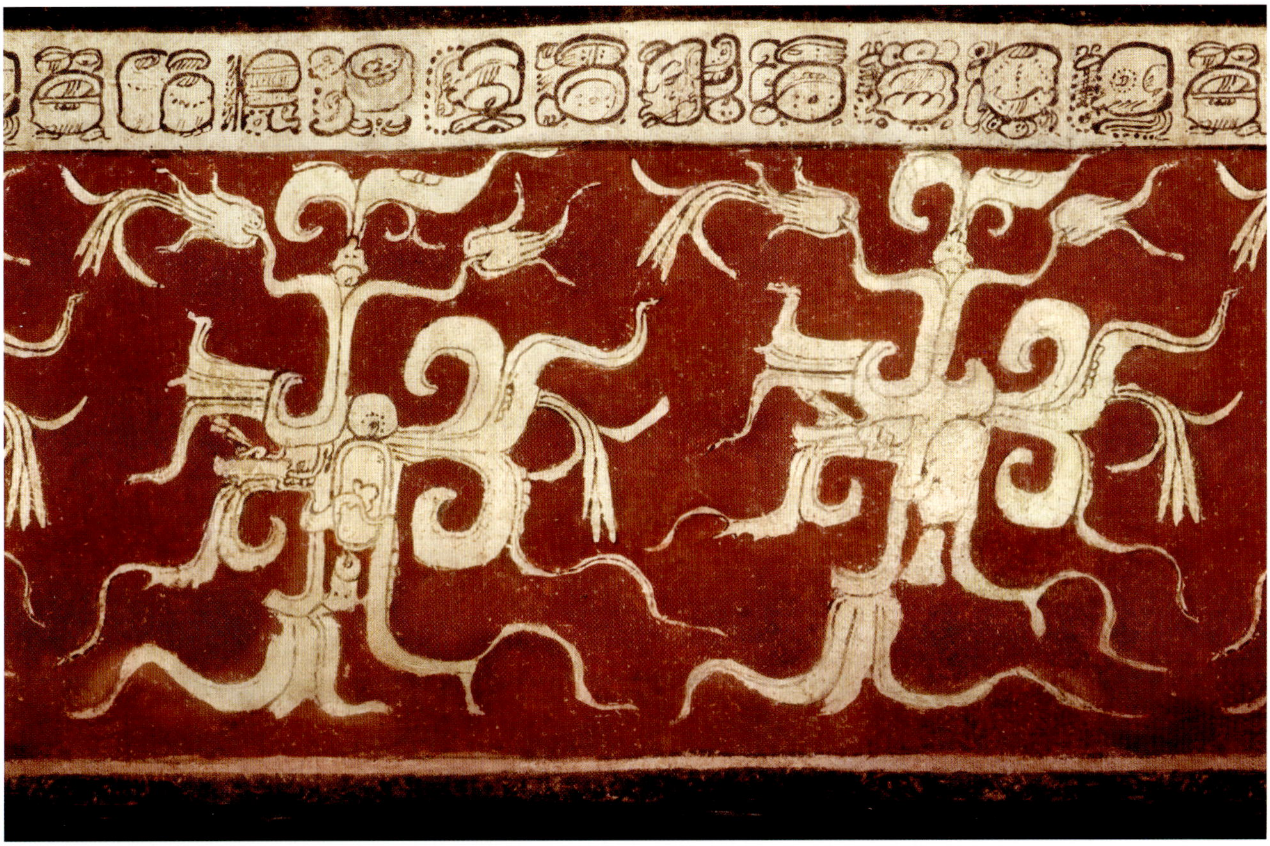

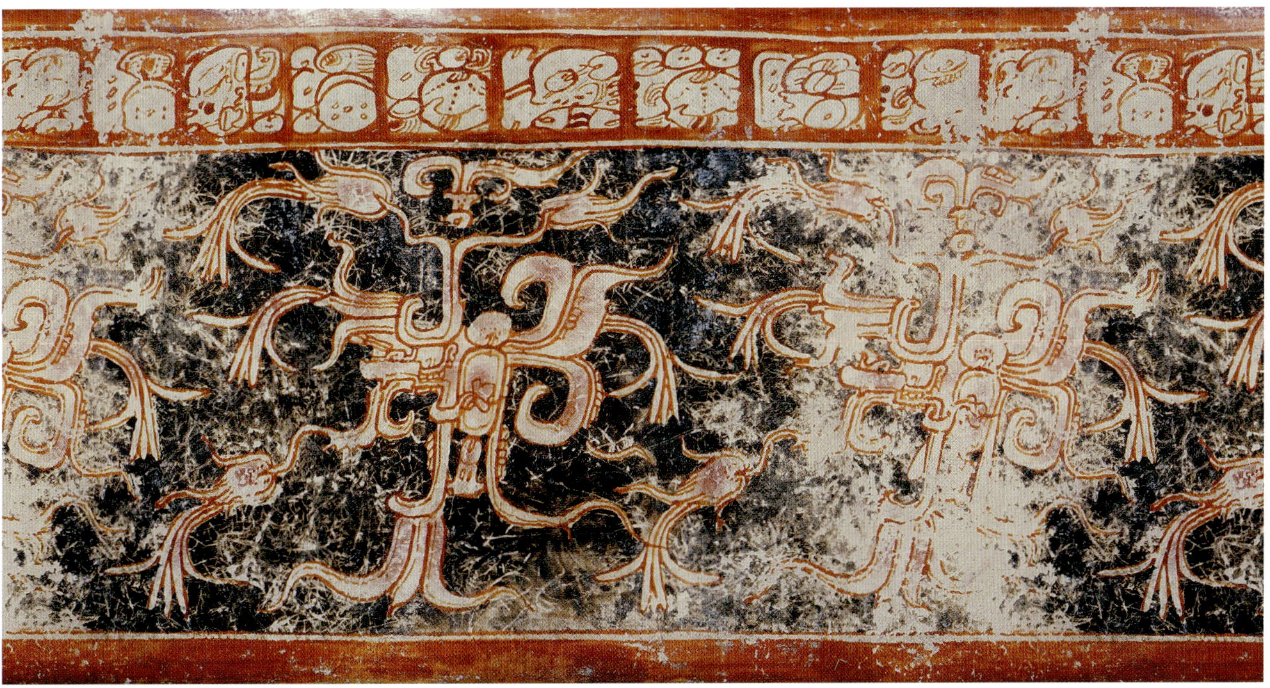

A

B

a prince of Hix Witz with a partially legible name, Chan Ahk. The imagery on one pot displays young gods, headbanded, in activities appropriate to energetic stages of life. They embark on the hunt, sit and speak in the garb of Hero Twins, the young and most clever tormenters of old gods; one is even a youthful Maize God. A headbanded youth, shorter than the other gods nearby, clutches his penis, testicles visible; he appears to jab his member with a thin blade. The owner is not described as a *ch'ok,* but the images and *yax ch'ahb* indicate a plausible, near-didactic purpose: the lord of Hix Witz would view exemplary youth from the mythic past. The set thus contrasted with many *ch'ok* vessels discussed in chapter 2. Those ceramics offered no such correlation of text and image. Other kingdoms joined Hix Witz in referring to *yax ch'ahb* on vessels. A perishable bowl, its stucco covering preserved by chance, advises the reader that its owner, a ruler of Tikal, was the *yax ch'ahb winkil.* The bowl may well have celebrated his completion of this ordeal.

Cut skin heals, and the mortified body can fill, after fasting, with food and drink. More permanent modifications must have taken place in infancy. Among the Classic Maya, the head could be shaped into tabular or elongated form by pressing or binding, and in ways that bridged levels of society. A modest burial might contain a body so shaped, as might a kingly crypt. A daily practice, affecting nearly all people in this part of the Pre-Columbian world, compression and constriction slowly worked the infant's head into desired form. Filed and inlaid teeth are another matter. No such modification is known for the very young, and the practice relates to the eruption of permanent teeth and teenage years. It imparted some new property to the orifice of breath, speech, and consumption, coding it as special. Perhaps it gave talismanic protection to those embarking on adult life. Enamel, common to all mammals, made way for precious stone, usually jade; or mirrorlike ferrous material, sometimes pulverized into a paste, was inserted into a tooth. Both substances were thought by the Classic Maya to contain vital essence or active spirits—a probable depiction of a mirror in the Postclassic Dresden Codex (pg. 42), the most skillfully produced Maya book, contains the face of a god. Filings into the shape of a sign for wind expressed breath or likened human to godly dentition. This was a momentous transformation, involving incalculable pain. The later Aztecs brought this to the level of metaphor, in that children imbued with life were thought to resemble precious beads drilled for suspension.[28]

The age when adult teeth appear varies. According to one survey, incisors are usually in place, visible above the gums by 7 to 9 years of age. Canines arrive by 12, the third molar as late as 20 or so. Frontal teeth are best for special display treatment, particularly those on the maxilla or upper jaw. Hard to shape, the teeth in the back are just as hard to see. Specialists in filing and inlay avoid them. In Bali, far away from the Maya region, the filing of canines neutralizes potential evil for young men and women by a painful act of self-discipline. Their animal nature diminishes, the passions subdue and balance, the human side asserts control. A Brahmin abrades the teeth, but the youth, about 6 to 18 years of age, must lie motionless for the 15- to 30-minute ceremony. A large percentage of the community, male and female, undergo the ordeal. In other parts of Southeast Asia,

FIGURE 56

Yax ch'ahb ceramics from northern Guatemala: A) New Orleans Museum of Art, on loan from Edward J. Howell; B) photograph by Justin Kerr (K9244); C) photograph by Justin Kerr (K1116).

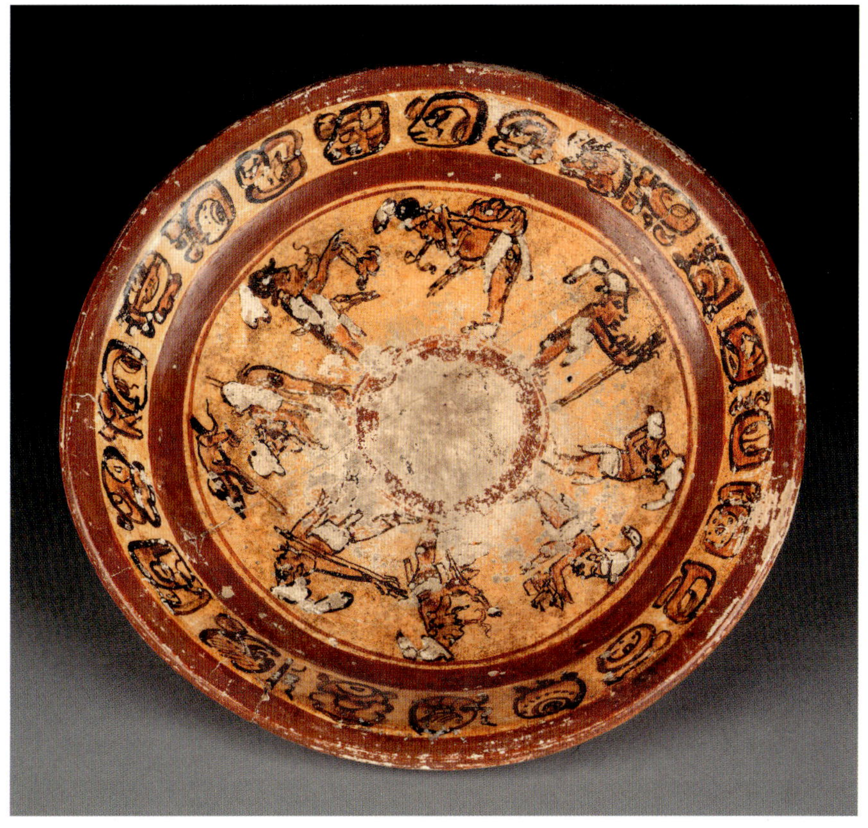

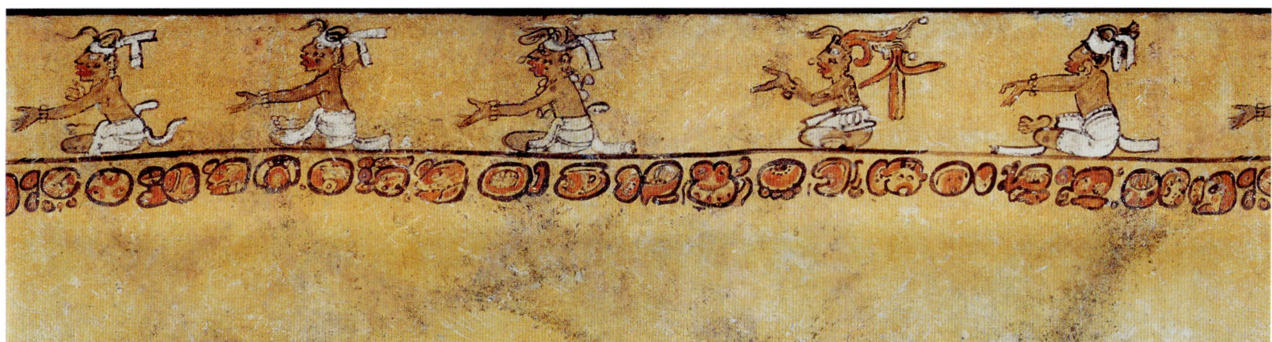

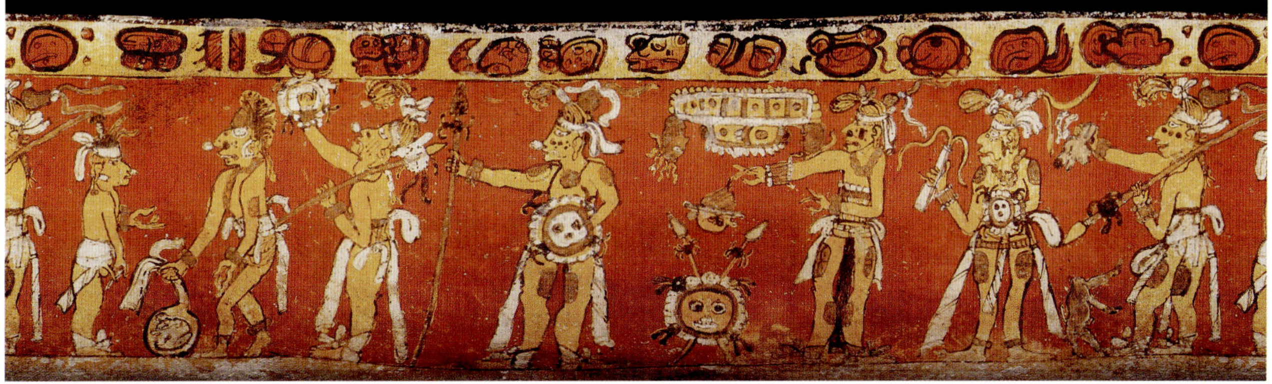

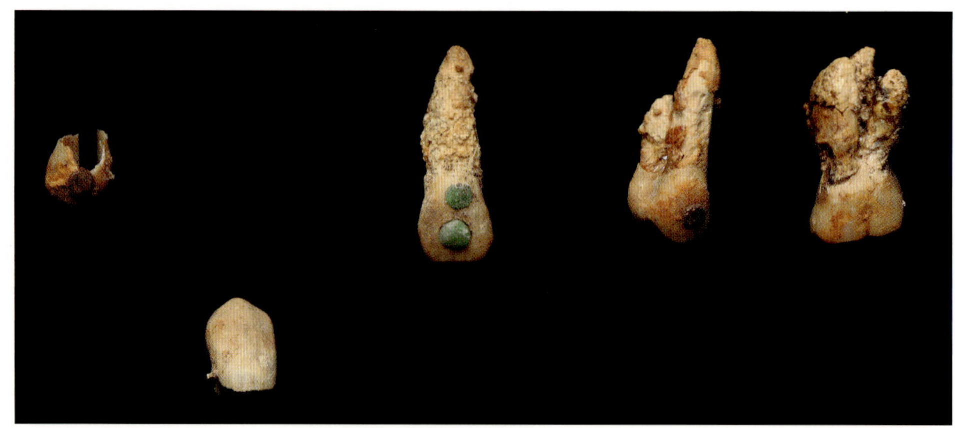

the motivation is beautification at the time of puberty; or, when pressed for an explanation, people might respond, "so one won't look like a dog." These ages roughly match the time frame of the *ch'ok,* when teeth became, for young men, a means of expression, the badge of a completed if protracted ordeal. For the Classic Maya, not all went through it, of either sex. But, to judge from surviving samples of skeletons, some 10 percent or more did. Andrew Scherer, an expert in Maya bones, observes that the percentage reaches nearly 58 percent in the Usumacinta region between Guatemala and Mexico.[29]

Dentistry on limited anesthetics would give some idea of the suffering (fig. 57). Edges were ground and filed, inlays inserted, after drilling, of jade or shiny hematite, especially in royal mouths. Some potion might have dulled the distress, but clearly this was an ordeal reserved for older youths. In the Usumacinta, as Scherer notes, the youngest person with mutilated teeth was between 18 and 20 years of age. The remains of boys did not possess inlays or filings. (The dates are "osteological," meaning they could deviate from physical norms, as many people do; actual chronological ages may differ.) A prince at Piedras Negras, whose stingray spine identifies him as a *ch'ok,* offers a telling example. He died aged 15 or 16, at about AD 700 or slightly later, yet his teeth show no evidence of modification. All other royal burials display dental work, and the remains were of older people. The apparent window of time, from 15 to 20 years of age, could not have been the time of most *yax ch'ahb* ceremonies—those were for boys.[30] Dental carving and drilling involved older youths, just before adulthood. They were closer to a real episode of physiological separation from the very young. This was the onset of andrenarche, an endrocrinological change involving new testosterone products of the adrenal glands.[31]

Beginning in the early first millennium BC, the practice endured. At a later period of the Maya past, in Postclassic Tipu, Belize, four young adults, none likely older than 25, had filed teeth. At Lamanai, Belize, a community of similar date, there were seven. A slightly later account, from sixteenth-century Yucatan, reveals another detail: old women performed the task, "filing... with certain stones and water." Whether the Classic Maya observed the same restriction is unknown. Drills, much like those for making beads, certainly made the holes for inlays. With teeth, drilling was probably not done all at once.[32] A female with inlaid incisor at the Classic ruins of El Kinel, Guatemala, was dead by about 16 to 20 years of age. Affected by decay, the inlay hole in an incisor might have been halfway through incrustation. Most Maya inlays are symmetrical. This one was not, suggesting more drilling and pain were to come or that the procedure was aborted.

No flesh survives from royal bodies of the Maya or, for that matter, of anyone from their kingdoms of the Classic period. The lone exception, to my knowledge, is carbonized flesh from a cremation found by the archaeologist Héctor Escobedo atop a pyramid at Dos Pilas, Guatemala. Lumpish and blue-white in color, it held no cultural information other than the fact that the Maya burned bodies at the end of the Classic period. But figurines indicate that age-related rituals may also have marked the faces of women and warriors. A few, not many, show patterns picked out in flesh, a skeletal jawbone over cheeks, the orbits of a god, horizontal cuts extending from the mouth or raised linear welts of scar tissue. No such scars appear on the rare depictions of young children, those cradled on mothers' hips or laps. Indeed, although impossible to prove, it may be that the intended recipients of some Maya figurines were, as among the Hopi of Arizona, the young or the "older" young on the cusp of adulthood.[33] Effigies called to mind models of good behavior and bad, in addition to offering fun and flexible use. That many are whistles underscores their value in performance, recalling the centrality of dance and music to initiation. Ear ornaments are less likely to be related to older youth. In the Bonampak murals, children of only a few years wear jade earspools, and such ornament must have come early in life.

A rite of passage, as discussed by van Gennep, also dealt with the dead. It would be a mistake to think only of the living. A tabulation by Andrew Scherer reveals the range of ages for children and youths inserted as probable sacrifices into royal or noble tombs.[34] (Because of variable preservation and maturation, not all are identifiable by sex.) From a set of twenty-two tombs at the cities of Kaminaljuyu, Piedras Negras, and Tikal, all in Guatemala, and at Palenque in Mexico, three were infants or children, but fully thirty-four were adolescents. A rite of passage is not only a positive matter, applied by well-intentioned people, it could also affect the unwilling, slaves or war captives, going on to future service or misery in the afterlife. A speculative option is that the sacrificed individuals corresponded to living offspring. A deeply embedded concept in Maya practice today, and probably in the distant past, is *k'ex,* a replacement offering that forestalled godly cravings. As sacrifices, the *k'ex* filled in for humans who would eventually relinquish their bodies, the food of gods; *k'ex* permitted, for a time, continued life for those with such replacements. The number of such offerings in royal tombs may not have been arbitrary: perhaps it matched a census of sons or daughters who, in spirit but through other bodies, accompanied their parent into future life. Regrettably, because of their ages, the skeletons cannot be sexed. As groups, sacrificial youths will be revisited later in the chapter.

Every rite of passage is to some degree personal, even if a subset of initiation ceremonies involved a larger group. This is so with *yax ch'ahb* or the infliction of pain through permanent body ornament. If van Gennep were to see them, he would note familiar themes: a setting apart, a time with activities out of the ordinary and emotions of elevated intensity, the emergence of a new identity and duties, along with a fresh relation to others. Yet the social features of these passages are never far away. Drinking vessels imply a single act of consumption by a *ch'ok* or *chak ch'ok* but also, probably, an act of sharing, whether of the contents or, as a gift, the pot itself. A *yax ch'ahb* event, painfully and personally felt, apparently needed validation by witnesses and help from courtiers. Parents stood by to supervise, gods arrived. Yet the strong impression is that this most personal event was for boys (though in one example, a princess soon to become a ruling queen, a great rarity). More hint than proof, the evidence suggests two overall trends: male youths went through several segments of life on their way to adulthood—others are to be described later—and some of those ceremonies were largely royal. If Maurice Bloch were to interject, there could be one proviso. Princes endured practices that could have been widespread; intent on legitimating royal practice, kingly parents simply appropriated them, and an experience shared with subjects ended up as a statement of profound difference. There is another set of life passages that is yet more social, seemingly for older youths, now as much noble as exclusively royal. This communion transports and molds an entire group of contemporaries, in joint activity that creates bonds, contrives consensus, and instructs the initiates in future responsibility.

ASSEMBLING YOUTHS

At the beginnings of a great Maya cycle, in 3114 BC, the Classic Maya believed the gods had been gathered (*tz'ahkaj*). Not willy-nilly, but in ordered rows. Two vessels from about AD 760, both belonging to youths, display the event. Gods in submissive postures sit in two lines. From his throne room, an elderly god, possessor of great wealth, a trader, addresses them. Presumably he commanded their presence. Dark backgrounds on both vases accentuate the predawn time, with brightness to come: the place is *k'inchil,* the essence of strong sun. It happens that humans also gathered in the same act of "ordering." On a pot at the Denver Art Museum, taken from the area of Río Azul, Guatemala, a seated lord collects around him a refined crowd (fig. 58). Partly hidden behind a curtain are two women, one called Ix Kanek', Lady Sky Star. They sit on a mat extending across a palatial platform. On the farthest side, still on the mat, are two subordinate lords, but not that lowly: sitting front and center is the "head lord," *ba ajaw,* first among princes at the court. The lord in the center, owner of the pot, has all he needs. There is a chocolate pot with a peaked cover pointing up the part of text referring to such vessels, an obsidian mirror for self-display, and, in his hand, a bouquet of flowers.[35]

Just behind, in a position of great prestige, sit four men. Like the main lord, the first sniffs at a bouquet, but the sense is of grouped, nearly equivalent men. The glyphs, while incompletely deciphered, refer to a joint plurality of four. The cluster of men is not

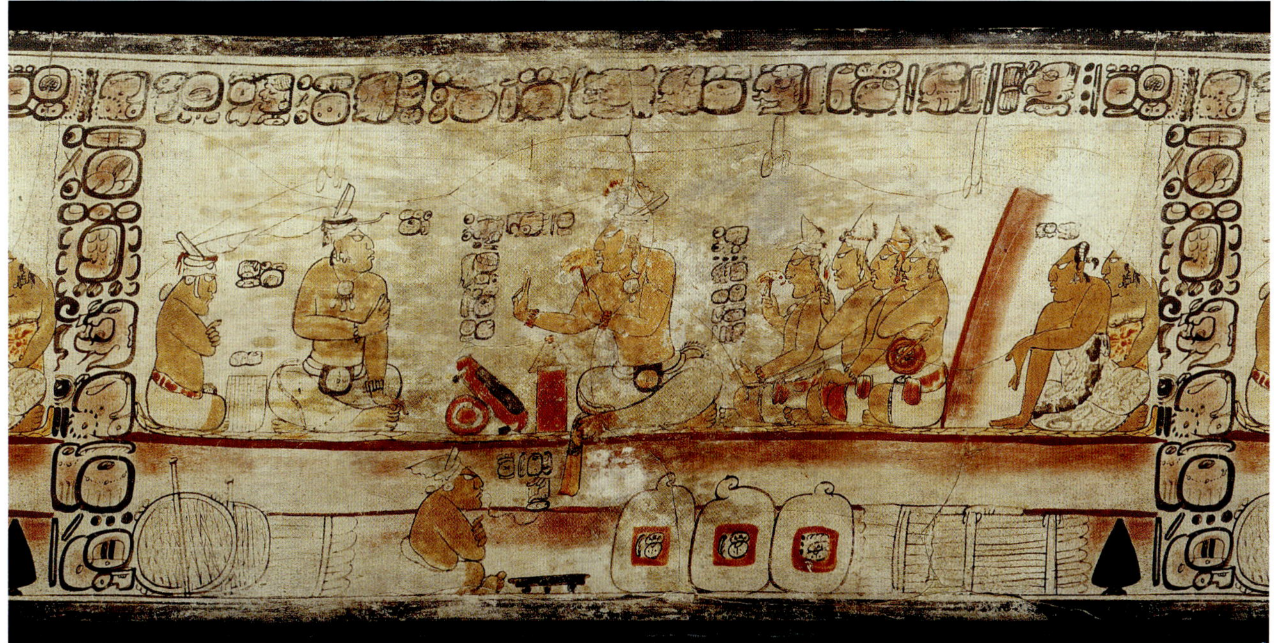

Río Azul vessel, AD 775. Poly-chrome ceramic, 11¼ × 6 in. (28.7 × 15.2 cm). Denver Art Museum, #2003.1. Photograph by Justin Kerr (K2914).

distinguished individually, yet they sit by the principal figure on the pot. Below, by heaps of wealth, bundles of beans and tribute mantles of plain cotton, sits the lone commentator. Possibly a dwarf—he is stunted, his back hunched—he alone speaks, saying *tz'akbaj keleem*, "the young man (*keleem*)" or "young men are placed in order."[36] *Tz'akbaj* is an unusual expression, a verb grafting a term for "order" with a suffix causing such action to take place. There is an alternative view of the phrase. The youths may be engaged in reflexive activity, ordering "themselves," *ba.* Whatever the intent, a self-organized act or not, the young men are assembled, and to what purpose remains unclear. The owner of the pot is the *kiit*—possibly the reverential term for "father"—of a ruler of Río Azul; the owner is also described as a kind of god, *k'uh,* most atypical for a living male. An unusual sign attached to his glyph for "portrait," *baah,* leads to the suspicion that he may no longer be alive (elsewhere, that sign serves to indicate an impersonation of deities). The scene may retrieve an event long gone.

A glimmer of explanation for such opaque events comes from another gathering of young men. Pieced together by David Stuart, the image is largely ruined, only a vestige left on the wall of Temple XVIII at Palenque (fig. 59).[37] But its message can be recovered from the fragmented, stucco figures; explanatory glyphs file neatly to the side. The time: in the past but vignetting the assembly of brothers, all sons of the renowned king Pakal, on January 27, AD 679. The older lord has only a few years remaining. Perhaps some premonition led to the gathering. In rare first-person reference, the king comments on "your heart" or "hearts" and "your placing in order." Two of the brothers would rule, the third went on to sire future kings. Crumbling from the walls of the temple then are retrospective claims

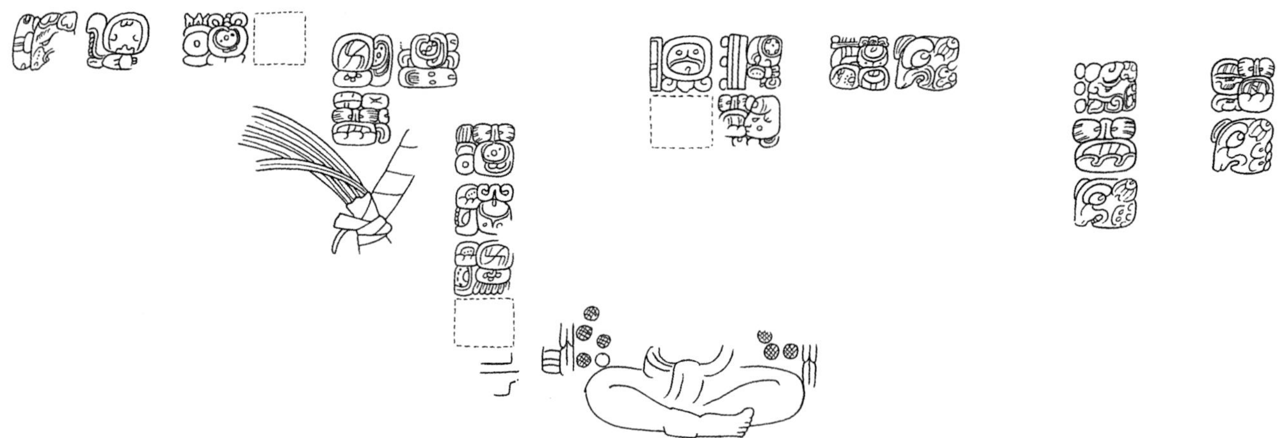

Gathering of princes, Temple XVIII, Palenque, Mexico. Stucco sculpture, showing events on Jan. 27, AD 679.

that Pakal had laid out the succession and that the arrangement enjoyed clear consensus among the heirs. Whether that was so cannot be proved, but it meant much to the grandson of Pakal, who probably commissioned the image. Offspring of the third brother, a lord who never ruled, he needed a stable claim to ascend the throne. The stuccoes, themselves fragile, perhaps replacing earlier works, offered precisely that evidence. At Palenque, glyphs might be popped off, alternative accounts devised, and new signs applied on another slurry of plaster. (Their detachability has, in fact, proved a temptation to past visitors; many such glyphs occur in collections elsewhere.[38])

To gather young men together implies a purpose—to consult, advise, even to task. It is also an invitation to joint adventure. Several pots make no open mention of youths, but the men are all young, serried in dance, setting off to war, returning with a harvest of captives. The scenes indicate what strong men are good for: assault, mutual help, and coordinated attacks going after human and animal prey. The weapons for hunting and warfare were much the same, aside from the blowguns used for birds. One bowl from the early seventh century AD—it is by the same hand as the *yax ch'ahb* vessels discussed before and most likely is from near Zapote Bobal, Guatemala—runs across the gamut of preparation (fig. 60). There is painting of the body with camouflage or odor-disguising ointment, a dark hand print here and there. Preparation blurs into results. Delicious little mammals, including an armadillo, are now in hand, along with a deer before and after butchering. Conches may confuse prey but also signal to other hunters in deep bush. A few hunters seem inept: one has dropped his bundle of spear throwers, to be poked at from behind. On other vases, the warriors return en masse from successful battle, a stripped captive in front of them. Yet the scenes come close to dance. Is the action an actual return to home with human spoils or a restaged version of it?[39]

Choosing between those options may misread Maya behavior. Formal movement of any sort could be as stylized as choreography. If young men went forth to hunt and battle,

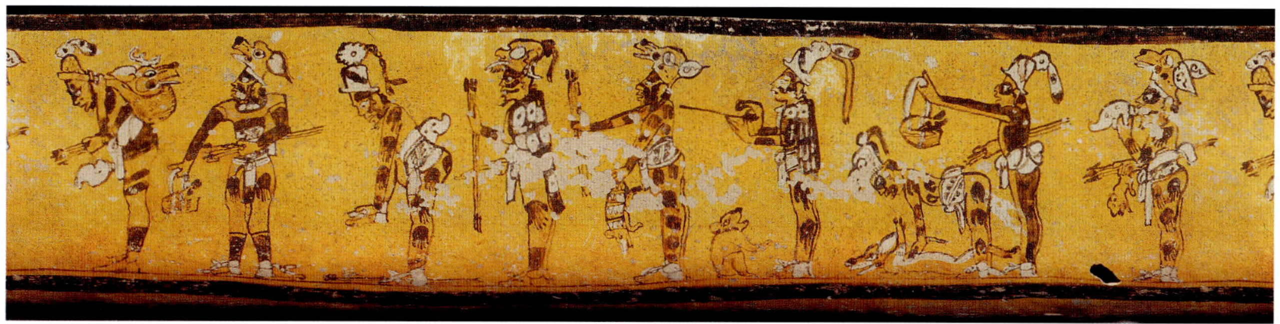

some might not have returned, or, as a set, others might have found their way into royal tombs as offerings—this was alluded to before, but there is a telling detail worth discussing. At Piedras Negras, royal tombs contain youths, including Burial 5, the interment of the ruler Yo'nal Ahk, and Burial 13, the tomb of his successor, Itzam K'an Ahk.[40] This contrasts with dynasties at Tikal and El Zotz, where such eternal companions tended to be infants or young children. A single youth is anomalous. In life and sacrificial death, their more usual condition was in groups, with the possibility that the number of such sacrifices corresponded to living family members.

The grouped nature of young men united in action comes to the fore in scenes with explicit mention of *ch'ok.* No guessing here: other scenes may show young men, but without glyphs their age must be inferred. From the barrel shape and handling of figures, both vases date to the final years of the Late Classic period, around AD 800. The first, at the Peabody Museum of Natural History at Yale University, displays a surface pockmarked by water damage. Enough remains of the scene to see a scene of ballplay. The opposed arrangement of three kneeling figures and three standing, a large ball in between, suggests an electric moment, perhaps at the beginning of play—everyone moving into position—or at its conclusion. Playing trumpets, holding conches, and waving fans is an apparent support staff, all labeled as *ch'ok.* The main players lack this title, suggesting a slightly older age. The youths are there to help and see, later to emulate, and that exposure to service explains the lone *ch'ok* in certain scenes, lugging in tribute for the ruler. The second pot, probably from the area of El Señor del Peten, in the Mexican state of Quintana Roo, may mix ages—most *ch'ok* did not associate exclusively with their own. But the youth leads a set of dancers with fans and weapons, many bearing a title, *lakam,* perhaps "banner," associated with subordinate lords. To walk first shows great prestige.[41]

RETURN TO THE HOUSES OF WEEPING

A setting apart for rites of passage could be notional. A celebrant may not need to visit some distant place, although authoritative control of the young becomes far easier, and the experience better managed and staged, by using special locations. Some surroundings are habitual, of daily use, prominent architecturally at the center of communities; others involve journeys to wild and unpredictable places. Away from dynastic protection, closer to snakes and beasts, these involve literal danger, but they also echo the unsettled state of liminal rites. In caves especially, day may seem like night, acoustics operate differently. Disorientation is common; as noted by many experiments, time or an integrated sense of the body begins to unmoor for most visitors. The mind plays tricks, optical effects occur, and the brain may "see" in ways unmediated by the eyes.[42]

Habitual locations for mature and young men are widely attested in history and ethnography—some of these were reviewed in the first chapter. The global evidence shows unsurprising diversity, and the meaning and use of the men's buildings seemed to have varied greatly. Some buildings were simply convenient places to gather, loaned by a member of the community; others could be regarded more abstractly, as "wombs" for re-creating males in adult form. Such sexual symmetry, a forced parallel between female menstruation and penile bloodletting, highlights some beliefs in New Guinea, along with segregation by gender, loosening of ties to mothers, and strengthening of bonds to men.[43] Indeed, the evidence from New Guinea is so rich, and the ethnography so perceptive, that its example can exert too strong and tempting an influence: the anthropologists Maurice Godelier and Gilbert Herdt write vividly of its isolation of boys from women, its centrality in social life during initiation, and the caring bonds between older and younger men—relations between older men and young lovers in classical Greece arise as obvious parallels. Then, suffusing the whole, is that hothouse sexuality so familiar from these accounts. A perceived build-up of sperm must be released by fellatio with other men. Men must be "made" outside of women's wombs, but by masculine efforts, as supervised by a "master of the first initiation ceremonies." Only then do young men re-enter a two-sexed world.

Among the Bororo of Brazil, men's houses lay at the center of settlements, embodying the "strength and virility" of a community, served by female "associates" who satisfied the sexual needs of "young unmarried initiated men." For the Igorot of the Philippines, a young men's sleeping house operated as a martial unit and training area for warriors, a place of teaching and punishment too. From it might come, every now and then, a work group under the control of adult males. In southern China, comparable buildings housed unmarried male youths of extended families—there might be several in a community— along with men whose wives were pregnant and thus prohibited from intercourse.[44]

In short, they were places where males reconfigured their relations to females, for a variety of reasons. The overt aim was to segregate the sexes, develop bonds within the families, provide energetic labor for family projects, and house itinerants such as traders. By the exclusion of perceived "misfits," it denied social participation to males who seemed unreliable or unproductive. Secrecy clouded the overall process.[45] Knowing things that others did not helped to define groups. As the sociologist Georg Simmel noted long ago, the paradox of secrecy is that it often operates best when others know that it exists but can find no way to pry open that store of information. Indeed the aim may have been mixed: to foster cooperation *and* competitive aggression. The operative term is "homosocial," a useful descriptive for a place in which people of the same gender meet or live; their gender counterparts are discouraged from entering. From Ireland or Andalusia, this might be a pub or bar, the domain of males, or, in rural America, a room set aside, even if only temporarily, for a women's quilting bee.[46]

In ancient Central America and Mexico, the gathering of men and youths in buildings or spaces set aside for that purpose is well attested in documentary sources, though less so in concrete examples. One report on the ancient Zapotec of Oaxaca, Mexico, assigns a central importance to men's houses. The claim is functional and evolutionary: village societies, not yet coalesced into cities, used such places as areas for competition over prestige and influence. The actual evidence is tenuous, however, consisting of "non-residential architecture" used by a hypothetical group of "full initiates . . . a subgroup of the men in the village." The overt inspiration appears to be the anthropology of New Guinea, the exemplary region in archaeological theory for societies of this sort.[47] That information is transposed to early settled life in Oaxaca, Mexico, yet with no mention of such structures for later periods. Presumably, according to such models, places for homosocial interaction were restricted to a societal type that existed before, and only before, the advent of pronounced and heritable hierarchy.

This cannot be so. Later periods provide the richest information, with increased likelihood that age grades and homosocial buildings connected to age grades were common features in Mesoamerican societies, at many levels of political organization. A key resource is the Florentine Codex compiled by Bernardino de Sahagún and his assistants in sixteenth-century central Mexico. This manuscript, an encyclopedic description of the Aztecs, an imperial group that extended into much of Mesoamerica, identifies houses in which the young were "trained and reared." Chapter 1 discussed these matters at length. The houses were known in part as *tēlpōchcalli*, "house of youth." Dedicated to duty but also to diversion, the *tēlpōchcalli* was a building where youths swept the house, tended fires, and, at night, sang, danced, and conversed. Sleeping together, youths were governed by a "master of youths" or "elder brother," a *tiāchcāuh*, who spoke for and disciplined his companions. The severity of punishment for excess and youthful fun was, as noted before, almost shocking, as it was for earlier ages.[48] In a dismaying page from the Codex Mendoza, an early colonial book, children were held over smoking fires full of chili peppers, their eyes gushing with tears. Parents pierced young wrists and bodies with maguey spines or struck their offspring with sticks. These abuses seem only to have taken place at 9 years of age, when, for the Aztec, boys and girls presumably achieved some measure of responsible decision making. Before, there were threats, and afterward the pain began, through increasingly brutal punishments and at a time according roughly with that for the *yax ch'ahb* of Classic Maya princes. In contrast, Maya ethnography suggests that indulgence in drink was, for the young, encouraged at certain times. The Dominican friar,

Diego Durán, describes the seclusion in Aztec places, the mortifications, the "praiseworthy exercises and customs," along with corresponding houses for women. Reverence to elders and service to lords, learning to be "at ease among them and charming in their presence," were central to such training, as well as song, dance, the arts of war, and "a thousand other refinements." Durán insists, however, that classes mixed in the *tēlpōchcalli,* although the sons of lords and rulers were "more highly respected and carefully attended."[49]

Aztec evidence needs repeating because it comes close to Maya practice. In the early historic period, centuries after the Classic period, the Maya showed ample interest in age grades and buildings of a homosocial nature. The highlands of colonial Guatemala had specialized houses where boys slept, issuing from time to time to run errands for priests.[50] For the period just before and during the conquest, Bartolomé de las Casas and others report on comparable "long houses" where young men lived near temples—this was touched on at the beginning of chapter 2. In general, this service seems to have been for a specified time, with the intent of introducing youth to civic duties and educating them under the supervision of older youth or priests. The offspring of priests, rulers, and scribes were targeted in particular, for training that would stand them in good stead when they inherited their father's offices and tasks. Such service and education took place over a number of years, in some cases delaying marriage.

Yet the buildings allotted to youths appear to have had varied functions: as barracks for guards or warriors; storerooms for sacred objects, arms, and tribute; and lodgings for merchants or other visitors. This was exactly the observation made by Charles Cheek and Mary Spink for their excavations at Copan, Honduras. In some examples the residences were described as little more than doorways or alcoves. This was where "young lords eight years and older slept" while they received instruction in ritual and maintained the fires of temple braziers. Such buildings could function as places where men of all ages retreated for periods of celibacy, especially when "participating in religious activities" or, as for the colonial Ch'olti', when their wives became pregnant. Among the Aztec, young women also received training in a special "seminary." The Maya lowlands record similar notices of homosocial buildings during the time of weak and erratic Spanish control over the region. One soldier, Nicolás de Valenzuela, noted that the chief settlement of the Ch'olti' Maya, Sakbalam, had three main buildings, including a "house of idols" and others for women and men, respectively, all oriented around a central plaza. At Classic-period Yaxchilan, two buildings mentioned before, Structures 21 and 23, are relevant. In their imagery and texts, they are strongly homosocial but in this case for royal ladies. Another must have been a chamber in a palace at Xcalumkin, Campeche, Mexico. The southern edge of a building yielded three texts, all of which record the names of women, all spouses of the king. In fact, Jamb 9 specifies four such queens, a decisive piece of evidence, if one were needed, for Maya polygamy (fig. 61). (Other buildings nearby highlight the pairing of ruler and son, so the homosocial spaces concerned men as well.) One deceased royal, the "Red Queen" of Palenque—so-named for her covering of cinnabar—even went to the afterlife with

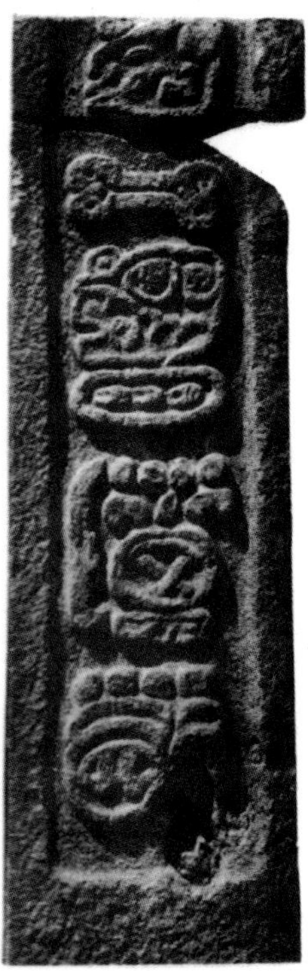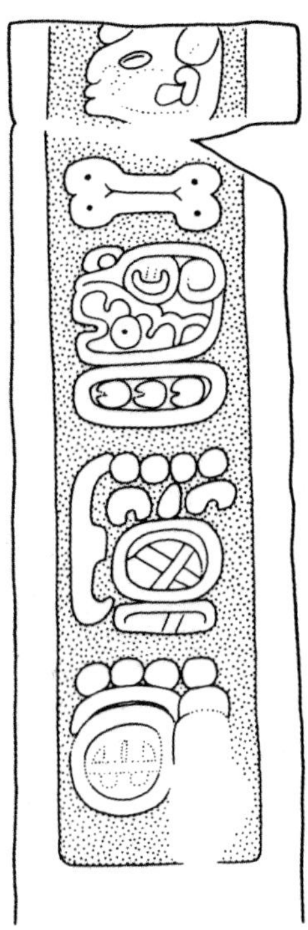

a female attendant.[51] On one point the early colonial documents are clear. Houses for unmarried men were widespread, from Yucatan to the base of the peninsula, and over to the multilingual port of Xicalango near the Laguna de los Términos in Mexico.[52] What appears to be missing is something like the Inka *aqllawasi,* a house of "chosen women" whose tasks included weaving and brewing.[53]

Las Casas deplored the supposed homosexual practices in such buildings. He saw a subversion of actual native morality: "They hold that sodomy is a great sin … and commonly the fathers despise it and prohibit it for their sons, but when they are instructed in religion they are ordered to sleep in the temples, where the older boys corrupt the children in this vice, and after they come out of there, they have bad habits and it is difficult to free them from this vice." This is implausible. If the practice were as abhorred yet frequent as Las Casas claimed, there would be little incentive for the continued existence of such houses. There is a more likely alternative: for colonial Maya, youth may have been a time of license and experimentation, of amity expressed physically and vice versa, or of more abstruse concepts involving the nature of emerging sexuality in males. For some, homosexuality was, of course, a lifelong orientation or entailed the occasional dalliance among adults—actual behavior of this sort is impossible to document, only the ways it was understood culturally. Las Casas also referred to "circumcision" in young men's houses, which the boys performed on each other. This may refer to penile bloodletting, well documented among ancient and historic Maya peoples.[54]

The theme of homosexuality is repeated in descriptions of seventeenth-century practices of the Itzaj Maya, who flourished as an independent force in northern Guatemala well into the colonial period. The main Itzaj settlement was said to contain *casas comunes nefandas apretiladas*, "abominable communal houses with railings around them," perhaps referring to open structures. Breezes and light might enter over low walls of masonry or wattle and daub. One Spanish account insists that the walls were covered with symbols or hieroglyphs and "sexual imagery," and that the role of the youth was to prepare food for Maya priests and to have sex with them. Thus: "They had a walled-around large house of very decorous construction solely for the habitation of acquiescents, into which entered all of those who wished to have their sodomitic copulations, especially those who are very young, so that they could learn there, these ministers of the Demon wearing women's skirts and occupying themselves only in making bread for the priests and in their obscenities."[55] To the north, in Yucatan, Bishop Landa comments on houses for "boys of marriageable age.... In each town [they had] a large house, whitened with lime, open on all sides, where the young men came together for their amusements ... [and where] they all slept together ... until they married." Aside from sexual (mis)adventures, as perceived through Spanish filters, those amusements included games of chance, ballplay, and, as documented in 1543 among Q'eqchi' of Verapaz, Guatemala, dances that drew on ingenious stagecraft, with false doors, masks and makeup, burning of fake trees to the accompaniment of trumpets, and percussion with shells and turtle carapaces.[56]

The age when youths first entered such houses, and the ages associated with them, may have been linked to notional puberty. This is unclear in the documents. At the least there was a need for instruction and guidance. Young males on the edge of puberty called for special management. On the whole, departure from the age grade was occasioned by marriage. According to Las Casas, "some fathers are very anxious to marry their sons as rapidly as they can in order to separate them from such corruption [the sodomy mentioned before], although they marry youths against their will and by force; but they have the custom never to marry their sons until they are 30 or more years of age, because the old men say that in the times that boys engender and girls give birth, the end of the world is near." However, the colonial Poqomam Maya probably determined age of marriage by class or social station, or could violate such mores through illicit, clandestine marriage. This contrasts with what is known of parts of colonial Yucatan, where boys might marry at 10 or 12 and have sexual relations with women at an age earlier than Spanish custom. A closer analogy exists with colonial Nahuatl-speaking groups of central Mexico. Young men about to marry were exhorted to leave behind the "misbehavior of youth—drunkenness, laughter, and joking." Some Maya youth did not make it to this stage. They were, as among the Itzaj and Yukateko Maya of the sixteenth and seventeenth centuries, a preferred item of sacrifice. The occupants of Classic Maya tombs hint at deep roots to this practice.[57]

Similar themes run throughout the colonial or ethnographic sources. Frequently, they form part of Roman Catholic associations, many of which blend with features of far greater age. In these sodalities, "minimal public validation of manhood" takes place, along with, in many cases, a physical separation from other ages and close attendance by an older male. In Chichastenango, Guatemala, service could be intermittent. Some young men worked only one week out of four, if in uncomfortable conditions. Not surprisingly, that kind of nuisance and bother led to disruptions. Anxious about expense and effort, some decided not to join or to drop out at a particular level. But good things came to those who kept at it. Courtship and marriage ensued with successful completion of service, a celebration often lubricated by final bouts of drinking.[58]

Among recent Maya, age grades are described as "seats" or "benches" of particular duties to the community. The grades correspond to well-defined roles, ties to particular buildings, and well-articulated links between various age grades. Some young males are even elected to positions of authority within their cohort. Indeed, there are usually two sets of youth: those just emerging from childhood, ready for limited service, and an older set, not yet married, with the right to dance and sing in public. The latter group could perform more onerous or challenging duties. The division between younger and older youth resonates with the Classic Maya evidence, which seems to distinguish between *ch'ok* and *chak ch'ok*. Among more recent Maya, marriage validates adult status. To the Tzeltal, who live in Chiapas, Mexico, males who did not marry are thought to be "shirking adult responsibility" through a "lack of independence." The placement and seating of the age grades are elaborated to a fine degree. To be a "youth" is, ideally, to form part of a larger group of finite duration but intense interaction. It is a time to obey esteemed members of their cohort as well as men at higher levels of age and authority. The rites of youth remind the young that older men are in charge. Punishments and fines, some levied by the cohort itself, await the disobedient. Indeed, psychological studies in Highland Guatemala reinforce the crucial role of such lateral, age-grade socialization.[59] Nonetheless, skills of varying sorts were transmitted effectively from older to younger generations without formal instruction or self-conscious parenting.[60] Youths tended to work alongside adults in a gradual escalation of responsibility.

For Mam Maya of the 1970s and 1980s, the first actual service by young males began at age 19 or so. The goal was to establish a man in society and delimit a period of licit drinking and carousing with age-mates of the same gender. Some kinds of service involved the possibility of "opting out," electing not to proceed to higher duties. Competence and attitude counted, too. Not everyone was worthy. Farther west, among the Tzotzil of the 1950s, the status of being a youth, *kerem*—the same term, allowing for a sound change, that is attested in the hieroglyphs—ended between 15 and 20, when marriage took place. The houses of young men, the taming or virile places, are seldom well described by ethnographers. There is one notable exception, that of "bachelor houses" or *posadas* or "gangs" around Lake Atitlan in Highland Guatemala.[61] A boy entered such a *posada* between about 12 and 15; he slept there but left during the day, staying until marriage at 18 to 30 years of age. Membership was fairly constant when the *posadas* were documented in the early 1950s. The building itself was usually loaned by an elderly widower. An old man offered space to young men, in yet another bond between youths and the elderly.

For the Maya, past and present, certain elements bear repeating. A rough checklist includes: the physical segregation of youths; the presence of stern, adult guidance that could approve occasional excess; the imparting of skills, some intellectual, some robustly athletic; more than a hint of homoeroticism and same-sex affection; concern with the ability to procreate, but only after ritual preparation; a harnessing, enhancing, at times neutralizing of the energies tied to male youth; the use of youthful labor for general benefit; and mention of homosocial places and shared journeys, as in the movement of young men to the court of Calakmul. This was not solely a feature of village life, a quirky rung on the evolutionary ladder from small-scale to more complex societies. Class and rank organized the formation of young men—a likely tack also among the courtly societies of the Classic Maya. Houses for women existed as well but were more shadowy, less to the forefront in surviving information.

INDECOROUS DECORUM

The Classic Maya probably had places for making men. In those buildings and courtyards, *ch'ok* were housed, shaped, and "grown." Colonial accounts point to deeper origins. But how deep can we go? Parts of the royal palace at Tikal have been identified as young men's houses, yet they have no imagery or artifacts to confirm or disprove that claim. It remains a guess. Columned halls at Classic sites such as Piedras Negras, Guatemala, and Blue Creek, Belize, have been likened to the open structures of the Itzaj—recall their "abominable communal houses." Again, the problem is thin evidence. Other dwellings of young men have been identified at Copan, in the northeast corner of the Main Group, another in the western building of Plaza A of 9N-8. The argument here is a bit stronger: the former contains a sweatbath and a set of dance masks, the latter ballgame equipment, all suitable for vigorous young men. Yet we know that older men bathed and played ballgames. In fact, the excavators, Cheek and Spink, perceive that we may be drawing an unnecessary distinction between a school for young men, a house for single men, and a man's house. They cannot choose between them, nor should they. Building function was likely to have been flexible. Cheek and Spink show less caution, however, in interpreting this or that chamber. One room belonged to a "priest-teacher," they say. In another slept "students" or "isolated men"; a final room was dedicated to "ritual purification."[62]

Places for young men may plausibly include the buildings associated with giant carvings of phalli, a noteworthy feature already discussed. Clustered mostly in the northern part of the Yucatan peninsula, their original locations can be difficult to reconstruct, which archaeologist Traci Ardren has pointed out. As mentioned before, large stone phalli frequently get hustled out of view by prudish explorers or later custodians of sites. Over 140 such phalli are known, some near caves or close to unexcavated buildings.

There is even a word for them in Yukateko Maya, *xkeptunich.* But only twenty-six appear to be in original position. The ruins of Oxkintok has one carving set into a stair, and at Huntichmul, Kiuic, K'uxub, and Sayil they occur in courtyards. They could not have rested on soil but were probably fixed or mortised into small platforms or small buildings—Structure 6E5 at Chichen Itza, Mexico, is one such example.[63] The question is whether the few buildings or platforms tied to sculpted phalli were houses or the places where adults transformed young men into mature ones. The divine associations of phalli cast doubt on that view.

A hieroglyphic throne in Structure 10K-4 at Copan provides a more personal association. It identifies the owner as a youth called "the person of the road-house" (*aj-bih-naah*), probably in reference to a Maya street or linear pathway nearby. Yet this is no house for groups; the sole possessor is a high-ranking young lord. Another example is probably also from Copan (fig. 62). On display in the Museo Popol Vuh in Guatemala City, it is said to come from the Río Polochic area of Guatemala, some 75 km from Copan. The stone and style make that unlikely, but the original find spot will only be known when more like it are discovered in place. There are good hopes for this, as the carving is a roof ornament—*almena* in Spanish—taking the form of a bat with its wings spread wide, and the text on the back, running backward in unorthodox layout but with perfectly legible glyphs, tells us the stone, a *tuun,* was raised up as a part of a set. In another unusual touch, the verb in the inscription is in plural form, implying an array of *almena* of comparable design, and these are the stones that will clinch the identity of the building from which the bat came.[64] The stones belonged to a "great youth," and the structure itself may have been his or the carvings his handiwork. Yet possessive phrases of this sort can be ambiguous. By another view, the great youth commissioned the pieces or wielded the chisel to make them. Several carvers are known to have been youths, probably in the middle of apprenticeships to older, more experienced sculptors.

The best candidates are not so much architecturally plausible or endowed with stray references to single youths. The first may occur at San Bartolo, in the room with Preclassic murals (c. 100 BC), low doorways, and almost didactic scenes of key mythic events, a room of "mysteries" for initiates, sequestered in an unusual location at the back of a temple (fig. 63). The images slope toward the viewer, and an instructor could point to, dilate on, any scene. A lintel from the Early Classic Structure 22 at Yaxchilan may indicate that it also was such a building.[65] A later text on the structure shows that it was built in AD 454 by the seventh king of the city. Nearly 300 years later, an upstart ruler of the city renovated it. One of the older lintels lists, for unclear reasons, a set of at least three, maybe four youths. Was this building, central to the city core, used in part by young men?

Another example is House C at Palenque, known to date to the time of Pakal the Great because of textual clues, and probably dedicated in AD 661 (fig. 64). The courtyard to the west of the building displays a series of stones that refer to various youths, in statements that still contain difficult phrases. Some names are baffling: the "elder brother of

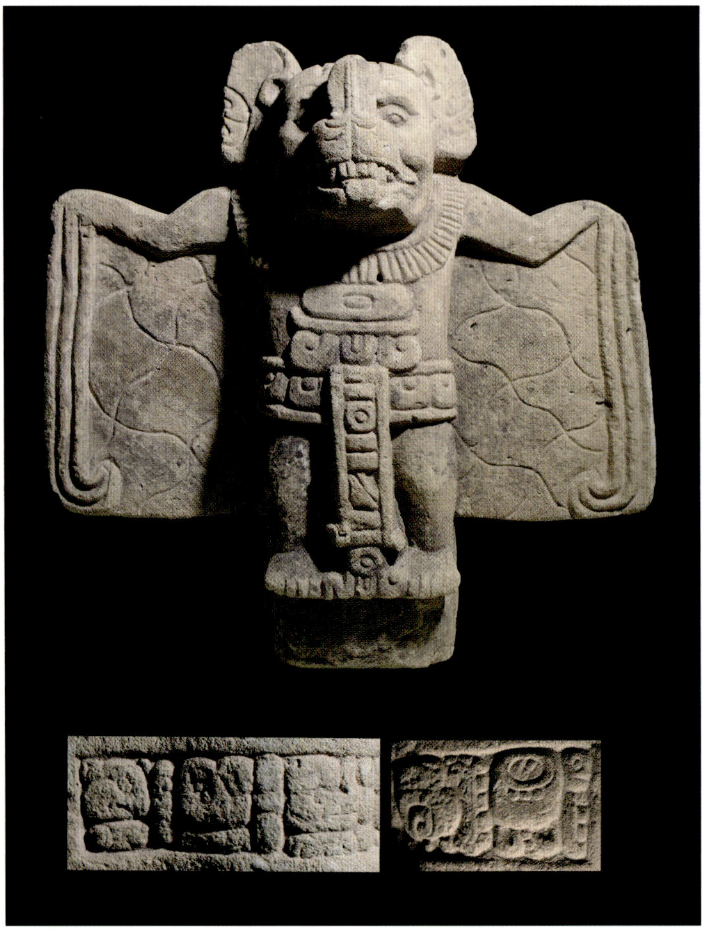

the obsidian," *sakuun taaj,* another possibly the "summoned god," *pehk-k'uh.*[66] The lead text refers explicitly to the death or "road-entering" of a lord from the site of Pomona, Tabasco. This was the seat of a dynasty intermittently under the thumb of Palenque, sometimes violently so. The mention of young men suggests that House C was a young men's house. Yet the foreign references give pause, as they probably refer to visitors or captives. Without exception, the youths appear to have come from the site of Santa Elena, Mexico, often an antagonist of the Palenque dynasty. Conceivably, the building at Palenque was a place for "pages" or thinly disguised hostages, perhaps even a special gathering point for the display of captured youths. The positioning of the glyphic panels is regular, their height approximating human stature. This suggests that they marked the orderly place-ment of young men or stood as proxies or memorials for them. Indeed, Simon Martin suggests that the panels once accompanied long-removed sculptures, leaving notable gaps where carved figures had once occurred.

The most secure young men's house has no texts, but it displays a set of rele-vant panels. This is a building at Rancho San Diego, Yucatan, from the later years of the

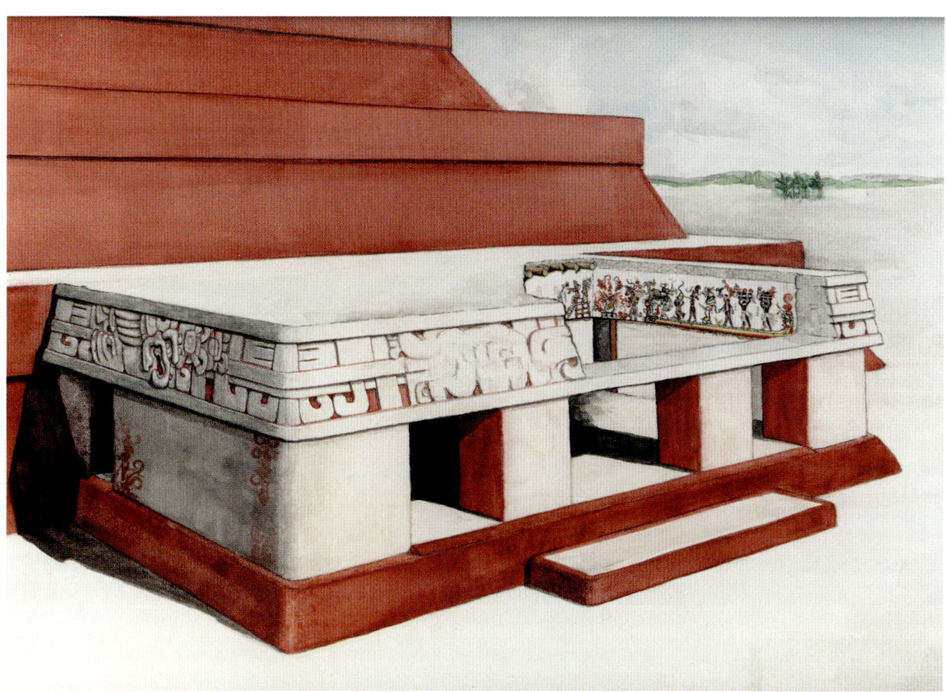

FIGURE 63

Las Pinturas, Sub-1A chamber,
Guatemala, c. 100 BC. Rendering
by Heather Hurst.

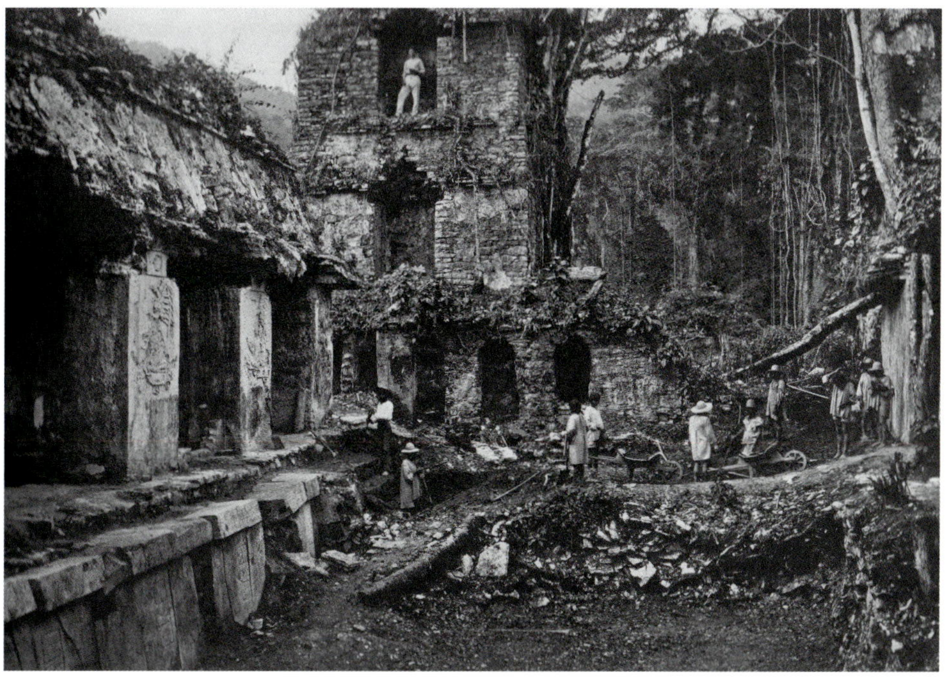

FIGURE 64

House C, Palenque, Mexico, dedicated Dec. 22, AD 661. Photograph
by Alfred P. Maudslay, 1890.

Classic period (fig. 65). The archaeologist Alfredo Barrera Rubio and iconographer Karl Taube linked a set of panels in the Barbachano collection in Mérida, Yucatan, with closely similar sculptures at Rancho San Diego itself, showing that these came from a rectangular structure on an elevated platform. The scenes on these panels, 13 in total, show scenes of drunkenness, enema insertion, revelry, stunned inebriation, dancing, homoerotic grappling—in short, many of the features attributed in historic accounts to Maya young men's houses. The Rancho San Diego find remains the most likely target for determining the material expression of a young men's house. Two scenes on Maya bowls highlight such binges, some perhaps intended to be amusing.[67] Both date to the mid-seventh century AD and probably come from northern Guatemala. The first, featured in chapter 1, highlights a distinction between drunken youths and supervisors, clearly sober, hands extended in restraining action or remonstrance; meanwhile, a young man vomits, another dips indecorously into a pulque vessel. Then, a messy fight, no holds barred, between two youths: a leg thrusts up to kick a face, hands yank hair, and noses gush with blood. Red scarves encircle the neck. The postures are highly unseemly for Classic nobles, nearly ridiculous or laughable. One of the supervisors is bearded, as older males might be in Maya imagery. The other vase has a more elegant rim-band text (fig. 66). A chocolate pot, it names an owner who appears to be the grandson, *mam,* of another person mentioned at the end of the text. The mayhem below is less violent than in the other vessel, but the group is larger, the drunkenness just as obvious. Pulque vessels are brought to another all-male group; the drink steeps, stuffed with maguey leaves, soon ready for drinking. Wild, careening dances, unsteady on the feet, appear twice on the pot, and a distinctive party "bib," perhaps of cotton, entwines the necks of two youths (the other bowl shows the same bib on one figure with hand in the pulque pot).

The glyphs are legible, but difficult to parse. The second vase, although itself used for chocolate, shows repeated *chi,* "pulque," glyphs on vases and in the text. The vessel recording youthful inebriation was not, it seems, used for stupefaction—it records the unusual scene, but in retrospective commemoration, for more decorous consumption. The events had taken place before, the drinking involved other kinds of ceramics. *Ch'ok* and probably *keleem* appear as labels, proving the link to young men. There may even be a reference to someone with mead, *aj kab,* and perhaps the spinning of drunken men, **wi-IL-la** in glyphs. An intriguing element, on this and the first pot, is the presence of terms for "guardian," spelled in a variety of ways. The appearance of older, or at least more sober, males may explain that usage: they are the supervisors or more responsible youths in charge. On the chocolate vase, one of them speaks, a line snaking from his lips to a column of glyphs. The same glyphs appear on the other vase. Difficulty remains in interpreting the decipherment, but it may be an imperative form, a scolding of the drunken youth near each such figure.[68] The two pots provide no setting for the dissipation, only a ground line on which to situate the brawling, drinking, restraining figures. Yet the knowledgeable viewer may have placed them immediately, in a building like that at Rancho San Diego.

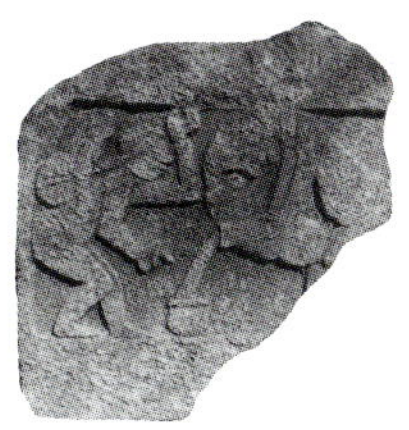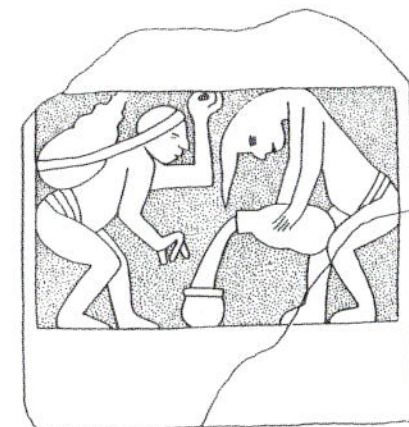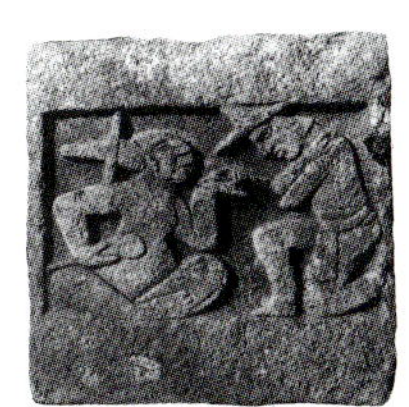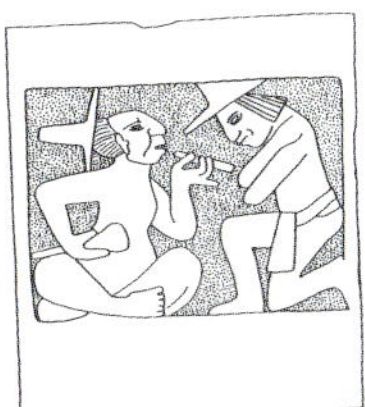

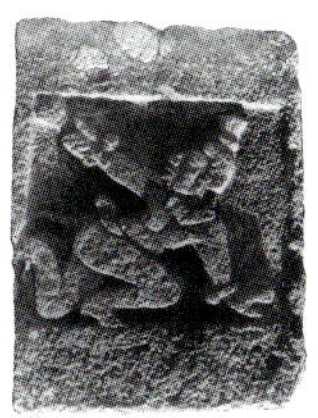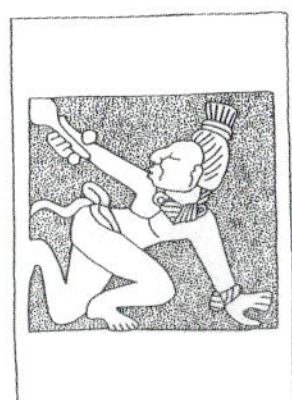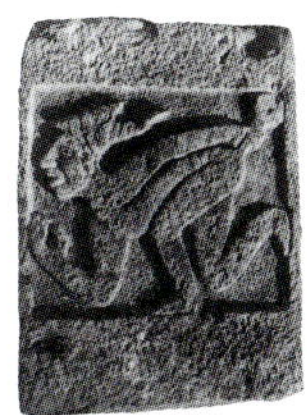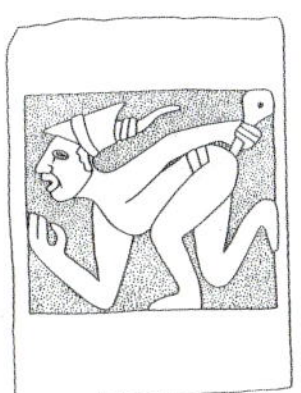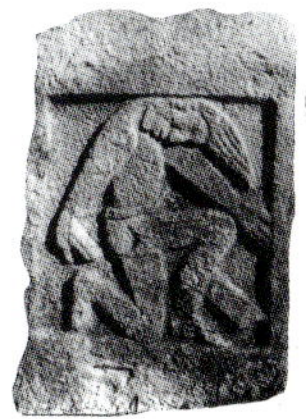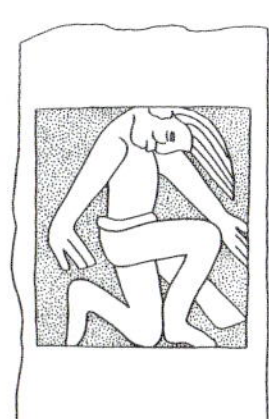

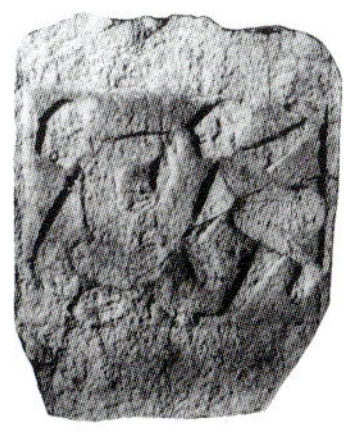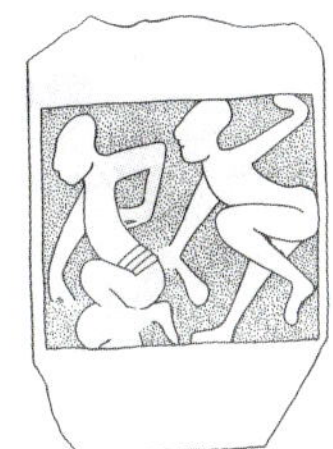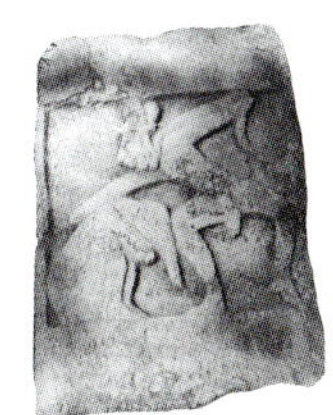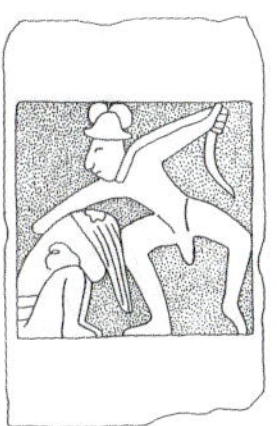

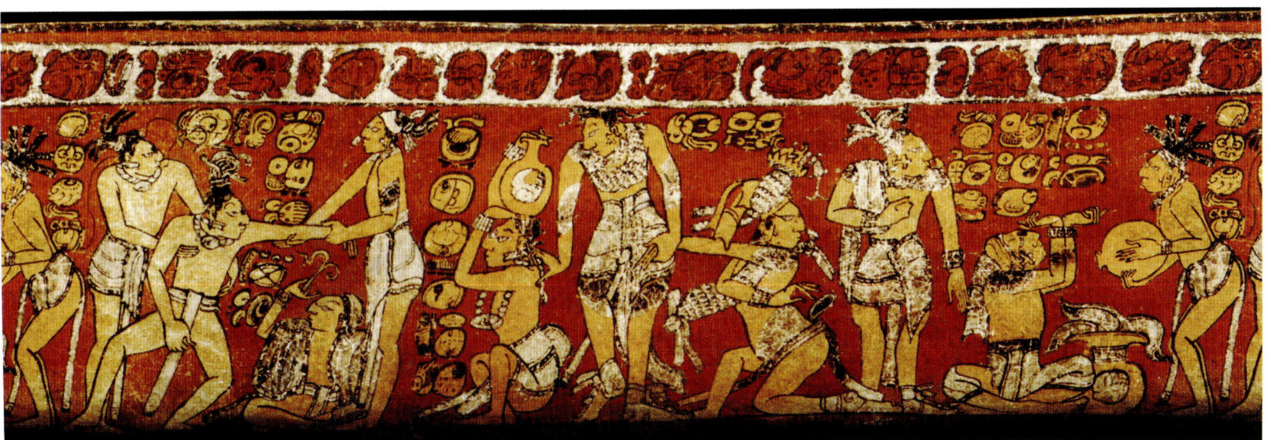

TOP **FIGURE 65**
Panels, Rancho San Diego, Mexico, c. AD 750. Photographs courtesy of Karl Herbert Mayer, drawings by Karl Taube.

BOTTOM **FIGURE 66**
Drunken scene with youths, c. AD 650. Polychrome ceramic. Museum of Fine Arts, Boston, #2003.775. Photograph by Justin Kerr (K1092).

The drinking will interest any reader familiar with present-day Maya. In certain villages of Chiapas, every male carries a bag with the essentials, including a bottle of cane liquor.[69] Most social encounters were sealed with drink, including every wheedling for favors. In one town, Zinacantan, young men were expected to drink more, emptying every round, while older men had to show some restraint.

A darker, less public place for young men takes us far to the south, to the cave of Naj Tunich on the border between Guatemala and Belize. A heartbreaking find, its nonpareil trove of texts and images, painted with highest skill on the cave walls, was partly destroyed by an irate guard in the 1980s. Fortunately, photos exist from prior to the damage. Maya caves doubtless had no one function or set of meanings; they were places of burial, ritual deposit, conduits to ancestors or telluric gods. At Santo Domingo, Guatemala, a text records the departure (*lok'oyi*) of the jaguarlike deity of the underworld sun from his home. A set of paintings in caves far distant from each other even shows the celebration by priests of an important calendrical ceremony on precisely the same date. But the Naj Tunich cave, studied by Andrea Stone and Barbara MacLeod, stands alone: it is exceptional for its abundance of texts and accompanying images.[70]

Two sets deserve special attention. After passing through the cave's majestic entrance, a visitor heads north, reaching a passage that zigzags to the north. This is the Western Passage. Twenty meters in, directly facing the visitor, is a more open chamber with an assemblage of texts and images that identify a variety of youths and show, for Maya art, extraordinary scenes: a floating penis, apparently with ejaculate, thrusts into the eroded midsection of a youth (fig. 67A). Another youth partly faces the viewer, an anomaly in itself, and appears to masturbate (fig. 67B). Close by is one of the few depictions of homosexuality in Maya art. An elderly male, his rump sagging, belly distended, clutches a young male, while his penis jams into the groin of the youth (fig. 67C). This is not a forced act, for the youth faces his older lover. The images seem even to be conventional types, or deities, not specific lords—a model for later visitors? The texts nearby, although still resistant to easy reading, refer repeatedly to youths, one of whom may be the painter of the texts, the son of a ruler. Farther down the Western Passage, after another zigzag, are other mentions of youths, including he who "sees the road, sees the night-soul," *il bih, il way.* A final cluster of youths are named in the North Passage, close to the turn off to the west. It records the "seeing" (*ilaj*) of a king, presumably a visionary experience, and attributes this painted text to his close relative, the prince whose name floats alone on the surface of the Western Passage. Another prince, from a different city, has his name nearby.

An earlier interpretation of the Upper Paleolithic cave art in France was inclined to see them as part of rites of passage for young men: they might stab at effigies of animals, leave handprints on walls, and delve into the sensory deprivation of caves.[71] That literature is vast but, because of the time and lack of texts, highly speculative. Naj Tunich differs fundamentally. Princes are named with great precision, their names

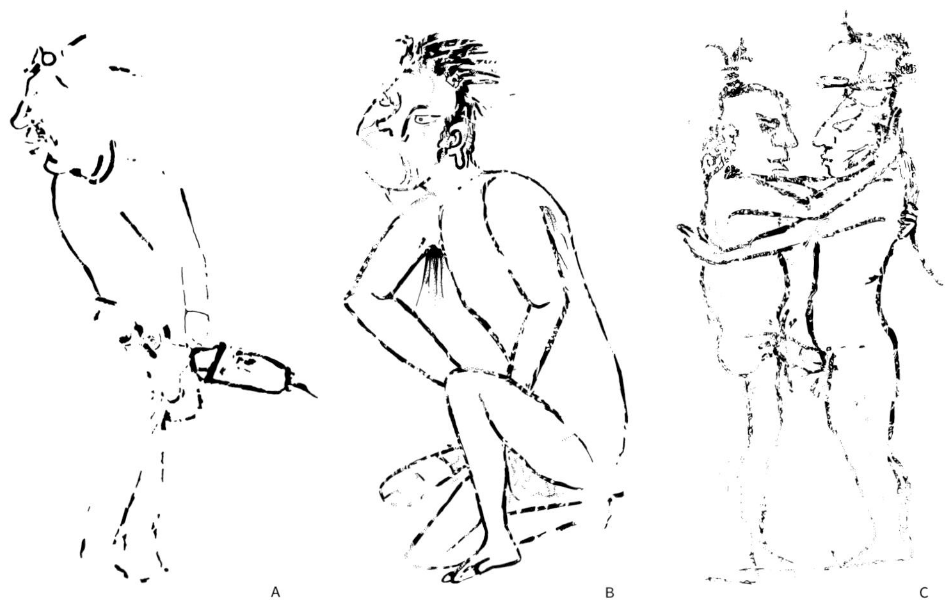

FIGURE 67

Young men at Naj Tunich, Guatemala, eighth century AD: A) ejaculating penis, Drawing 17, Western Passage; B) possible masturbation, Drawing 20, Western Passage; C) old man and youth in lovemaking, Drawing 18, Western Passage. Drawing by Andrea Stone, photograph by Chip Clark.

clustering in certain parts of the cave. One set collects, as nowhere else, highly erotic scenes and, in one secure instance, same-sex lovemaking. What may be the footprints of a youth, documented by the archaeologist James Brady, occur deep in the cave (fig. 68). They may even have been placed deliberately, with their neat edges and solid impressions. The events mentioned in the cave vary, but many dwell on acts of "arrival" (*huli*) and "seeing," suggesting both a place of pilgrimage—the diversity of royal titles implicates several cities—as well as profound visions. There is something else. Many of the dates in the cave, meticulously recorded by scribes of great accomplishment, accord with no known calendrical system. Their day and month signs are often incongruous. As a result, the cave texts seem to distort time, just as the winding passages and absolute darkness, alleviated only by flickering torches, affect the sense of space. That darkness may well have led to the visions experienced by visitors, when the brain, deprived of light, populated sight with things unseen. A stray text alludes to a *chil k'uh*, perhaps "pulque god," hinting that inebriation assisted in the general disorientation. Naj Tunich is also strongly homosocial. Not a single woman is clearly mentioned in its texts nor displayed in its imagery. If certain houses were young men's houses, supervised by older males, monitoring binges and controlled fighting, Naj Tunich could illustrate a very different experience. It involved a visit to politically neutral locations, young men in tow, intent on transformative visions. Their names at times appear in isolated phrases, to indicate their presence but not explaining why they are there. In the cave, homosexual practices noted by Spanish clerics occur precisely where young men are named.

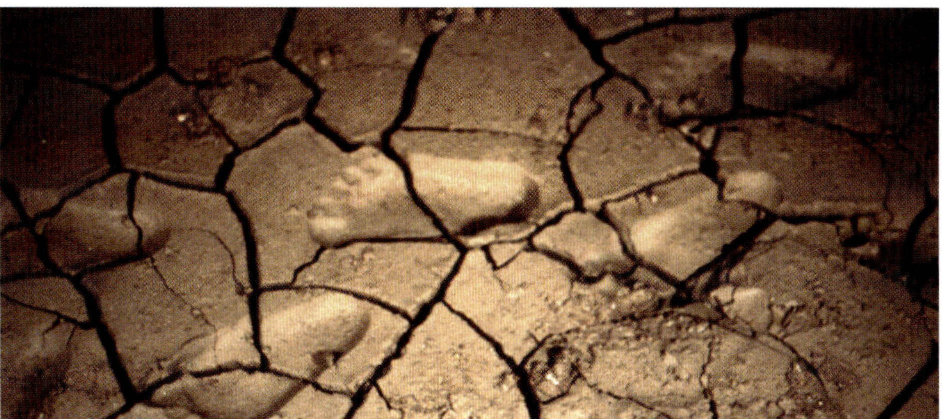

PERSONAL PASSAGES IN GOOD COMPANY

The rites of passage assembled so far extol shifts in individual lives. The walking, sentient young, capable of speech and intelligent discourse, are the first to transform, brought to their duty as bloodletters by parents and ritual specialists. These new abilities, to be employed throughout life, became especially relevant when there might be doubts about the dynastic legitimacy of a boy or, in one case, a girl. There is little doubt that it involved ordeals. Later, as young men develop, there is ample evidence, both from distant and more recent sources, that their separation, training, and controlled excess were worthy of social investment. The symbolism, especially in the lush and detailed ethnography, is emphatic about its sexualized, procreative import. The colonial authorities speak with disapproval of homosexuality, cultural and affective practices that surely go back centuries, into the Classic period itself, and with liaisons between older men and younger boys. (The scene at Naj Tunich may involve mythic, godly prototypes, but it could still offer a charter for human actions.) There were mundane, everyday motivations, too: enlisting young labor to useful tasks, testing them, evaluating those of merit, and promoting, during the Classic period, the princes above all. A contradiction creeps into the data—there is separation into groups, with all the implied virtues of equality and joint activity, the sheer fun of a thorough debauch and alcohol-fueled fight. But there is also a persistent stress on nobles set apart from boys and youths of comparable age.

Ultimately, it is the future king who is set apart on his transit to the throne. A final text lays out his own special challenge (fig. 69). Throne 1 at Piedras Negras, crafted by two named sculptors of supreme ability, tells us how the final known king, "Ruler 7," came to the throne.[72] He is a puzzle: patron of sculpture celebrated by Mayanists, he also reigned with the help of an *éminence grise*, a lord, raised in part at Piedras Negras, of the smaller community of La Mar. His name literally backs the throne, and the ruler would lean back against his comforting, textual presence. Ruler 7 was energetic in claiming ties to an earlier king, at least two rulers before, entering his tomb with purifying fire, but his claim must have been weak. His predecessor was evidently forced to abdicate, and the

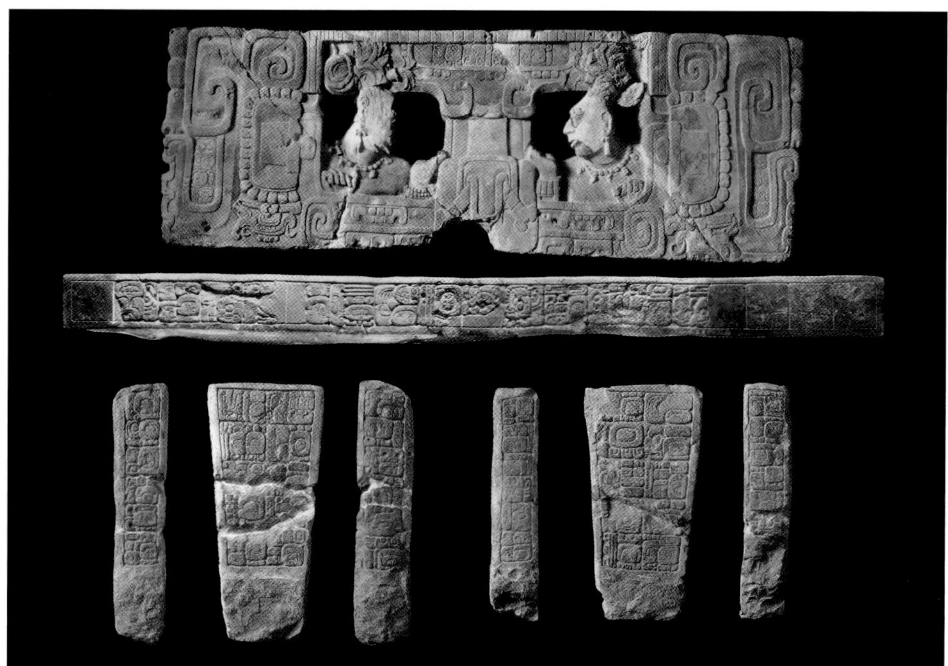

young ruler, a *ch'ok,* went through strenuous, ritual motions to assure his rule. A luminous or polished stone object, a sacrum to top all sacra—remember Turner's emphasis on such objects—was transported by mysterious means at the behest of the prince. The object "rested," then eventually returned, and only then could the king be crowned. There was formal movement, an esoteric effigy or fetish of supreme but unspecified relevance. The ritual circuit done, the object came back, presumably in the company of the prince. Set apart, the new king found a way to fold again into society, reincorporated: van Gennep would have been encouraged by its orderly logic. The lord was now ready for a monarch's lifetime of rule and lawful authority. He had passed through the taming places of his world.

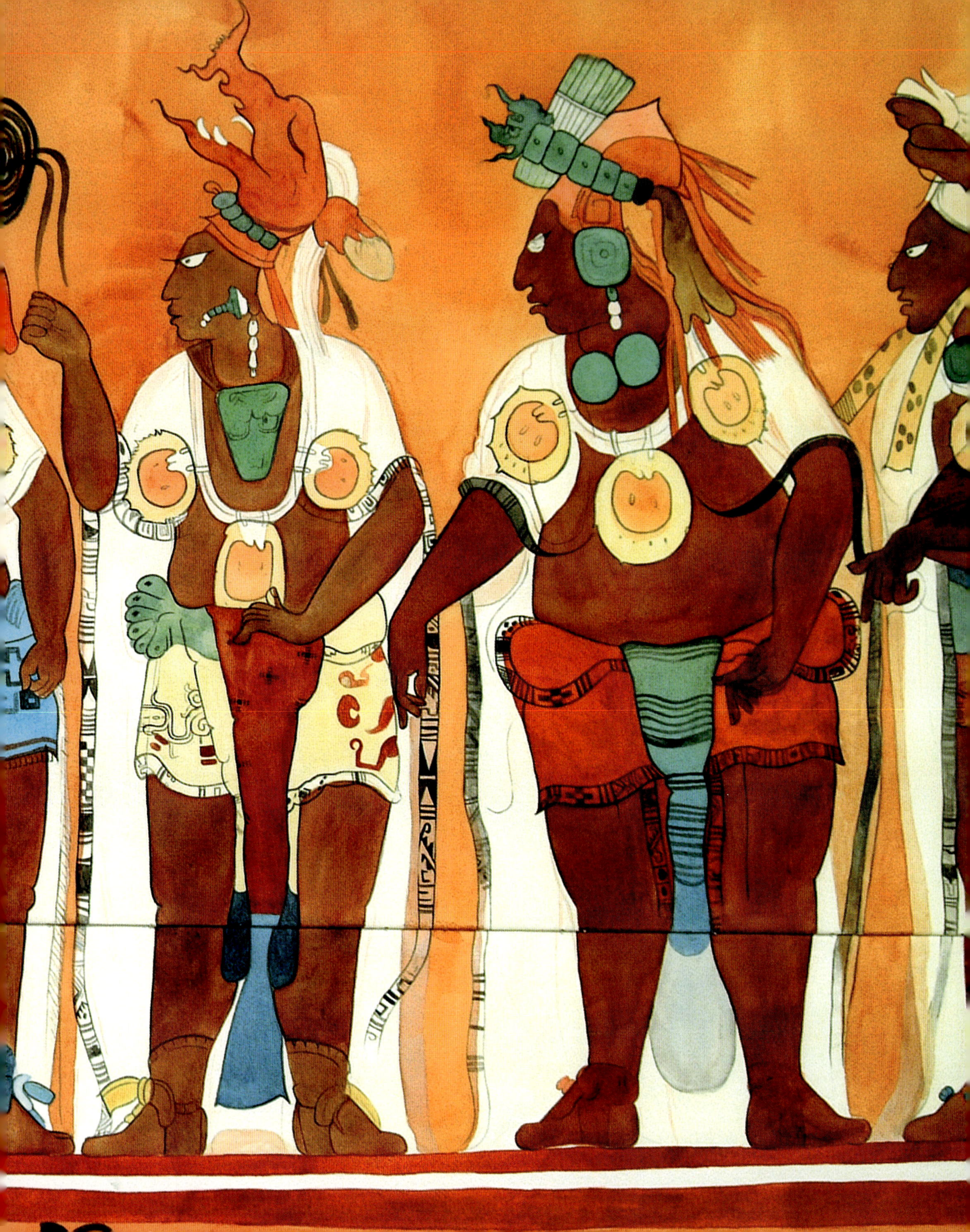

5 The Good Prince

The heir to a throne attracts a blend of hope and anxiety. There are wishes that the heir will prove viable as well as real concerns that he or she might not. The most illustrious bloodlines do little to reduce that worry. Sighs of relief attended the abdication of that hapless playboy Edward VIII of the United Kingdom. No such luck awaited the Spaniards, who in the sixteenth and seventeenth centuries endured the pitiable rule of Juana *la loca* ("the Mad") and her descendent Carlos II *el hechizado* ("the bewitched"). Don Carlos of Spain died in prison at the order of his father, King Philip II, alarmed by his son's vagaries and presumed treason. For different reasons, the Hanover rulers of Great Britain showed unfailing dislike of their heirs. George II gloated about Frederick, the recently expired Prince of Wales: "I lost my eldest son—but I am glad of it."[1]

The Classic Maya had, to judge from current evidence, many of the same fears and aspirations. They wanted to know whether an heir was capable, or at least that he or she be seen as capable. A case had to be made to a kingdom that the selection of the heir was just, correct, and necessary. The royal courts in which rule took place deepened these concerns, in that royal families and their members operated as nodes of cooperation and faction. They could settle on an heir or, over the long term, find endless ways to quibble and quarrel over succession. For the Maya, there may be no more elaborate display of such courts than the Bonampak murals of Chiapas, Mexico, dating to AD 791.[2] They illustrate the problem of heirs to the fullest extent in ancient America. The evidence consists of murals painted in three rooms and their less-preserved entrance jambs (fig. 70). As a program, the murals populate the royal court of Bonampak with over 272 figures, including some repeats from room to room. Perhaps the largest single collection of Maya names, the paintings link certain figures to captions, provide headdresses that label the wearer (especially in Room 2 of the murals), and supply an array of titles. Other texts, centrally placed, describe dates and actions. The Bonampak murals provide something else as well: they offer an unprecedented glimpse into the weaving of texts and images in Classic Maya civilization. The story they tell is daring yet sad. A prince is poised to rule, a young man suspended at the tense intersection of generations. But we, the viewers, know something he does not: the prince will soon confront an irreparable period of chaos. His kingdom will not survive for very long.

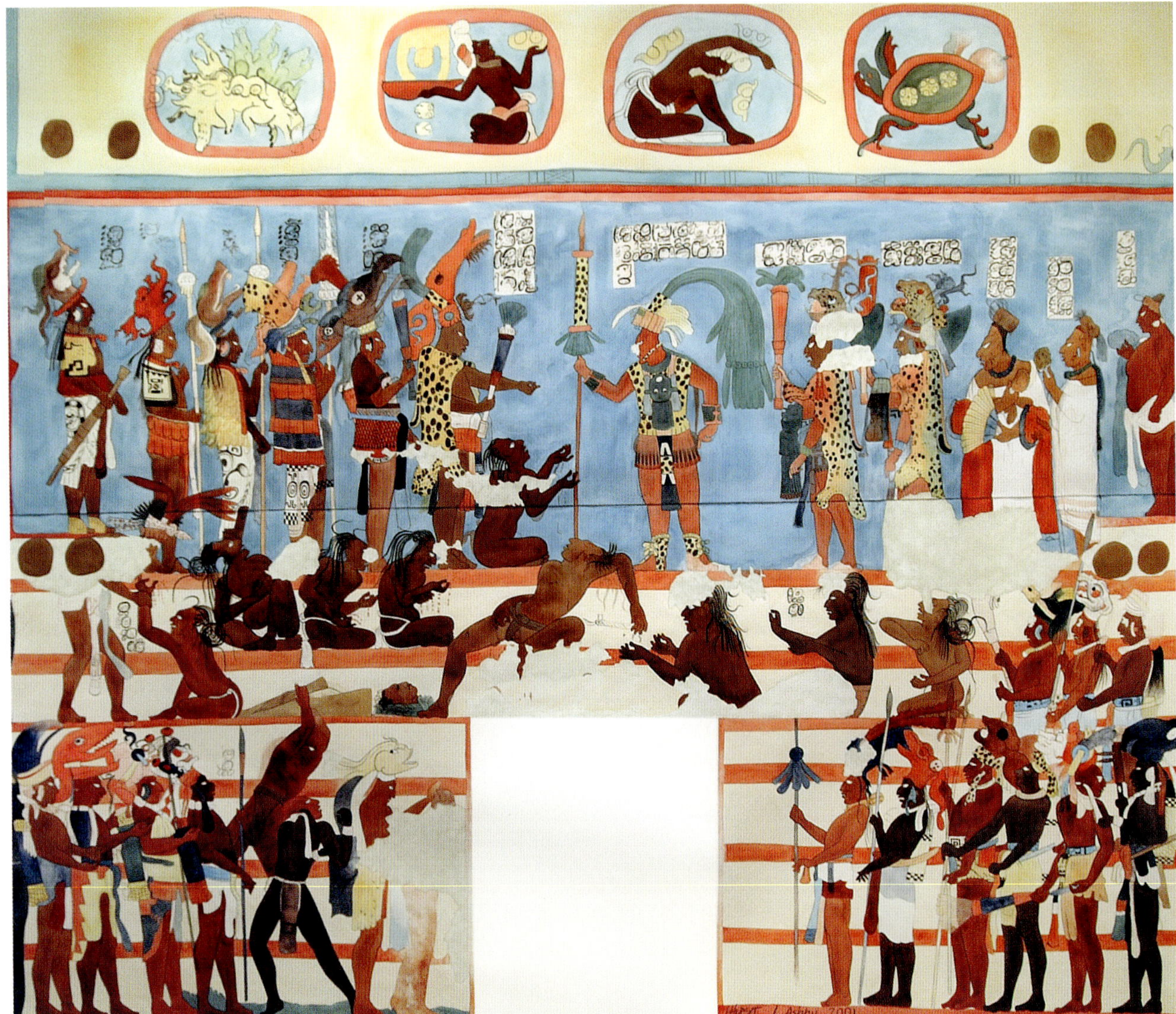

A

FIGURE 70

Murals, Bonampak, Mexico:
(A) Room 2 detail, north wall;
(B) Room 1 detail of main prince,
north wall. Reconstruction, Yale
University Art Gallery, Gift of
Bonampak Documentation
Project. Illustrated by Heather
Hurst and Leonard Ashby.

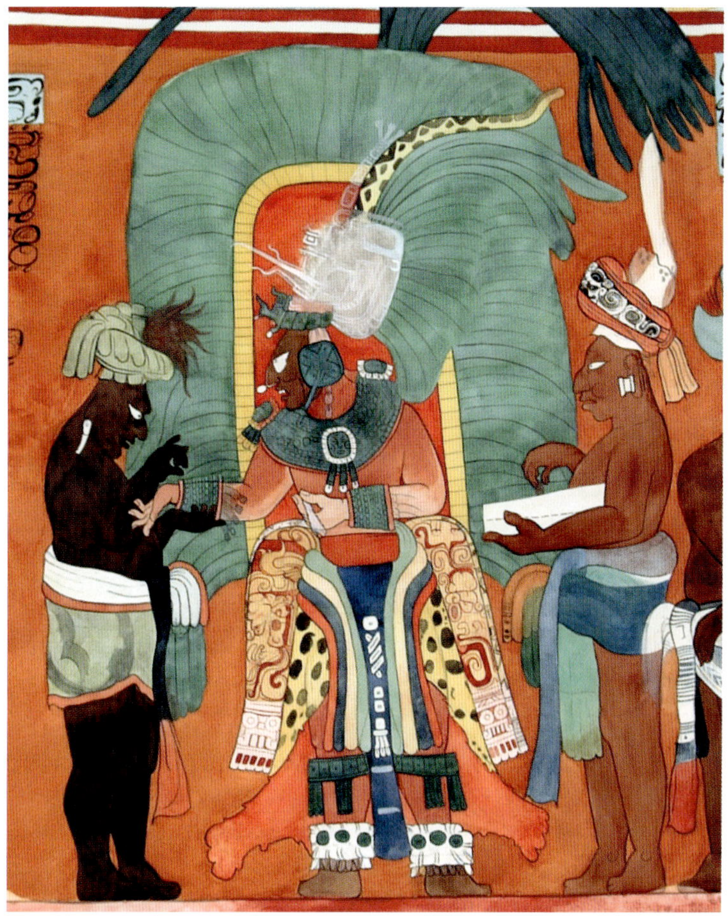

B

A VOLATILE SPACE

In systems of hereditary rule, the questions are always the same. Who should succeed, how should they be selected, and what attributes should attach to the heir? Since the time of Sir James Frazer and before, scholars have understood that royal succession involves peril, consequence, and meaning. His approach has been called an example of "extreme comparativism." This is not an approach beloved of many historians, who believe it ignores local subtleties. Yet, in modified form, comparison lies within the comfort zone of anthropologists. In a classic study, Jack Goody did justice to the choices at hand, some of them overlapping.[3] Heirs could be appointed by superior authority, elected by courtiers of inferior station or accede to the throne by brute force and civil war. They might even be detected, as was the infant Dalai Lama in Tibet, through miraculous signs. Eligible people needed to be identified. To assure the smoothest passage across reigns, a mechanism had to be found to narrow that pool. By definition, kingship was and is restrictive. Were it not, every pauper—or every person with aggressive attitude, weapons, and a following—would strive to be a prince.

At one range of succession are the unambiguous examples of real or adoptive primogeniture. The eldest must succeed, even if a drooling fool. Or, as in early Ireland, a ruler might choose his heir before his own death. The other extreme is "blood tanistry," of Mongol origin, found in early Tang China and enduring until the sixteenth century within the Ottoman court of Turkey and the Near East: those eligible to rule, often brothers but also members of a broader cohort, eliminated each other through battle or homicide.[4] Among the Ottomans, throttling by silk cord was the favored method. (Later, in a gesture to family feeling, brothers were simply shut away in the *kafes* or "cage" of the royal palace.) As a system for succession, primogeniture focuses on uninterrupted institutional flow. By contrast, blood tanistry personalizes monarchy, rewarding talent and ruthlessness. Each has its dangers. The first risks the ascension of an incompetent or a psychopath. The latter undermines the very principle of inherited office, suggesting that aggression by any party will remove obstacles to rule. For most societies this approach is profoundly destabilizing.

Royal transition occupies the volatile space between generations. In slow burn until the death of the king, it plays out across vertical and horizontal dimensions. Uncles, cousins, aunts, nephews, nieces, brothers, sisters—all have an interest in what happens. As a focus of emotions, transition convulses with affection, ambition, worry, and antagonism. Often, younger generations crave ascent so as to fulfill the promise of their rank and training. Being close to the summit inclines people to climb there. Members of a single generation push hard against those within their group. Or they might lie low for reasons of self-preservation, like Uncle Claudius in Robert Graves's novel *I, Claudius.* In the book, Claudius, the most unlikely of imperial candidates, watched with horror and fear while rivals eliminated each other; he was the one person left standing. The expedient of fraternal succession also does away, at least potentially, with Hamlet's uncle, an older relative ravenous for power yet without a clear path to achieving it. Such succession gives a nod to rights at all levels of the court, reducing tension in the process.

Among the Classic Maya, the evidence is overwhelming for father-to-son transmission of thrones, passing through female lines when dynasties appeared to fail. In the western Maya region, there is a tendency to fraternal solutions during the final centuries of the Classic period. The emphasis on brothers is not new among the Maya, going back to the sixth century AD at least, and it seems also to have been an ordering principle among nobles or even members of artist's families. Yet the greater visibility of brothers along with other members of royal courts signals an open admission that rulers did not govern alone. The Maya texts also hint, mostly by omission or later erasures, that some successions were highly troubled. A good instance is the celebrated interregnum at the site of Yaxchilan, Mexico. The ruler who presided over this period is attested not at Yaxchilan, but at Piedras Negras, Guatemala. With a prince from his court, he visited this much-loathed neighbor and participated in a feast. A big mistake: his very existence was blotted out later at Yaxchilan.[5] A Hatfield, he had cozied up to the McCoys, a hereditary enemy.

At Piedras Negras, for its part, fraternal succession occurred when an heir, perhaps a young ruler, was captured by a noble of Yaxchilan. They probably went down the list to select the next king.

A constant aim is to avoid discord. Resolution of competing claims occurs within specific constellations of history, personality, and the varied meanings and roles of kingship. For the past, much of this conflict channels into texts and images. It stands to reason that succession of the good prince, the right prince, ready to rule, accords with ideas about the proper route to kingship. Visual and textual declarations are likely to be moralizing and prescriptive. They claim to describe actual events, but ideals and wishful projection massaged the whole.

THE MORAL PATH OF PRINCES

In Europe, great energy went into the instruction of young princes and their guidance by stereotyped example and expectation. Erasmus's *The Education of a Christian Prince*, written with an eye to employment from its subject, the future Emperor Charles V, was intent on securing that objective. But it also extolled monarchical wisdom and continuity of policy at a time of present and future insecurity: "the prince can leave no finer monument to his good qualities than a son who is in every way of the same stock and who recreates his fathers' excellence in his own excellent actions." A good deal depends on perspective. A manual for becoming a king is not the same as a narrative of the steps that could lead to such rule. In one genre of these texts, the intent is reportorial, presenting a sequence of events that brought an heir to the throne. Such statements can be normative too, bound up with ideal expectation. They urge all who follow to place themselves on the worthy course set by former rulers. The reality of those reigns is less relevant than their imagined example. Or, as another alternative, an account can be completely impersonal, distilling the essence of a good lord into a series of maxims or desirable qualities. These alternatives are not mutually exclusive. A purported life of a king often draws on standardized themes. A general treatise can mine the past for its contents. The mix of wishful projection and a specific, princely object of entreaty find solid expression in Niccolò Machiavelli's *The Prince*, a volume that praises the notorious Cesare Borgia. Later, affected by changing loyalties, it ends up as an offering to a Medici, Cesare's mortal enemy.[6]

In Mesoamerica, a manual for the handling of heirs appears in Bernardino de Sahagún's Florentine Codex, that supreme record of Aztec civilization cited in earlier chapters. In it, Sahagún, or those writing the document for him, describes the training of lords within special houses for noble youth. Along with the rigors mentioned before, it operated through a metaphor of craftsmanship, as though forging metal or shaping stone. After youths had gone to war and taken captives, the emperor might reward them with precious tokens of his esteem. Separate passages by Sahagún stressed an "exemplary life" and, through a list of polarities, contrasted a good lord with a bad one, "a causer of riots, a braggart . . . miserly . . . gluttonous."[7] Examples, after all, can be positive or negative. They help people hew to the right course.

In these sections, Sahagún was focusing on noblemen, not rulers per se. Yet, on accession, even kings addressed gods in tones of abasement, with pleas for divine guidance.[8] All levels needed help. For his part, Erasmus clearly saw the future of kings in Christian terms. This does not diminish his broader claims or differ markedly from what the Aztecs believed. Rulers mattered. Their formation involved decisions about which features to encourage or discourage. The transition from one reign to the next induced unease, and the wish was that the heir be well picked. The wrong person might take charge, with disastrous results.

TEXTING

The Bonampak murals came to the attention of explorers in 1946, as part of an unsavory scuffle that involved competition, large doses of nationalism, insensitivity, self-promotion, and duplication of effort. Still, these early visits were crucial, for they documented the murals in relatively good condition before the deterioration of later years. From these early images came an insightful study of glyphic content at Bonampak and a numbering scheme, viable but incomplete, for the texts themselves. In 1985 and 1986, further cleaning by the Mexican authorities revealed a brighter, more accessible surface, resulting in a valuable set of photographs and essays. A team led by art historian Mary Miller in 1996 undertook a program of imaging that included conventional infrared and color photography, digital multispectral recording, and, perhaps to greatest effect for glyphs, a television camera or "vidicon."[9] Over a period of weeks, I used this device alongside the brilliant engineer Gene Ware. We worked long hours in the hot, airless rooms of the mural building. The frame of the camera shook annoyingly when moved, and our patience was taxed to the limit. But the experience was well worth it, and we were able to recover details invisible for centuries.

The most commonly accepted narrative interpretation of the murals is that the paintings show the designation of an heir for the kingdom of Bonampak. In earlier studies, the three rooms were thought to highlight the designation itself (Room 1, with dressing and dancing by various lords), a ferocious battle and its aftermath (Room 2, with capture and captive sacrifice), and a later dance (Room 3). In essence, that narrative remains true, and Miller deserves credit for her sustained insistence on this point and her other insights about the paintings. The overall program of iconography matches this sequence, even to the murals in the upper vaults. Room 1 highlights jeweled diadems, consistent with the accession mentioned in the long text below. Room 2 presents the dark arc of night over a bloody melee. Completing the cycle, Room 3, a scene of sacrifice, mentions the sun and portrays the blood imbibed by that hungry being. In Maya archaeology, the murals have been central to interpreting the Classic Maya as a warlike people, at least at the elite level.

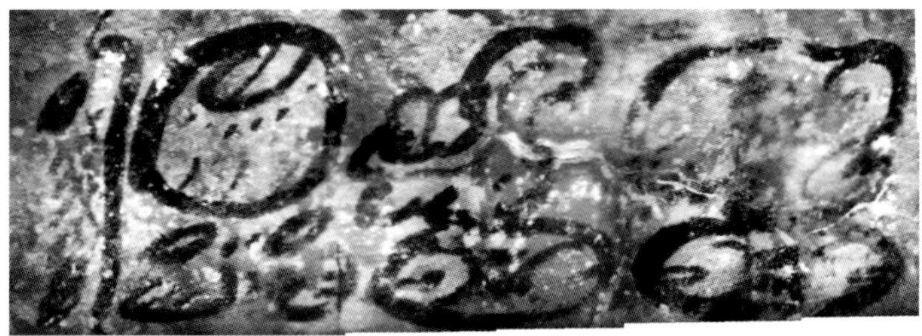

The violence of Room 2, with its colliding bodies, trumpet blasts and terror, was particularly influential. The murals also buttressed a view that warfare among the Classic Maya synchronized with moments in the Venus calendar. Yet, at Bonampak and elsewhere, that interpretation has become doubtful. Misread dates and events weaken the argument.[10]

The evolving question is emphasis. There is a stronger sense, only enabled by a rereading of the captions, that the reigning lord and his ally at Yaxchilan need demotion in our understanding of the murals. Above all, there is the identity and positioning of the heir—one interpretation stressed a small figure held by a courtier in Room 1—along with the nature of the men attending such rituals. With better images, "central" figures at the court of Bonampak can be seen, especially in Rooms 1 and 2, as nearly anonymous messengers from foreign tributaries. Another suggestion, that the murals were not finished because of impending societal collapse, is still being debated.[11] The evidence is baffling. Certain chambers, especially the micro-glyphs in Room 3, show minute finish and detail, as though unhurried by the press of larger events.[12] However, many texts in that room are ghostly: there is space set aside for glyphs but nothing inside, an emptiness that speaks volumes. Hypothetically, perhaps a later king decided not to invest in the building, or, as another possibility, political disarray led to the unraveling of the kingdom and there was no longer support for literacy or the making of images.

Despite unanswered questions, much can be read. For reference, the glyphic texts have been labeled by room number with Roman numerals (I, II, III), then by caption within each room (1, 2, 3, etc.). The carbon content responds well to the vidicon camera, sometimes with surprising resolution and a smoother, less grainy, more contrastive result than with infrared film (fig. 71). A few texts hidden to the naked eye became entirely legible.

Several captions in Room 1 disclose a red tinge, thus being among the few to be clarified by color photography. Notably, these occurred near figures painted in similar tones.[13] The brush may have wandered from one to the other, or perhaps the artist sought to cohere the two with shared pigment.

We have mentioned missing glyphs, especially in Rooms 2 and 3. The calligraphers took pains to block out spaces for them, in seeming expectation of a predetermined number of signs.[14] The vidicon confirmed that the blocked areas were left blank, a pattern attested in certain carved texts at sites such as Dos Pilas, Guatemala.[15] The areas with incomplete captions were usually near one another and were strongly concentrated in less martial scenes. The micro-glyphs and delicate painting in these same rooms underscore the paradox of inconsistent finish. Nonetheless, the clustering of blank texts suggests a task orientation by sector of wall. In other words, the figures were left unlabeled not because certain people had fallen into disgrace (a political explanation, rather like the airbrushing of a Soviet-era photograph) but because someone had failed to finish an area (an oversight in image making). The curious parity between the incomplete number of captions in Room 1 and Room 2 (about thirteen in each) hints at systematic exclusion. Against this is the baffling omission of clear labels for royal ladies or a male (the king) on his throne in Rooms 1 and 3. In one Room 1 text the ruler is securely identified—why not everywhere? The same holds true for an obese servant described by Miller, in conversation, as the "eunuch." (An association with royal ladies makes this description more than humorous, recalling male attendants of the Forbidden City or an Ottoman harem. A castrated man cannot introduce his bloodline into a royal family.) This figure is labeled in Room 2 but not in Room 3, although the person is certainly the same. What can be said is that in parts of the murals texts were painted last, after the figures were rendered. The painters must have had preparatory drawings, strong memories, or cues from named headdresses, body size, and recognizable costume elements to keep the figures straight. As with all past imagery, the viewer was intended to carry much of the interpretive burden, supplying context that remains irretrievable today.

Glyphic captions are about naming people. Ultimately, names imply an engagement with society. Someone has exercised the right to assign one, seldom randomly and most often in relation to other names. Such words are more than convenient code: they classify, group this person with that one, or distinguish one from the other. Names may even be described, rather grandly, as part of a "representational economy" that "controlled, treasured, handed on, manipulated, and resisted." Names do not just identify a person, they work to form that identity. But more than naming itself, the most relevant decisions for the Bonampak painters and their patrons were whom to depict and whom to label. There are at least 272 people depicted in the murals (the thin paint in some areas makes for ambiguity about the absolute number) along with at least 127 captions and texts.[16] In Maya sculpture, during the Classic period, almost all figures, with a few exceptions, are accompanied by a caption. In Maya painting, whether on walls or pottery, this is not so, especially

in large-scale compositions. One of the many enigmas in the Bonampak murals is whether
the lack of labeling was social, with certain individuals not receiving a caption because of
low or captive station, or because these unnamed bodies were so much "wallpaper." They
simply filled a scene and communicated, as in Room 2, an impression of unspecified warriors, legs and arms akimbo in hot battle. The fluttering limbs almost convey a sense of ani-
mation and blurred motion, yet the striking attention to details of individual dress suggests
real people, if included and arranged for pleasing effect. The painters could have named all
the figures had they wanted to. In Room 3, some figures are identified by small-scale notations of their names and titles, often on weaponry, but the majority have no such caption.

In a sense, names recorded in the Bonampak murals express a double form of presence. A depiction is fortified by naming and thus becomes more concrete. A name is
rooted in material form by appearing with its referent. Such features are familiar elsewhere. In scenes of the Annunciation from the Italian Renaissance, texts intrude into
images when incarnating the living word of God or when showing heartfelt appeals
to divinity. Western imagery has a long tradition of this. In certain Renaissance images,
texts name sitters or artists, or they might allude to literary themes. When referring
to people, Maya glyphic captions had two basic forms. A few labels, as at Bonampak, affirm
that someone of high status was present. In such texts, a name often follows the glyph
for *baah*, "body," a word that carries a secondary meaning of "image." By this means the
Maya conflated, particularly in royal portraiture, an actual body with its depiction.[17] This
practice stemmed from the idea that there could be multiple versions of the ruler's body.
Images replicated the presence, even the essence, of kings, queens, and courtiers. The
difference was that royal bodies might die and decay, but images lasted beyond a lifetime.

A second kind of caption records speech, words uttered at some time in the past.
Employing first- and second-person pronouns, such texts often appear as glyphs on scrolls
tethered to speakers' lips. This convention recalls the oral performance that many scholars
attribute to the act of glyphic reading. But the sense of immediacy differs: the Bonampak
texts distance the reader because of their impersonality. Most use the third-person pro-
noun, the standard for monumental glyphs. Reported conversations, largely on pottery,
are filled with first- and second-person references. The scenes may involve far times
and beings, but the texts bring them closer, into earshot. As in archaic Greece, "the practice of writing words . . . was [likely] bound to the strength . . . of orality." The image and
text establish a joint authority, creating a truth elicited from two modes of communication: pictures and writing. Both are pictorial, yet they discharge different functions.[18]

A thorough study of captions in Maya imagery does not exist. A few features
come to mind, however. As a practice, captioning goes back to the beginnings of
Maya script, as part of a general tendency to link words and images. Most captions, at
Bonampak included, occur close to or slightly above the face of the person they identify.
This placement is violated when such space is absent or is crowded out by more pres-
tigious figures; then the caption appears to the front or lower still, by the legs. In other

Maya imagery, groupings of assembled lords, stressing their unity, may be accompanied by texts that are so compressed the captions cannot be easily separated. With war captives, another pattern appears: the thighs, stomach, or chest are now scored with names, or the glyphs appear on loincloths above the groin. Abundant in Classic Maya script, perhaps even central to it, such "name-tags" identify the ownership of an object. They can be properly understood as captions for the things they designate: a sculpture was made by this person, a pot owned by another. As things seen and held, they testify that such statements were true—they give them weight and reality.[19]

Most captions are in bounded areas, and areas of contrast enhance legibility. If on a darker background, zones with glyphs tend to be lighter, as at Bonampak. If on a lighter backing, captions float against darker bedding. Raised captions accompany higher status people (rulers, principal nobles), incised ones accompany those of lower status or those absent from a carving (captives, sculptors). Texts physically closer to the reader correlate with the prominence of their content, so that an outthrust block conveys high status. Painted captions reproduce that relative prominence by imitating a sculpted text, with doubled or contrastive outlines to simulate a raised inscription for figures of greater importance. In contrast, a simple black outline suggests the recessed or incised caption of a less important person. Notably, captions with reported conversation have no such contrasts. The texts hover as though part of the scene, without need of graphic distinction from the background. This appears also to characterize captions in the limited palette of, say, "codex-style" vessels that use no more than two pigments on a beige background. The intent may also have been deliberate, to bring the texts close to those being depicted. Rather than separating text and image, the painting flattens them into the same plane.[20]

A TYPOLOGY OF CAPTIONS

The texts in the Bonampak murals conform to distinct types. Room 1 features a long text, an "Initial Series" with multiple dates and events; Room 2 contains a lone "Calendar Round" caption with abbreviated chronological information. More frequent, especially in Rooms 1 and 2, are statements (*u baah*) declaring that a particular person is present, in dance, or holding objects. By an order of magnitude, there are also names or titles only in all rooms, along with dedicatory texts on textiles in Room 1, the chamber dedicated to tribute. Diverging from their usual role in Maya texts, the dedications actually "conceal" the name of the owner or maker, their epithets artfully hidden behind a fold of cloth, implied but not visible. A final set is the most enigmatic of all: micro-glyphs of acutely reduced size that embellish Room 3. Some categories contrast with others because they are intended to exist *within* the image. They are depicted on objects or on what may be images of cloth or paper, as in the micro-glyphs directly across from the entrance to Room 3. The experience of the murals could vary. Viewers could pass through the separate rooms as they wished. Yet, as noted before, the overall sequence is secure, with only a few modifications of interpretation. Room 1 is a scene of tribute, dressing, and dance. Room 2 records war and its bloody aftermath. The concluding segment, Room 3, lays out a pageant of dance and blood sacrifice.[21]

Initial Series Text

Where preserved, the Initial Series text, which presents a lengthy, more detailed positioning of a Maya date, is fully legible (fig. 72). It contains two dates in total, which correspond, in the most accepted correlation of Maya and European calendars, to the Initial Series itself, December 10, AD 790, and a second date, November 11, AD 791. The first date marked an accession to the office of *ajaw*, "lord," by someone who was the sacred lord of Bonampak and its area. A man of substance, he also held the *bakab* and *kaloomte'* titles, markers of the highest rank. This event took place under a regional overlord Shield Jaguar IV from the city of Yaxchilan. At Bonampak, Shield Jaguar used not his royal name but a title of martial prowess, a clue to the basis of his clout and prestige. The second date refers to the dedication of the building (*ochi k'ahk'*, "fire-enters," a dedicatory phrase) or the phase of the building. There is also the name of the structure, less readable than one might like, and mention of a dance of deity impersonation. The god doing this service was the Sun God, supplied with the weapons of war (*took'*, "flint," and *pakal*, "shield").[22]

The final section records the names of the ruler of Bonampak, Yajaw Chan Muwaan, a person highlighted in Room 2. According to other evidence, he came to the throne some years before, in AD 776. His father, Aj Sak Teles, is also cited. Both appear in the carved lintels of the mural building, above the doorways leading into the three rooms (Aj Sak Teles is also painted on the jamb leading into Room 3, just beneath a carved lintel that features him). Lintel 1 of the mural building depicts Yajaw Chan Muwaan capturing an enemy in AD 787. Lintel 3 displays Aj Sak Teles, probably in AD 780. Lintel 2, the middle sculpture, just outside Room 2, shows the probable overlord from Yaxchilan in AD 787—none other than Shield Jaguar IV. Lintel 2 also bears a sculptor's signature, which indicates that the carver, almost certainly the maker of all three lintels, was loaned to Bonampak by the king of Yaxchilan. If there is a looming figure, a guiding force, this king plays that role. He had been a formal witness, so the glyphs tell us, to the accession mentioned in the Initial Series text. In much the same way, Stela 1 at Bonampak confirms that its sculptor belonged to this ruler of Yaxchilan. All such references raise the chance that the murals were not purely local in planning or execution. Yaxchilan has a few murals, and an apparent, poorly preserved reproduction of an unfolded Maya codex garnishes a palace interior at Tecolote, a site under the control of Yaxchilan. Lintels 1 and 2 at Bonampak record events that lie a short time apart, probably in reference to a conflict against a mysterious site known as Sak Tz'i', "White Dog." Unfortunately, the ambiguities of the Initial Series text are difficult to resolve. The name of the person reaching *ajaw* status is unclear. Because of erosion, it is not clear whether he is the same as any other lord in the murals.

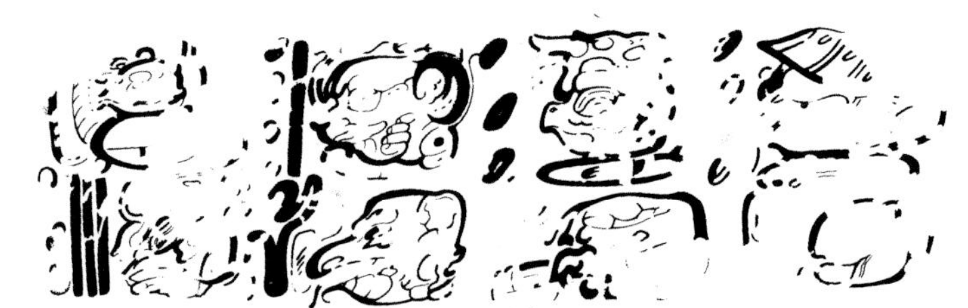

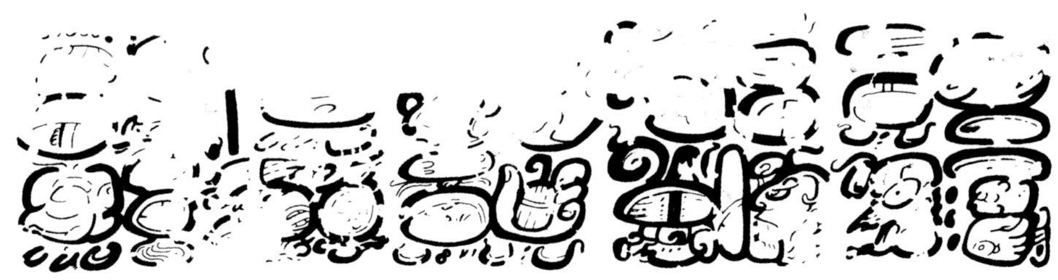

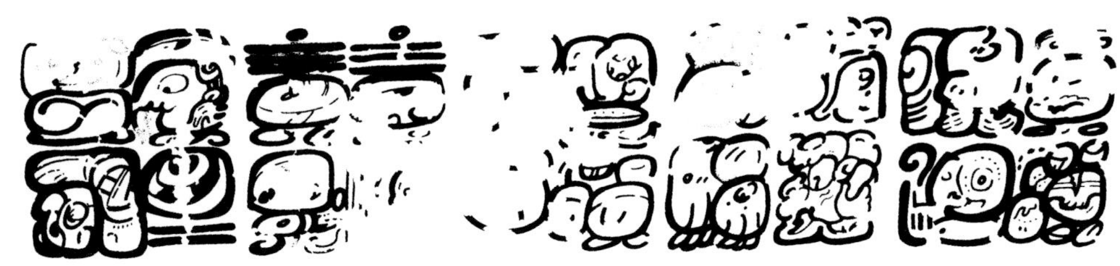

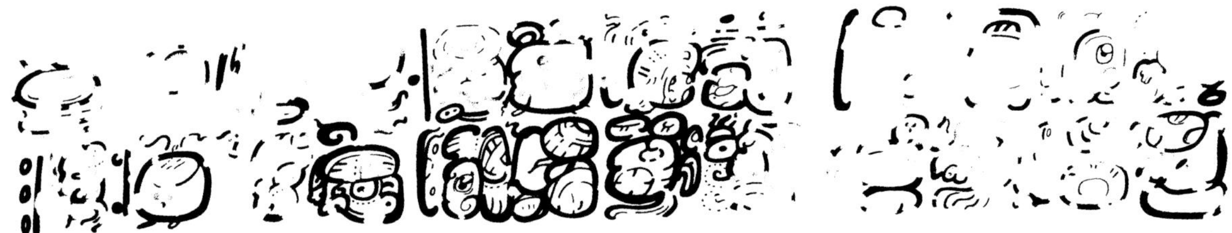

FIGURE 72

Bonampak murals: Initial Series text, Room 1.

The sculptures clearly relate to the murals, but the paintings may gloss, extend, or build on those carved messages. They may even be later—paint can always be added to a plain wall. Inserting a new lintel is far more laborious, and there is no evidence this was done. In some respects, the Initial Series text arcs over events in the paintings. Physically, it spans a good section of Room 1, but its content ties more firmly to Room 3 and its solar imagery.[23] The Initial Series unites the rooms into a chronicle of dynastic transition, success in war, and ritual duty.

The Calendar Round Caption

The next-longest text is a long caption of twenty-three glyph blocks in Room 2 of the mural building, found near the head of Yajaw Chan Muwaan. The dates have long been a puzzle, but the most likely choice remains July 19, AD 786. The text records a capture by Yajaw Chan Muwaan, along with what may be a second name, of a lord who uses one of the two local titles for sacred rule. All else in Room 2 ensues from this event and its central claim of agency. The main captive on the opposed wall, staring up at Yajaw Chan Muwaan, is likely to be the captive mentioned here. At the same time there seems no special need to fix the date in absolute time, a role played by the Initial Series.

Statements of Bodies in Dance or with Objects

These kinds of captions occur only in Rooms 1 and 2. A lord's body or image, marked for possession as *u-baah,* is in "dance," *ak'oot,* or is shown with a variety of objects. In two cases, the objects in dance, and so depicted in the costuming, are green plumes. The glyphs spell this out explicitly as *ti-k'uk'uum,* "with plumes" or "feather, quetzal." The dancers are the literal embodiments of feather tribute, now incarnated as royal youths. They are the wealth of the kingdom. The captions in Room 2 refer less to legible objects, although one possible reading, *ti-jaw,* "with face-up," works persuasively with the supplicating captives below. In Room 1, the figures identified by *baah* statements are royal youths. In Room 2, they are the ruler, Yajaw Chan Muwaan, and, in face-to-face position, the *u-mam keleem,* "grandfather of the youth" (fig. 73).[24] The *baah* reference serves to annotate and highlight the focal figures of Rooms 1 and 2, especially those in immediate, face-to-face contact. The intention may have been to single out some bodies over others, to prioritize their presence in the scenes. They also draw attention to those who complete the narrative in the murals through dance or review of captives.

Names or Titles Only

By far, most captions at Bonampak record names only, without any dates or events. At least 112 of these are known, and they may be divided into several kinds: there are impersonal references, names appearing with titles earned by merit or success in war, attendants of treasured objects, names with courtly functions, and, as part of longer texts, royal and noble titles. This is treasure trove, the largest set of names on any monument of

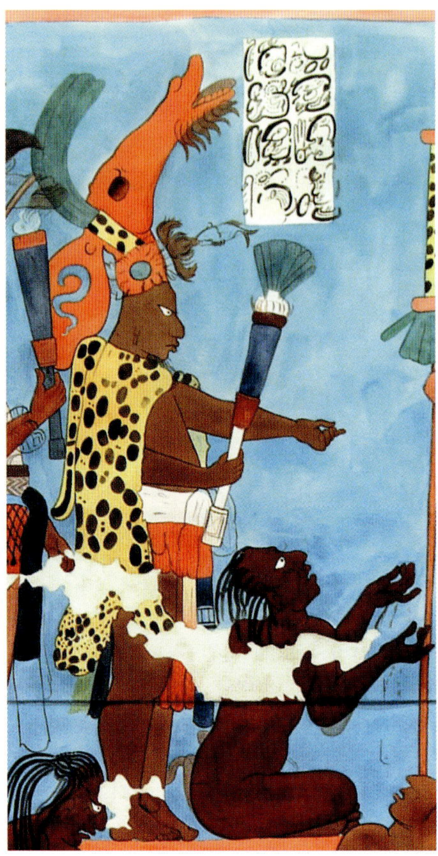

the Classic period. The texts have another trait beyond their quantity. Most have a high degree of what might be called "syllabicity"—that is, a heavy reliance on glyphic syllables and not just word signs. In Maya writing, syllables strip meaning, leaving only sound, while word signs focus instead on both sound and meaning. Syllabicity—the extent of syllabic usage—may be measured as a ratio using the number of syllables against the full number of glyphs, including word signs. That ratio at Bonampak signals a need for heightened clarity of sound. In part, these preferences for syllabic spellings may shift by time, a feature of later texts in the Classic period. But they could also reflect privilege. The youngest prince, a figure to be discussed soon, and a female—either the mother of the ruler Yajaw Chan Muwaan or her namesake (*etk'aba'il*)—have more syllabic spellings of their names. But they are the exceptions. The highest-ranking figures possess names with a high percentage of word signs (Yajaw Chan Muwaan, Chooj, "Bird" Bahlam).[25] Colors and certain titles, especially "lord," *ajaw,* favor presentation in this form. Other names, now pruned of their syllables, appear as word signs in headdresses. This is true of Room 2 and two youths in particular: Chooj and "Bird" Bahlam. Perhaps such spellings were practical. As prominent displays, they identified captains on the field of battle, which helped in the rallying of supporters and the coordination of attacks. In fact, their use in Room 2 may also explain

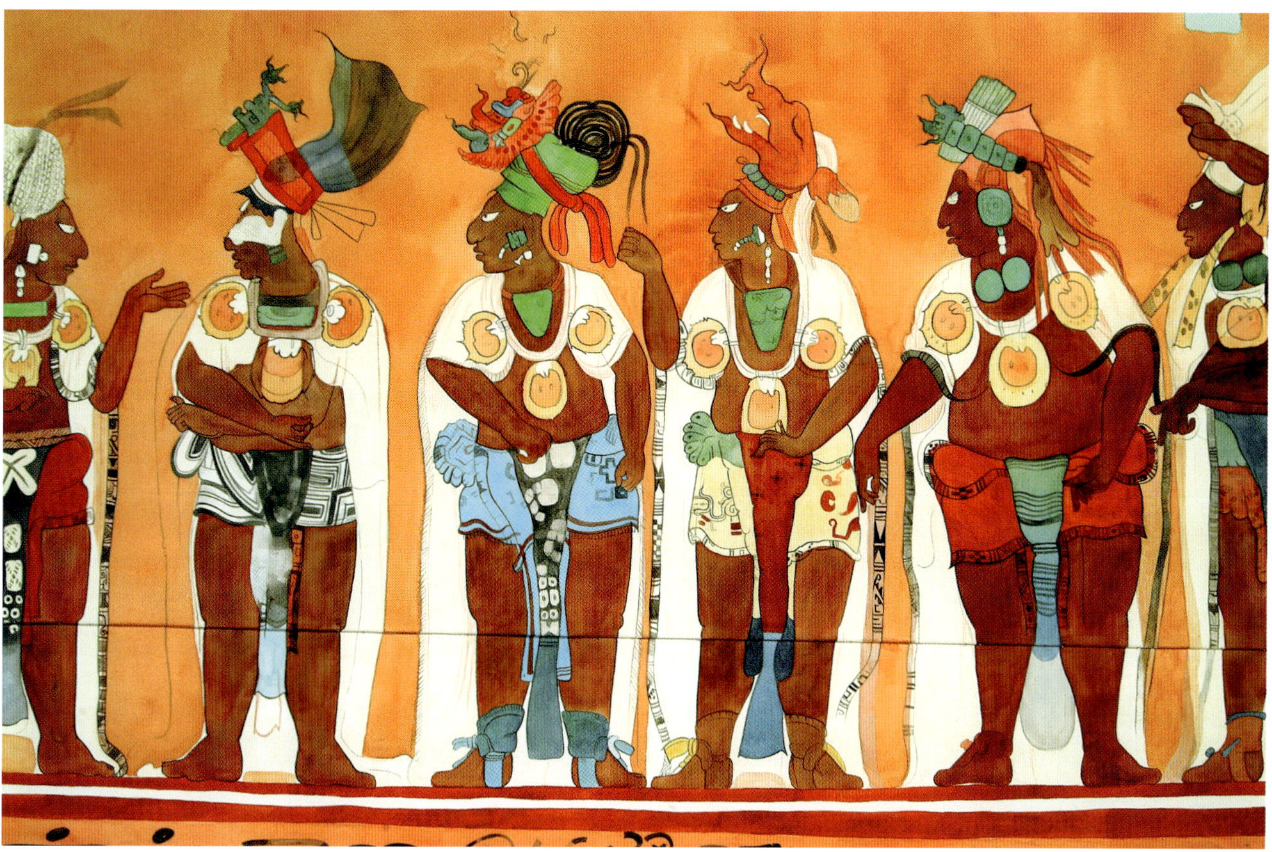

the dearth of names amid the welter of bodies in that chamber. Glyphs in great number would become lost in the dark and complex image. Costuming, so richly supplied by the painters, did a far better job as labels of people.

Ebeet, "messengers," are a notably anonymous set of figures in Room 2. Seemingly of high status, they are, I believe, dressed as walking tribute, soon to be divested at the throne of the lord. Their feathers, cotton mantles with embroidered or woven selvage, and titles leave little doubt they are the emissaries of foreign lords (fig. 74). They offer tribute, but gingerly. Getting too close to the ruler of Bonampak risks abduction as a hostage—better to send an expendable proxy.[26] One such subordinate is from *Lam,* another from "Red" or "Great Water," *Chak Ha'.* Neither of these places is identified in other texts. This raises the suspicion that the "catchment" of tribute at Bonampak, the region that sustained it, was, at least in this case, relatively small. The date of the event is uncertain, but the subsequent scene of battle in Room 2 implies a political motive, perhaps to reaffirm alliance and subordination prior to conflict. Or was this a pretext for war, in that someone had neglected to supply tribute?

The earned titles are a looser set. Some employ an indirect form of reference, a person described in relation to a captive. Such use is common in Room 2, in the battle scene.

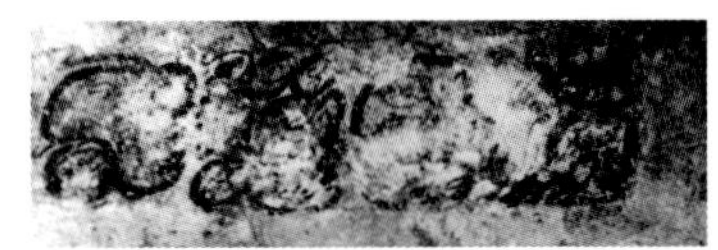

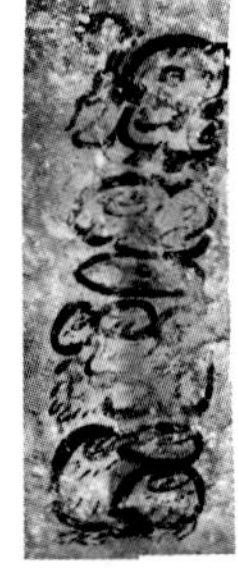

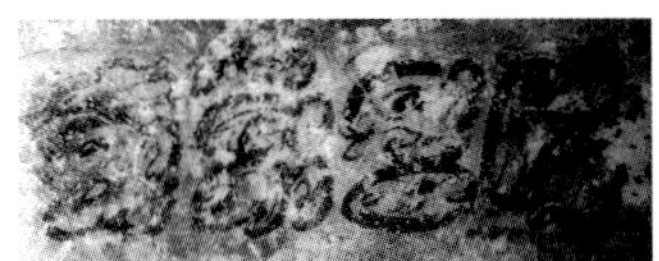

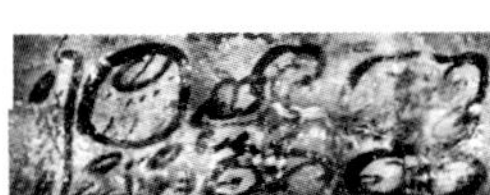

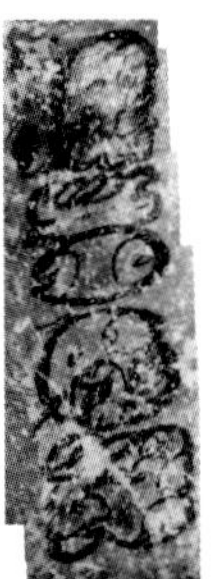

FIGURE 75

Royal youths in Bonampak texts: Chooj in top section (Caption II-33), "Bird" Bahlam in the second (Captions I-23 and II-34), and Aj Bahlam at bottom (Captions I-20 and III-7). Images by Stephen Houston and Gene Ware.

The title of dancers in Room 3 tends to be *aj jol,* "he of the head." It may describe head-hunters, in logical consequence to the fights in Room 2. Their ubiquity in the dance scene of Room 3 and the challenge of finding their names elsewhere in the murals raises a possibility. This courtly privilege came to successful warriors, now performing key roles in sacrifice. An unusual spelling of "4" probably records the guardianship of captives. One lord was the "guardian of the first-lord," *baah-ajaw,* another of a "lord" more generally or, perhaps a "person," *winik.*[27] Not surprisingly, these references cluster in the battle scene and the presentation of captives in Room 2.

Another category consists of courtiers who employ or guard objects. In Room 1, they are the "head" (*baah*) person associated with the physical "thrones," *tz'am.* Others serve as bailiffs with staffs (*baah-te'*). In Room 2, the objects change systematically, congruent with the theme of conflict. Now there are titles of war like "head-shield," *baah-pakal,* and "head-flint," *baah took',* the latter linked to someone letting blood from captives. One of the few prisoners to be identified is *Chak Mo'te' Baak,* the final word being a term for war captive. A dresser, arranging a feathered back rack for the prince "Bird" Bahlam, seems labeled solely by function. He is a *tikoom,* possibly from a term for "unwrapping" or "opening" cloth or stiff textile. Again, the correlation with rooms is striking. An enigmatic title, *'anahb,* appears only in Room 1. The term is connected to courtly service but

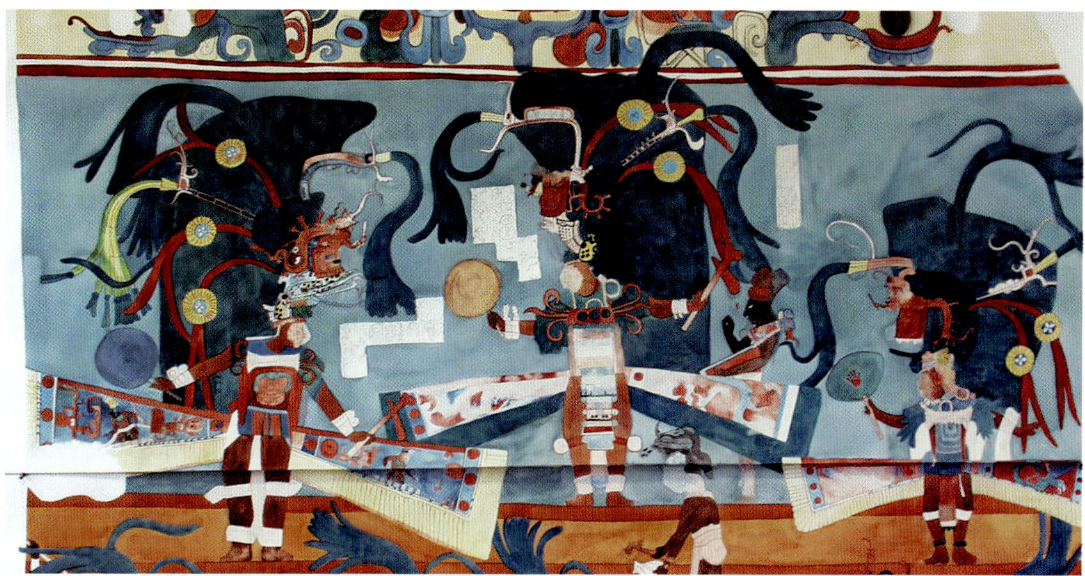

in ways not yet understood. It may come from the notion of a "runner," tied to a root for "run," *ahn.* The same room identifies the main musical performers, maracas in energetic play, as *k'ayoom,* "singer." Also present is a label for courtiers, but in one place, *ti'hu'n,* perhaps "mouth (spokesman) of the book" or "royal regalia." A number of lesser ranks, *sajal* or an enigmatic related term, *saaj* (mostly in Room 3), scatter throughout the murals. It appears with the second most prominent woman at court, the mother of the ruler or her namesake.[28]

Along with these titles are royal epithets, found throughout the murals. These refer to lordship of a place and, with added luster, "sacred lordship." The two in use within the murals are those of Ak'e, for the general area of Bonampak, another of the place called the "Bat"-*kal-naah,* probably in reference to a particular structure, *naah,* "building." Only the ruler, Yajaw Chan Muwaan, and what appears to be his second son, "Bird" Bahlam, use both titles. This may advertise broader dominion than held by others in the murals, or it might be due to variable preservation: the senior brother once displayed a full set of titles, which are now mostly gone. The youngest brother, Aj Bahlam, employs the high title only once, even when his caption is well preserved. The presence of brothers brings us to the reason for discussing the murals. They are all *ch'ok,* "youth" (fig. 75). The title marks the only known figures to appear in all three rooms: Chooj and "Bird" Bahlam. The third, Aj Bahlam, does not appear in the battle scene, possibly because he was younger than the other two. Clearly, he was shorter, a difference of scale that emphasizes his age in relation to the others (fig. 76). One lower-ranking individual exhibits the age-grade title, too, but, in general, the mural scenes identify few such youths.[29] A child thought at one time to be the heir can be seen in Rooms 1 and 3, but he or she is never labeled. In Room 1, the toddler is shown in an obscure corner of the scene, difficult to make out and concealed above cross-beams for the room vault. Room 3 displays what may be the same figure in a woman's lap, in front of a throne with women letting blood. This was perhaps yet another offspring of the royal line but so young as to be marginal, thus shown but not named. At that age, survival would have been uncertain for most children in Classic cities.

Dedicatory or Enumerative

A few texts are not so much captions as statements of ownership or manufacture. They involve a full or abbreviated dedicatory expression referring to the object being depicted *u-buhk*, "his/her cloth," or the painting itself, *u-tz'ihb-il*, "his/hers/its painting." In other examples, such dedications reveal the name of an owner. As noted in chapter 3, they preserve the identity of the original donor as it passes through social networks. A noteworthy feature here is that the names of these donors are nowhere visible. The cloth is always folded precisely where one would expect to see those glyphs. All are in Room 1, the chamber dedicated to tribute and its acceptance. A subset of labeled offerings would include the quantification of tribute in the chocolate bundle under the throne on the east wall of Room 2, *5 pi[h] kakaw*, 5 × 8,000 [beans of] cacao.[30]

Micro-glyphs

These signs, of minute size, only legible inches from the surface, appear to adorn a book or painted textile on the back wall of Room 3, just across from the entrance.[31] The texts refer explicitly to Shield Jaguar IV, accompanied by tiny figures of warriors in a battle scene. The sense is of a guiding, authoritative template, a book or painted cloth or paper near an act of human sacrifice.

DRAMATIS PERSONAE AND A DRAMATIC PERSONALITY

When seen as a totality, the texts and captions of the Bonampak murals exhibit several characteristics. Most titles, other than royal ones, occur in distinct rooms. They are apparently assigned because of the themes dominant in those chambers. In Room 1, the themes are tribute, dressing, dance, mummery, and musical performance. Room 2 almost roars with violent conflict against a dark and grassy setting, away from settled places. Its narrative concludes with a human cull of captives to be presented, tortured, and killed in the company of the highest members of court and upper echelons of the victorious force. In Room 3, there is a dance with observers. It targets sacrifice and the display of what appears to be a central, if miniature, text. It is this scene that keys back to the final passages of the lengthy text in Room 1. Scholars have long understood that these rooms conform to a sequence. They follow a narrative that, because of separate entrances to the rooms, requires physical repositioning of the viewer within an enveloping story. Here is, as Mary Miller suggests, a "virtual reality," prefiguring Silicon Valley by centuries. The sequencing itself, through rooms that are self-contained, even hermetic, hints at stylized staging. Each room packages the necessary events that lead to the next. The overall narrative embraces the sum of the chambers, but there is a measure of didacticism in the rooms, for future instruction, exposition, and proof of past merit.[32] In this, they echo the earlier murals at San Bartolo, Guatemala. Did young men also gather in the mural building, and was this edifice dedicated to their training?

Perhaps the central, most surprising attribute is the discontinuity of clearly labeled figures. For all the chance to duplicate actors—many did sustained service at court in the palace, on the battlefield, and in dance—the painters would have none of it. The sole labeled figures to appear in all three rooms are two youths, Chooj and another, his probable sibling, "Bird" Bahlam. The smaller, younger prince, Aj Bahlam, disappears in Room 2 but reappears for the dancing scenes in Rooms 1 and 3. Perhaps his age and inexperience prevented direct involvement in bloody conflicts.[33] The risk of death and capture was too high. Of course, there are other figures with pivotal roles. The ruler, Yajaw Chan Muwaan, makes an unambiguous appearance in Room 2. He is the main figure in several bloody displays, both during and after battle. Although unnamed, he is almost certainly the figure on the throne in Room 2. Tribute of feathers, *Spondylus* shell, and chocolate is heaped below his seat. In the display of captives in Room 2, there is the "grandfather of the youth," or perhaps "youths." The spouse of Yajaw Chan Muwaan, a queen who came from the locally powerful site of Yaxchilan, stands just to his side, along with his possible mother or daughter. They, too, make an appearance in Room 3, but now, mysteriously, Yajaw Chan seems entirely absent. The throne, studded with jade or spotted with green paint, is the setting of women's bloodletting, along with the women's attendant, the "eunuch." He was by their side in Room 2, and now he comes back to offer stingray spines for their ritual.

Sensitivity to hierarchy shapes and dominates Maya imagery. The figures in central position, facing to the viewer's left, are usually of the highest rank and, with few exceptions, the main focal points of dynastic displays. The lone exceptions are when an overlord is present. Placement with respect to that main figure then organizes outward according to descending status and by relative importance in the narrative. The youth known as Chooj, the only person to be tied to the place-name of Bonampak, occupies the principal position in scene after scene.[34] Room 2 plays a different game, now extolling the prowess of the dynasty, but still with a special place for Chooj. By one reading, although not the only one, the battle scene across from the tortured captives shows the two princes, identified by their jaguar headdresses, doing the heaviest, fiercest work of the conflict. The father, identified by his feathered, broad-brimmed hat, stands to the side, as if in admiring approval.

In Room 1, Chooj is the chief figure to be dressed. He is the person his probable brothers face in dance. In Room 2 he stands beside Yajaw Chan Muwaan, and in Room 3 he repeats the arrangement of the dance in Room 1, mimicking precisely the choreography and relative positioning of the dancers. His principal companion is always "Bird" Bahlam. Unlike his brother, "Bird" Bahlam uses the *Yajaw K'ahk'*, "Fire-lord," title that appears to involve martial or priestly roles, and perhaps both. This would suggest a division of responsibilities that complement those of Chooj. Indeed, the pattern prefigures Aztec practice, in which brothers and uncles toiled as war leaders and architects of expansive polices.[35] To his side in dance, in a less prominent yet almost sheltered position, steps Aj Bahlam. The young man is seldom accorded the lengthy titles of his companions.

The murals do not stress the ruler, Yajaw Chan Muwaan, but rather they shine a spotlight on another single figure, Chooj. There is no genealogical evidence to prove it, but the series of three youths, all using comparable titles, including ones ordinarily assigned to rulers, suggest a descending birth order. Their kinship is buttressed by the presence of royal ladies, perhaps sisters. In watchful attendance, the females undertake duties like bloodletting while the young men dance. Seen from this vantage, the sequence of events propels a basic and necessary claim for any heir. A good prince must be valiant and obedient to established wisdom and practice of the reigns that came before. That claim requires another—that the heir be the right one, as validated by the rules of succession and confirmed by deeds. Those qualities are plainly shown and cadenced in the painted rooms of Bonampak. They record an exemplary performance, even leadership, of a good prince. He celebrates the joys of tribute through a song and dance of dynastic affirmation. He does masterful service in battle, the literal right-hand man of his presumed father. Finally, he performs a dance of sacrifice that impersonates the Sun God, a being associated with rulership in the Classic period and before.[36] It is thus highly plausible that he is the heir. All activities, however, relied first and foremost on his age cohort, and then, in expanding circles, the ascending generations of his family and larger groupings of courtiers. An heir, the story seems to say, can only thrive through vertical and horizontal support.

The Initial Series text is revealing. Miller showed decisively that it refers to an accession to *ajaw* status.[37] The final passage, which refers to Sun God impersonation, alludes to the dance in Room 3, under vivid yellow skies and images of solar beings gorging on blood. (In one headdress, detailed in infrared, a dancer carries the face of a blood-eating bat.) Yet, the names that follow and conclude the Initial Series text are of Yajaw Chan Muwaan, then the name of his father, Aj Sak Teles, and perhaps others. To a worrisome extent, a case can be made that Aj Sak Teles was dead at this point, but so too was Yajaw Chan Muwaan. As one hypothesis, the program of lintels can be detached from the murals (again, a masonry wall with finished door lintels must stand before it can receive paint). The sculptures focus on a triad of father, son, and their probable overlord from Yaxchilan. The father's actions, earlier ones, are likened to the son's, who captures his victim at a time just after the success of his overlord. Both conquests affect the same foreign kingdom. In contrast, the murals deflect this attention and shift it radically to the three youths, one among them in particular.

The recent discovery of a burial under Room 2 is intriguing in light of the murals. The burial contains no surviving cranium, but it is rich in grave goods. The body had a supposed age of "approximately" 35 to 42 years at death. If correct, this aging would eliminate the presence of a youth in the burial, but it could pertain to older personages in the murals. The murals could then be seen as the record of an exemplary path for a prince, of someone who actually came to the throne. He used the mural program to highlight his role in a slightly earlier building. He also sharpened his profile as an obedient and legitimate heir to throne. Yajaw Chan Muwaan recedes in salience because he is dead—is the burial his? The succession statement in the mural should be taken at its word, as a record of a young prince shown, by vivid evidence of the murals, to be a worthy heir. He was an example to all other youths in his royal line. The murals look back to an unblemished career and anticipate a model for future rule. The acute irony of the mural building and this budding career is that, within a few decades, the Maya collapse would convulse Bonampak and adjacent regions.[38] This parable of a perfect prince, a visual manual like those known from other monarchical societies, would soon fall on uncomprehending eyes.

A candid appraisal would acknowledge that this scenario—of a dead ruler, an account from his life that targets an eventual heir—is circumstantial. The precise genealogical relation between Chooj and Yajaw Chan Muwaan, although likely to be close, cannot be decided without better evidence. An eroded sculpture at Bonampak, Stela 15, may show Yajaw Chan Muwaan with a woman and a younger male—Chooj? But there are no remaining, readable glyphs. In the Initial Series text, the name of the heir, maddening in its poor preservation, might possibly resemble the head of Chooj, the head of a man-eating cougar. Yet the outlines are sufficiently distinct to question that claim. Perhaps in this region there were multiple, simultaneous rulers from the same family. This possibility receives guarded support from the unusual joint use of "sacred" titles of kingship by younger lords in the murals.[39] This usage could have been a dynastic response to the perception and reality of encroaching disorder. By commissioning the murals, perhaps Yajaw Chan Muwaan and his overlord wished for general acknowledgment of Chooj.

What can be established with greater certainty is that the captions of Bonampak, unprecedented in number, provide a moral narrative for the transition of generations. Theirs is a boisterous but chaptered arc into royal life. General virtue, locally conceived, entwines with a distinctly personal narrative. "Truth," the paintings seem to say, exists within a framework of tradition and precedent. Like all good stories, the rooms offer a model career, with beginning, middle, end, and a desired, even propulsive conclusion.[40] The chapters focus on energetic reception of tribute (Room 1), a dark time of conflict and its bloody consequences (Room 2), and a dance and offering that brought the Sun God to earth (Room 3). Enabled by young men, just exaction led to just conflict and finally to just and necessary sacrifice. Paintings that had appeared to highlight a mature ruler appear, from multiple lines of evidence, to praise the epitome of a good prince. Beholden to kin and court, the youth was able to rule—he was ready to rule—on the testimony of the murals.

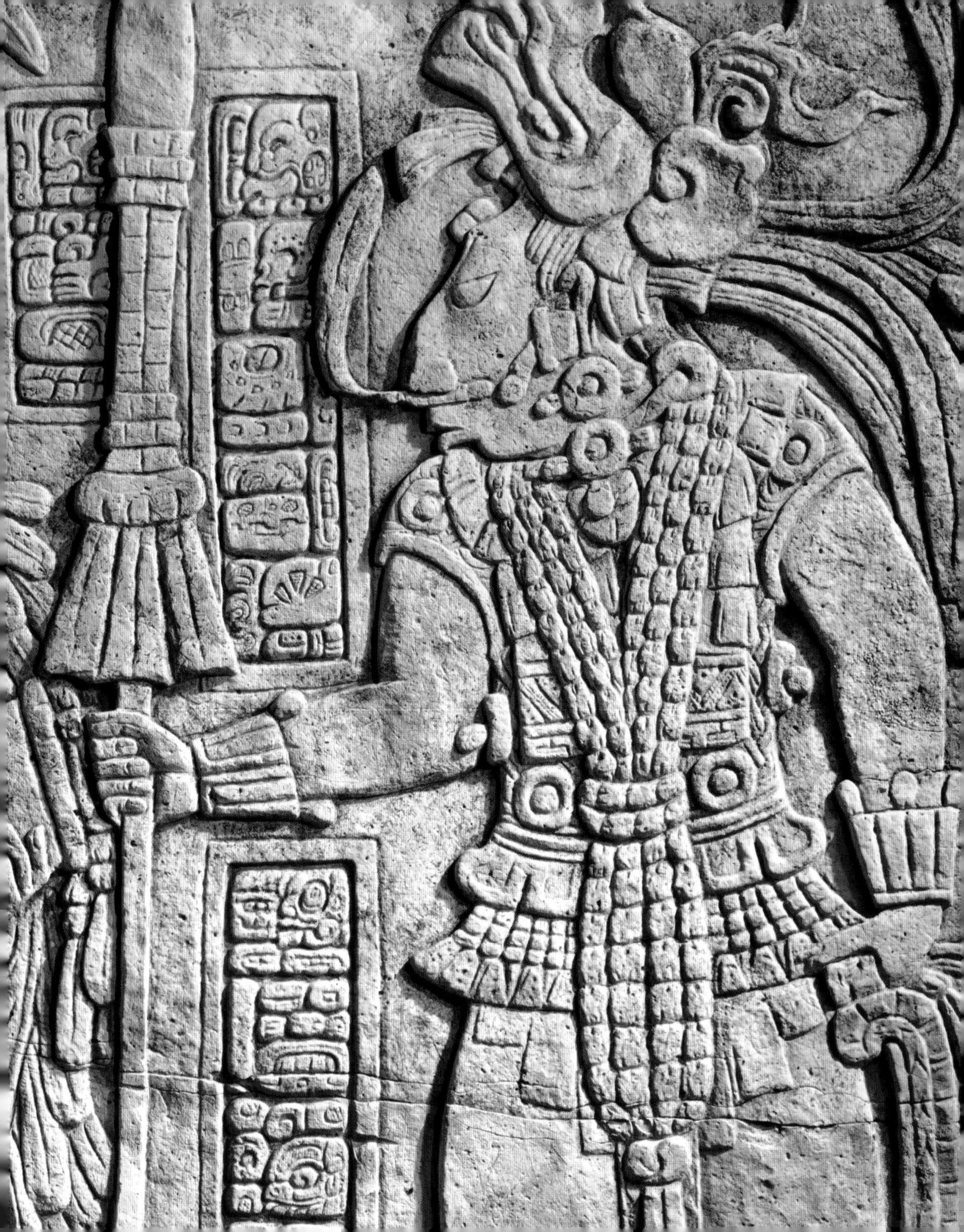

6 Draining the Cup

—Edmund Waller, "Of the Last Verses in the Book"

If lucky, young men grow old. They pass through the rigors of adulthood, thrive, and survive. Then they wait for the inevitable. Aching and weary elders of 80 seem far from their time as youths. But for the Classic Maya that distance is less than one might think. A joint label for grandsons and grandfathers underscores their reciprocal relation. In name and fact, the first replaces the second. *Ch'ok* cannot be understood without looking at those of very different appearance and physical capacity. There is also a more surprising belief: the sexual urges of *ch'ok*, especially those in the second decade of life, seem, from the visual evidence, to be shown as homoerotic and the youths' gatherings homosocial. Heterosexual encounters appear to occupy not the young men, where one might expect these attentions, but older, often divine males. These include the Maize God, a likely embodiment of polygamous adulthood, and a set of wrinkled deities with sparse teeth and hunched backs. Seemingly powerless, these figures are anything but. Filled with wisdom and the energies of earth, stone, and water, they express, in some images, an almost irrepressible lust toward younger women. In the words of the poet W. H. Auden, they combine "eros and dust."[1] With them may appear a class of courtesans, far younger, and perhaps motivated by profit. Daubed with bright body paint, the ladies are also richly dressed, ornamented, and solicitous of wrinkled lovers. Such young women not only help to define the nature of old men but also illuminate a category of females overlooked by Maya scholarship. To grow young men is also to anticipate their old age. For the Classic Maya, elderly men of necessity mirror and contrast with younger selves.

RECIPROCALS AND REPLACEMENTS

As we have seen, Maya writing reveals a great deal about objects and images. It permits us to identify *ch'ok*, *chak ch'ok*, *keleem*, and the essence of maleness, *xib*. There is often, as

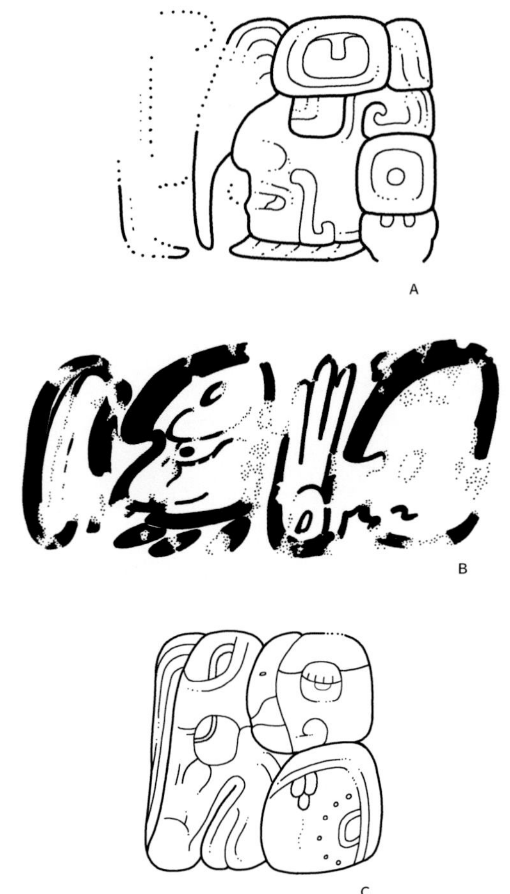

in many advertisements of gender, an exaggeration of attributes, a ratcheting up of what was thought essential to that unstable identity.[2] Another sign, deciphered as *mam* by David Stuart, labels old men. The glyph shows a hairy elder (fig. 77A). Long bangs cover his face, although like many gods he has sharp, eagle eyes in the earliest versions. Presumably, little gets by him. A circular element adorns his forehead, and he tends to wear a prominent ear-spool, perhaps inserted years before in the passage to adulthood. An alternate glyph proba-bly has the same reading, *mam,* but a different meaning of "grandson." It absorbs all but the old man's profile and replaces it with the head of a vulture, sometimes marked by a mirror or polished stone in the forehead (fig. 77B). For unknown reasons, the Maya linked the vul-ture to statements of maternal parentage. A rare variant in the Dresden Codex and a few other texts incorporates the head of an opossum and the long hair of the *mam.* In Room 2, the Bonampak murals refer to such an opossum *mam* as the "grandfather" of a youth, a *keleem.*[3] Ordinarily, that creature was *uch* in the language of the inscriptions, but in the Dresden Codex the *mam* opossum merges with an aged being known as an *Itzam,* traveling and dancing during New Year's ceremonies. (*Itzam* appears again later in this chapter.) A glance at this mammal affirms its similarity to aged men. It is whiskered, white-faced, slow-moving, and snaggle-toothed. Its self-protection is not ferocity but playing dead.

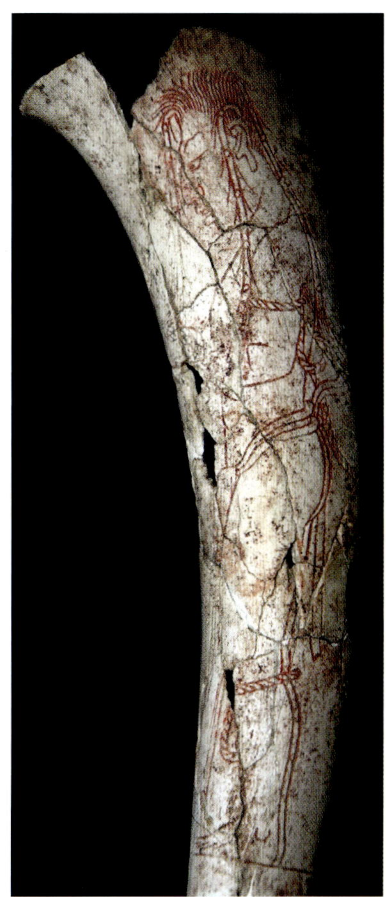

Young captive, grandson of
Calakmul king, MT39, Burial 116,
Tikal, Guatemala, c. AD 700. Bone,
4¾ in. (12.06 cm). Museo Sylvanus
G. Morley, Tikal, Guatemala.
Photograph by David Stuart.

Mam appears in most Mayan languages, with meanings that mostly target
"grandfather" but also "ancestor," "elder," and in Ch'orti', all male kin in ascending
generations. Not a single woman is named as such. Another important feature is
that the word occurs reciprocally to identify a "grandson" (granddaughters were not
labeled in this way). In Yukateko, the blood relation goes through the maternal line,
and as Stuart notes there are hints of this in glyphs at Yaxchilan, Mexico. Mention
on a stuccoed text at Holmul confirms this view, in that the local lord is the maternal grandson of an important foreign lord. Indeed, it is probably the same "Ruler
A" of Naranjo, Guatemala, who commissioned so many pots in his youth (recall the
discussion in chapter 3). A ruler of Tikal is said to have been the maternal grandson,
perhaps, of that same king.[4] Marriage had its political benefits. Commentators said
of the European Hapsburgs, "Bella gerant alii, tu felix Austria, nube!" Let others
wage war; you, happy Austria, marry! For the Classic Maya, the youth so named
generally held lower rank than his maternal grandfather. An exquisitely incised
bone from a royal tomb at Tikal (Guatemala) highlights a captive who is the "grandson" of a ruler from Calakmul (Mexico), Tikal's hereditary enemy (fig. 78). This
must have been a grievous blow, and the loss is made sharper by the evident beauty
of the youth. In much the same way, a block looted from La Corona, in Guatemala,
ties a local to his grandfather, also one of the mightiest kings of Calakmul.

Almost all references to "grandson" come from the Late Classic period.
With a few exceptions, *mam* as "elder" or "grandfather" is early. Perhaps, with
an increased need for alliances, maternal descent grew in importance. Strength
came from having friends, in the aggressive milieu of that time. Consider, too, dynasties
with many stakeholders, obscure relatives at the margins who may hunger for power.
Illustrious descent in both lines, maternal and paternal, solidified claims to rule and made
marginals even more so. The asymmetries between the early and late periods express
themselves through another pattern. We have seen much evidence that pottery, painted
with skill by literates, belonged to youths. A number of pots may have been used by those
of more advanced standing or slightly greater age, the *chak ch'ok.* In the Early Classic,
by comparison, certain pots of unusual finish belonged to *mam,* not the "grandsons"
emphasized in later texts but the "grandfathers" or "elders" spelled out with the hairy,
wizened face. Some are on chocolate pots, apparently as expressions of ancestral piety
or as gifts to elders (fig. 79). Had something happened to motivate those gifts, the birth
of a grandson, admission to some senior council, or was there simply a higher count of
katuns to celebrate? An Early Classic ceramic, the so-called Deletaille tripod, hints that the
donor might have been a grandson.[5] The owner of this chocolate vessel was *u mam k'an-
witznal ajaw,* "the grandfather" of the lord of the city known today as Ucanal, Guatemala.
Presumably, the younger lord gave the pot, and his grandsire was around to receive it.
Other references to *mam* appear as pectorals in the shape of ancestors—that is, to a deceased rather than still-present grandfather. The owners of such jewels were not those

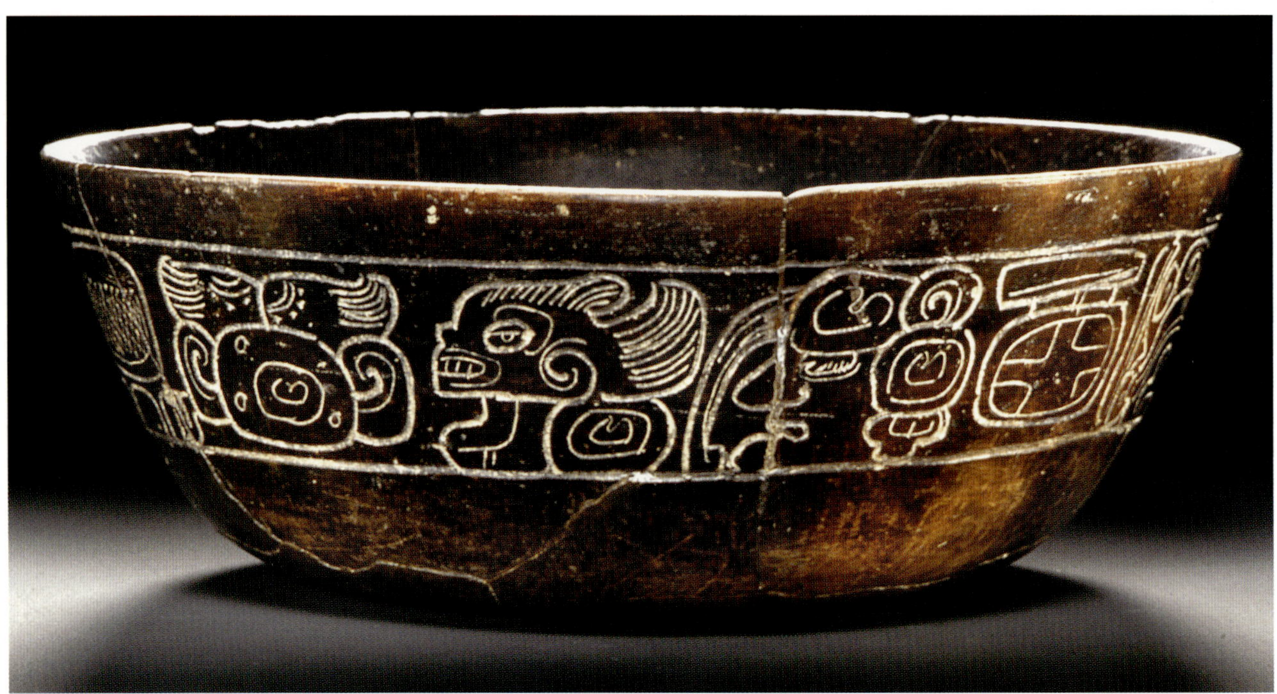

wearing them but those beings within, an internal presence to be displayed by those seeking ties to ancestors. If the Late Classic emphasized *ch'ok,* these earlier texts, and possibly those on Preclassic fetish objects, extolled elders and grandfathers. This implies a more definite marking of that time of life, a stress on the old rather than the young, on length of accumulated authority rather than mere birthright.

The reciprocal identity in *mam,* grandfather melding with grandson, needs its own explanation in ideas that are widespread among the Maya. The Tz'utujil believe that "a man's or woman's face must remain on the face of the earth through the replacement of their eyes, noses and mouth in the eyes, nose and mouth of their grandchildren." Over time, a grandfather switches out with a grandson. It may be for this reason that, in a well-known custom, some dynasties, especially those along the Usumacinta River between Guatemala and Mexico, alternate royal names by generation.[6] A Shield Jaguar has, as his own grandson, another Shield Jaguar, and so on, if with interruptions and anomalies that may arise from fraternal succession. Younger brothers, not expected to rule, receive other names. Such concepts are attested in other parts of the world. In Melanesia, there was apparently almost a "cyclic trajectory" of reincarnation; everyone embodied, to some extent, a person who had gone before. Rights, goods, and powers attached themselves to that cycle. In Africa, where ancestors are of long-standing interest to anthropologists, people may think of themselves through ancestral experience, often fathomed through dreams. The names of the esteemed dead, the "most generous, powerful, or handsome, or the best warrior(s)," are given in central Africa to newborns "without delay." The deceased themselves pass through "initiation rites," their crania "cradled like children" to which "lullaby-like songs" might be sung. They have become "full persons" and the seeds of a "future community." With such comparative evidence in mind, the anthropologist Maurice Godelier specifically examined the meaning of reciprocal terms. They reveal not an unending succession of different people but almost an erasure of such distinctions, a cycling through in "every three generations."[7]

As I write, kinship studies lodge in a sleepy, even moribund corner of anthropology. Earlier scholars had placed this work front-and-center, and some of us can remember as students the numbing nature of that work and its near-algorithmic complexity. But the social attributes of being an elder—the structures of kinship that embed that category—speak directly to the Classic Maya. (And indeed some anthropologists have found renewed interest in what Marshall Sahlins, a distinguished analyst of culture, calls the "mutuality of being."[8]) To revere the elderly, and those who have gone beyond to ancestorhood, is to honor and obey filial loyalty. For kingdoms, it goes further. A "lord-father" analogy takes a common feature of society—that of valued elders—and narrows it to a ruler and his line. Selective amnesia may result, and village elders are eventually forgotten.[9] How many of us, aside from genealogists, can recall the names of great-great-grandparents? Dynastic ancestors, as in ancient China but among the Maya too, affixed their identities to buildings and sculptures that could be revered and ceremonially accessed over time. On a human level, they energized the presence of the dead. The living kept ancestors around, not least by sharing their names and cherishing the things they once owned. Yet for the Classic Maya that early emphasis on the old and revered gave way, if incompletely, to fervent interest in the young. Both retained an unbudging purchase on Maya thought and creative expression, but the shift from *mam* to *ch'ok* indicates profound differences between their times of maximum emphasis. Elsewhere such shifts relate to demographic changes, as in early modern Europe. Greater populations, higher rates of survival, burgeoning elites—all might lend themselves to a more youthful focus. After all, these people were the predicament, the destabilizing element needing attention. We be can sure that stable rule was an objective in most periods. The Maya of the Early Classic period seemingly looked back to the bases of tradition, to the ancestral origins of social and ritual authority, and to the solid wisdom of elders. Later Maya glanced elsewhere. Their target: future youth to be guided to courtly service or confirmed in valid, dynastic succession.

PARADOX AND POTENCY

Older men are full of contradictions, and in ways that affect our views of young men. Their experience is vast, yet folly can be there in abundance. Bernardino de Sahagún, writing of the Aztec in the sixteenth century, offers his usual contrast between the good and the bad—his two-part moralizing is familiar from earlier chapters. The revered old man is "famous, honored, an adviser, a reprehender, a castigator, a counselor, an indoctrinator. He tells, he

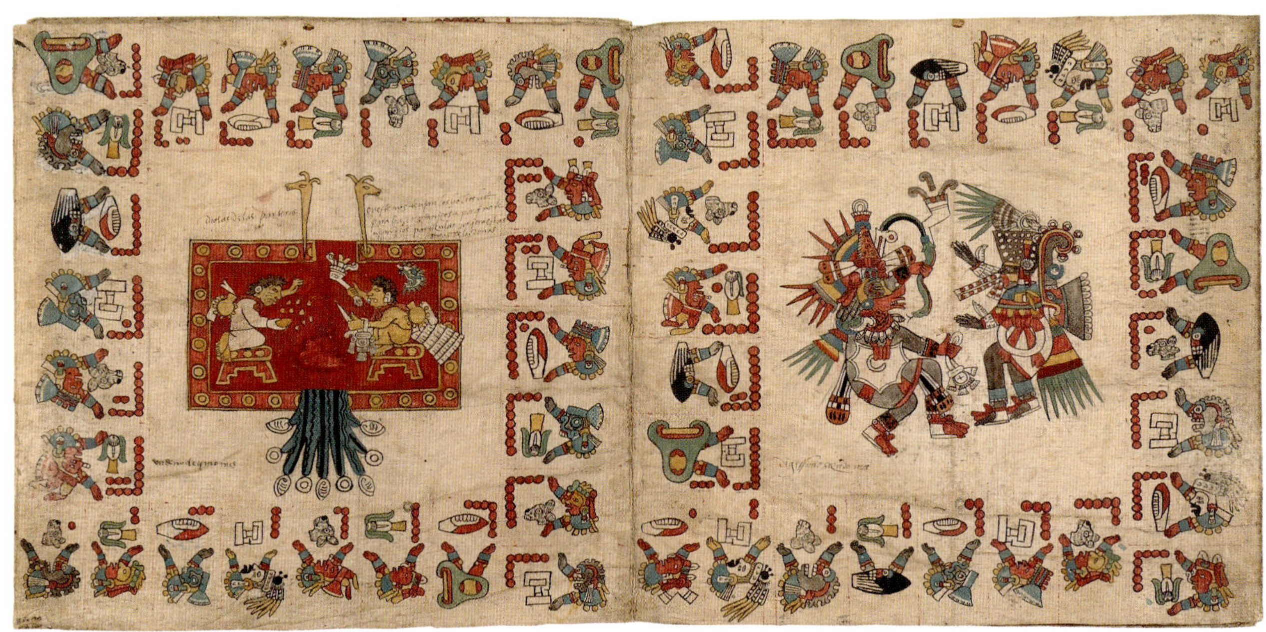

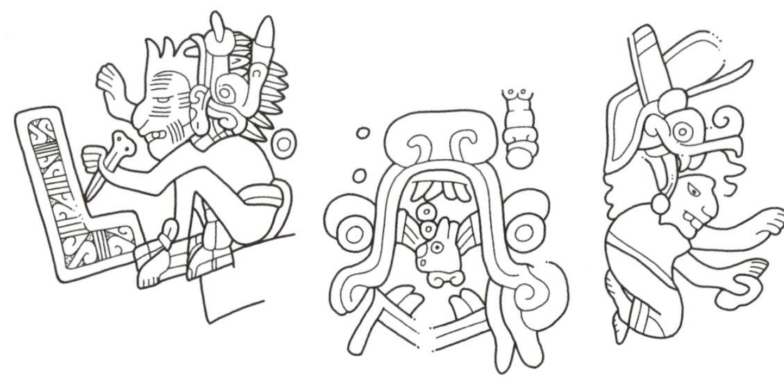

relates ancient lore; he leads an exemplary life." This is wisdom indeed. Others do not live up to that standard. The bad old man is "a fabricator, a liar, a drunkard, a thief; decrepit, feeble; a gaudy old man, a luxurious old man, an old fool, a liar. He invents falsehoods." For the Aztecs, old men have become "very big," possessing an internal fire (*tōnalli*) of spirit force likened to the warmth of the sun. But, in the worst case, they descend to second childhood. Spirit force, hot and irradiating, combines with mental deficits to make them dangerous. They may not be able to control the energies seeping out from their bodies.[10]

Benevolence cannot be assumed from the old. As noted by the epigrapher Simon Martin, "where there was once athleticism there is now acumen, where strength there is sorcery." Occult, terrifying knowledge is one aspect of experience. Learning helps but also harms. It is no coincidence that, among the Aztecs, a primordial couple—aged, gap-toothed, shrunken, wrinkled—practice prophecy. Even at the beginning, they can know all, see all. In one scene from the Codex Borbonicus, prepared about the time of the Spanish conquest, the creator goddess scatters corn kernels or seeds for prediction

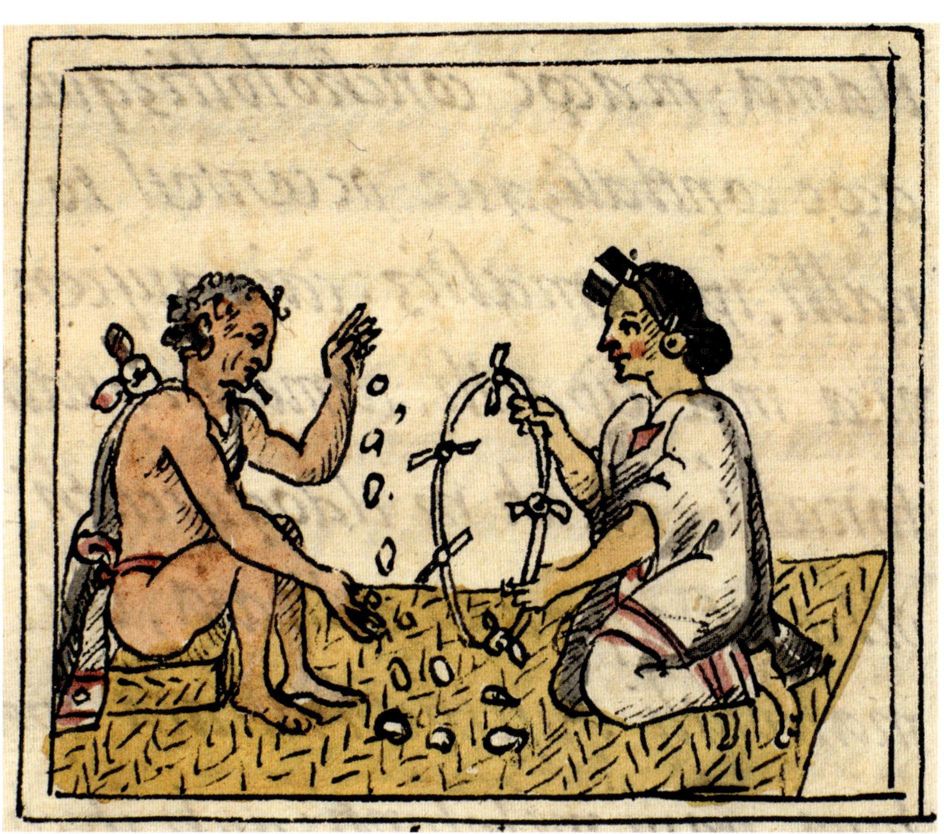

(fig. 80). Their eventual order will allow her to see future events, a capacity passed down
to successors. The Codex Magliabechiano, a document prepared in the mid-1500s but
based on a prototype from a generation before, shows one of them. A female "doctor"
throws twenty kernels of corn, one for each day of the Aztec calendar. The patient must
have gotten bad news, for he weeps in misery or pain. As for the primordial male in
the Borbonicus, he is a quintessential priest, burning incense with one hand while his other grips a bone awl for bloodletting. He is the first human agent and giver of offerings, the
first painter and scribe. They are linked to the initial day of the calendar, Cipactli, a crocodile tied to the origins of the world. A rock carving, the Piedra de Coatlan, from Morelos,
Mexico, shows them emerging from a crocodilian cave, a place of first emergence (fig. 81).
The old man uses a bone awl to carve a text—the act implies a permanent record—and
the female seems now to grasp a divinatory tool, perhaps a cup or shell for throwing the
seeds or kernels of augury. These helped her "see" and recount a narrative of how time,
space, and identity intersect, and how potential misfortune might be mitigated. The
Florentine Codex, by Sahagún and his associates, filters the couple through European
modeling and perspective, but declares the pair to be the authors of all "astrology" or
"necromancy," implying that they were inventors of the day count, indeed, of writing itself
(fig. 82). The female holds a knotted cord. As suggested by Colonial sources, the cord may
relate to the use of hand measurements in curing.[11]

Evidence from the colonial Maya attests to similar pairs of progenitors. The crone is the first midwife—a gloss in the Borbonicus describes her as the goddess of such specialists—and Karl Taube has identified a similar being among the Classic Maya (fig. 83).[12] Feline in nature, an elderly sorceress with hanging breasts, the Maya goddess presides over birth and death. On a cosmic level, she is there at the beginning of the world and at its destruction. The Dresden Codex places her against a blood-red sky, pouring out a deluge from an upended water jar. As a midwife, she is also present at childbirth. Like a Norse Norn, cutting thread to determine lifespans, the goddess is seen on one pot wearing a spindle with cotton thread. The spindle appears near her head, as though perched behind an ear. Most likely, she was also the main patron of Maya curers. This role accounts for a sculpture from the first years of the Early Classic period (fig. 84). The goddess leans forward over the square holder of a long-gone mirror. Among the Aztecs, a reflective surface helped curers in detecting disease.[13] Looking into it, a person reflected with a light face revealed a slight indisposition, something that would soon pass; a dark face foretold serious disease. The carving of the old woman is active, in a sense, and unsettling. By peering into the mirror, a viewer faced the goddess and her unwavering eyes. The goddess, her mouth open, seemed to talk in turn. But who really wanted to listen? For most people, a grim diagnosis is hard to bear. Knowing one's destiny, if bad, must have been disagreeable. Yet the power of that knowledge carries uncommon force. The feline nature of the crone suggests the dark origins of that wisdom. The carving is not large, but in use it likely inspired dread, even fear.

Her spouse is also found in Classic Maya texts and imagery. He is a god called, based on studies by David Stuart and Simon Martin, *Itzam*, a god we have already encountered, and a pure distillate of the powers of aged men. If the goddess helps at childbirth, he offers scribal knowledge to newly emergent humans. In one scene, *Itzam* instructs in mathematics or tabulation. He is a generous god, a repository of learning, and he is shown on one pot, now at the Kimbell Museum of Art, Fort Worth, Texas, with attentive students nearby. He also discharges an unimaginable strength. Often, *Itzam* functions as an Atlantean figure, bearing on his back the weight of the world or, in images that fuse cosmos and politics, the thrones of kings. At times he lifts the sky itself. Atlas, supporter of the heavens in Greek mythology, did so as punishment by Zeus. Ultimately, the Maya god's labor also implies obedience to higher authorities. Often found in groups of four, each identical to the other, he is indispensable to the vertical ordering of space as an Atlantean figure. Nonetheless, his duties suggest he took orders from others. *Itzam* is seldom shown on a throne, as someone in charge. When he does, as on one pot, his court consists of misshapen people—hunchbacks and the obese.[14]

The Classic Maya probably saw old men in ways similar to the views of their descendants in present-day Guatemala, Mexico, and Belize. In much of the Maya highlands, old men occupy the top ladder-rung of civic responsibility, having held weighty and expensive office over the years. (Many of these hierarchies are now gone or fading fast.)

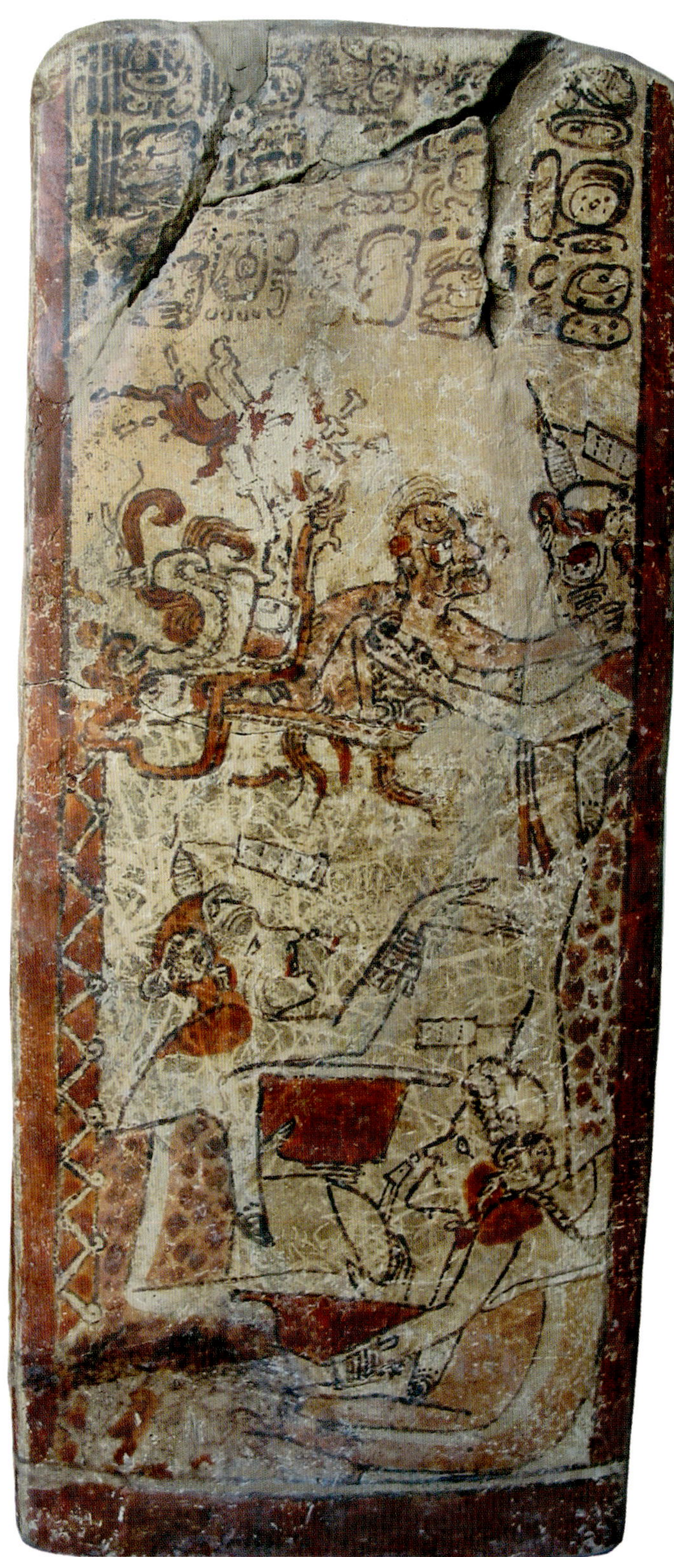

FIGURE 83
Maya midwife goddesses,
Guatemala, c. AD 750. 9⅘ × 4³⁄₁₀ ×
4³⁄₁₀ in. (24.89 × 10.92 × 10.92 cm).
Los Angeles County Museum of
Art, purchased with funds pro-
vided by Camilla Chandler Frost
(M.2010.115.452).

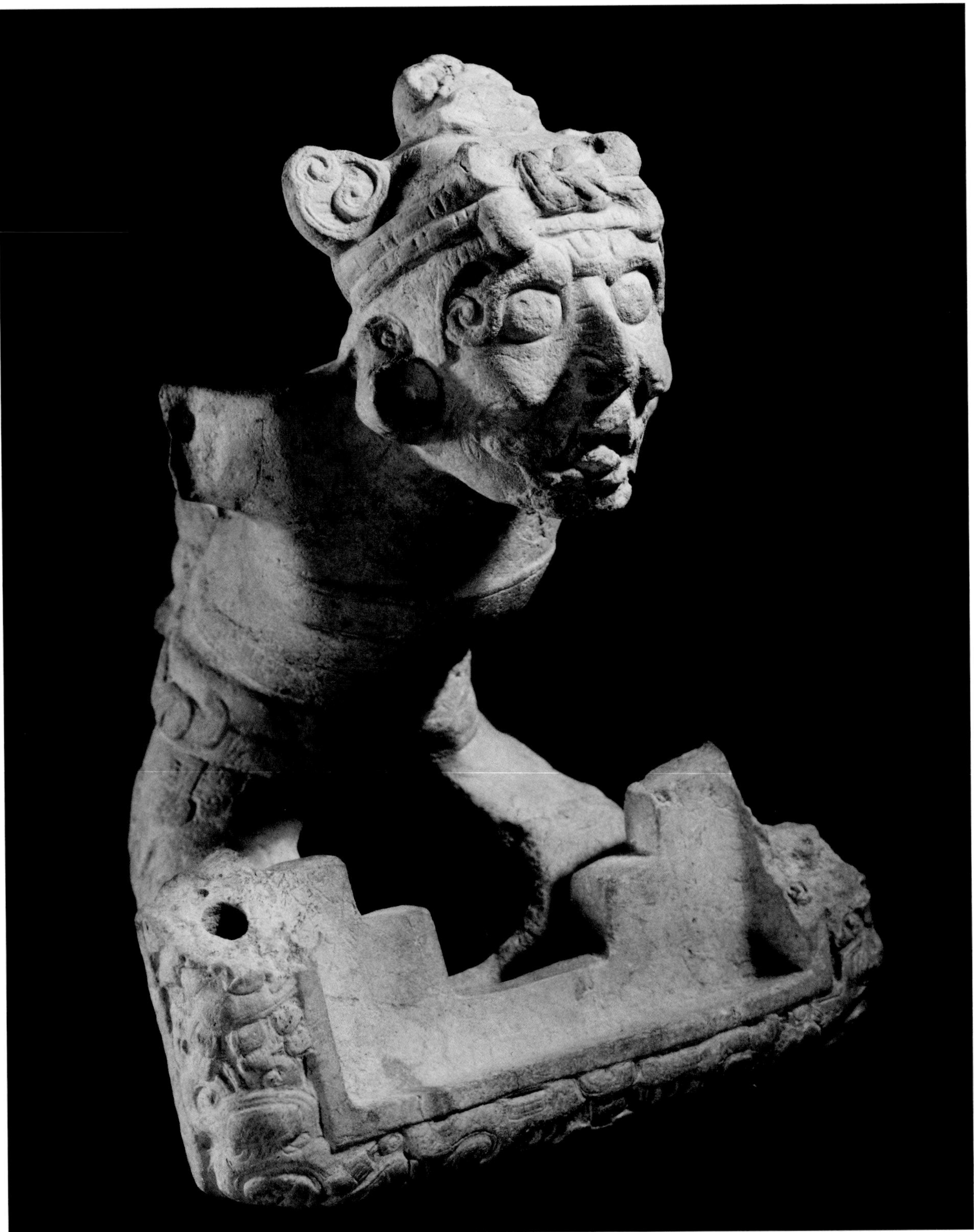

With increased service, ritual garments become more impressive, badges or tokens of office more gleaming, and likely to have been passed down over the generations. Among the Tz'utujil of Santiago Atitlan in Guatemala, older men are well on the road to becoming "perfect ancestors" with deep wisdom. They may transform into the *lab* of the Tzeltal Maya, an "invisible old folk . . . personifications of the soil."[15] Hazardous to humans, they thieve souls. But there is no clear cutoff, no time when men become definitively old. Senescence may be linear, only one direction for all, but for humans it broaches many dimensions. Chronological age does not equate to functional age; the body may go soft before mental acuity or vice versa. Life expectancy often defines the elderly in a particular society, and not just for the Maya. As I write, situated near illustrious hospitals, a death at 55 seems premature. It begs explanation, maybe a lawsuit. Not so in the Jamestown colony of Virginia four hundred years ago.[16] Surviving into one's thirties was good fortune indeed. In agrarian settings, the time also arrives when men can no longer walk to, or work in, distant fields. For that, youths will do just fine. That group includes those, such as among the Mam Maya, who are still in their twenties but living under paternal roofs. During the Classic period, for elites, old age may have been when men no longer went to battle.

Classic Maya imagery displays some men in all their wizened ruin. A carving from Copan, Honduras, of a less than impressive *Itzam* is almost undignified (fig. 85). Drool trickles, one imagines, out of the gaping, tooth-deprived mouth. For kings such images are rare to nonexistent; royal vanity and a wish to project physical strength precluded such representation. A lintel looted from the kingdom of Yaxchilan features a king who ruled from AD 681 to 742 (fig. 86). To his side stands a youth, a nobleman, already adept at war—he has taken four captives in battle. The king is a shade taller, but nothing in his physique betrays his actual age of over 80. Not a wrinkle mars his body, his muscles are full, his thighs thick. There are no stigmata of old age. Portly kings are seen, especially in the extraordinary dynastic narratives on pots from the area of Motul de San José, Guatemala, but that heaviness may stress their actual appearance, along with good health and access to a rich larder. Captives are another matter. An elderly nobleman from Yaxchilan, a victim of Piedras Negras, Guatemala, downstream, kneels in front of his captor, his knees knobby, his body scrawny, the protruding ribs pointing to weakness. He is a study of misery and the effects of wear and tear. By coincidence, he is also a nobleman or possible kin of the vain ruler on the lintel. The images could not present a stronger contrast between vigor and frailty or with the frail bones and poorly healed fractures of known Maya kings. The founder of the royal dynasty at Copan left a skeleton with strong evidence of trauma.[17]

For all their power, and perhaps because of it, gods are the ones shown old. There are a few exceptions, such as aged porters, male and female, detected by Simon Martin in the murals of the Chiik Nahb building at Calakmul.[18] Poor people—their loads are too heavy by far: the woman's burden, a huge basin, could almost fit her entire body; the man tries to steady his pack with an awkward, twisted arm across his back. The images

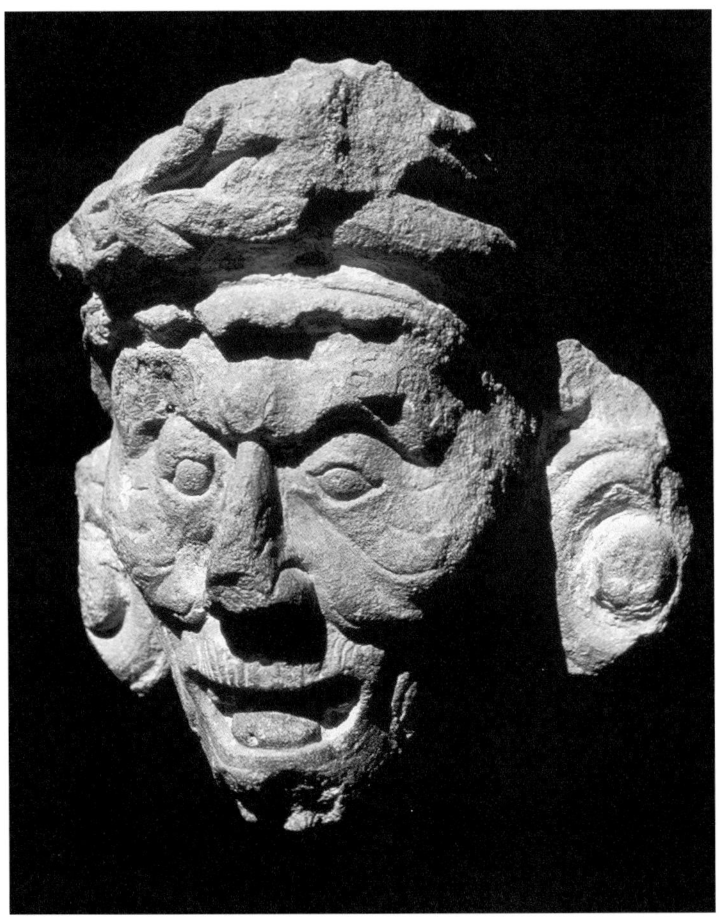

seem close to jokelike. But it is the gods who provide a comprehensive view of what it looks like to be elderly. Unlike most Maya in Classic imagery, the gods sprout facial hair, wispy beards, here and there a mustache. The jaw droops open—are they losing muscle tone or making endless speeches? In human bodies, the nose often grows in size, as there is no stopping the effect of gravity on cartilage, and old gods have prominent, aquiline noses, accentuated by bone loss around the mandible, a common by-product of tooth loss. Muscles have weakened, joints seem disproportionately large, backs stoop; several images may depict an abdominal hernia or everted umbilicus, perhaps from ascites, an accumulation of fluid; a thin and muscled belly gives way to bloat. Gods, however, do not follow human development. A vase at the Los Angeles County Museum of Art proves that old gods were born old, their skin wrinkled and hair scraggly. Among these gods, a baby is anything but helpless, with potentials far greater than any human infant. Some gods had other kinds of midwifery: the Sun God, evidently a newborn with flowery umbilicus, has an elderly god of trade sawing through that tissue with an obsidian blade.[19] A younger god sits nearby with a bowl containing another, more stylized blade and a bowl intended for

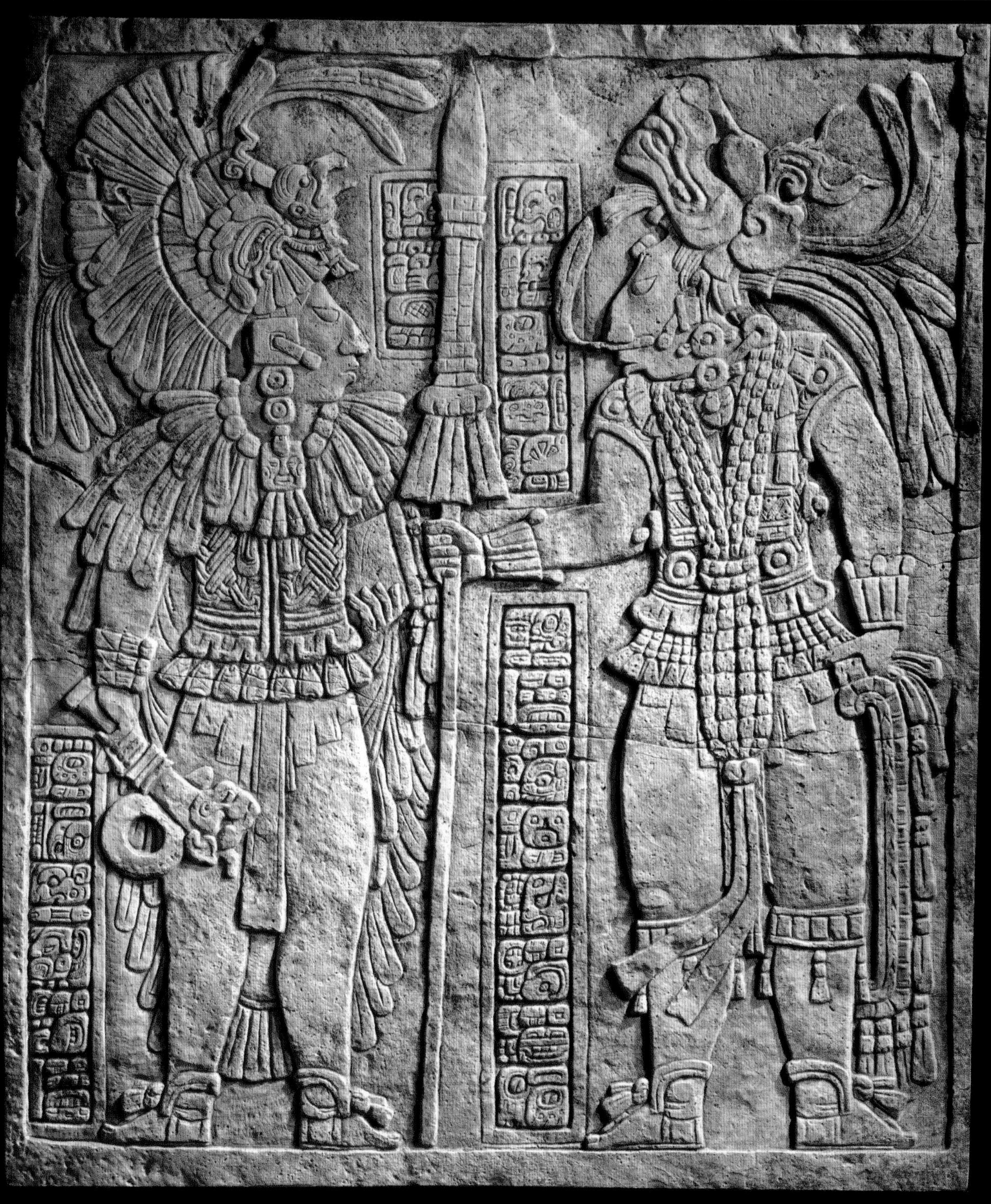

the navel string. The reference may be doubled, nodding not just to birth but to death by heart sacrifice (both beginnings and endings may be implied in the scene): the long umbilicus is tagged with the word *ohl* for "heart." Whatever the reality of great age, its infirmities and diminishing energy, the beings in this image and others reveal uncommon knowledge and skill. They act with a robust purpose that warrants respect and fear. If old men were close to draining their cup, they did so, it seems, with vigor intact.

AGED LUST AND PRETTY LADIES

Most human bodies, especially of royalty, are depicted in flattering ways. Recall that kings are hearty and full grown. Plump men and women may reflect the body types of the affluent, never short of food. There are also, as noted in earlier chapters, a solemnity and formality to their presentation. Excess and erotic abandon occur in only a few places, including at Naj Tunich, on a few pots, and on the reliefs from Rancho San Diego in Yucatan. Lovemaking, either in seduction or flagrant expression, involves gods. On a broken dish from about AD 700 at Uaxactun, Guatemala, spider monkeys and bugs mount receptive women. An old god sits nearby, smoking a cigarillo and receiving tribute in the form of feathers. Perhaps the setting is his debauched court.[20] Some pictures take us into the nature of comedy and satire. They not only describe gods but, in subtle reproach, the behavior of humans. Ill-matched couples are rife in European art. A hideous old man paws or is stroked by a young woman. Viewers look carefully at the female reaction. Is there a disgusted rebuff or an invitation to further cuddling? The same occurs throughout Late Classic Maya art, especially in the figurines, which represented the broadest disseminations of Classic Maya imagery other than bowls, plates, or vessels. As portable objects, their circumstances of ownership and view were not as controllable as a stela or a stucco façade. Although a carving has a carefully arranged, thought-through placement, not so a small figurine. Many figurines show winter-spring pairs, an old god hitching up the skirt of the young female (fig. 87). Yet the image is not wholly censorious or clowning. There may have been a sneaking approval of such vim among elderly men. The energy allowing them to support earth and sky can find other outlets. A vessel now at the Museum of Fine Arts in Boston displays a large assembly of unequal pairs, young ladies being gifted, it seems, to a passel of randy *Itzam*.[21] Another vase, at Princeton, depicts him with his harem. He tinkers with the bracelet of one lady, possibly as a valuable present for her attentions. To be sure, the moralizing contrasts with views of the more august elderly, the enthroned Sun God and the lord of royal wisdom, known to specialists as "God D" (his real name remains elusive). They are, like the Chinese ancients, less affected by decline than the figures whose longevity gave proof of virtue and accumulated experience.[22]

The sexuality of old men brings us back to the young. It is only here, and with images of the polygamous Maize God, that erotic encounters between genders appear with any frequency. Where youths show erotic experiences, these take place—with admittedly

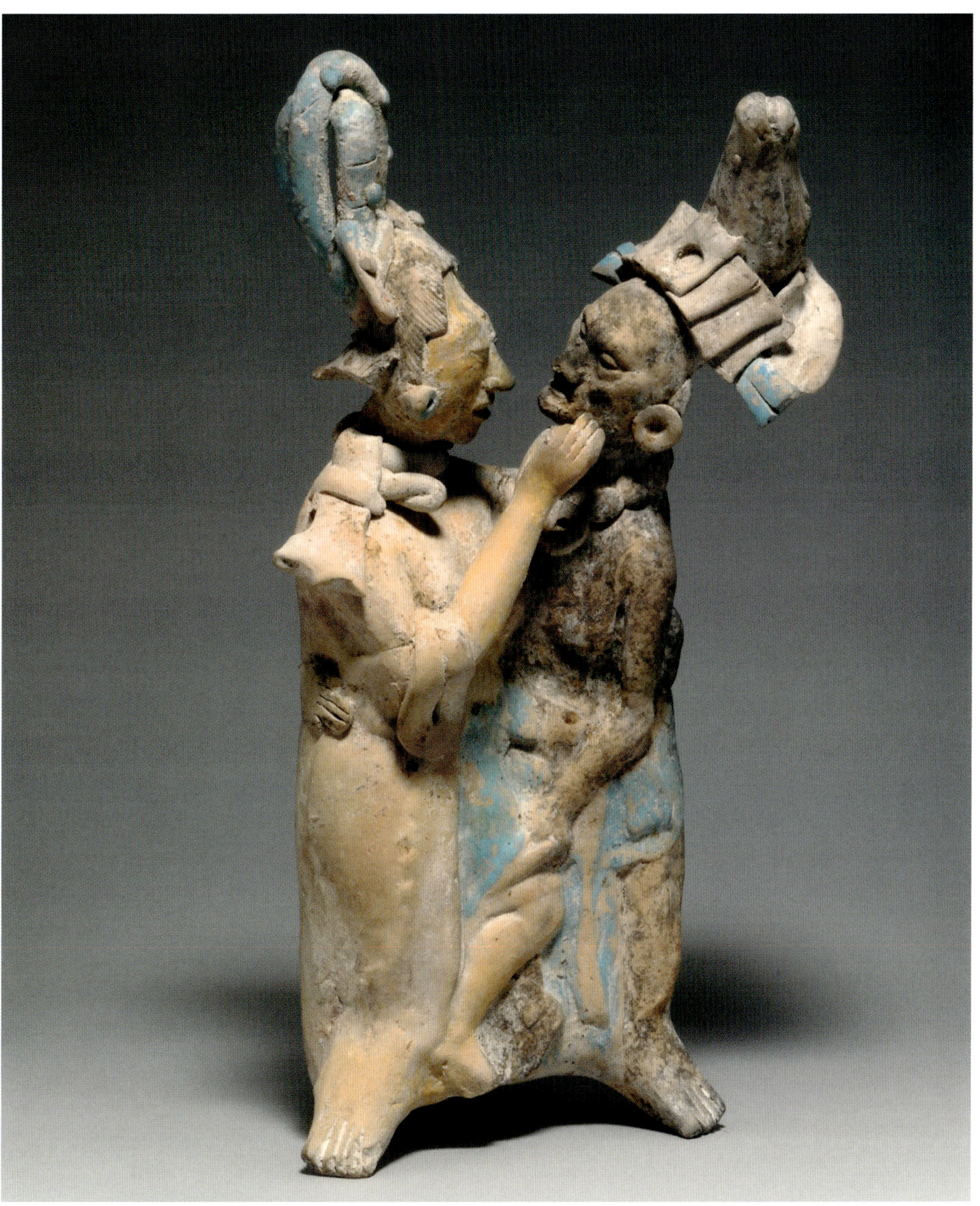

a small sample—in conditions of homosexual practice and homosocial gathering. To state the obvious: it is highly implausible that *ch'ok* of the Classic period avoided heterosexual liaisons. But the available imagery strives to avoid or mute that probability, associating such activity with the elderly, and always in dalliances between aged men and much younger women. Their companions may have been motivated by other, more mercenary needs. The Aztecs knew of such women, although they have been largely ignored in Mayanist scholarship. Diego Rivera's murals of the Aztec market at Tlatelolco—completed in 1945, visible today on the second floor of the Palacio Nacional in Mexico City—buzz with scenes of imperial commerce. Vendors hawk while merchants bicker, counting with upright fingers. Slave traders nearby examine the teeth of human stock. Tortillas are there, too, close to belly-up frogs. Dogs, deer, iguana, and fish lie in good order or, like a fat little *xolo* dog, they mewl and squirm. All will soon be purchased, cooked, and eaten. The most arresting figure, however, is a woman in white (fig. 88). Central to the composition, she hikes her skirt and invites the attention of several leering men. One of them, to upper left, looks like a Rockefeller, a family Rivera would have loathed: Nelson, future U.S. vice president, sanctioned the destruction in 1934 of Rivera's mural at Rockefeller Center in New York City. At Rivera's coy insistence, it seems, we are all voyeurs. Almost alone in the murals, the woman's body faces the viewer. Her bright red lipstick, elaborate costume, and long loose hair, described and illustrated in Aztec sources, heighten the wanton allure. Never one for nuance, Rivera surrounds the lady with an aureole of calla lilies, which may have been Rivera's coded image for female privates. His portrait of Natasha Zakólkowa Gelman, painted a year earlier, voluptuous on her couch, uses the same framing device.[23]

Rivera's lady was an Aztec prostitute or *āhuiyani*, someone who gave pleasure but in debased or self-indulgent ways, a "flower woman."[24] She "lives in wickedness . . . she goes about in gaudy dress, drunk, besotted," "shamelessly, presumptuously, conspicuously washed and combed." She "sells her body" and "paints her face . . . her hair falls loose"; she goes "about . . . in the market place . . . places herself at the market, adorns herself at the market place."[25] But the stern judgment in these phrases from Benardino de Sahagún does not offer a complete picture, for such women performed openly in sacred dances with warriors.[26] A peculiarity is that depictions of young and older harlots in the Florentine Codex show them standing on water, grasping flowers in one hand and, oddly, the glyph for water in the other (fig. 89). It is possible, but on reflection unlikely, that this sign merely reinforces the first letter in their name, *āhuiyani* (from *ā-tl,* "water"). Underfoot, gripped in the hand, the symbols point to deeper and more complex meanings.

Most treatments of female identity among the ancient or colonial Maya do not mention prostitutes or allude to them in indirect ways. One source describes female prostitutes in Yucatan, but as beings "constructed as an ethnic outsider and an enemy" and, in the Books of Chilam Balam, a figure whose very label was an insult thrown at others.[27] Early Maya dictionaries, a window into past thought, refer widely to such figures, hinting that they were a common sight. Relevant words relate to adultery, fornication,

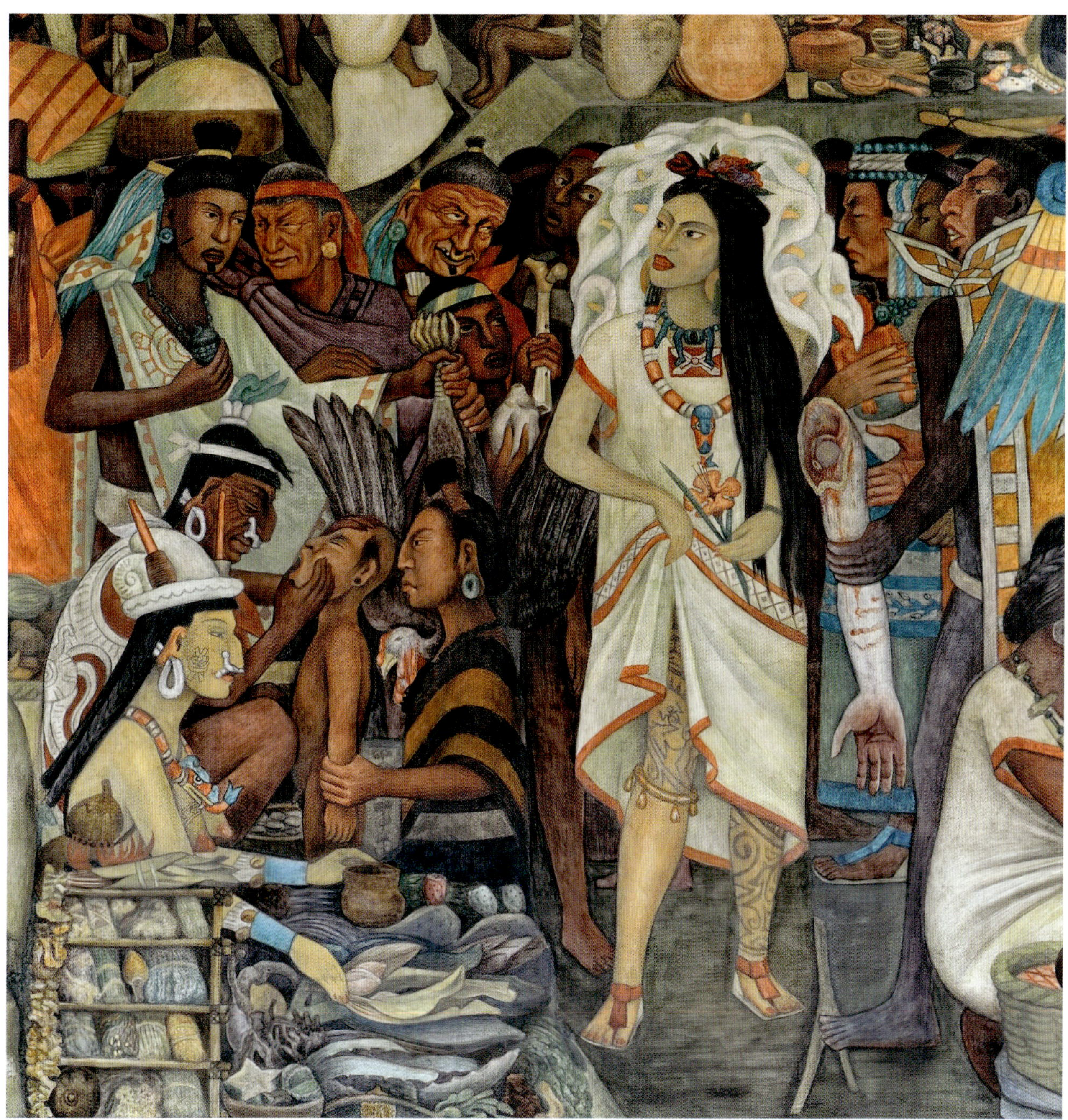

FIGURE 88

Diego Rivera, *El tianguis de
Tlatelolco* (detail), Palacio
Nacional, Mexico City, 1945.

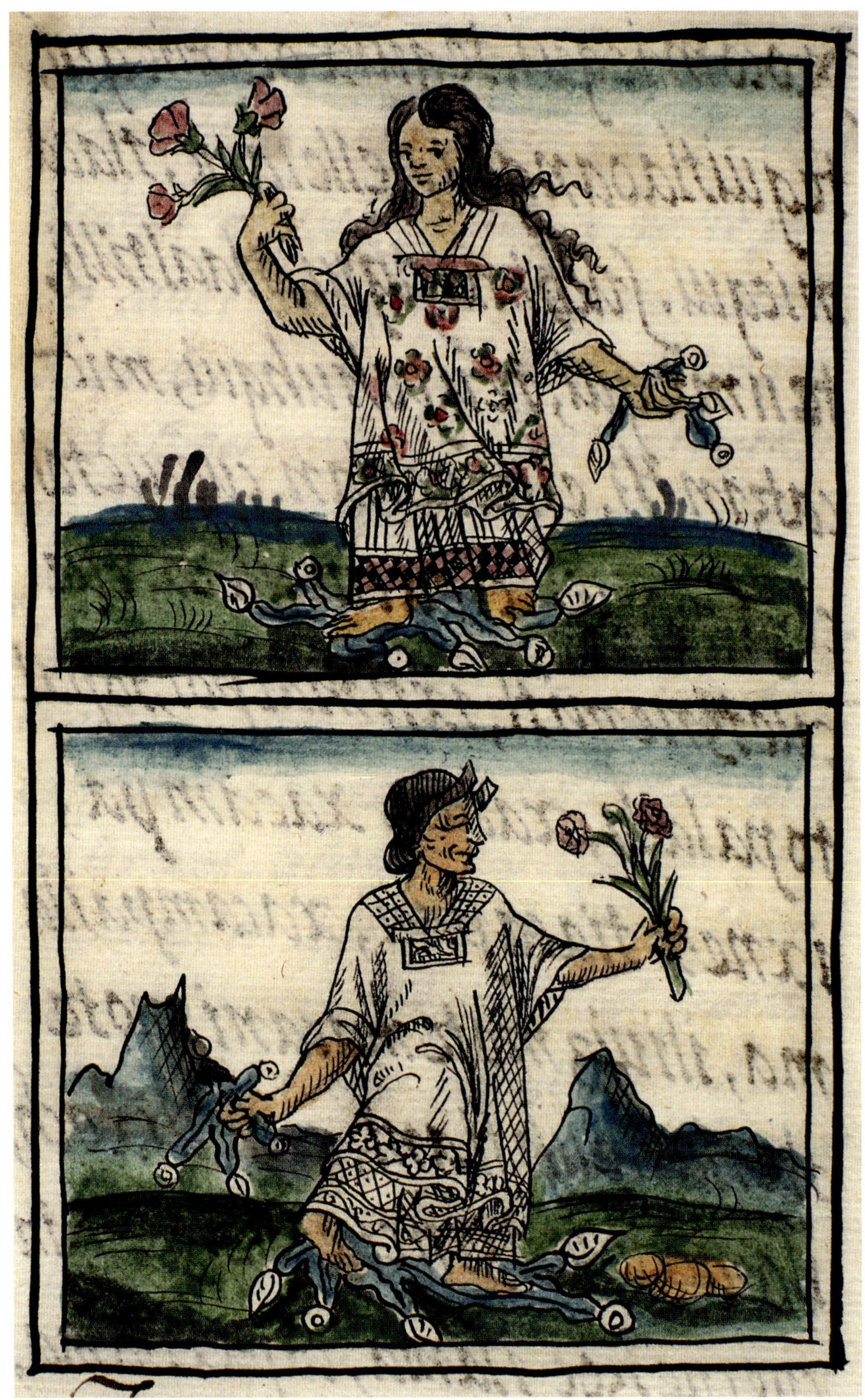

FIGURE 89
Prostitutes, *Florentine Codex,*
Book 10, fol. 39v. Biblioteca
Medicea-Laurenziana, Palat.
218–220.

sexual penetration, scourging, and lust, with the added nuance of concubinage. Colonial Yukateko correlated these acts and urges with agouti or hares (*tzub*), the latter a well-known companion of the Moon Goddess and a symbol of procreation. For *tzub,* the meaning is quite explicit: these are "the bad women whose body may be public or not," and, in a cognate word, "the whore who invites and sells herself."[28]

The Classic Maya probably had such women, and these may have been some of the females shown with old men. Key evidence comes from the Chiik Nahb murals at Calakmul, most of which date to the seventh century AD (fig. 90). Concerned with trade, these paintings appear within a market facility built at the height of competition between the great cities of Calakmul and Tikal. The murals focus on the erotic beauty of the serving ladies, their body paint and jade jewelry. The women pour drinks and offer *atole* while dressed, at times, in diaphanous clothing. Glimpsed underneath are breasts, areola, and full thighs. One in particular repeats in different sections. She is best labeled, from her dress in a well-preserved scene, the Lady in Blue. Overtly sexualized, the woman offers hospitality and welcome accommodation or participation in marketing. Similar trading ladies, brought to my attention by Karl Taube, occur as figurines from the Alta Verapaz, in Guatemala, also bejeweled, gowns slung low, hair coiffed.[29] Vending women exist in other traditions of Lowland Maya figurines. Many wear hats, perhaps to show they came from far away, but possibly to protect their delicate complexions. They both are and are not standard vendors, involved in trade yet outfitted in ways that imply other kinds of service.

A more overt example of such ladies of pleasure and erotic hospitality comes from a bowl dating to about AD 600, which links them to water.[30] These women, certain to be goddesses, fondle *Itzam* who leer in delight. The ladies stroke their sides, fan faces, or hold up mirrors while the men daub their mouths with snuff or pigment. Most carry exactly the same name, possibly a token of multiple or shared identity, or they use a sparse description, *ixik,* "female." The watery attribute of Aztec prostitutes seems to be more than a coincidence. They conformed to a widespread notion of "watery women" or "women of watery locales" whose sexual behavior differed, in disquieting, less manageable ways, from that of other ladies. The women are unlikely to be spouses. A plausible view is that they traffic in generous reception and consumption, with physical favors to come.

At Calakmul, the Lady in Blue embodied, if not a historical person, then the essence of gracious hospitality. Or, as a bolder suggestion and with a gesture to the eroticism of the murals, she operated as an exemplary or deified procuress, employed rather than punished by the state, a catalyst for other kinds of business. She labored, it seems, away from direct male supervision. She took charge herself, with no overt partner, no husband, no pimp. In one image, a young woman, perhaps a unique depiction of a Maya slave, toiled as her assistant. The Florentine Codex says of the procuress: "She is of a house. . . . She induces, seduces with words, incites with others. Adroit of language, skilled of speech, she is a fraud. . . . She receives guests. She secures recompense, payment from others. She robs

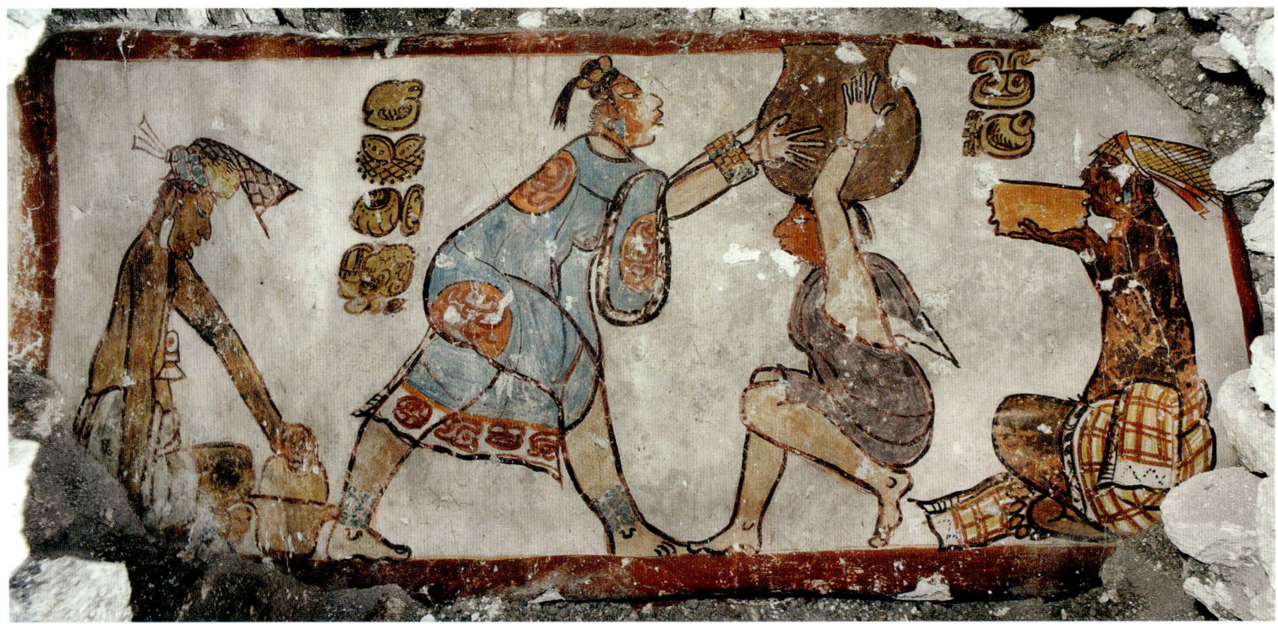

one—she constantly robs one."[31] However, if present at Calakmul, such women performed a role of some respect and importance. Even their female servants might have been courtesans, a category well documented in other parts of the world, from twentieth-century New Orleans to Edo-period Japan.[32]

The Lady in Blue raises basic matters of identification. Scholars often refer to "noble" ladies or "idealized elite" women and goddesses in imagery of the Classic Maya period. This applies to Jaina figurines as well, said to come from an island off the coast of Campeche, Mexico. But what if an entire category of Maya society has been overlooked in retroactive prudery or distaste, one that serviced older men and their sexual demands? As the eminent Mayanist Michael Coe observed to me, the females participating in enema rituals could have been ladies of pleasure. Some elite ornament or jewelry, thought to have been commissions of dynastic figures and other nobles, may have been baubles ordered in quantity by courtesans. Sex work has its own history. As one example from archaic Greece, the high-status *hetaera*, the most polished of courtesans, was probably fashioned under the impetus of aristocratic males.[33] Men defined their own masculinity by interacting with such females. Through women's bodies and, tragically, through their abuse, men worked out what it meant to be men. Such were the "relational identities" mentioned in the first chapter. Wrinkled men and lusty ladies surely diverted those who looked at them. Contempt blended with amusement. Maybe there was a little envy. In old men, young men saw the possibility of future license. According to the Codex Mendoza, the Aztec regarded old age as a time for liberal drinking and intoxication. There were new powers, potentials, and freedoms to come. Of course, among the Maya, younger males could get rambunctious, too: one pot shows the Maize God trampling and kicking a set of older gods who

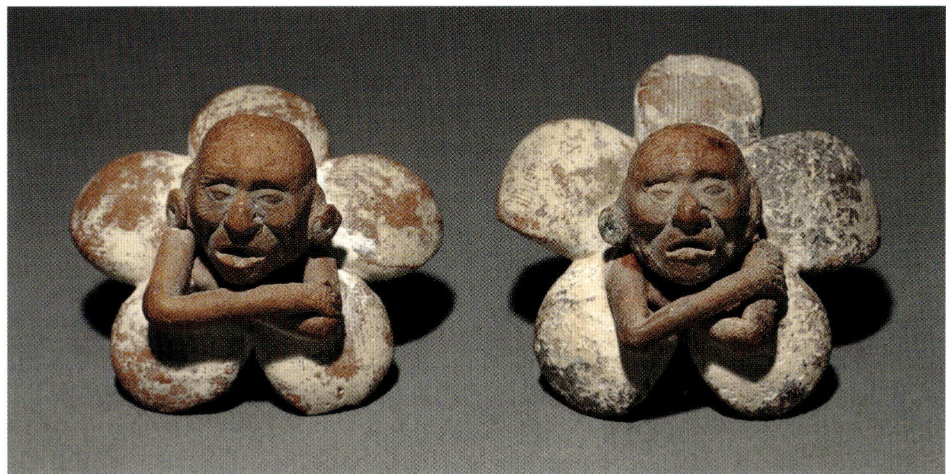

have been stripped of their finery.[34] As for women, the crone could no longer bear children. She had no sexual allure, her body was thin and slumped, but her abilities, the effects of her wisdom and incantatory power, determined whether someone might live or die. Being postmenopausal gave some comfort too: the dangers of childbirth lay behind her.

The paradox here, of old men with lush sexuality, depends on more subtle ideas. Among the Tz'utujil of highland Guatemala, the *mam,* explicitly named as such, ripen fruit through their internal heat. They are the pathfinders for younger men undergoing agricultural pilgrimages. Succulent fruits come back as gifts to the *mam,* in fulfillment of youthful duties before marriage. This may account for Classic-era flutes, whistles, and ear ornaments from the island of Jaina (fig. 91).[35] Daubed with Maya blue or bright yellow, they represent flowers or corn in which old gods appear with crossed arms. The motion implies respectful service, but the main point is that, with musical instruments, new growth, fragrance, and pleasing sound are associated with grizzled faces and bodies. This is a surprise. With age, most voices become lower and rougher—the last thing one thinks of are trilling flutes. The vitality of fresh vegetation ordinarily relates to younger beings like the Maize god. Yet, with these objects, older gods project their own earthy fertility and possession of the energy that ripens plants. The traits of the young pass to old men, their logical and nomenclatural counterparts.

A WORLD OF GROWING MEN

Centuries ago, the *ch'ok* of the Maya world became old men. This came to pass if they were lucky enough to live long enough. Some turned out to be ancestors of renown. Intervening centuries forgot them, however, and their resuscitation in this book has required several steps: close study of texts and imagery; a probing for later ideas that descended, by twisting path, from Classic beliefs; and, more abstractly, examination of organizing principles from other cultures, some relatively close, others an ocean or two away. This volume has looked at how ancient peoples interpret and use the human body. It reflects on the condition of being male through a Maya prism, at how they infused masculine identity with meaning and social resolve. Some features of young men are proven. In Classic times, they existed as a central category of being, motivating the commission of paintings, buildings, and valued objects. Of course, evidence is not always of the same quality. Buildings for young men would be difficult to identity without accompanying texts or images.

What does seem certain is that, as a group, young men coalesced in the distant past. According to some clues, their formation and early naming resulted from martial needs and the impress of Teotihuacan, Mexico. They were clearly organized into groups, especially of those past the endrocrinological portal of andrenarche, when new chemicals issued from the adrenal cortex. Yet, at the highest level, the course of individual youths received special inflection. Testing of merit took place, and some did not make the grade. A "wilding time" of controlled excess worked certain urges out of their system while reinforcing others. Young men learned to work in unison. Those figures who come closest to view are the princes of Bonampak, the striplings at Caracol, Dos Pilas, Naranjo, and Palenque, the Hamlets, pawns, and cunning operators of their period. Personalities and dynastic details influenced them as much as wider, general patterns. Other youths, known only by general titles, received, held, and gave away pots of fine finish and literate phrasing. The relative number of these people should, on the slightest reflection, astonish by their quantity. Their presence, along with that of various buildings, needs mention, as, indeed, does the possession of things by old men and ancestors in the Early Classic period.

The confession that we are all humans brings young men close to hand. Their energy, which exhausts, their forward impulses, which worry, their newfound sexual urges, which must be harnessed and controlled, are all recognizable. They had wild fun, auto-erotic experiments, drank too much, consorted with a variety of sexual partners, if under the eye (and with the involvement) of older men. The fluid sexuality may raise the accusation of seeing the Maya as truly the Greeks of the New World, not only for their aesthetic sophistication but the selective allowance of homosexuality. The very young had to do painful things to their bodies in ritual duties, but the Maya appear to have observed certain distinct phases of youth. At the summit, probably, were the *chak ch'ok*, on the verge of aging out. There are also the vegetal metaphors, the nomenclatural separation of "maleness," the evidence of waves of production, even sets of pottery found by chance in excavations or by looters, and the principal link of sexual imagery not to the young but to old men, gods at that.

Then there are indications of varying prominence. A few dynasties reported at length on young men, others paid little heed; not a single reference to *ch'ok* occurs at Tikal, and those at Copan veer to gods or divine youths. What seems evident is that at times of transition young men achieved a singular prominence, when kingdoms were being created or new dynasties formed, or when polities seemed in precarious state. The Early Classic period had some *ch'ok,* if named with Teotihuacan-style signs, but its focus was on steady, patient, and wise elders and ancestors. That era appeared to have operated according to a different strategy of continuity, looking upward to ancestors, not down to the spread of elite youth. The Late Classic, source of most of our evidence, offers a different account. Its attention steers to young men through spirited stories and pictures, buildings and spaces, many created by the greatest carvers and painters of the age. Subtle anxieties flit behind this large cultural investment, along with an abiding sense of admiration and wonder. Restive courts would soon use and use up such youths. For some centuries, though, boisterous boys had fun and adventure as focal points of their societies. At times alone, initiated into painful rites, they also gathered in groups and romped, danced, feasted, drank to excess, scuffled, played ball, and let sacrificial blood. Making love, raging in war, they worried and delighted their elders. Then, having sprouted, the *ch'ok* grew at last, with adult help, to the duties of manhood. The gifted passage had come to an end.

NOTES

1 A SPLENDID PREDICAMENT

1. The scenes come from Thomas Cole's *Voyage of Life,* the series of paintings in the National Gallery of Art, Washington, D.C., Ailsa Mellon Bruce Fund 1971.16.1; 1971.16.2; 1971.16.3; 1971.16.4; see Schweizer, *Voyage,* 17–37, 44–49.

2. Wallach, "Popular Art," 235, 241.

3. Shakespeare, *As You Like It,* II, vii, 139.

4. Ehmer, "Life Stairs," 54; the conceit of the "life stairs," *lebenstreppe,* goes back to 1540, an innovation, perhaps with Calvinist shadings, of printers in Augsburg (Jörg Breu der Jüngere) and Amsterdam (Cornelis Anthonisz). The notion of an arc-like life, the midpoint its moral and physical summit, the height of the sun in each day, descends from Aristotle, Solon, and Dante. On the genealogy of such ideas about aging: Burrow, *Ages of Man,* 1–7; Chew, *Pilgrimage of Life,* 147–60, esp. 156, for discussion of seasonal correlations; Sears, *Medieval Interpretations,* 153–54. On seasonality and ages: Kammen, "Life Cycle," 39. The dominant metaphor, from the sixteenth century on, binds each step to a ten-year span. The summit, vigorous middle age, segues by bumpy descent to infirmity and fear. In some diagrams, a zoo of yapping and howling proverbs, Aesop-like, encapsulate each defining attribute of the male life. The vignettes provide plenty of comment about the attributes and failings of each span. A print by Albert Alden (1812–1883) from nineteenth-century Massachusetts states: at eighty, craving comfort, "the cat keeps house and loves the fire. At eighty, we the same desire"; Kammen, "Life Cycle," 48, fig. 8; also Boston Athenaeum, wood engraving, "The Life and Age of Man," #1978.58. On animals and human life stages: Sears, *Medieval Interpretations,* 154.

Writing long before, and building on classical precedents, Dante would have understood this as part of natural order that shifts by phase of life: "certain ways are suitable and laudable at one age which are foul and blameworthy at another"; Dante: *Convivio,* 4. Folk rhymes, stage designs, and imprecision about age: Cole, *Journey,* 11, 24. Elderly forbearance: Ehmer, "Life Stairs," 59.

5. Danish source: Dal, with Skårup, *Ages of Man,* 8. For distinctions between the robust and decrepit elderly: Cole, *Journey,* xviii, fig. 2, for an eleventh-century link of the four seasons to spans of life. Related reflections on spiritual age occur in a 1380 sermon by Thomas, Bishop of Brinton: Cole, *Journey,* 6.

6. Shakespeare, *The Winter's Tale,* III, iii.

7. For Greek analogies of "tasteless behavior," marginal figures, and comic disdain on Attic Greek vessels: Sutton, "The Good, the Base, and the Ugly," 199–202.

8. Bribiescas, *Men,* 113. Lifespans, reproduction, and juvenility: Hewlett, *Adolescent Identity,* 1–2. On physical shifts: Ellis, "Risky Adolescent Behavior," 45. On maximum height and breadth: Laes and Strubbe, *Youth,* 62. Primate attributes: Hewlett and Hewlett, "Hunter-Gatherer Adolescence," 80.

9. Translation from Neubauer, *Culture of Adolescence,* 112–13.

10. On risk-taking and negative attributes: recital in Guthrie, *Paleolithic Art,* 179 (for quotations), 186–88 (pie charts and graphs for rash behavior).

11. Guthrie, *Paleolithic Art,* 168 (braid pulling). On libido: Udry and Billy "Coitus," 851, for evidence of hormonal drives in early intercourse, cited by Guthrie, 170. "Access to sex": Guthrie, *Paleolithic Art,* 365.

12. Guthrie, *Paleolithic Art,* 186 (chromosomal block), 189 ("heritable component"). Disputed chromosomes: Munafó et al., "Personality Traits." On dysfunctional American youths: Kimmel, *Guyland,* 13, 25–28. Prior studies of teenage wildness in the post–Civil War period: Hall, *Adolescence;* Coleman, *Adolescent Society;* Erikson, *Identity.* For historical comment on such literature: Arnett, "Storm and Stress" and "Brilliance and Nonsense."

13. "Essentialist" view of men: Alberti, "Masculinities," 407. On youths recruited for war, below: Vautravers, "Child Soldiers," 98 (for early modern Europe), 99 (weaponed *Hitlerjugend,* used late in World War II), 104 (thought to be easily disciplined or "gregarious").

14. Quotation on "diversities": Plummer, "Male Sexualities," 192, and 181, 187, for strong critique of biological arguments about gender. Plummer stresses how, to a unique extent, humans attach meaning to sexuality. On the Andes: Dean, "Making of Men," 148 fn. 5, 152, 157, 160, 164, 169–70. On the necessity of contrast: Arnold and Brady, "Introduction," 3–4; Connell, *Masculinities,* 44, 71, who decries biologically reductive theories; Gutmann, "Trafficking," 386–87; Kirkpatrick, "Liminal Category," 385–88; Knapp, "Masculinist Approaches," 92; see also broader oppositions among the Kabyle of Algeria in Bourdieu, *Masculine Domination,* 7–11.

15. Butler, *Gender Trouble,* 175, 178, 179 (on "performance"); *Bodies,* xxi–xxii, 71, 172. On group coercion: Foucault, *Discipline and Punish,* 170–94. Connell et al.: "Introduction." Mayanist use of Butler's work: Joyce, *Gender and Power,* 187–88; "Girling the Girl," 474; *Ancient Bodies,* 99, 122, 127.

16. Connell et al.: "Introduction," 10.

17. On making men "better": Connell, *Masculinities,* 228–48.

18. On such "choreography": Bogin, *Patterns,* 214, 216; Worthman, "Adolescence," 38.

19. Doubts about the "trans-historical core" of masculinity: R. Stone, "Masculinity Without Conflict," 86.

20. Bribiescas, *Men,* 120. On the Aka: Hewlett and Hewlett, "Hunter-Gatherer Adolescence," 13–21, fig. 4.2. "Frontal lobes": Kolbert, "Terrible Teens," 84, citing Jensen and Nutt, *Teenage Brain;* similar horror stories appear in Steinberg, *Age of Opportunity.* On competitive urges and Darwinist-tinged research: Archer, "Aggression"; Deaner et al., "Predisposition"; De

Block and Dewitte, "Darwinism"; Lombardo, "Evolution of Sport." On primate aggression and human youths: Anestis, "Testosterone"; Newton-Fisher, "Female Coalitions"; Rowe et al., "Testosterone"; van Bokhoven et al., "Salivary Testosterone." Psychology of youthful aggression, as life-long or intensely correlated with adolescence: Moffitt, "Anti-social Behavior," "Psychopathology"; assessment by Skardhamar, "Reconsidering."

21. On the penis and the phallus: Bordo, *Male Body,* 87, 96, 242, 248; Plummer, "Male Sexualities," 179. "Double binds": Bateson et al., "Theory of Schizophrenia," 251; *Ecology,* 276–82. Concurrent masculinities: Dunlop, "Mightier Than the Sword," 161–62; Yarrow, "World Historical Category," 118. Friedman and phallic odium: *Mind of Its Own,* 120–35 (racist views of the African phallus), 159 (blood libels against Jews).

22. Phallocracy in ancient Athens: Keuls, *Reign,* 3–15. Mediterranean ethnography: Brandes, *Metaphors,* esp. 75–96; Herzfeld, *Poetics of Manhood,* esp. 123–36. Gilmore on "man-playing": *Manhood,* 220. On "hegemonic masculinity": Connell, *Masculinities,* 77–81; Connell and Messerschmidt, "Hegemonic Masculinity," 832 ("normative . . . honored way of being a man"), 846 ("consent, discursive centrality, institutionalization . . . marginalization or delegitimation of alternatives"), 848 (male and female models); also Plummer, "Male Sexualities," 180 ("works to essentialize the male sexualities of some men into the sexualities of all, as well as . . . a bipolar feminine essential sexuality"). On "lived consensus": Vale de Almeida, "Southern Portugal," 141; see Bourdieu, "Social Space," 729, 732, for equation to "the common sense"; war and hegemonic masculinity: Resić, "Masculine Ideal."

23. On the Mead and Freeman controversy: Mead, *Coming of Age;* Freeman, *Mead and Samoa;* Shankman, *Trashing,* and "Hoaxing."

24. Pipher, *Reviving Ophelia,* 19, 20. For its male counterpart, decrying the "silence, solitude, and distrust" of American boys and teenagers: Kindlon and Thompson, *Raising Cain,* xix.

25. Able work on children: Ardren and Hutson, *Childood;* Joyce, "Girling the Girl." And in anthropology: Meehan and Crittenden, *Childhood.* "Fully formed adult humans": Hamann, "Murderous Children," 222. "Boys" of 14 and 20 as indistinguishable from 5-and-10-year olds: Joyce, *Gender and Power,* 124, 127, 128.

26. On what has been termed "iconic masculinity": Arnold and Brady, "Introduction," 8.

27. Freud on developmental stages: Kohlberg, *Moral Development*; Piaget and Inhelder, *Psychology*.

28. On emerging adulthood: Arnett, "Emerging Adulthood," 71–72; Arnett, Žukauskienė, and Sugimura, "New Life Stage," 574–75. On the delights of being young: Arnett, "Storm and Stress," 677. Attributes of emerging adulthood: Arnett, "Emerging Adulthood," 9. Gloomy views of adolescence abound in Gillis, *Youth and History*, 32–42.

29. Ariès and his critics: Ariès, *Childhood*, 33, 39, 125; Hutton, *Philippe Ariès*; A. Wilson, "Infancy," 150–52; see also Laes and Strubbe, *Youth*, 7–8. For *Émile* and religion: Rousseau, *Émile*, 348. On *Émile* as "breakthrough": Bedaux, "Introduction," 11. Classic adolescence, presence or absence: Kleijwegt, *Ancient Youth*, xii–xv; cf. Eyben, *Restless Youth*, 5–41. On "supra-historical givens": Laes and Strubbe, *Youth*, 10.

30. Useful overview of "virility" and its history: Corbin et al., *History of Virility*, esp. 1–164. Theran youths and phases of boyish and youthful life: Chapin, "Boys," 255; also Rutter, "Children," fig. 23. Greek gravestones and age classes: Stewart and Gray, "Confronting the Other," 248–49. Greek terms: Herrmann and Kondoleon, *Games*, 125; also Davidson, *Greek Love*, 90. Horace: *Ars poetica*, lines 161–65. Youths as elite concern: Laes and Strubbe, *Youth*, 252. On Roman feelings about youths: Laes and Strubbe, *Youth*, 44, 45. Aristotle on youths: Byzantine adolescence: Hennessy, *Images of Children*, 3.

31. Devilry, Venus, and youth, albeit with variant duration: Sears, *Medieval Interpretations*, 90, 109. Misrule and "abbeys": N. Davis, "Reasons of Misrule," 51, 54, 73–74. On Renaissance youth: Taddei, *Fanciulli e giovani*, 87; Trexler, "Ritual in Florence," 202, esp. 237 for "baleful influences of women," 243 for quotation from Platina (1421–1481), author of a celebrated cookbook, about "harmonious" movement. Evidently, Platina "cooked" young men, too, to a desired outcome. On the "misrule" of young men: N. Davis, "Reasons of Misrule." Ages of "adulthood," by gender: Chojnacki, *Women and Men*, 187.

32. Chojnacki, *Women and Men*, 203, 204.

33. "Uneasiness" about Puritan youth: Lombard, *Making Manhood*, 52–57. Enslaved teenagers: Murray, "Children and Culture," 48.

34. Schlegel and Barry, *Adolescence*, 198. Andean bears: Dean, "Making Men," 175, citing Urton, "Animal Metaphors," 270–72. Marquesas: Kirkpatrick, "Liminal Category," 385–86, 388. Societal conflict and young men: Comaroff and Comaroff, "Occult Economies, 288–89; Graff, *Conflicting Paths*, xiii, 6–13.

35. Labor, agility, strength: Bogin, *Patterns*, 207, 209; Worthman, "Adolescence," fig. 1. On average age of Olympic medalists: Berthelot et al., "Performance Evolution," 1001, figs. 1–2. Across sports, performance levels peak perceptibly between 15 and 20 years of age. Before that: exponential growth in ability; thereafter: far slower improvement.

36. China: Furth, "Birth to Birth," 179; L. Miller, "Children," 219.

37. Age grades and age sets: Radcliffe-Brown, "Age Organization," 21; Lowie, *Primitive Society*, 257–337; F. Stewart, *Fundamentals*, 130–31, 229–30, 243, 283.

38. Baxter and Almagor, "Introduction," 5 (implies replacement and continuity), 7 (equality and "jerks"), 14 (role of gerontocracy), 16 ("act wildly to the edge of delinquency," templates for military organization), 18 (lack of controlling powers or corporate action), 24 (aging as an ascent to a "superior, because senior, condition"), 25 ("age-systems create figurative representations of time as well as being parts of time").

39. Family training: Greenfield, *Weaving Generations*, 69–88; also Lave and Wenger, *Situated Learning*. Apprenticeship: Farr, *Artisans*, 34–35; Yarborough, "Apprentices as Adolescents"; Wendrich, "Archaeology and Apprenticeship," 2–7.

40. Bourke, *Dismembering*, 124–26, 128, 133 ("absence of women" promoted these affinities).

41. Japan: Norbeck, "Age-Grading," 377–78. Royal heirs and nobles, while marked by special dress or hairstyles as youths, did not pass through such age classes. On rules of transition: Baxter and Almagor, "Introduction," 21–25. The authors stress the functional tasks for certain age organizations. On the American Plains: Lowie, *Primitive Society*, 257–337.

42. Guthrie, *Paleolithic Art*, 115 ("a significant segment of these Paleolithic handprints and tracks were made by young people"), 124 ("handprints of adolescents are the most numerous among the Paleolithic sample . . . the vast majority of these individuals were males"), 125 ("individuals falling between ten and sixteen"), 156 (new

form of parenting), 180 ("testosterone events"), 399 (art as instructive play). Criticism: White, "Looking." On female handprints: Snow, "Sexual Dimorphism," 755.

43. Guthrie, *Paleolithic Art*, 159.

44. On the late formation of *epheboi* in Athens: Chankowski, *L'Éphébie hellénistique*, 90–114; also Kennell, *Ephebeia*; Kozak, "Greek Government," 315–16. Graham Oliver kindly assisted with these sources.

45. Athenian youth: Beaumont, *Childhood*, 21 ("protracted affair"), 16 (enrollment in ranks of *epheboi*), 209 (changes in depiction and emphasis). Vidal-Naquet, *Black Hunter*, 97 (military service), 98 (duration), 99 (seclusion from society), 107 (departure on marriage), 107–8 (service on frontiers), 118–19 (as hunters and solitary youth), 147 (Spartan analogues). Criticism of Vidal-Naquet's "historical anthropology": Chankowski, *L'Éphébie hellénistique*, 1–34. On Sparta: Davidson, *Greek Love*, 390, with mention of "herds" and "herd-leaders" or "magistrates"; also Laes and Strubbe, *Youth*, 49. Spartan traditions: Kozak, "Greek Government," 305 (the *agōgá*, or, in later stages of military formation, the *krypteia*, sent off to wilderness to train on sparse diets and kill Spartan serfs). Standard work on Greek homosexuality: Dover, *Greek Homosexuality;* for reaction and extension, Davidson, *Greek Love*, 139, 611, disdaining Dover's reluctance to accept the wide existence of sodomy, male "wedded couples," and the diversity of "homosexualities." On male-to-male courtship in Athens: Shapiro, "Fathers and Sons," 99, also 104–5, for satyrs as emotive counterparts to stern Athenian parenting. For comparable liaisons between older and young males in Renaissance Florence: Rocke, *Forbidden Friendships*, 94–95, 102. On Rome: Williams, *Roman Homosexuality*. Homosexual liaisons between age grades: Herrmann and Kondoleon, *Games for the Gods*, 29, 127. Eros and the beloved: Davidson, *Greek Love*, 19, 20–21. Desire and conduct: McNiven, "Immature Gestures," 99. Fantasy and play in Greek imagery: Walsh, *Distorted Ideals*, 276–77.

46. On beautiful youths: Topper, *Imagery*, 53–54.

47. On Greek concepts of beauty: Konstan, *Beauty*, 39, 170–71, for *kállos* as "physical beauty," conducive to desire, and *kalós*, which could "connote moral excellence or courage." Konstan emphasizes that there is no disinterested, Kantian contemplation of a beautiful thing. Instead, there is

emotion, attraction, lust, passion; *Beauty*, 183–86.

48. On *kouroi*: Neer, *Greek Art and Archaeology*, 110 (as signs or proxies), 113 (dating), 115 (Egyptian prototypes), 156 (Homer and fallen dead who "acquire youth and radiant beauty").

49. Studies of *kouroi*: Andrew Stewart, *Art, Desire, and the Body*, 63 (origin of term from Vassilis Leonardos), 64, 65 (quantity), 65 (tragic implications), 67 ("perfect object of male desire"). "Heroic paradigm": Langdon, "Awkward Age," 174. *Kouroi* as wealthy, privileged youth: Neer, *Style and Politics*, 91, 101, 118. Concrete specifications of ideal beauty: Jenkins and Turner, *Greek Body*, 11. Tripod handles and evolving concepts of male beauty: Papalexandrou, *Visual Poetics*, 161, 162 ("spear-brandishing warriors"), 163 ("golden youths," *chryseioi kouroi*), 167 ("external appearance and internal constitution of self"). Divine models for youths: Shapiro, "Fathers and Sons," 97.

50. On male beauty and the motivation of such depiction: W. Davis, *Queer Beauty*, esp. 2–5, 114–15; Potts, *Flesh and the Ideal*, 118, for quotation.

51. Inversions of adolescence: Dowden, "Fluctuating Meanings," 238. Liminality of youths: Mitchell-Boyask, "Trials of Manhood," 43. "Princes of youth": Fraschetti, "Roman Youth," 78–81. Medieval youths: Duby, *Hommes et structures*, 213–25.

52. On social reproduction among youths: Collins, "Social Reproduction," 43–45.

53. On male and female natures among the Aztec: López Austin, *Human Body*, I: 292.

54. Sahagún, *Florentine Codex*, Book 10: 2, 12, 13.

55. On stages of men: López Austin, *Human Body*, I: 285. On the complementary nature of Aztec sexuality: Powers, *Crucible of Conquest*, 15, 17. Codex Borbonicus: Anders, Jansen, and Reyes García, *Libro de ciuacoatl*, 206–7, and fol. 28. Written descriptions of the pole-climbing ritual: Durán, *Book of the Gods*, 208–9. Comparable evidence of body ornament and ear-piercing to mark age grades: G. McCafferty and S. McCafferty, "Crafting the Body Beautiful," 190.

56. Analogies for young men's houses: Durán, *Book of the Gods*, 82, 112, 113.

57. Houses of weeping: Sahagún, *Florentine Codex*, Book 6: 214. Pannock, *Bonds of Blood*, 72, believes some of the confusion in descriptions of these houses reveals their flexibility and diversity.

58. Youths as "offering": Sahagún, *Florentine Codex*, Book 10: 213. Tedious duties, including

bloodletting, cleaning, and tending of fires: Sahagún, *Florentine Codex*, Book 2: 59, Book 6: 214. Training in arms: Clendinnen, *Cost of Courage*, 9–10. Masters of youths and older youths as leaders; Sahagún, *Florentine Codex*, Book 8: 43, 72, 76. Punishment of transgressions: Sahagún, *Florentine Codex*, Book 8: 43. Occasional permissiveness: Sahagún, *Florentine Codex*, Book 8: 18, 61.

59. Becerra Rodríguez and López Arenas, "Hallazgos," 20.

60. Youths as sacrifices: *Florentine Codex*, Book 2: 9. Young women: Burkhart, *Before Guadalupe*, 24; Durán, *Book of the Gods*, 84; also Sahagún, *Florentine Codex*, Book 6: 209–18.

61. Merchants: Sahagún, *Florentine Codex*, Book 9: 14, "Accompany them carefully. Imitate them as they go, as they travel.... Let them be made to prepare for the others the little seats, beds of straw, grass seats. And [instruct them in] all the penances, the fixing of the divisions of the night, the vigils: take care of them; keep them firmly in your grasp."

62. Homosexuality: Pannock, *Bonds of Blood*, 68, 145, in which she writes that "legally and morally, homosexuality was officially and unambiguously deplored"—chewing gum or chicle was thought especially effeminate. Olivier, "Homosexualidad," 305, states unequivocally that homosexuality was seen with "disgust and categorical rejection" (de asco y de rechazo categórico) by the noble informants of Bernardino de Sahagún. But he also acknowledges ("Homosexualidad," 307) a certain degree of "tolerance" for such practices in restricted contexts. A similar if more tendentious view: Sigal, "Queer Nahuatl," 16, 21–24, who argues for a berdache-like figure among the Aztecs, a man who fills the roles of a woman; see also Kimbell, "Aztec Homosexuality"; Klein, "Gender Ambiguity," and "Androgyny"; Sigal, "Cuiloni"; Trexler, "Gender Subordination," and "Making the American Berdache." On the Classic Maya and homosexuality: Houston, Stuart, and Taube, *Memory of Bones*, 209–17.

2 GROWING MEN AMONG THE MAYA

1. Las Casas, *Apologética historia sumaria*, 2: 515; Tozzer, *Relación*, 124.

2. Las Casas, *Apologética historia sumaria*, 2: 515: "los mozos mayores en aquel vicio a los niños corrompían; y despúes salidos de allí mal acostumbrados, difícil era librarlos de aquel vicio."

3. Quotation: Villagutierre, *Conquista*, 457: "Gastaban lo mas del tiempo en idolatrar, bailar y emborracharse a todas horas y tiempos con los Fuertes brebajes que saben confeccionar."

4. Testing endurance in dance: Barrera Vásquez, *Dzitbalché*, 26. Erotic parties, Barrera Vásquez, *Dzitbalché*, Cantar 7, 50–51.

5. Productivity: Kramer, *Maya Children*, 34, fig. 2.1. Tojolobal: Ruz, *Legítimos hombres*, 118, 141, with clear division of labor by age 6 or 7, including the offering of special food; also Ruz, "Ecosistema." Tzotzil: Groark, "Pathogenic Emotions," 183.

6. Phalli: Amrhein, "Phallic Imagery," figs. 4–10, figs. 1a–22a; Pollock, *Puuc*, 262 (Uxmal), 541, fig. 908 (Acanmul). Genital piercings: Hogan et al., "Genital Piercings," table 4; the transverse piercing might be a "shaft ampallang" in the typology of such modifications; see parallels in the Boxer Codex, 41, Lilly Library, Indiana University, LMC 2444, c. 1590, Philippines. Stelae showing main figures with large phalli: Amrhein, "Phallic Imagery," figs. 24 (Sayil), 26 (Musée de l'Homme, Paris, #67.37.1.), 30a (Bilimtok, Campeche), 35a (Keuic, Yucatan). Architectural setting of phalli: Lincoln, "Ethnicity and Social Organization," 439–40.

7. Telantunich: Ardren and Hixson, "Telantunich," esp. figs. 3, 4, 6. Maya clowning: Taube, "Ritual Humor." Pre-human monkey men: Christenson, *Popol Vuh*, 90. On events before the dawn of humans: Hamann, "Social Life," 354–55.

8. The association of skeletons and phalli recalls comparable scenes of over-sexed, merrymaking, even dancing cadavers in Moche imagery of coastal Peru: Donnan and McClelland, *Moche Fineline Painting*, fig. 3.16; Quilter, *Moche*, 55, pls. 18, 19; Weismantel, "Moche Sex Pots," 501. On phallic pots among the Moche: Bergh, "Death and Renewal," 88–89. My thanks go to James Doyle for reminding me of these images that depict the very lively dead.

9. Hegemonic masculinity and idealized males: Ardren, "Phalli Stones," 53, 54. "Sexualization": Joyce, "Male Sexuality," 267. On Śiva: R. Davis, "Origin," and throughout his *Oscillating Universe*. Tzotzil joking: Bricker, *Ritual Humor*, 106–7; Laughlin, *San Lorenzo Zinacantán*, 479. On hermaphrodites: Blackless et al., "Review and Synthesis," 157–59. Hermaphrodites in the past: Brisson, *Sexual Ambivalence;* Daston and Park, "Hermaphrodites"; Long, *Hermaphrodites.* For a

somewhat tendentious review of Nahuatl (Aztec) evidence: Sigal, "Queer Nahuatl," 24–25.

10. Aguateca phallus, from Structure M8–8, dating to c. AD 800: Inomata and Eberl, "Stone Ornaments," 115, fig. 6.35. Palenque: Maudslay, *Archaeology,* 4: pl. 13. I thank Mary Miller for reminding me of this example, which emphasizes grotesque shifts of size and proportion in the kneeling or standing figures. Nixtun-Ch'ich': Pugh et al., "Chak'an Itza Center," 8, fig. 8. Captives and phalli: Houston, Stuart, and Taube, *Memory of Bones,* 210, 213, figs. 6.7, 6.9, 6.10. Bonampak: Taube, personal communication, 1995. Santa Rita figurines: Finamore and Houston, *Fiery Pool,* pl. 52.

11. Rope-dance with bloodletting: Madrid Codex, 19b.

12. Mary Miller, personal communication, 2016. On comparative studies of menstruation: Buckley and Gottlieb, *Blood Magic.* On Maya mention of moons and menstruation: Houston, "Heavenly Bodies." On slang for menstruation, below: http://www.helloclue.com/survey.html.

13. Cahal Pech: A. Stone, "Commentary," fig. 1. Penis sign: Stone and Zender, *Reading Maya Art,* 60–61; cf. Joyce, "Male Sexuality," 273, who does not discern its linkage to gods; for discussion of Joyce's proposals, see Houston, Stuart, and Taube, *Memory of Bones,* 211, 213.

14. Ardren on watery meaning: "Phalli Stones," 60, commenting on "water," "liquid," and the "life-giving power of rain." Xkipche: Schlegel, "Xkipché," 118, fig. 2. Waterspouts: Amrhein, "Phallic Imagery," fig. 15 (Rancho San Pedro); Pollock, *Puuc,* 262 (Uxmal). An image in the Postclassic Madrid Codex (8) shows *Chahk* sitting on a craggy, celestial mountain covered, graffiti-like, in numbers—the import is obscure. Supporting it is a death god. Water gushes down everywhere, but some of it is urine streaming out from the penis of the skeletal deity.

15. Identification of the Maya Maize God: Taube, "Maize God." Corn maidens, as identified by Karl Taube: Saturno, Taube, and Stuart, *Murals of San Bartolo: North Wall,* 18–19, 34. Mourning maidens and the mummified Maize God: Grube and Gaida, "Katalog," Abb. 12.

16. Head deformation: Houston, Stuart, and Taube, *Memory of Bones,* 45; Scherer, *Mortuary Landscapes,* 26–29; Tiesler, "Cranial Vault Modifications," 17, who nonetheless feels that other gods were emulated with modifications from infant cradle-boarding. Shaping the head, brain, and senses among the Tzeltal: Pitarch, *Jaguar and the Priest,* 89.

17. "Dual gender" theories and indeterminate gender of Maize God: Joyce, *Gender and Power,* 81, 82. Berdache and "third-genders": Looper, "Women-Men," 198–201. The standard on North American practices: Roscoe, *Changing Ones.* On mythic maidens: Chinchilla Mazariegos, *Imágenes,* 59–63.

18. Dual expressions for ancestors and priests: Hull, "Poetic Tenacity," 88–89, citing Wisdom, *Chorti Indians,* 409–10. On the Tzotzil: Vogt, *Zinacantan,* 32. On gender complementarity among the Tzutujil Maya: Tarn and Prechtel, "Constant Inconstancy." Tzeltal "mothers-fathers": Pitarch, *Jaguar and the Priest,* 120–21.

19. Complex sexuality: Sigal, *Sexuality and Ritual,* 117, building on Klein, "Gender Ambiguity," in an interpretation unrecognizable to another authority, Olivier, *Aztec God,* 48–56. A classic source on godly fusions: Nicholson, "Religion," 413–14; see also Bassett, *Earthly Things,* 95. Quotation on Ch'orti': Wisdom, *Chorti Indians,* 409–10.

20. Creator couples: Houston and Inomata, *Classic Maya,* 257, fig. 9.5. The Tzutujil refer to creators as an old couple, the "great-grandfather" and "great-grandmother": Stanzione, *Rituals of Sacrifice,* 21. A scholar of Aztec religion, Miguel León-Portilla, saw its creator deities as a single, transcendent being, Ometeotl: *La filosofía,* 157–58. But when depicted, as in the Aztec Codex Borbonicus, 21, they are distinct, gendered male and female, if in complementary pairs.

21. Palenque "goddess": Stuart, *Inscriptions from Temple XIX,* 180–83. Skirts and gender: Joyce, *Gender and Power,* 81–82. Berdache and "third-genders": Looper, "Women-Men," 198–201.

22. Maize God glyphs: Zender, "Maya Portrait Glyphs," 5–9, figs. 5, 6, 8.

23. Young lords and Hero Twins: M. Coe, "Hero Twins." On the dual nature of the twins: Taube, "Maya Conceptions," 469, 471–73. My thanks go to Andrew Scherer for reminding me of their relevance. Old gods as newborns: Taube, "Birth Vase," 664. Newborns: Stone and Zender, *Reading Maya Art,* 30–31, *unen,* "baby." In 2016, Marc Zender noted to me that two paired Maize Gods are featured on an unusual scene that highlights a chocolate pot in the Kislak

Collection, Miami. To my eye, they graft details of the male Hero Twins onto this pair; in fact, one carries the spots of a Twin.

24. Villagutierre, *Conquista*, 456, "Y cuando no había de esta caza, sacrificaban los muchachos o mozuelos mas gordos que había entre ellos mismos en aquellas islas." Beautiful captives and sacrificial dance: Barrera Vásquez, *Dzitbalché*, Cantar 13, 77, "aquella donde atado esta aquel viril muchacho, impoluto, virgen, hombre" (*leil-xibil pal-h-zac-zvhvy-vinic*). Sacrificial dance: Barrera Vásquez, *Dzitbalché*, Cantar 1, 26–27, "Mocetones recios, hombres del escudo en orden, entran hasta el medio de la plaza para medir sus fuerzas de la Danza del Kolomché. Enmedio de la plaza está un hombre atado al fuste de la columna petrea, bien pintado con el bello Anil. Puestole han muchas Flores de Balche para que se perfume; Así en las palmas de sus manos."

25. On timocracy: Houston, Stuart, and Taube, *Memory of Bones*, 202–3. On honor and slights: W. Miller, *Humiliation*, 118–19.

26. Individuals and groups: Douglas, *Natural Symbols*, 57–60. Douglas's views evolve yet expand on the earlier ones of Émile Durkheim; Spickard, "Guide," 168.

27. On gladiators: Taube and Zender, "American Gladiators," and Houston, "Gladiatrix." On the Huron: Heidenreich, "Huron," fig. 4.

28. Against a notion of single ethnicity: Houston and Inomata, *Classic Maya*, xiii.

29. *Xib*: Kaufman, "Etymological Dictionary," 138; Kaufman and Norman, "Outline," 135. Yukateko Maya: Ciudad Real, *Calepino*, 587. Acalan Chontal: Smailus, *Maya-Chontal*, 35, *nucxibilbaob*, "grandes ancianos."

30. Decipherment of *xib*: Barthel, "Regionen," 92; Kelley, *Maya Script*, 193. Female Rain God: Dresden 63, which pairs **IXIK-ki CHAHK-ki**, *Ixik Chahk*, "Lady Chahk," with **mu-XIB-bi CHAHK-ki**, probably *Mun Xib Chahk*, "Immature Male Chahk." For *mun*: Barrera Vásquez, *Diccionario*, 540.

31. Centzonhuitznahua: Matos Moctezuma and López Luján, *Escultura*, 336–37. Four hundred boys: Christenson, *Popol Vuh*, 101–4.

32. The pot: K1299; the stela: Naranjo Stela 35, positions D1–D6; Graham and von Euw, *Naranjo*, 91–92. Interpretation: Grube, "Monumentos esculpidos," derived from observations by Simon Martin (personal communication, 1997). Stripes

as "red": Stone and Zender, *Reading Maya Art*, 124–25. Incense burners: Stuart, "Fire Enters," 402–9.

33. Quirigua: Maudslay, *Archaeology* 2: pls. 7, 25, and Quirigua Stela A, glyphs C8-D9, **4 ch'a-jo-ma? 4 TE' IHK' XIB**, *4 ch'ajoom 4 te' ihk' xib*, "4 incensors, 4 Black Males"; Quirigua Stela D, glyphs B18, A19, **4 TE' IHK' XIB**, *4 te' ihk' xib*, "4 Black Males." Yaxchilan dwarves: Hieroglyphic Stairway 2, Step VII, glyph U2, Graham, *Yaxchilan* 3: pt. 2, pl. 160. Cuckolded god: K1182, 2794, 8927. The name may have had dynastic connotations. Oxkintok, Yucatan, was also named 7 Xib; García Campillo, "Informe epigráfico," 194–97.

34. Gladiator: K7749, Los Angeles County Museum of Art, #M.2010.115.875. Bone awls: Kidder, *Artifacts of Uaxactun*, 54–55, figs. 41, 82c; Moholy-Nagy, *Utilitarian Artifacts*, fig. 121a–e, fig. 123f.

35. Singers, *k'ayoom*, with *xib* heads: Houston, "Hill of Beans," 40; Houston, Stuart, and Taube, *Memory of Bones*, fig. 4.19; K954, preceded by *itz'aat*, "skilled person." The *hay* decipherment for vase, later read *jaay*, was first discovered by Kerry Hull in the 1990s (personal communication from Hull, 2015).

36. *Tz'ak* sign and its pairings: Hull, "Poetic Tenacity," 112 fn. 12; Knowlton, "Diphrastic Kennings"; Stuart, "Paired Variants."

37. Reading for *keleem* by Nikolai Grube: MacLeod and Reents-Budet, "Art of Calligraphy," 161 fn. 19; also MacLeod, "Primary Standard Sequence," 427–29, 440 fn. 2, fig. 16.3. Variant forms exist in the heads composing part of the *keleem* spelling, of which the most frequent is that of a spider monkey. But there are also youthful or even female heads, as on blocks in the Hecelchakan museum documented by Ian Graham; files, Corpus of Maya Hieroglyphic Inscriptions project. "Strength": Kaufman, "Etymological Dictionary," 138. Tojolobal: Ruz, *Legítimos hombres*, 118. Río Azul vessel: K2914, Denver Art Museum #2003.1. The *keleem* often follows *chak ch'ok*, "great youth," to be discussed in later sections of the chapter; see Tokovinine, "Two Vessels," 18, table 1. This pattern, of "strong" coupled with "great," further suggests that it pertains to older youth. *Keleem* in the Calakmul murals: S. Martin, "Hieroglyphs," 71–72.

38. Xcalumkin: Graham and von Euw, *Xcalumkin*, 161 (Lintel 4, the wife), 183 (Panel 5, the older

male), 185 (Panel 7, the younger). The full name of the youth is *Keleem Batuun,* with *keleem* probably functioning as an adjective. Other *ch'ok* and *keleem:* Graham and von Euw, *Xcalumkin,* 157, 175, 177, 185, 190, 197.

39. Caracol: Beetz and Satterthwaite, *Caracol,* fig. 8, of Stela 6, position Z1, but misdrawn in the published illustration.

40. On Maya pots: M. Coe, *Maya Scribe,* 21–22, tables 1–2. *Ch'ok* reading: Grube and Stuart, "Observations," 7–8; Houston, "Phonetic Decipherment," 132; Ringle, *Mice and Monkeys,* 12–14; Stuart, *Ten Phonetic Syllables,* 46. An unusual variant replaces the "rat" head with a human face and a smoking torch where his eye should be; K5452.

41. Quotations: MacLeod and Reents-Budet, "Art of Calligraphy," 133–34. Following a suggestion from Marc Zender, Alfonso Lacadena and Søren Wichmann propose another term for "youth": *ba'k,* spelled **ba-ku** on Yaxchilan Lintel 18, position B5; Lacadena and Wichmann, "Glottal Stop," 138. The reading is plausible but unconfirmed.

42. Chontal: Knowles, "Chontal Maya," 415; also Keller and Luciano, *Diccionario Chontal,* 45, 104–6, and the precursor language, Acalan Chontal, Smailus, *Maya-Chontal,* 67. Reconstructions of early Mayan forms: Kaufman, *El proto-Tzeltal-Tzotzil,* 117; Kaufman and Norman, "Outline," 119. Ch'orti': Pérez et al., *Diccionario Ch'orti',* 58; also Ch'ol, Aulie, de Aulie, and Scharfe de Stairs, "Diccionario Ch'ol-Español," 5, 40–41. Some of the spellings have been modified to underscore equivalences between Mayan languages. Spellings can vary, not by actual sounds, but by scholar or period of recording. Colonial sources can be particularly taxing. In listening to native speech, some ears were more discriminating than others.

43. Chontal has *chäcch'oc,* "baby, infant"; Keller and Luciano, *Diccionario Chontal,* 79; also Grube and Gaida, "Katalog," 81. Here the intensifier identifies small size, not great status, potency or size, always an alternative possibility with *chak.* The usage in Chontal precisely inverts Classic practice, which likely stresses older youths; see chapter 2. For colloquial Spanish terms, I thank Charles Golden; a source: http://madeinguatephoto.blogspot.com/2012/03/babosadas-de-los-chapines.html, accessed Mar. 25, 2016.

44. "Earth sprouts": Sandstrom, "Weeping Baby," 270.

45. Feldman, *Poqom Maya,* 168; Miles, *Pokom-Maya,* 762, table 7. Still unexplained in Maya script is the ubiquity of exalted titles related to "trees" or "plants," as in *yajawte',* "the tree's lord," common in many Classic-era texts.

46. *Ch'ok* in Yukateko: Barrera Vásquez, *Diccionario,* 139. *Mun:* Kaufman and Norman, "Outline," 126; Barrera Vásquez, *Diccionario,* 540–41. Enslaved orphans: Tozzer, *Relación,* 63, 73. Stucco frieze at Tonina: rendering by Ian Graham in the Corpus of Maya Hieroglyphic Inscriptions, Peabody Museum, Harvard University; in all likelihood the frieze dates to Oct. 10, AD 721. Aztec slave collars (*quauhcozcatl*), as Karl Taube reminds me: Berdan and Anawalt, *Codex Mendoza,* 206, see fol. 66r.

47. Lacadena, "El anillo jeroglífico," 183–84; Stuart, "New Year Records," and "Brief Introduction," 120.

48. Grube and Stuart, *Observations,* 7–8, fig. 8. Plano-relief vessel, Museo de la Cultura Teotihuacana: Taube, "Tetitla," fig. 11.6.

49. Magisterial survey of this evidence: Stuart, "Arrival of Strangers"; also Martin and Grube, *Chronicle,* 29–31. Bellicosity of the connection and admiring Maya evocations: A. Stone, "Disconnection," and Taube, "Temple of Quetzalcoatl." My thoughts reflect discussions with Karl Taube.

50. Photographs on file in the Corpus of Maya Hieroglyphic Inscriptions project, Harvard University; Carnegie Institution of Washington photos, #CI708709 to CI708720. For excavation: A. Smith, *Uaxactun,* pl. 50.

51. Another early example with goggle-eyes, in the Dumbarton Oaks collection: S. Martin, "Carved Bowl," fig. 55b, d. Palenque bowl: Fields and Tokovinine, "Carved Bowl," 106, fig. 54. It is possible that the bowl was carved at a later time, an object assigned to the youth of a deceased or elderly king.

52. Martin's suggestion: personal communication, 2008; photographs of this monument were shown to me by David Stuart. Stucco heads from Governor's Palace, Uxmal: National Museum of the American Indian, presented by James B. Ford, 8/72; two others from scanned slides in Dumbarton Oaks; http://academic.reed.edu/uxmal/galleries/Mid/Other/PP/Other-PP-10.htm.

53. El Cayo: Maler, *Usumatsintla Valley,* pl. 35. Dumbarton Oaks panel: Houston, "Carved Panel," fig. 25.

54. The lunar portion of Maya texts records an expression, *u-ch'ok-k'aba'*, "its youth-name," in reference to another series of signs ("Glyph X") that pertain to the current lunation of either 29 or 30 days: i.e., in translation, " 'Glyph X' is the youth-name of a particular moon." Another text, from Itzan Stela 17, positions I3–J4, refers to a building that also has a "youth-name," *ch'ok-k'aba'*. Perhaps Classic Maya buildings could experience name changes when repurposed or covered by new layers of masonry.

55. Fraternal succession at Palenque: Stuart, *Inscriptions from Temple XIX*, 151–54, fig. 118. Brothers: Martin and Grube, *Chronicle*, 75–77, 162, 183, 186. Older and younger brothers: Stuart, "Kinship Terms," 5, fig. 6. At La Corona, Guatemala, these often precede *winik*, "person," sometimes followed by *ch'ok*, as on La Corona Panel 3, section B.

56. Palenque bowl: D. Stuart and G. Stuart, *Palenque*, 233. Caracol: Beetz and Satterthwaite, *Caracol*, fig. 16, Stela 6, position G1. The published drawing is poor, but scrutiny of the original confirms the presence of *ch'ok*, just after a personal name. Brothers and obsidian: Rossi, "Brothers Taaj," 129–41, fig. 1.12, noting that those at Copan occur with deities or supernaturals. As Rossi points out, such analogies also appear in Tzotzil: Rossi, "Brothers Taaj," 130; Vogt, *Zinacantan*, 238. First-born of woman: Stuart, "Kingship Terms," fig. 2. "Head youth": Houston, Stuart, and Taube, *Memory of Bones*, 62, fig. 2.5. Palenque lord: Martin and Grube, *Chronicle*, 174; Stuart, *Inscriptions from Temple XIX*, 155. A fragmentary Late Classic panel coming from the site of Jonuta, Tabasco, associates a figure with the same title—although clearly not the same Palenque lord—with the payment (*tojil*) of tribute (*ikaatz*), often in the form of hard-stones.

57. *Bakab*: Houston, Stuart, and Taube, *Memory of Bones*, 62–64. *Chak ch'ok winik*: Grube and Gaida, "Katalog," Abb. 33; also K6551. *Itz'aat*: Stuart, "Maya Artist," a rare confirmation that royal males were characterized explicitly as literates. Example: Becquelin and Taladoire, *Tonina*, fig. 142b.

58. *Ch'ok* as sculptors: Houston, "Crafting Credit," especially El Peru Stela 34, Naranjo Stela 12, Piedras Negras Stela 12, "San Lucas" Stela, and Yaxchilan Lintel 45. El Cayo Altar 1 is the work of a young scion of the overlord's family. 1 Witzil Chahk: Yaxchilan Lintel 45, positions D1–D5,

and Dos Caobas Stela 1, back, positions W1–W2; Skidmore, "Two Stelae." Palenque, Death's Head: scrutiny of original, now missing its head, in the Museo Nacional de Antropología. Piedras Negras student carvings: Satterthwaite, "Stone-Carving," figs. 2, 6.

59. Tikil: Aulie, de Aulie, and Scharfe de Stairs, "Diccionario Ch'ol-Español," 117; Schumann, *La lengua Chol*, 31; Stuart, "Brief Introduction," 119, for decipherment. Pole dance: Stuart, "Great Bird's Descent." Pole dance with eagle impersonators: K2356, Houston, Stuart, and Taube, *Memory of Bones*, fig. 1.49, original observation by Karl Taube. *Yookte'* as rite of young men: Schele, "Office of Heir-Designate," 288–95. Alternatively, the *yookte'*, which means "upright stick" to the Ch'orti' Maya who use it to rasp maguey leaves, refers to perishable wooden supports of braziers: one vessel shows such a brazier with a caption of *yook*, "its foot/support," along with *ch'ajoomtaak*, "the incensers" who presumably worked the brazier (K1645).

60. J. Thompson, *Maya Hieroglyphic Writing*, fig. 58.

61. Nonhuman scribe: K8393. Drunken feline: ex-Ranieri collection, Crystal River, now Los Angeles County Museum of Art. *Ch'ok Xib* deity: K593.

62. Pusilha: Stela C, Prager, "Inschriften von Pusilha," 213, from Stela C, position pA1. "Watchers," *koknoom*: Bernal, "Dignatarios"; original reading David Stuart. New Year rites and youths: Stuart, "New Year Records." Newborn gods: Stuart, *Inscriptions from Temple XIX*, 141; also S. Martin, "Baby Jaguar."

63. Female *ch'ok*: Graham, *Part I: Yaxchilan*, 121, in Lintel 56, Structure 11. Her name, in glyphic transcription: **IXIK-ki ch'o-ko IX-SAK-bi-ya-ni**; also Stuart, *Inscriptions from Temple XIX*, 152, fig. 117.

64. Warrior dances with *ch'ok*: K5763. Musicians with conch shells: K3814. Dos Pilas: Structure L5–49, Houston, *Dos Pilas*, 44. Cell construction: W. Coe, *Tikal Report: Great Plaza*, fig. 170. Youthful journeys: S. Martin, "Court and Realm," 182–84.

65. Courtesans: Houston, "Courtesans"; also K530, Boston Museum of Fine Arts, #1987.719. Mirror of *ch'ok* and wooden effigy: Miller and Martin, *Courtly Art*, pl. 16.

66. Berjonneau and Sonnery, *Rediscovered Masterpieces*, pl. 367. Kislak mirror back: Kislak pc 0132, K4829.

67. Youths and tribute: K1728; also Just, *Dancing*, 149–53, pl. 15. Palenque youth: Stuart, *Inscriptions from Temple XIX*, fig. 95. Museo Regional de Chiapas: photograph of vase on display by Andrew Scherer. Companions to warrior kings: panel in Merrin Gallery, April 2015, New York City.

68. Photographs from David Stuart, who also points out the extraordinary "font" of the pot. Each glyph appears to have a nonlinguistic outline of an animal.

69. Sacrificed youths: Ruz Lhuillier, *Templo*, 50–51, fig. 179; Cucina and Tiesler, "Companions"; Houston and Scherer, "La ofrenda máxima," 185–88. Piedras Negras burial: Fitzsimmons et al., "Guardian," 458–59, fig. 10.

3 A GIFTED PASSAGE

1. A topic that still needs study: Maya vases and their varying volume of liquid. Narrow, straight-sided cylinders, to be held by one hand, develop in the late seventh and early eighth centuries AD. Exquisite examples occur at Tikal, Guatemala, and vicinity, with diameters of 2⅜ in. (6 cm; K2707), 2½ in. (6.5 cm; K8007), and 3⅛ in. (8 cm; K8008). Within a century or two, as in the Pasión region of Guatemala, vases elongate and rims draw inward for narrow openings, Sabloff, *Excavations at Seibal*, figs. 384, 400, 405. For an exceptional study of such changes in shape: Eberl, "Heterogeneity and Integration," 80–118. Serving lady with vase: M. Coe, *Maya Scribe*, pl. 32.

2. Small tumblers: Culbert, *Ceramics of Tikal*, figs. 83c, 91i, from Burial 196. On feasts: Tozzer, *Relación*, 101, 217. For the drinking dwarf, see a vase now in the National Gallery of Australia, NGA 82.2292, K1453. Claudia Brittenham notes that the container is likely a perishable gourd. Pot showing drink preparation: S. Coe, *First Cuisines*, 141–42. A recent doctoral dissertation claims that many vessels were not usable for drinking. A narrow opening would "hit the bridge of the nose on an adult face before the vessel is fully tilted": Loughmiller-Newman, *Analytical Reconciliation*, 303. Yet no large imagination is needed to see a drink being poured down a gullet—was drinking always dainty?—and the remainder left as ostentatious waste or poured into a smaller container. The dimensions of some such pots was perhaps less about ideal function than the display of images or designs on them. My thanks to Claudia Brittenham for leading me to this source. For the Calakmul murals, from Chiik Nahb Structure Sub 1–4: S. Martin, "Painted Pyramid," 64, 68, figs. 4, 7, 10, 13, 18. Simon Martin urged me to think of these figures as providers rather than consumers. Indecorous drinking on Classical Greek vases, often by satyrs: Lissarrague, *Greek Banquet*, 13–14, 28. On Greek symposia as anticipated experience: Topper, *Imagery*, 4. For the Greeks, the satyrs were "masters of exaggeration," in permanent erection, cravers of heady, unmixed wine, examples of pure farce because they do resemble humans; see Mitchell, *Visual Humour*, 306–7, 309–11.

3. Examples of *Humpen* mugs from sixteenth-century Bohemia and Germany: Los Angeles County Museum of Art, William Randolph Hearst Collection #48.24.186 (4½ in. [11.4 cm] dia.), #48.24.197 (5⅞ in [15 cm] dia.) #48.24.218 (4½ in. [11.6 cm] dia.). Examples of later vases with restricted rims: R. Smith, *Ceramic Sequence*, fig. 42b8, 44f. On competitive consumption of fish oil: Kan, *Potlatch*, 230.

4. Statements of possession without clear owners—"his [or her] pot" for a certain recipe of chocolate—include K544, K758, and K796. Several appear to be reduced versions of longer statements. Lack of space truncated them: K544 concludes with a preposition, *ti*, perhaps to indicate a vessel for an unnamed person; K796 also ends with a preposition, *ta;* another boils down *yuk'ib*, "his drinking vessel," to a **yu** syllable (K1355). A codex-style vase, so called for its resemblance to bichromatic Maya books (and now in the Los Angeles County Museum of Art), mentions an owner, but generically so: the pot belonged to a *K'uhul cha?-tahn winik*, a title used by many lords in the area of Calakmul, Mexico (M.2006.41, K531; see also K1810, K2723, K3221, K4644). Several pots in the same style omit even that (K1181, K1182, K1203, K4546). Other pots are equally vague or abridged, referring to *chak ch'ok* (K595). The Kerr database: www.mayavase.org, with the relevant search heading of "Primary Standard Sequence." A search for *ch'ok* references beyond the Kerr database hints at many more such references, e.g., Chase and Chase, *Investigations*, fig. 38; Villela, *Civilizations*, 57. A fair prediction is that the number will only grow steadily and proportionately. See also on Thomas Aquinas's nuanced understanding of private property: Chroust and Affeldt, "Private Property," 182.

5. Classic Maya personhood: Houston, Stuart, and Taube, *Memory of Bones*, 76–81, 97–101. On property and moral dispossession, much of it Marxist in tone: Hann, "Dispossession," 17; Hann, "Embeddedness," 1, 4–5, 36.

6. Tzotzil terms: Laughlin, *Santo Domingo Zinacantán*, I: 156, 246. On mountain lords, the greedy, unpredictable owners of animals and animal souls: Pitarch, *Jaguar and the Priest*, 219 fn. 10, 226 fn. 4; Vogt, *Tortillas*, 16–17; Vogt, *Zinacantan*, 302; Watanabe, *Maya Saints*, 75, 87, 102. *Ah yum:* Wisdom, Materials on the Chorti Language, 445; also in Ch'olti', Robertson, Law, and Haertel, *Colonial Ch'olti'*, 314, for *dueño*, "owner."

7. The sole use of *yum* in a Classic text, from a vessel found at Río Azul, remains unclear. Possibly it expresses the idea of "father," but this cannot be proved; Stuart, "Kinship Terms," 3–4, fig. 3.

8. For such coverings of pre-existing texts and designs, see K8575, which leaves exposed an earlier set of rim-band glyphs that name the first owner. Repeating a depiction of spider monkeys, it alters and eroticizes them by adding male genitalia. A second text, painted vertically over the layer of stucco, may append the name of a new owner. Tikal example, from Burial 195: Culbert, *Ceramics of Tikal*, fig. 51. The survey is taken from www.mayavase.com, drawing on so-called Primary Standard Sequence tags that identify ownership. The most skilled study of dynastic pots in foreign kingdoms: Just, *Dancing*, 102–23, 142–48. On "Animal Skull": Martin and Grube, *Chronicle*, 40–41.

9. Ethnography of looting: Paredes Maury, "Surviving in the Rain Forest," esp. 12–24.

10. On pseudo-glyphs: Calvin, "Between Text and Image," esp. 11, 213–20; also Houston, "Routine, Mass-Made, Pseudo." Earlier discussion: Longyear, *Archaeological Investigations*, and *Copan Ceramics*, 61–62.

11. Nonetheless, Yucatan and Campeche do have a larger number of monumental texts with pseudoglyphs; see, e.g., Pollock, *Puuc*, figs. 236 (Sayil), 385 (Tabi), 792 (San Pedro).

12. Texts on ceramics: Stuart, *Glyphs on Pots*. Houses as *otoot*, "dwellings": Houston, "Classic Maya Depictions," 349, fig. 13; see K6028, Museum of Fine Arts, Boston. Reciprocal metaphors and ceramics as cosmic models: Houston, "Classic Maya Depictions," 349.

13. Recent review of such contents: Beliaev, Davletshin, and Tokovinine, "Sweet Cacao," 267–69. A divide exists among scholars: some wish to see complex grammatical particles in ceramic texts; others are "minimalist," focusing more on descriptions of drinks and a less elaborate argument for grammatical suffixation. Consider the poorly understood spellings **ji-chi** and **yi-chi**. In personal communications to David Stuart (*Glyphs on Pots*, 37), Terrence Kaufman and John Justeson suggest that the preceding glyphs determine their occurrence, and that the terms convey the sense of "already,"*-ich*, descended from a yet more ancient **-ik*. Thus, *k'ahlaj* is followed by **ji-chi**, *t'abayi* by **yi-chi**—note the consistency between final and initial consonant, *j* followed by *j*, *y* by *y*. The pattern of sounds is violated in several texts, K796, K1256, K1892, K2292, K3230 (*k'ahlaj* + **yi-chi** or *t'abayi* + **ji-chi**), yet these may be errors of habitual spelling, slipped in with little thought. They do appear to express the flow of sound. A minimalist suspicion: the presence of *ich* in both implicates "chile," *ich*. As a flavoring, chile is perfectly appropriate for drinking vessels. An unusual rendering of **yi-chi-li ja-yi** appears on a vessel looted from Xultun and now at the Boston Museum of Fine Arts; the syntax points to *ich* as an adjective for *jaay*, "cup," thus "his[*y-*] chile[*ichil*]-cup[*jaay*]": see also Stuart, *Glyphs on Pots*, 37; for vowel-harmony (e.g., *ich-il*) in glyphic adjectives, Houston, Robertson, and Stuart, *Quality and Quantity*, fig. 15. Equally enigmatic, also relevant to minimalist views: **-na-ja-la** (later **-na-ha-la**). Alfonso Lacadena interprets this as a passive *tz'ihbnaj(al)*, "it is painted"; Lacadena, "Passive Voice," 183–84. An alternative idea is that it reflects an adjective, *najal*, qualifying the following glyph for "drinking vessel." To be sure, Lacadena's proposal has linguistic merit, but it does not account for several texts. One records *t'abayi naj jich* (K1080). Logically, a "passive" particle *-naj* cannot follow a mediopassive *t'abayi*. The sequence has no precedent in Mayan grammar. Another text reads *u-tz'ihbil u* (or 2?) *-naj* (K1398). Here, a possessive particle and another sign come between elements that, in Lacadena's interpretation, cannot be separated; see also M. Coe, *Maya Scribe*, pl. 35, and K3026, **u-tz'i-ba-IL na-ja yu-k'i-bi**, again with an interpolated **IL**, contrary to Lacadena's proposal. The minimalist view: a possible term in Yukateko, *na'ah*, "satisfied, full,"

leads by conjecture to glyphic *naj[~h]al yuk'ib*, "full, plentiful, is his drinking vessel"; see also Kaufman, "Etymological Dictionary," 971, for proto-Ch'olan *naj, "full." A descriptive before the term for "drinking vessel" is known to occur. An Early Classic stone bowl from Santa Rita, Belize, prefaces *yuk'ib* with *ixi'm tuun*, "maize-stone"; Chase and Chase, "Early Classic Period," fig. 7a.

14. In a somewhat reductive study, scientific assays purport to show that, in two collections, one looted, the other from Calakmul, Mexico, vases labeled for chocolate retained traces of maize detected by scientific means; Loughmiller-Newman, *Analytical Reconciliation*, 296–97. That vases served other uses beyond their stated ones does not surprise—a coffee mug could also cradle tea or milk, and a whisky glass, if the user were so inclined, a club soda. This hardly qualifies, however, as a debunking of decipherment or the projected and recorded function of a pot. On signatures: Stuart, *Ten Phonetic Syllables*, 4–8, figs. 6–9; Houston, "Crafting Credit."

15. On *alay* as "here is": Macleod and Polyukhovich, "Deciphering the Initial Sign." As a marker of past time: Tortuguero Monument 6, positions E6, E13. Another vessel, K1728, confirms the temporal nature of the sign, replacing it with **HA'-'i**, perhaps to be understood as "now." For *t'ab*: Stuart, "Fire Enters," 416–47. For *t'abayi* as foot ascending a stone platform: K508, a vase that also specifies the precise date of the "raising up," Mar. 30, AD 773. Some time ago, in unpublished research, Peter Mathews noted what may be the same verb on a Zapotec monument, MA-J-14, at Monte Alban, Oaxaca. The only difficulty is that the footstep descends in this sign, and its verbal status is unclear. Other vessels with firm dates: 9.11.0.0.0 12 Ahaw 8 Keh, Oct. 10, AD 652, Stuart, "Kings of Stone," fig. 15c; K8622, 9.14.9.15.10 7 Ok 13 Yax, Aug. 25, AD 721; K791, 9.16.3.13.14 4 Ix 12 Kumk'u, Jan. 19, AD 755; K3394, 4 Ajaw 13 Yax; K8121, 8 Ajaw 3 Wayeb. Another term, *k'ahlaj*, is thought to involve "binding," in a trope for the dedication of sacred things; see Stuart, "Kings of Stone," 155–56. According to syllabic clues, **K'AL** is doubtless correct as a reading for the relevant sign. *K'al*, "to bind," occurs in most languages of the Guatemalan and Chiapan Highlands; Kaufman, *Etymological Dictionary*, 1000; it may also figure in Yukateko as a reference to "trap," "button," "enclose," or "imprison," or as *ch'al*,

"braid," a cognate in colonial Tzotzil, cf. Barrera Vásquez, *Diccionario*, 367–68; Laughlin, *Santo Domingo Zinacantán*, I: 195. But Simon Martin and I have also considered an alternative meaning of "rise" or "raise up," a reading buttressed by a medley of evidence; see S. Martin, "Maya Polity." Where depicted, the action of *k'al* glosses the lifting up or offering, often by subordinates, of headdresses and royal headbands with jade jewels; see Berjonneau and Sonnery, *Rediscovered Masterpieces*, pl. 395, also, Dallas Museum of Art, #1988.129; Bonampak Sculptured Stone 5, position A2-C1, Palenque Palace Tablet, Miller and Brittenham, *Spectacle*, figs. 286, 298. These scenes pertain unequivocally to enthrone-ment. An unprovenanced lintel from the area of Bonampak links *k'al* to a lintel (*pakbu-tuun*, "face-down stone"), presumably because the stone was raised above a doorway. A variant spelling appears in the rim-band text of a pot. As pointed out by Martin, it substitutes a small human figure for *k'ahlaj*, the passive form of the verb (Martin, "Maya Polity," 98 n. 61, K3120, the famed "Altar de Sacrificios" vase, R. E. W. Adams, "Comments," fig. 2e). Looking rather like Humpty Dumpty, with enlarged head and weakling arms, it lifts up the small, polished celt of the **K'AL** sign. Just after comes *t'abayi*. This sequence hints at a poetic couplet with *k'ahlaj*, both conveying the same meaning of "raising" yet in divergent, subtly distinct ways: one may communicate the muscular fact of lifting, the other its upward physical trajectory. In the Postclassic Dresden Codex, too, the *k'al* verb may record the "rising" of Venus in particular sectors of the sky; e.g., D46–50. For its part, Ch'orti', a fecund source for decipherment, offers *k'ar*, a root signifying "hold on" or "possess"; Wisdom, Materials on the Chorti Language, 500. That meaning departs from "lift," however. Debate will surely continue about this crucial set of ritual terms.

16. The narrative at Dos Pilas involves the harass-ment of a local scion of the Tikal dynasty. Having taken possession of this swampy area far from Tikal, he came under repeated attack by his dynastic enemy, a ruler of Calakmul. Enough was enough: abandoning ties to kin, he embraced an alliance with Calakmul, now his protector. The arrangement must have been of mutual convenience. For Calakmul, it encour-aged an irritant of its enemy, and a possible

claimant to the Tikal throne. As turncoat, Ruler 1 (Bahlaj Kan K'awiil) of Dos Pilas would have found the same advantages. Another use of *t'abayi* occurs over a century later, at Piedras Negras, on Throne 1. By one reading, it refers to the slicing (?, **ja-ta-wi**) and abdication of an earlier ruler, followed in short order by an enigmatic passage without clear agent; see Martin and Grube, *Chronicle*, 151: **u-chu[ku]-wa i-ki-tsi T'AB-yi LAM-NAAH**, either "he carries" or "he seizes the burden/bundle, it/he rises up in a certain building or place." The absence of an agent suggests that the person undertaking these acts is none another than the abdicant, the last figure mentioned in the text. By comparison with Dos Pilas, the text savors of exile.

17. Roys, *Chumayel*, 101, 150. Tikal plate: Martin and Grube, *Chronicle*, 39, or K8121.

18. The vessel was discovered at Tikal, MT 219; Stuart, *Glyphs on Pots*, 34.

19. For such titles, but explained as general designators, not youthful ones: MacLeod and Reents-Budet, "Art of Calligraphy," 133–34. "Youthful power": Grube, "Hieroglyphentexte," 78, "Die Fürsten und Könige der Maya beanspruchten Jugendlichkeit und Kraft als ihre Attribute und ließen sich deshalb auf öffentlichen Monumenten trotz fortgeschrittenen Alters stets jugendlich idealisiert portraitieren. Vielleicht aber sind diese Titel in den Weiheinschriften viel konkreter zu verstehen, als Verweis auf die kräftigende un belebende Wirkung des Kakaogetränks." Titles for owners of pots: Colas, *Maya-Personennamen*, 154.

20. For youthful accession: the Lady of Tikal [6 ya]; "Aj Wosal" at Naranjo [12 ya]; K'ahk' Tiliw Chan Chahk [5 ya] and "Itzamnaaj" K'awiil [13 ya] of the same city; "Itzamnaaj" Bahlam IV of Yaxchilan [at most 17 ya]; Itzamk'anahk of Piedras Negras [12 ya]; Pakal the Great at Palenque; K'inich "Ich'aak" Chapaht [14 ya]; Martin and Grube, *Chronicle*, 38, 71, 74, 82, 134, 143, 162.

21. Pots with Emblem glyphs and youthful owners: K1547 (Xultun, Guatemala); K2803 (Hix Witz, but perhaps painted at the so-called Ik' site); K3500 (Xultun); K3743 (Xultun); K4332 (Palenque); K6618 (El Zotz?); K7149 (Xultun); K8665 (Hix Witz). The limitation to a few sites is striking. Two of the Xultun pots identify generic owners without personal names (K1547, K3743, K7149); one mentions a specific lord (K3500). The Hix Witz pots identify two different rulers by name.

22. Xultun vessel: K7055. On Xultun and such pots of young men, Garrison and Stuart, "Un análisis preliminar," 836, fig. 11. Tikal examples with female owners: K1941, K2695. Only the last, belonging to a "holy woman," *k'uh(ul) ixik*, has solid provenience, being excavated at the Mundo Perdido Complex at Tikal. Woman's plate: K9072. A possible example of female ownership, from the general region of Calakmul: K2777. Nonetheless, the woman's name is indicated solely by the female head **IX**, followed by a title not otherwise used by that gender; the deity with whose identity "she" merges appears to be masculine too.

23. Female potters, male painters: Houston, *Life Within*, 60; comparative evidence from the American Southwest: Crown, "Pots and Potters," 678–79; also Guthe, *Pueblo Pottery Making*. An excellent study of gender and pot making: Callaghan, "Polychrome Vessels," 123; citing, Reina and Hill, *Traditional Pottery*, 70, 77, 200–201; also, for Puebla, Mexico, Druc, "Ceramic Production," 79.

24. Tayasal cup: K2707. Nonetheless, one small cup is labeled as the possession of a king; Culbert, *Ceramics of Tikal*, figs. 83, 84.

25. Context for the vessel: Laporte and Fialko, "Reencuentro," 82, figs. 70, 71. On the occupant's age and teenage years: Wright, "Immigration to Tikal," 349, table 1. Andrew Scherer cautions that the anomalous isotope may indicate access to high-quality supplies of water.

26. For an *atole* bowl with rounded sides, belonging to a prince, *chak ch'ok keleem*: K2730; for a plate (*lak*) owned by a provincial lord, a *chak ch'ok keleem*, near Calakmul: K3876. For *u k'aba'* pot: K7460.

27. On the value of chocolate: Tozzer, *Relación*, 95 fn. 417. A basic resource on cacao: Blom, "Commerce," 536–38; S. Coe and M. Coe, *True History*, 39–66. Popol Vuh Bowl: K3395, **yu-k'i-bi ta-*u-lu**. Scott Hutson drew my attention to the effort involved in preparing *atole*; see also S. Coe, *First Cuisines*, 138–40.

28. Themes: flowers (K1547, K4379, K4991, K6395); feathers (K1335); water-bird, fishing (K6551); horizontal bands (K3743); dance and dressing, some of humans (K532, K764); dancing Maize God (K5648, K5746); dressing of Maize God (K7268);

Maize God at court (K5720); *Chahk* with fat beast (K555) or spearing mythic fish (K595); feasting animals (K744); mythic owls (K758); heart eating, on an over-painted pot (K1337); insect and half-figure in human form (K6998); Itzam in Venus serpent (K2774); K'awiil in smoke or flames (K3025, K3500); black centipede head (K7149); seated K'awiil (K8118); Maize God with bloodletter (K8741); elderly deities (K8939); "birth" of music from mountain (K8947); snake heads emitting smoke or flame (K8815); mythic decapitation scene by stela (K8719); Principal Bird Deities (K2704); water snakes (K2292, K3155); mythic youths, *hu'n* jewel in basket, bloodletting Maize God on throne (K8665); a deity known as "G1" (a sharklike variant of *Chahk*, K4333); mythic image of Maize God, women, birds, and sacrificers with jaguar ears (K5043); a probable orgy with Itzam and young females (K530); naked woman on armadillo (K3876); *hu'n* jewel (K4572, K7459, K9153); half-figures in recumbent *hu'n* jewels (K8257); young women brought in marriage, a mythic scene (K5847); four eagle-men with acrobatic Maize God (K8242); warriors with staffs or blowguns (K5390); palace of high god, "God D" (no Kerr #); palace scenes of more conventional, not clearly mythic sort (K1186, K1775); specific historical images (K1728, K2695, K7997).

29. For this lord, the thirty-fifth in the royal sequence at Naranjo: Martin and Grube, *Chronicle*, 71–72. A recently discovered sculpture, Stela 47, reiterates his subordination to a king of Calakmul. Yet Aj Wosal mimicked certain carvings at the enemy of Tikal: cf. Tikal Stelae 8 and 9, and Naranjo Stelae 16 and 17.

30. I am indebted to Bryan Just for showing me the pot: the owner of this *atole* bowl, from a province of Calakmul, was a *ch'ok winikha'b ch'ajoom*, "[the] youth, the incenser of *1x20-year span [0–20 ya]." A unit of 20 years (*winikha'b*) was signaled by the absence of any number. Similar usage occurs in the Postclassic Dresden Codex and the Classic-era Tablet of the 96 Glyphs at Palenque, positions I4, K8.

31. The vessel is now on display in a vitrine of Maya objects; Houston and Tokovinine, "Caracol." Paperwork kindly provided by a curator, Chris Wingfield, indicates that it was a 1963 donation from A. Hamilton Anderson, an early official of archaeology in Belize. The find spot appears to be have been "burial chamber B-5."

Unfortunately, records of Anderson's excavations at Caracol were swept out to sea during Hurricane Hattie in 1961. Arlen and Diane Chase report that it was a tomb in Structure D18 re-excavated by their team; Chase and Chase, "Home in the South," figs. 63–68.

32. The anomalous pot is K7716. Its image displays a ruler, presumably Aj Wosal; behind appears a tribal god linked to the Naranjo dynasty; S. Martin, "Tikal's 'Star War,'" 227. At first glance, the number with this glyph for units of twenty years (the *winikh'ab*), appears to be "4," thus recording someone of 60 to 80 years of age. With Aj Wosal, a long-lived figure, this stage of life is certainly possible. Indeed, Alexandre Tokovinine has suggested to me that Aj Wosal was "socially young" and perhaps unmarried for much of his life. The style of the glyphs, especially a rare **AJ** sign, is in any case later than other members of this set. It ties the pot to the other example with advanced age notation yet lacking in youthful titles (K6813). The historical scene, too, contrasts with all other vessels in the series, being a dynastic tableau. More usual notation from area of El Zotz, Guatemala, with *keleem*: M. Coe, *Maya Scribe*, pl. 38.

33. Alabaster drinking vessel from Palenque area: K4332. Also: mace-head, K6631; mirror, Miller and Martin, *Courtly Art*, 45.

34. For a Caracol example: Chase and Chase, "Interpreting," fig. 87. For looted counterparts: K2292, K8242.

35. On Caracol vessels: Structure A3 Tomb, Late Classic period, Chase and Chase, *Investigations*, fig. 1; Holmul, finds from Tepeu 1 burial by Estrada-Belli, http://a57.foxnews.com/global. fncstatic.com/static/managed/img/fn-latino/ lifestyle/0/0/Holmul%20ceramics%20Latino. jpg; Tikal, Culbert, *Ceramics of Tikal*, figs. 86–90, all from the Late Classic Burial 196. For Holmul, see also: Callaghan and Neivens de Estrada, *Holmul Region*, fig. 7.4.

36. Assemblage: K633 (Art Institute of Chicago, 1986.1081), K635 (Art Institute of Chicago, 1986.1080), K2796, and K4379. The last is over-restored, and K2796, while theologically dense in its scene of gods in primordial time, has a far leaner, almost scratchy line. It may come from a different moment in the calligrapher's career or use of a quill or *chehb* rather than a fine brush; see also Herring, "Royal Artist," 39, for isolation of the calligraphic features of this

assemblage. Square vessel: K7750. An earlier, plausible view, that the painter was a prince, cannot be sustained (cf. Stuart, *Ten Phonetic Syllables*, fig. 6): the owner's name, designating a prince, leads to a lower band containing the names of his royal father and mother, and only then refers to the painter. The calligrapher's genealogy is, alas, wholly unclear. A dynastic chocolate pot from Naranjo occurs at Buenavista del Cayo, Belize, at an earlier date, c. AD 720; Reents-Budet et al., "Palace Dumps," 117.

37. Example of tandem ownership: K5452. On Wak Chan K'awiil: Martin and Grube, *Chronicle*, 39. On the queen and her co-ruler: S. Martin, "Early Classic Co-Rulers," "Line of the Founder." At first, I had seen the final phrase on the top row as "cross-sex sibling," spelled **yi?-TAHN-na**, *y-ihtahn*, "her brother": Kaufman and Norman, "Outline," 121, #173. That was wrong. Simon Martin urged me to re-examine a higher-resolution image, which yielded another reading: **u 1-TAHN-na**, "her first-of-the-chest" or, less literally, "her son." The **1** appears as, evidently, a single human finger, a known variant of that number. It is preceded by an equally rare **u** sign occurring elsewhere in the text as a free-standing sign (see, for example, its use in **u tz'i ba li**). The woman mentioned on the vase would thus be the *mother* of the first owner.

38. The vessel is K0954. For "singer" decipherment: Houston, "Hill of Beans," 40. On deity impersonation: Houston and Stuart, "Gods, Glyphs, and Kings," 297, 299, figs. 6, 7; A. Stone, "Aspects of Impersonation"; also Houston, Stuart, and Taube, *Memory of Bones*, 271–72; for a useful review, see: Knub, Thun, and Helmke, "Divine Rite of Kings," esp. 190–93. Another impersonator of god of music: K1728.

39. Possession by impersonators of the Sun God: K6437, K7224, K7750. These record the Sun God as a "lord," *K'inich Ajaw*, a bird (an eagle?), and a being radiating seven beams of light, conceived as centipedes. For "Black Hole Lord": K791, cf. K1609. God of primordial events: K635. Illustrious parentage: K635, K1383, K7750. A possible youthful owner in state of impersonation appears on a bowl excavated at Holmul, Guatemala, but likely from Naranjo; Reents-Budet, *Painting*, fig. 4.12.

40. K3876, with a title associated with provinces of the Calakmul region. Its central image has no

precedents and borders on the folkloric: a naked woman kneeling over a supine armadillo on a rock.

41. Tobacco containers: Jay I. Kislak Collection, Rare Book and Special Collections Division, Library of Congress, #41–1 to 5; also Smith and Kidder, *Motagua Valley*, fig. 2. Residue analysis of tobacco: Zagorevski and Loughmiller-Newman, "Detection of Nicotine," 410; also Loughmiller-Cardinal and Zagorevski, "Maya Flasks," 9–10. Tobacco use among the Maya: Groark, "Angel in the Gourd," 9–13. Several show conversation between K'awiil and the deity of trade, God L; one vessel from the Puuc area of Yucatan takes that relationship further, as God L holds up the head of K'awiil; M. Coe, *Maya Scribe*, pl. 56. The vessel belonged to a *chak ch'ok* and the bearer of an important local title, the *sajal*. Similar to an epithet of subordinate lords in the Usumacinta region of Guatemala and Mexico, it nonetheless differs by referring to higher-ranking figures; see Houston and Inomata, *Classic Maya*, 176. A recent study of a container from Copan found at Tazumal, El Salvador: Card and Zender, "Miniature Flask," 285–87.

42. Snuff as medicine: S. Martin, "Painted Pyramid," 66; J. Thompson, *Maya History*, 118–20.

43. For mirror backs: Jay I. Kislak Collection, Rare Book and Special Collections Division, Library of Congress (034.01.00). Images with men holding mirrors near a lord: K764, K787, K1454, K1463. A courtesan or young woman lifts a mask to an elderly god on K530. Topoxte mirror from Burial 49: Grube, "Hieroglyphentexte," Abb. IV.3; Hermes, "Secuencia," 155, fig. 15; Miller and Martin, *Courtly Art*, 45. On age of tomb occupant: Wright, Schwarcz, and Acevedo, "La dieta," fig. 114. In an email, the main author, Lori Wright, has indicated that the sex is weakly proven at best, and the age would range from 20 to 35. Still, it is neither an aged individual nor excluded as a male.

44. "Holy lord" solely as *ch'ok*: K1728.

45. Alexandre Tokovinine was generous with images of this plate. The find, "Vessel 1," was made in Tomb 1, Building F, Group 1, by Raymond Merwin, who began work at the site in 1911; Merwin and Vaillant, *Holmul*, 13–15, fig. 7, and sensitive exegesis by Callaghan, "Polychrome Vessels," 114–18, fig. 8.5. For historical discussion: Martin and Grube, *Chronicle*, 80–81, which also discerns the hand of Tikal at

this time in Naranjo's dynastic politics. Greek krater with line of ships and reflection of drinker: Lissarrague, *Greek Banquet*, 112–14.

46. Colonial Tzotzil: *tekpanil*, "gift, generosity, nobility," and associated as well with "eloquence"; Laughlin, *Santo Domingo Zinacantán*, I: 229–30, 278, 311. On *matan:* Kaufman, *Etymological Dictionary*, 785. *Sih:* Kaufman, *Etymological Dictionary*, 786. Ch'orti': Wisdom, Materials on the Chorti Language, 572, 639, 642. On Christian and philosophical discussions of the gift in early modern Europe: N. Davis, *The Gift*, 11–22.

47. David Stuart and Marc Zender were helpful with comments on gifting. For *ak':* Caracol Stela 3, position D13; La Corona Hieroglyphic Stairway 3, block VIII, positions C3–D3; Naranjo Hieroglyphic Stairway 1, block 4, position H1; Naranjo Stela 32, position A'1; Palenque, Temple of the Inscriptions, positions O4, P11, Q4–R4. For "feathered flute": La Corona "Element 39," position B2–A3. Ch'olti': Robertson, Law, and Haertel, *Colonial Ch'olti'*, 313; same source, *sii (çii)*, 313. On Yukateko practices: Hanks, *Referential Practice*, 362–80. The "counting out" of gruel offerings in rectangular patterns on altars recalls numbers placed before some verbs on rim-band texts related to drink; K3642.

48. *Mayiij* in the texts: with female bloodletting through the tongue, **ma-yi-hi**, on Yaxchilan Stela 35, position F1, involving the mother of Bird Jaguar IV; M. Coe, "Wooden Box," figs. 1–3, 7, as **ma-yi-ji**; Bassie and Zender, "Wooden Offering Container," 14–15; Comalcalco Urn 26, Pendant 17b, 18b; Zender, Armijo, and Gallegos, "Vida y obra," 48–49, fig. 17. Other such boxes: Anaya Hernández, Guenter, and Mathews, "Wooden Box"; Pendergast, *Actun Polbiche*, fig. 11a; possible vestige of one belonging to a youth at Piedras Negras: Fitzsimmons et al., "Guardian," 462, fig. 9.

49. Examples of paternal statements: Itzan Stela 17, positions C1–D1 (**u-si-hi u-CHIT-*ti CH'AHB-?-?**); Tamarindito Hieroglyphic Stairway 3, Step V, position E1, Step VI, positions A1–B1 (**si-hi-ja u-chi-ti ch'a-CH'AHB**); unprovenanced panel, Denver Art Museum, 1997.149, positions B10–C1 (**u-si-ji ch'a-ba**). Related text: Machaquila Stela 6, position B1 (**u-chi-ti CH'AHB**). *Sij* as "gift": Kaufman and Norman, "Outline," 130, although reconstructed there, contrary to glyphic spellings, as **sih*. On *huun tahn:* Stuart, "Kinship Terms," 8.

50. The lone dynastic exception may be a slate mirror back that may be the "gift" (**si**) by an important lord of El Peru, Guatemala, to a lord at the smaller city of El Zotz; Schmidt, de la Garza, and Nalda, *Maya*, pl. 434; the object was found in the Nicoya region of Costa Rica.

51. On sacrifice: Hubert and Mauss, *Sacrifice;* later comment by Allen, Mauss, *The Gift,* with perceptive foreword by Mary Douglas, esp. vii (Douglas on the "escalating contest" for honor) and xiv (importance of public visibility and adjudication); and, in Mauss, 17 ("contract sacrifice" for gods), 39 ("three obligations: to give, to receive, to reciprocate"), 65 (systems of "courtesies"). Mauss's nostalgia is on full display in his conclusion (106): "This is what tomorrow, in our so-called civilized world, classes and nations and individuals also, must learn. This is one of the enduring secrets of their wisdom and solidarity." For Derrida: *Given Time*, 7.

52. N. Davis on "gifts gone wrong": *The Gift*, 67–84, esp. 74, with Davis's translation from Montaigne's *Essais*.

53. On the emotional charge of gifts: Thoen, *Strategic Affection?*, 223–29. For gifting as communication: Cheal, "Showing Them," 155–57. On the "management of meaning": Algazi, "Doing Things with Gifts," 12. On potlatch and the generational transmission of titles: Roth, "Tsimshian Potlatch," 143–44.

54. Appadurai, "Introduction," 21.

55. On "moral memory": Simmel, "Faithfulness and Gratitude," 45. Pierre Bourdieu and contradictory claims for domination and subjective altruism: *Logic of Practice*, 122–41; also Silber, "Bourdieu's Gift," 183. Bourdieu and temporal delay: *Logic*: 198, 200.

56. Trait lists: Osteen, "Questions of the Gift," 25–26. Thomas on the "gift": *Entangled Objects*, 205; also N. Davis, *The Gift*, 136 fn. 8.

57. Weiner, *Inalienable Possessions*, 7 ("serial world... always subject to loss and decay"); 46 ("Samoan fine mats and Northwest Coast coppers remained attached to their original owners even when they circulated among other people"); 61 (burial with high-born dead); 141 (on the complexity and layering of gift transactions). To envision the "formula for maintaining the social sphere" as a whole, Maurice Godelier (*Enigma*, 36) refines the distinction to "*keeping-for-giving and giving-while-keeping*" (italics in original). Yet his definition of a valuable, also italicized as "*of*

no practical use" or *"unusual in the daily activities of living and earning a livelihood,"* would deny any such value to Maya dining services; Godelier, *Enigma,* 161. Mauss on things with "soul": *The Gift,* 16. On exclusion: Komter, *Social Solidarity,* 133–43. The material overemphasis in much discussion: Rosenwein, "Francia and Polynesia," 371.

58. E. Thompson: "Folklore," 258; further critical comment on Mauss: Wagner-Hasel, "Egoistic Exchange," 159–65. At an extreme: Patrick Geary ("Gift Exchange," 140) sees Mauss, in "a meager harvest from so prominent a scholar," as engaged largely in reflection on the West, with evidence contaminated by contact with European traders and colonial powers.

59. On Attic vases: esp. Neer, *Style and Politics,* 130–31, including quotations here and in the subsequent paragraph. Homoerotic images with "beautiful" youths: Lissarrague, *Greek Banquet,* 32. Gift giving in Greece: Kurke, *Traffic in Praise,* 85–107; Seaford, *Reciprocity,* 204, 217–19. On *hetaerae*: Kurke, "Inventing the Hetaira," 145–46. Procession of warriors: K638, K1206, K5763. Greek courting with animal gifts: Shapiro, "Fathers and Sons," 99, cat. 45. Erotic content of Greek vessels: Andrew Stewart, *Art, Desire, and the Body,* 156–81. "Primitive" pasts in Athenian scenes of feasts: Topper, *Imagery,* 157–59. Maya comparisons: Houston, Stuart, and Taube, *Memory of Bones,* 102–3, 129.

60. Quotations: Neer, *Style and Politics,* 130–31.

61. Dietler on "diacritical" feasts: "Theorizing the Feast," 73–86; see also Appadurai, "Gastro-politics," 507.

62. Inalienability of Maya ceramics: Callaghan, "Polychrome Vessels," 124. The emphasis on labor is perceptive, but one wonders about the salience, say of paste preparation or basic forming in establishing an inalienable trace of those involved in production; also Mills, "Establishment and Defeat," table 1, emphasizes the "highly gendered" production of such objects, their separation from mundane exchange, and their use "to authenticate individual as well as collective identities."

63. On Q'ekchi' patterns of inalienable possession: Kockelman, "Inalienable Possession," 25–26, 62. For glyphic study of intimate possession: Zender, "Morphology," 195–209.

64. Cf. K3395; the presence of a ruler's name, Jasaw Chan K'awiil of Tikal, brackets the Uaxactun

vase to that temporal span. Same artist: K0595. The Uaxactun vase has reportedly been purchased by La Ruta Maya Foundation in Guatemala.

4 THE TAMING PLACES

1. Rites of passage: van Gennep, *Rites of Passage,* 65–115. This paragraph draws on La Fontaine, *Initiation,* 16 (mutilation), 24 (on van Gennep), 26 (criticism by Max Gluckman of van Gennep), 28 (subdivision of rites), 38 (gender segregation), 48 (varying emphasis within rites), 63 (spirit possession), 67 (purification), 102 (dual-purpose initiations), 102 (metaphors of death and rebirth), 102–3 (dual-purpose initiations, admitting novices, and transforming children), 105 (supposed breaking of ties with mother, incorporation into male world), 108 (linked to social rather than physical maturity), 109 (restriction to one sex), 111 (penile bloodletting in New Guinea), 127 (spirit impersonation and performance in New Guinea), 128–29 (menstruation identified with penile bleeding, New Guinea), 133 (feasts and drum-laying in men's house), 137 (separation from family house into men's houses, New Guinea), 140 (initiation and introduction to public duties), 181 (value of sheer entertainment).

2. On youthful gods: Doyle, "Creation Narratives"; Taube, "Birth Vase," 664, prefers to see the newborn old god, a *mam,* as a deity "summoned at the birth of a child."

3. Criticism: Gluckman, *Essays,* 9, cited in La Fontaine, *Initiation,* 26.

4. Turner's doctrines of ecstatic communion, social leveling, wild states during liminality, and "timelessness": *Dramas,* 238–39, 253, 268–70, for "timeless condition, an eternal now" (238); "sacra" and "storage bins," "cosmologies, values, and cultural axioms" (239). Turner on the emotionally laden, creative, and "breakthrough" nature of liminality: *Ritual Process,* 128–30, 133. For an appreciative review: St. John, *Victor Turner.*

5. Noncombatant status: Babcock, "Turner," 461, who also comments on his stays in gypsy camps. Rock concerts: Turner, *Dramas,* 261–65.

6. Madagascar: Bloch, *Blessing to Violence,* 48 (age of circumcision, "clean," "sweet or beautiful"), 48–49 (enable sexual potency of boys), 55 (role of older youths, including nature of plants), 74 (such youths ensuring "strength in this life and the continuing existence of the descent groups"), 88 ("continuing chain of moral life

and blessing"), 131, 142 (royal appropriation in 1844), 143 (youths as "wild, strong cattle"), 171 (wild vitality tamed), 184 (timeless inevitability). Kratz: *Affecting Performance*, 25–26, 28 (criticism of Bloch), 73 (instilling a "hierarchy of gerontocratic authority"), 94 ("roaming together, visiting girls, hunting, climbing for honey, and raiding cows"), 235, 254, 308 (music and oratory).

7. Four syllabic spellings reinforce the reading for *ch'ahb*: (1) Caracol Stela 3, position B19 (**YAX-ch'a-CH'AHB-wi**), dating, perhaps, to Jan. 28, AD 633; (2) Tamarandito Hieroglyphic Stairway 3, Step VI, position B1 (**CH'AHB-ba**), c. AD 710; (3) Yaxchilan Stela 35, position C1 (**ti-ch'a-CH'AHB-ba-ti-AK'AB-li**), July 2, AD 741; and (4) a panel from the Denver Art Museum (#1997.149) dating to Dec. 3, AD 780, position C1 (**u-ch'a-ba**). Another example, with suffixed **ba** sign, may occur on Yaxchilan Lintel 24, positions C1, E1, c. AD 726. As supposed obsidian: Stone and Zender, *Reading Maya Art*, 74–75. Frontal examples: Balser and Instituto Nacional de Seguros, *Jade precolombino*, 44c, 45, 117; also, Copan Papagayo stone: Fash et al., "Hieroglyphic Stairway," fig. 5.

8. Quotation: Tozzer, *Relación*, 184.

9. Prior discussion: Houston, Stuart, and Taube, *Memory of Bones*, 130–31. *Ayuno*, "fast": Kaufman and Norman, "Outline," 100, descended from Common Mayan **k'ajb'*. Ch'olti' for "ayuno": *çapi* (*sahp* in Ch'orti', see Wisdom, "Chorti Language," 623); *pocti* (*poki uti*, "rinse one's mouth," Wisdom, Materials on the Chorti Language, 569); *hitz* (*hie'*, "hunger," in Chontal Mayan, Knowles, "Chontal Maya," 423). See also Robertson, Law, and Haertel, *Colonial Ch'olti'*, 296; Ch'orti', *ch'ajb'eyij*, "fast, go without food," Hull, "Abbreviated Dictionary," 25; colonial Tzotzil, *ch'abaj*, Laughlin, *Santo Domingo Zinacantán*, I: 194; Kaufman, *Etymological Dictionary*, 714; Yukateko, *ch'ab*, glossed as "abstenerse de deleites carnales, ser casto y hacer penitencia" (abstain from carnal delights, to be chaste and make penance) but also "create," Barrera Vásquez, *Diccionario*, 120. Note the internal *h* in many spellings of *ch'ahb*, proving its presence during Classic times, if unremarked in spellings. Sexual abstinence prior to rituals in colonial and more recent times: Colby and Colby, *Daykeeper*, 101, for the Ixil; R. Wilson, *Maya Resurgence*, 63, 69, for Q'eqchi'. Diego de Landa on fasting, avoidance of sex, links to

bloodletting, and calamity for those lapsing in duty: Tozzer, *Relación*, 150, 152, 156, 162, 184, 219; quotation on 184. Sacred incense: J. Thompson, *Ethnology*, 104. Abstinence and separate quarters for men with pregnant wives: Scholes and Roys, *Chontal Indians*, 43, noting this practice for the seventeenth-century Cholti Maya. Fasting prior to ritual, often combined with sexual abstinence: Orellana, *Tzutujil Mayas*, 101; J. Thompson, *Maya History*, 172–73, and citing Bartolomé de las Casas, 177. Young men, fertility, and planting: R. Wilson, *Maya Resurgence*, 64–65, 111, 135. Tzutujil young men or *alcila*: Stanzione, *Rituals of Sacrifice*, 15, 57–58, 158, 167–168, 200. *Alcila* is doubtless a version of *alguacil/aguacil*, a Spanish term from Arabic used by other Maya to designate lower ranks in civic hierarchy; Vogt, *Zinacantan*, 697.

10. De Coto, *Vocabvlario*, 408–9.

11. *Ch'ahb-ak'ab*: Stuart, "Ideology," 79.

12. Yaxchilan Stela 35 and relevant queens: Martin and Grube, *Chronicle*, 125–27, 129. Rendering and photo of the back are in Corpus of Maya Hieroglyphic Inscriptions Project, Peabody Museum of Archaeology and Ethnology, Harvard University.

13. Predawn world: Hamman, "Pre-sunrise Things," 354, on this pervasive and presumably ancient trope, "For 20th-century Mixtecs, Chinantecs, Mitleño Zapotecs, and Yucatec Maya, the past was a time of darkness in which no sun shone."

14. Anthropological studies of blood: Carsten, *Blood Will Out*, which nonetheless focuses heavily on present-day concepts.

15. Piedras Negras princess: Stuart, "Four Shell Plaques," 176–82. Young queen of Tikal: S. Martin, "Early Classic Co-Rulers," and "Line of the Founder," 18–19. Excavated by Vilma Fialko, the stela, from Tres Cabezas, is unpublished but thoughtfully brought to my attention by Simon Martin. Dates are reconstructible in part: the first, **9.3.9.13.4, 9 K'an 12 Mol, Sept. 5, AD 504, is the queen's birth, one day later than its other record, a possible indication it took place at night; see also Tikal Stela 23, positions A1–C4: Jones and Satterthwaite, *Monuments*, 50–51, fig. 36; for her co-regent's *yax ch'ahb*: Jones and Satterthwaite, *Monuments*, 26, fig. 14. A calendrical event comes next (9.3.10.0.0, 1 Ajaw 8 Mak, Dec. 10, AD 504), then her probable "covering" or "enclosing" at 9.3.13.0.0, 2 Ajaw 13 Keh, Nov. 25, AD 507, and accession at 9.3.16.8.4,

11 K'an 17 Pop, Apr. 22, AD 511. The text closes with the date 9.4.0.0.0, 13 Ajaw 18 Yax, Oct. 17, AD 514. Child brides in tribal Pakistan: Nasrullah et al., "Girl Child Marriage," 540; marriageable girls could show breast growth, enter into their first menstrual cycle, or prove capable of domestic tasks such as lifting a bed or water jar; Rutgers WPF Pakistan and Adolescent Girls Empowerment Project, *Puppeteers*, 11.

16. Early stela: Princeton University Art Museum, 1999–232, K152. As "first penance": Stuart, "Childhood Ritual"; also Fields and Reents-Budet, *Lords of Creation*, pl. 56; Schele, "Hauberg Stela," 138.

17. Palenque: Martin and Grube, *Chronicle*, 171; D. Stuart and G. Stuart, *Palenque*, 216–19. Relevant text: Palace Tablet, positions F6–F14. The date is 9.10.18.17.19, 2 Kawak 12 Keh, Oct. 20, AD 651. Images by Marc Zender: http://www.mesoweb.com/monuments/DPLHS2.html, accessed Feb. 2, 2015.

18. On the Dos Pilas tomb, Burial 20: Just, *Dancing*, 112–15, figs. 44–45.

19. Yaxchilan Stela 35: Tate, *Yaxchilan*, 197.

20. In Room 2 at Bonampak, Chiapas, a head lies on such a bed of leaves, perhaps to sop up blood; Miller and Brittenham, *Spectacle*, fig. 210.

21. Headband title and distribution: Stuart, *Inscriptions from Temple XIX*, 133–37, figs. 105–10, 112, "some undeciphered title applied to important priests or members of the royal court." *Ebeet* as "servant," "worker," and "messenger": Kaufman, *Etymological Dictionary*, 58; Kaufman and Norman, "Outline," 119; Robertson, Law, and Haertel, *Colonial Ch'olti'*, 332.

22. Page service: S. Martin, "Court and Realm," 182–84. David Stuart kindly shared his drawing of La Corona Panel 1; the departure of the lord took place on Nov. 7, AD 673; six days later he was "called" or "summoned," possibly *u-pehkji*, by his overlord—was this into the king's very presence, after some cooling of heels at court? Twelve days passed before the undeciphered event with the sons of the king. For "summons": Houston, "Parliaments." Birth of summoned lord: Feb. 22, AD 645.

23. Houston, "Maya Multilinguals." Mayan language contact: Law, *Language Contact*, 175–85.

24. Aguateca vessel, from Structure M7–35: Inomata, "Last Day," fig. 15.

25. Bonampak area: Houston, "Archaeology and Maya Writing," figs. 5b, 5c. Buenavista del Cayo: Reents-Budet et al., "Palace Dumps," fig. 6.

26. Xultun-area vessels: K7055, K8728, K9153.

27. Hix Witz set of Chan Ahk: Green, "First Blood," citing personal communications from Erik Boot and Michel Quenon. New Orleans Museum of Art plate: on loan from Edward J. Howell, along with a bowl by the same hand, K1373. *Winkil*: Stuart, "Four Interesting Logograms." Ch'orti', as noted by Stuart: Wisdom, "Chorti Language," 757. Tikal example, below: MT218.

28. Tiesler, "Cranial Vault Modifications," esp. 11: "Overall, Mesoamerican head modification practices are evident in up to a hundred per-cent of prehispanic skeletal populations." Aztec children and drilling: López Austin, *Human Body*, I: 209, from the *Florentine Codex*, Book 6: 202; also, Houston, Stuart, and Taube, *Memory of Bones*, 132. Mirror in Dresden Codex with face of deity: page 42, right side.

29. Eruption of teeth: Moorrees, Fanning, and Hunt, "Age Variation," figs. 3–6; B. H. Smith, "Standards," fig. 1. Maya dental modification: Fastlicht, "Dental Inlays," 399; Romero, "Dental Mutilation"; Williams and White, "Dental Modification," esp. 141, table 3. I thank Andrew Scherer for discussion of these themes. Balinese tooth filing: Fischer and Estiti Andarawati, "Tooth-Filing in Bali," 40, 45; Forge, "Tooth and Fang," 7–12; A. Jones, "Dental Transfigurements," 99–101; Pindborg, Möller, and Effendi, "Dental Mutilations," 190–93, esp. tables 1 and 2 for percentages. "So one won't look like a dog": Headland, "Teeth Mutilation," 55.

30. General discussion: Scherer, *Mortuary Landscapes*, 30–37. Pain: Geller, "Altering Identities," 285–86, 288, who stresses "group initiation rituals" and also its "ongoing process." Prince at Piedras Negras: Fitzsimmons et al., "Guardian," 465–66.

31. On endrocrinology and andrenarche: Campbell, "Middle Childhood." Possibly, this phase had to do with heightened glucose metabolism. Ultimately, according to Benjamin Campbell, it was a time "subsidized by adults," with much emphasis on "self-directed play"; Campbell, "Middle Childhood," 229–31.

32. Preclassic dates: Saul and Saul, "Preclassic Population", 45–46; Williams and White, "Dental Modification," 141. Old women filing: Tozzer, *Relación*, 125–26. Long-term process: Gwinnett and Gorelick, "Inlayed Teeth," 576–80.

33. Facial marks: Piña Chán, *Jaina*, pl. 12; K271, K2661, K2821, K2384, K2865, K3325, K3552. Hopi kachina dolls: Colton, *Hopi Kachina Dolls;* Teiwes, *Kachina Dolls*. A perceptive treatment of Maya figurines: Halperin, *Maya Figurines*, esp. 44–142.

34. Rites of passage and the dead: Metcalf and Huntington, *Celebrations*, 30–33. Adolescent sacrifices: Scherer, "Osteology," 207. *K'ex:* Taube, "Birth Vase," 669–74; also Love, *Maya Shamanism*, 40–56.

35. Deity vessels: K2796, M. Coe, *Maya Scribe*, 106–9, pl. 49; K7750, see chapter 2. Río Azul pot, Denver Art Museum: K2796. The owner of the vessel, Nabnal? K'inich Lakam, comes from Río Azul, but has an unknown relation, as *kiit*, to a ruler of that city, yu-ku-no-ma K'AWIIL. Transcriptions of glyphs: first subordinate male, yo-ko-wa-?; second subordinate male, ba-AJAW; main lord, u-BAAH-hi-nu yo-OTOOT-ti na-ba-NAL?/WINKIL? K'IN-ni-chi a?-chi-ma 5-?-ni; set of 4 lords (see below), u-BAAH-hi 4-na-?-? to-ba yi-chi-NAL u-sa?-ku?; lady, IX-KAN 'e[k'e].

36. Are the assembled young men the younger brothers of the main lord, their *sakuun*, "older brothers"?; see Stuart, "Kinship Terms," 5, fig. 6. The speaking dwarf: tz'a-ka-ba-ja ke-le, with an omitted, final ma that would have completed the spelling.

37. Palenque scene: Houston, Stuart, and Taube, *Memory of Bones*, 189; D. Stuart and G. Stuart, *Palenque*, 162–63.

38. For Palenque glyphs in collections: Houston and Stuart, "Hastily."

39. A pot close in style and content, probably by different hand but possibly from the same atelier: Museum of Fine Arts, Boston, #2003.776, gift of Landon T. and Lavinia Clay. Blowgunning of birds: K1116, with decapitation of a deer, also spears, knives, shields of war; K4151, Museum of Fine Arts, Houston, bagging flying birds; also K1345. Preparation and result: K1373. Return of triumphant warriors: K8933, Brooklyn Museum 1998.176.2.

40. Sacrificial burials of youths: Cucina et al., "Companions," 109, 113, table 8.1. Piedras Negras: Scherer, *Mortuary Landscapes*, 151, "Children and adolescents were generally preferred over adults, with adolescents selected more often than infants and children."

41. Ballplaying scene with youths: K3814, Yale Peabody Museum, ANT 232318, h. 8⅝ in. (22 cm), dia. 4¾ in. (12.1 cm). *C'hok* in service: K1728, Museum of Fine Arts, 394.1985. Dance of *lakam:* K5763, see Tokovinine, "Painted Vessel," 344–53, pl. 62; Cortés de Brasdefer, "Maya Vase," 6.

42. Lewis-Williams, *Mind*, 121–35.

43. Men's houses: Gregor, "Men's House"; Rodman, "Moving Houses," 58, 63, 68. "Wombs": Lattas, "Poetics of Space," 76–79. For gender complementarity in New Guinean men's houses: Strathern, "Men's House," 46–49.

44. Bororo: Crocker, "House Associates," 239–40. Philippines: Eggan and Scott, "Ritual Life," 47–51. Southern China: Spencer and Barrett, "Bachelor House," 472–76. Papua New Guinea: Godelier, *Great Men*, 31 (removal of boys from women, with "all the other boys of his age," as guided by a "master of the first initiation ceremonies"), fig. 3 (re-entering a "bisexual world"), 52 (sperm accumulation, and violence of fellatio), 53 (couples of young males and older partners).

45. On secrecy as property and buttress of power: Simmel, *Sociology;* also Bellman, "Paradox of Secrecy"; Murphy, "Secret Knowledge." Related to initiation: Beidelman, "Secrecy and Society," 43–46.

46. Homosocial: Sedgwick, *Between Men*, 1–2, emphasis on social bonds, not physical setting. Male domains: Brandes, "Sex Roles," 364–66.

47. General evidence for men's houses: Joyce, *Gender and Power*, 121, 139–40. Zapotec houses: Marcus and Flannery, *Zapotec Civilization*, 78, 87 for "full-initiates" quotation. New Guinea as model: Yoffee, *Myths*, 27.

48. *Tēlpōchcalli:* Clavigero, *Historia antigua*, II, 199ff; Sahagún, *Florentine Codex*, Book 4: 2, 49, 53–55, 57; also Karttunen, *Analytical Dictionary*, 221. Physical punishment: Berdan and Anawalt, *Codex Mendoza*, 123 (fol. 59r).

49. For an intriguing comparison of such training and kivas in southwestern Pueblos: Parsons, "Aztec and Pueblo," 629. Calmecac: Karttunen, *Analytical Dictionary*, 22, 142. Durán: *Book of the Gods*, 110–15. Role of class: Kellogg, "Woman's Room," 563. The encyclopedic Aztec sources provide moral exhortations in the form of dichotomies between "good" and "bad" kinds of people, not so much on an individual level as according to placement in the social categories of indigenous society. Punishments of escalating pain and severity are specified for those who transgressed established norms.

50. Colonial Maya: Miles, "Summary," 281, 283, 286. Orellana, *Tzutujil Mayas,* 205; J. Thompson, *Gage's Travels,* 231.

51. Function of buildings: Miles, "Summary," 278. "Young lords eight years and older": Carmack, *Quiché Mayas,* 188–89. Abstinence and residence: Miles, "Pokom-Maya," 769; J. Thompson, "Chol Mayas," 596. Women's "seminaries": Carmack, *Quiché Mayas,* 189. Sakbalam: De Vos, *No queremos ser,* 131; see also Bernal, "Dignatarios." On Yaxchilan Structures 21 and 23: Miller and Martin, *Courtly Art,* 99–101, 106–9. Xcalumkin: Graham and von Euw, *Uxmal, Xcalumkin,* 161, 170–71. Jamb 8 identifies the building as the "dwelling," *otoot,* of the queens; Jamb 9 refers to the four consorts of the "wise man": **u-4-ya-?ATAN-IL 'i-tz'a-ti.** The *-il* suffix is suggestive, in that it would more likely apply to deceased individuals. Father and probable son: Xcalumkin Panels 5–8, both enthroned. Red queen: González Cruz, *Reina roja,* 126, 128–29, 221.

52. Xicalango: Remesal, *Historia general,* Book 5, ch. 10; Ximénez, *Historia,* Book 2, ch. 37, in which the "unmarried youths were still sleeping in the municipal men's house, as was customary in Mexico and Yucatan," this in the early seventeenth century. Eric Thompson claims such houses existed two centuries before, in Mayapan, the regional capital of Yucatan; Thompson, *Rise and Fall,* 142.

53. On Aqllawasi: Bauer, *Cuzco,* 128–30; d'Altroy, *Incas,* 301. James Doyle kindly reminded me of their relevance to production by sequestered genders.

54. Las Casas on homosexuality: Miles, "Pokom-Maya," 763. Penile bloodletting: Miles, "Pokom-Maya," 764, 766 fn. 96; see Boon, "Circumcision/Uncircumcision," for comparative discussion.

55. Itzaj men's houses: G. Jones, *Conquest,* 333, 334 ("sexual relations"). "Walled-around large house": Sigal, *Moon Goddesses,* 202, 290 fn. 90. In the absence of any more detailed description, it is impossible to know what the author meant by "women's skirts"—that they were long garments not worn by other men he had seen, or transgendered clothing?

56. Landa quote: "… en cada pueblo una casa grande y encalada, abierta por todas partes, en la cual se juntaban los mozos para sus pasatiempos. Dormían aqui todos juntos casi siempre, hasta que se casaban"; R. N. Adams, "Bachelor House," 590. Landa: Tozzer, *Relación,* 124. Q'ekchi' Maya: Estrada Monroy, *K'ekchi',* 172–73.

57. Las Casas quote: Miles, "Pokom-Maya," 763. Poqomam in general: Miles, "Pokom-Maya," 756, 762. Carnal relations in Yucatan: Chuchiak, "Secrets," 89. Nahuatl youthful behavior: Sousa, "Tying the Knot," 35. Sacrifice of youth: Jones, *Conquest,* 332, who nonetheless questions some of these reports; also Tozzer, *Relación,* 116 fn. 535.

58. "Minimal public validation of manhood" and alcohol: Moore, "Cargo System," 54, 57. Chichicastenango: Bunzel, *Guatemalan Village,* 108. Oaxaca: Weitlaner and Hoogshagen, "Grados de edad," 184, 298–99.

59. Tzeltal marriage: Stross, "Tzeltal Marriage," 330. Flux of age grades: Weitlaner and Hoogshagen, "Grados de edad," 188, 194, fig. 3.

60. Socialization and instruction: Rogoff, "Adults and Peers," 19, 30, 33–34; also Lave and Wenger, *Situated Learning.*

61. *Mam* age and service: Watanabe, *Maya Saints,* 97, 111–12, fig. 7. Kerem among the Tzotzil: Guiteras-Holmes, *Perils,* 70, 71. *Posadas* and "gangs" in Guatemala: R. N. Adams, "Bachelor House," 590; Paul and Paul, "Life Cycle," 187.

62. Tikal: Harrison, "Central Acropolis," 304; Haviland and Haviland, "Glimpses," 306. Itzaaj: Driver, "Colonnaded Building," 78. Copan: Cheek and Spink, "Grupo 3," 83–91; Webster, "House of the Bacabs," 20–22.

63. Phalli: Ardren, "Phalli Stones," esp. 56–60; Stone and Zender, *Reading Maya Art,* 61. Comprehensive tabulation: Amrhein, "Phallic Imagery," esp. 46 (original position), 48, fig. 15 (waterspouts), Chichen Itza temple with interior phallus (fig. 7), Coba temple with interior, upright phallus in situ (fig. 61), 239–98, fig. 3 for tabulation.

64. Hieroglyphic throne: Baudez, "Iconographic Analysis," fig. 69. Museo Popol Vuh bat sculpture: #2005–0032, Easby and Scott, *Before Cortés,* pl. 183. Three epigraphic details need mention. The text is slightly eroded, and the *chak* resembles another color designation, *yax,* "green/blue." That color is unprecedented in this setting, however, and *chak* is more likely. The **TUUN** word sign also looks like the sign for "hill," *witz,* because of a small split on its top. "Hills" are not human in origin, so *tuun* is the preferred reading here. Finally, the verb as three dots, a likely pluralizer pointed out in other contexts

by David Stuart. Sculptors as *ch'ok:* Houston, "Crafting Credit," 417–18; one, in fig. 13–17, went by an evocative name, **yu-CHAN-na**, *yu[uh]chan,* probably "jewel" or "bead" of heaven and a plausible allusion to the Aztec concept of children as drilled beads.

65. San Bartolo: Karl Taube, personal communication, 2004; Saturno, Taube, and Stuart, *Murals of San Bartolo: North Wall,* 4–7; Taube et al., *Murals of San Bartolo: West Wall,* 4–5, figs. 1–2. Structure 22 and Lintel 18: Tate, *Yaxchilan,* 200–202. *Ch'ok* appears three times in the text, at positions B2, B3, and B4, with a possible **ba-ku**, "boy"; see Lacadena and Wichmann, "Glottal Stop," 138. The problem with the reading is that the word appears only in Yukateko, and the other supposed examples probably yield an unrelated reading, **ba-TUUN**. House C: Martin and Grube, *Chronicle,* 162, 165, also, S. Martin, "Classic Maya Polity," 362–63, fig. 186.

66. The **ta-ji**, "obsidian," was read by David Stuart.

67. Rancho San Diego: Barrera Rubio and Taube, "San Diego," 3–18. Some panels are now in the Gran Museo del Mundo Maya in Mérida, Yucatan, e.g., #10–426044. The first vessel, in a private collection, has a buff background, and red characterizes the other, K1092; the latter is now in the Museum of Fine Arts, Boston, #2003.775. A panel likely to come from the building appeared on eBay in 2015. Mary Miller suggested some of these scenes might have been thought humorous, a view I share. Another possible young men's house, linked to *ch'ok keleem,* occurs in the West Quadrangle, Ichmac, Campeche; Pollock, *Puuc,* fig. 803,

68. Imperatives: S. Martin, "Painted Pyramid," 64, from an observation by Kerry Hull. The glyphs here are **ku-?xu ba-ni**, with K1092 presenting the **?xu** frontally. As a tentative reading, *kux* may be referring to the concept of being "wet," a hazard with vomit and spilled drink; see Wisdom, Materials on the Chorti Language, 497. "Guardian" is spelled in two different ways, as **ka-na-na** on a vessel in a private collection, **u-cha-nu** on that in the Museum of Fine Arts. The latter spelling is found in the Usumacinta drainage, on a panel at the Kimbell Museum of Art, AP 1971.07. "Spin": **wi-IL-la**, Kaufman and Norman, "Outline," 136.

69. Maya drinking: Bricker, *Ritual Humor,* 55, 60, 70, 92; Vogt, *Tortillas,* 34–38; Vogt, *Zinacantan,* 398–99.

70. Naj Tunich: A. Stone, *Images,* esp. 185–233, with a chapter co-authored by MacLeod and Stone, "Hieroglyphic Inscriptions," 155–84, esp. 158–62. Homoerotic images: Stone, *Images,* fig. 8-17 (Drawing 17, the floating penis), fig. 8-18 (Drawing 18, older lover and young male), fig. 8-12 (Drawing 20, masturbation). References to *ch'ok:* fig. 8-20 (Drawing 20), figs. 8-28a, c, 8-67 (Drawings 28, 29, 67, painter prince), fig. 8-65 (Drawing 65), fig. 69 (Drawing 69). Possible pulque god, **chi-IL K'UH**: fig. 8-90 (Drawing 90). Note, there may be two female names out of the dozens in the cave, but they could also represent syllables: fig. 8-65d (Drawing 65).

71. Paleolithic rites of passage for youths: Lewis-Williams, *Mind,* 79; Pfeiffer, *Creative Explosion,* 123; Whitehouse, *Arguments and Icons,* 22–23, 63; for a shamanic emphasis of the same, Clottes and Lewis-Williams, *Shamans,* 20–24.

72. Ruler 7: Martin and Grube, *Chronicle,* 152–51; also Houston, "Game."

5 THE GOOD PRINCE

1. This chapter is an edited and emended version of Houston, "Good Prince." Don Carlos of Spain: Parker, *Philip II,* 79–95. George II: Walpole, *Memoirs of King George II,* 152.

2. Royal families: Houston and Inomata, *Classic Maya,* 150–58. Definitive report on Bonampak murals: Miller and Brittenham, *Spectacle.*

3. Royal succession: Beard, *Frazer,* 217; see also Ackerman, *Frazer,* 199, 200, on Frazer's "tissue of conjectures." The selection of heirs: Goody, "Introduction," 15–23.

4. Blood tanistry: Chen, "Succession," 389, 391; Fletcher, "Turco-Mongolian," 238, 240.

5. Fraternal succession: Martin and Grube, *Chronicle,* 151–53, 168–74; Stuart, *Inscriptions from Temple XIX,* 151–57. Joint governance: Houston and Inomata, *Classic Maya,* 171, fig. 6.5. Interregnum: Martin and Grube, *Chronicle,* 127. A captured heir at Piedras Negras: Martin and Grube, *Chronicle,* 151; Safronov, "Yaxchilan."

6. Known in Europe as *speculum principum* or *Fürstenspiegel,* the "mirror of princes," such discourse describes "princes," usually sovereigns rather than heirs. Yet these exemplary manuals did serve as instruction for potential successors. The European tradition shows a long genealogy, perhaps going back to prehistoric times, but each version is awash in the anxieties and expectations of its period (e.g., Born, "Perfect

Prince," 503; R. Martin, "Hesiod," 32). One commenter emphasizes not their shared messages but their diversity, which proved "adaptab[le] as a tool for criticizing the faults of particular rulers" (Nederman, "Mirror Crak'd," 19). Erasmus, *Education*, xxiv; "the prince can leave no finer monument," 7. *Res gestae* and "things done": Boone, *Stories*, 15–16; Cooley, *Res Gestae*, 40. Machiavelli, *Prince*, 3–4, 28–32.

7. Handling of heirs in Sahagún: Sahagún, *Florentine Codex*, Book 4: 62; 8: 71–74; 10: 20.

8. Kings addressing gods: Sahagún, *Florentine Codex*, Book 6: 44–45.

9. Discovery of the Bonampak murals: Bourne, *Recollections;* M. Miller, *Murals*, 14–17. Importance of early documentation: M. Robertson, "Bonampak Photographs"; Ruppert, Thompson, and Proskouriakoff, *Bonampak.* Bonampak glyphs: Mathews, "Dynastic Sequence." Numbering scheme: R. E. W. Adams and Aldrich, "Reevaluation," figs. 1–3, updated in Miller and Brittenham, *Spectacle*, unnumbered folder reproductions. Mexican restoration: Staines Cicero, *Pintura;* see especially Arrellano Hernández, "Diálogo." Additional cleaning took place in 2010, with the detection of two new pentimenti or graffiti of human heads (Orea Magaña, Sandoval, and González Correa, "Recientes intervenciones"); Mary Miller kindly shared this reference. Vidicon: Ware et al., "Infrared Imaging." The documentation has unavoidable gaps for reasons of limited field time, along with the press and challenge of completing large-scale copies of the murals. The doorjambs contain the images of local rulers, along with their name captions, as does an external cornice, in line just above the three doorways. Watercolors of these were made by Augustín Villagra in 1947, 1948, and 1951 (Staines Cicero, "Augustín Villagra," lám. 1–9). The exterior glyphs appear in a copy made by Rina Lazo, now on display in a mock-up outside the National Museum of Anthropology in Mexico City, and in a watercolor by Villagra published in Mexico (Miller, *Murals*, 15; Staines Cicero, "Augustín Villagra," lám. 13).

10. Room 3: M. Miller, *Murals*, 149–51. During unpublished fieldwork at Bonampak in 1995, Karl Taube discovered the solar emphases of Room 3; the consumption of blood is shown by the volutes gushing from solar beings in the vault; for further images, see Miller (*Murals*, pl. 3); Miller and Brittenham, *Spectacle*, 225. Room 2 violence: Miller and Brittenham, *Spectacle*, 94–112; Miller and Martin, *Courtly Art*, 163–74; Schele and Miller, *Blood of Kings*, 216–17. Warfare and the Venus calendar: Lounsbury, "Astronomical Knowledge." In part, Floyd Lounsbury built this argument on the undeniable presence of star signs and constellations in the vault of Room 2, all hovering over the dark mass of violence below. He conjectured that the scene mirrored a well-known sign for conflict that included the glyph for Venus; Lounsbury, "Astronomical Knowledge," fig. 1; also Miller, *Murals*, 47. Lounsbury, a scholar of great perception, was nonetheless in error about the accompanying date, with negative consequences for his argument. Closer scrutiny of the month sign in the text shows not Yax, as Lounsbury supposed, but Ch'en. His identification of the day sign was likely incorrect too: the days Oc or Men are just as likely as the Chicchan he discerned. At the time, most specialists focused on the Venus in the verb that had interested Lounsbury. The sign has another element, however: torrents of water gush to either side, and the likelihood is strong that the more direct metaphor related to storms, perhaps with seasonal timings, and not solely to Venus. Simon Martin (personal communication) is pursuing such leads in work not yet published. The overall scene of Room 2 is, to judge from the dark background, a nighttime scene, so the presence of stars and constellations may cue a nocturnal setting.

11. Anonymous messengers: Houston, Stuart, and Taube, *Memory of Bones*, 244–51. Unfinished murals: Miller, *Murals*, 150–51. Collapse: Miller and Brittenham, *Spectacle*, 175–76.

12. Details: Miller and Houston, "Algunos comentarios," 253, fig. 6.

13. Vidicon clarity: I-33, I-37. Color images: I-43, I-45. For illustrations: Miller and Brittenham, *Spectacle*, 228–37.

14. Missing glyphs: I-5 to I-17, II-2 to II-3, III-1 to III-3, III-11 to III-12, and III-14 to III-20.

15. Dos Pilas: Houston, *Dos Pilas*, figs. 4–16.

16. Names: Bodenhorn and vom Bruck, "Entangled," 3, and "representational economy" quote. Names as part of a person: Bodenhorn and vom Bruck, "Entangled," 11; Battaglia, "Problematizing the Self," 2. For tabulation of names at Bonampak: Miller and Brittenham, *Spectacle*, table 2, although their tally may be overgenerous.

17. Annunciation: Tarr, "Visible Parlare," 225, fig.
15. Embedded texts: Sparrow, *Visible Words,*
62–65, 76–83. There is a noteworthy contrast
with medieval images, in which, by theological
claim, truth lies behind and beyond images, as
an "energy" that was both "invisible and intan-
gible": de Nie, "Seeing and Believing," 74. For
baah: Houston, Stuart, and Taube, *Memory of
Bones,,* 72–81. Royals as body fetishes: de Huesch,
"Symbolic Mechanisms," 214.

18. Speech scrolls: Houston, Stuart, and Taube,
Memory of Bones, 163; see also Hurwit, "Words in
the Image," 187. Oral exposition of Maya texts:
Houston, "Literacy," 39. This exists not just
among the Classic Maya but also in a description
of Hogarth's mordant caricatures from eighteenth-century England: "Every picture (even a
still life) may *suggest* a story but it is the viewer
who *tells* the tale, frames the narrative and fills
the gaps" (Uglow, *Hogarth,* xv). "The practice of
writing words": Hurwit, "Words in the Image,"
197. "Fraternize": Gombrich, "Image and Word,"
215. Despite their authoritative impulse, the
Bonampak murals also display what appear to be
"marginalia" or unauthorized images, especially
in Room 3. The expertise is such that there could
not have been much time between their making
and the execution of the murals.

19. For a study of glyphic names in captions see
Colas, *Maya-Personennamen.* Captioning in the
beginnings of Maya script: Saturno, Taube, and
Stuart, *Murals of San Bartolo: North Wall,* figs.
31–33; Taube et al., *Murals of San Bartolo: West
Wall,* supplements. On use of space: Hurwit,
"Words in the Image," 180. Compressed captions: Schele and Miller, *Blood of Kings,* pl. 40a.
At Tonina, Mexico, to consider one example,
captives show their names on bodies or on loincloths, above the groin, an invasion of corporeal
space that fails to occur with the naming of
rulers or their family (e.g., captives with body
glyphs appear on: Tonina Monuments 27, 83,
84 [Graham and Mathews, *Tonina,* 71, 113, 114],
Monuments 133, 147, 148, 155 [Graham et al.,
Tonina, 71, 80, 81, 89]; captives with glyphs on
front loincloths, above the groin on: Tonina
Monuments 151–54 [Graham and Mathews,
Tonina, 85–88]). One records a set of glyphs on
the back, but the figure of the captive is almost
in quadrupedal, bestial position (Monument 10
[Mathews, *Tonina,* 35]); this recalls the carving of
a dog, marked on his back with *u tz'i,* "his dog"

(Monument 89 [Graham and Mathews, *Tonina,*
118]; see also Stuart, "Chocolatier's Dog")—a real
creature beloved of its owner or a metaphoric
depiction of a reviled captive? Such images of
captives may literally have served as pedestals
for rulers standing on them, a use consistent
with depictions of captives underfoot, the
backs of such figures positioned upward to
support the lord's feet (Graham and von Euw,
Naranjo, 53). In other instances, the glyphs "slip"
down to the shield on which the ruler kneels
(Graham and Mathews, *Tonina,* 102). Rulers
do show glyphs on their backs of their cloaks,
yet this is more by way of standard glyphic
display, like the glyphs on the back of a stela
(e.g., Monuments 3, 9, 13, 14, 20, 26, 28–30, 47, 56,
71, 85, 101 [Mathews, *Tonina,* 15, 18, 34, 43, 45, 56,
63, 73, 77, 95, 100, 105, 116, 124], Monument 176
[Graham et al., *Tonina,* 121]). The Tonina stelae
differ only because, in place of a slab monolith,
the depiction of the ruler is fully in the round, a
freestanding figure. At Naranjo, Guatemala, the
scoring of names on captives' bodies, usually
the thigh, is just as invasive (Naranjo Stelae 8,
11, 13, 21, 24, 30 [Graham, *Naranjo,* 27, 33, 37, 53,
63, 79]). Such invasions are almost nonexistent
in the painted captions that appear on pottery.
Name-tags: Stuart, "Hieroglyphs on Maya
Vessels."

20. Legibility of captions: Schele and Miller, *Blood
of Kings,* 153. Some of the earliest texts on Maya
stelae impart a distinct sense of their own
physicality. Figures stand to one side or flank
the inscription as though it were itself a free-
standing object rooted firmly in the ground
(e.g., El Baul Stela 1 [Schele and Miller, *Blood of
Kings,* fig. 8]). In a sense, the image reproduces
an all-glyphic stela in use, but now with its array
of human and supernatural participants. Raised
vs. incised captions: Miller and Martin, *Courtly
Art,* pl. 2. Painted captions: Schele and Miller,
Blood of Kings, 153. Captions with conversation:
Miller and Martin, *Courtly Art,* pls. 14, 17. As such
they differ greatly from the "cartoon bubbles"
that characterize eighteenth-century satirists
such as James Gillray: often, those with bubbles
are "demotic" or essentially wise commentators
(Bindman, "Text as Design," 317). Captions on
codex-style vessels: Robicsek and Hales, *Maya
Book of the Dead,* 15–34.

21. Bonampak mural sequence: M. Miller, *Murals,*
150–51.

22. Initial Series text: M. Miller, *Murals,* 27–38; Miller and Houston, "Algunos Comentarios"; Miller and Brittenham, *Spectacle,* 70–72. *Ak'e/ Usiij Witz:* Stuart, "Bonampak's Place Name." For house dedications, see Stuart, "Fire Enters," which also addresses the personal names of buildings. Impersonations are discussed in Houston, Stuart, and Taube (*Memory of Bones,* 27–75). The form of the "dedication" verb, "fire-enter" may use a unique near-homophone for "enter" or *och:* a possible "opossum," *och* in Yukatekan languages, *uch* in the Ch'olti'an language recorded in the Classic texts and spelling as **u-chu,** *uch,* on one unprovenanced pot from northern Guatemala (M. Coe and Houston, *Maya,* pl. XVIII; for Mayan words, see Kaufman, *Etymological Dictionary,* 577).

23. Bonampak dynastic sequence: Mathews, "Dynastic Sequence," 64–68. With careful reasoning, Peter Mathews concludes that the date of Lintel 3 cannot be fixed in absolute time, leaving the matter in "abeyance" (Mathews, "Dynastic Sequence," 67). Nonetheless, two of the possible dates come after the time when the mural building was dedicated—an unlikely occurrence for sculptures that had to be in place before. Another possibility falls decades earlier. The date preferred here lies within a few days of Lintel 2. Stela 1: Houston and Inomata, *Classic Maya,* fig 6.15. Tecolote murals: Golden, Scherer, and Muñoz, "Exploring," 15, fig. 5; Tate, *Yaxchilan,* 234. Sak Tz'i': Martos López, "Plan de Ayutla," with a more likely candidate, found by Charles Golden, Andrew Scherer, and their team at the site of Lacanja-Tzeltal in Chiapas, Mexico. Solar iconography: Karl Taube, personal communication.

24. A lord in dance: Grube, "Classic Maya Dance." Green plumes: Houston, "Feather Dance." Embodied tribute: Houston et al., *Memory,* 244–50. *Ak'oot:* I-42. *Ti-k'uk'uum:* I-21/22 or "feather, quetzal," I-42. The *jaw* lexeme appears in terms for broad dishes, as in *jawante'* or *jawte'* (Houston, Stuart, and Taube, "Folk Classification"). For the reading of *mam,* see Stuart, "Hieroglyphs for *Mam*"; also Houston, "Splendid Predicament," 159.

25. Syllabic spellings: Wichmann, "Mayan Historical Linguistics," 290–91, fig. 3. *Etk'aba'il:* Mathews, "Dynastic Sequence," fig. 2, position D6; W. Coe, *Piedras Negras,* fig. 43d, position L2. To Marc Zender goes credit for the reading of *Chooj,*

'cougar' (personal communication; see also Robertson, Law, and Haertel, *Colonial Ch'olti',* 328). It displays a feline head consuming the sign for "person," *winik,* and remains today, in northern Guatemala, the most feared of the jungle cats, attacking humans with less hesitation than the jaguar. The final syllable **ji,** often present in glyphic versions, signals the final consonant *j* and internal vowel length *ō.*

26. Expendable proxies: Houston, Stuart, and Taube, *Memory of Bones,* 248–49. Place of origin of emissaries: I-1, I-52.

27. Simon Martin ("Broken Sky," 4 fn. 10), identifies a relevant glyph, in certain names, of a skull suspended through the eye sockets by rope. The likelihood of head-hunting trophies is strong, and in Room 2 on the south wall several figures bear such skulls, usually inverted, a few still covered by flesh. Guardianship of captives: Houston and Martin, "Abbreviations." Head-hunters: III-4, III-9, and III-10. Earned titles: II-3, II-6, and II-13. Guardians: II-30 (*baah-ajaw*), II-26 (*ajaw*), and I-53, II-4 (*winik*).

28. Courtiers: Houston and Inomata, *Classic Maya,* fig. 6.13. *Tz'am:* Stone and Zender, *Reading Maya Art,* 96–97. *Tikoom:* Barrera Vásquez, *Diccionario,* 792. "Runner": Kaufman and Norman, "Outline," 116; independently noted by Beliaev, "*Wayaab'* Title," 127. *K'ayoom:* Houston, Stuart, and Taube, *Memory of Bones,* fig. 4.19. *Ti'hu'n:* Zender, *Classic Maya Priesthood,* 219. *Tz'am:* I-34, I-36. *Baah-te':* I-26. *Baah-pakal:* II-23, II-30. "Head-flint," *baah took':* II-39. *Chak mo'te' baak:* II-41. *Tikoom:* I-19b. **AJ-na-bi,** or **a-na-bi:** I-33. *K'ayoom:* I-38, I-39. *Ti'hu'n:* I-51. *Sajal* or *saaj:* I-43, I-45, II-37, III-4, and III-9. Royal female: II-36.

29. "Bat"-*kal-naah:* Mathews, "Dynastic Sequence," fig. 1. In a personal communication, Alfonso Lacadena observed that in the Usumacinta river drainage names with animals tend to attach an *aj* prefix, possibly as an expression of dialect. Aj Tihl, "He of the Tapir" also appears in the Bonampak murals, in II-6: **AJ-TIHL-la.** Eroded text with titles: I-42. Individual with age-grade title: I-32.

30. Full dedicatory expressions: I-5C, I-49B. Abbreviated version: I-6B. Painting: I-5B. Cacao: I-18. Quantification of tribute: Houston, "Hill of Beans"; see also Stuart, "Jade and Chocolate," for discussion of *pih.*

31. Micro-glyphs: Miller and Houston, "Algunos comentarios," fig. 6; Miller and Brittenham, *Spectacle,* 237.

32. Didacticism: Houston, "Splendid Predicament," 171; Karl Taube, personal communication.

33. It is striking that names with "cougar" are used most often by princes, "jaguar" by rulers. The attribution of special ferocity may have been intentional.

34. Visual hierarchy: Houston, "Classic Maya Depictions." *Chooj:* Stuart, "Bonampak's Place Name."

35. "Bird" Bahlam might have been named after a close relative, the great Bird Jaguar ("Bird" Bahlam) the IV of Yaxchilan (Martin and Grube, *Chronicle*, 128–34). His probable line of descent would thus have passed through Yajaw Chan Muwaan's wife, the woman from Yaxchilan (Room 2). This would make Shield Jaguar IV, who is highlighted in the central lintel of the mural building, a likely uncle. *Yajaw K'ahk':* Stuart, *Inscriptions from Temple XIX*, 123–25; also Zender, "Classic Maya Priesthood," 195–210. In his study, Zender sees this as a counterpart to an Aztec "fire priest," *tlenamácac*, but I would go further, suggesting a specifically non-Maya, Teotihuacan heritage behind the title—see the Teotihuacan-related, "goggle-eyes" turban adorning a *Yajaw K'ahk'* portrayed on a censer support from Building 1, Group IV, Palenque; Schmidt, de la Garza, and Nalda, *Maya*, pl. 131. Division of duties in Aztec practice: Durán, *History of the Indies*, 74–101; M. Miller, *Murals*, 149.

36. Sun God: Taube, *Major Gods*, 50–56, "Structure 10L-16."

37. Accession to "ajaw" status: M. Miller, *Murals*, 35. Miller tells me that Péter Bíró, in unpublished independent work, has come to a similar possibility, namely that a new ruler commissioned the murals.

38. Room 2 burial: http://www.inah.gob.mx/index.php/boletines/14-hallazgos/4077-descubren-entierro. Maya collapse: M. Miller, *Murals*, 151.

39. Readable glyphs: Tovalín Ahumada and Ortiz Villareal, "Avances," 87, fig. IV.2. Joint use of the highest titles: I-23, I-41, and III-6.

40. Truth: J. S. Turner, "To Tell a Good Tale," 30–40, 43. Good stories: Brooks, *Reading for the Plot*.

6 DRAINING THE CUP

Epigraph: Edmund Waller, c. 1686, "Of the Last Verses in the Book" http://www.poetryfoundation.org/poem/174707, accessed Aug. 17, 2015.

1. W. H. Auden, "September 1, 1939," https://www.poets.org/poetsorg/poem/september-1-1939, accessed Dec. 3, 2016.

2. For examples of exaggeration and anxious definitions: Courtine, "Impossible Virility," 399–401.

3. Stuart, "Hieroglyphs for *Mam*." Examples are especially abundant in the Early Classic period. Monumental examples include, in chronological order: Tikal Stela 31 (Oct. 20, AD 445), B19, F10, J1, N1; Tres Islas Stela 1 (May 16, AD 475); Tres Islas Stela 2 (May 16, AD 475), B7; Tikal Stela 10 (Aug. 12, AD 527), D7; Tikal Stela 5 (June 15, AD 744), A3. An unpublished example was found in 2015 at Achiotal, Guatemala, as drawn by David Stuart. Unlike the others, which appear as stand-alone titles, this example is possessed, **u-MAM**. Earlier, Oswaldo Chinchilla Mazariegos, *Observaciones*, had isolated the sign and labeled it *mechudo*, a figure with "unruly hair." Vultures and mothers: M. Coe, *Maya Scribe*, pl. 3, position D4; see also Chichen Itza, Temple of the Three Lintels, Lintel 3, G2. *Mam* as opossum: Dresden 55–58. Bonampak example: Houston, "Good Prince," 163, fig. 5, caption II-31. Stela with opossum-*mam:* Stierlin, *Mexique*, pl. 215. One hairy *mam*, on a stone sphere in the Los Angeles County Museum of Art, formerly Ranieri collection, has fishlike attributes, as though of different kinds of ancestors.

4. Holmul discovery: Estrada-Belli and Tokovinine, "Apotheosis," 162, fig. 6, table 1. Tikal: MT39, Burial 116, Moholy-Nagy, with Coe, *Ceremonial Artifacts*, fig. 200a–c. Grandfather of Tikal ruler: Grube and Gaida, "Katalog," 106–7, Abb. 9.4–9.5, who nonetheless read the sign as "Großvater" (grandfather), with the proviso that another interpretation ("Deutung") is also possible. La Corona: Hieroglyphic Stairway 3, block V, pB3, unpublished drawing by David Stuart. Other vulture versions of *mam*: Art Institute of Chicago Altar, #1971.895, E1 (**MAM-'a-ku**); carved human femur, L1 (**u-MAM**); M. Coe, *Maya Scribe*, pl. 82; Palenque Temple XVI Panel, pG8 (**ch'o-ko JANAHB-?K'UK'-BAHLAM u-MAM K'INICH-JANAHB-PAKAL**); Palenque Temple of the Sun, north jamb, G4 (**u-MAM**, just after the name of the ruler's mother, Lady Tz'akbu); Pomona Panel 8, pB2 (**u-MAM CHAN-la-CHAHK**), the grandfather of unknown status; Pomona Panel 11, pD3 (**u-MAM**); Pomona Stela 4, pA2 (**u-MAM**), in reference to the grandson of a local king; Tikal-area vase lid, D1 (**MAM**); Quirigua Stela 5, B11–A12 (**u-tz'a-pa-wa u-MAM-PIH-AHK?-**"name"); Río Azul-area earspool, B1 (**u-MAM**); Ruta Maya altar,

Grube and Luín, "Drum Altar," fig. 5 (**u-MAM**, although not identified as such by the authors); Tonina Monument 146, B7 (**u-MAM-ba-ka-ba**); Uxul Stela 17, pA4 (**u-MAM-ma**); Tortuguero wooden box, Kislak Collection, J2–L1, #f1434.64 no. 215 (Bassie and Zender, "Wooden Offering Container," 15, albeit with differing view of the *mam*, which they read as "grandfather"); Yaxchilan Lintel 14, G5 (**u-MAM-AJAW**), in what appears to be the namesake or companion (**ye-ta**) of nobleman. The pattern of maternal descent may have exceptions. The inscription at Tonina may suggest paternal descent, in that the grandson of a *baahkab,* an exalted title, is said to have been his *mam.* At Tonina, all *baahkab* (from **ba-ka-ba**) are kings, although the distribution is restricted to a few rulers: Monument 7, R1; Monument 16, pG1; Monument 26, B13; Monument 42, pA1; Monument 44, O1; Monument 104, J1; Monument 170, H1. But the reader should beware: the mother of the lord may have been of high rank, and her father a nonlocal *baahkab.* The text is broken off and its reference unclear. A mythic scene describes a newborn as the "grandson" of an older god, the turtle (**a-ku**), followed, after further names of the grandfather, by mention of mother; K5164.

5. Objects belong to "grandfathers" or "elders": e.g., Boot, "Portraits"; Grube and Gaida, "Katalog," 11; Houston, Stuart, and Taube, *Memory of Bones,* fig. 1.54. A jade turtle carapace with a *mam* owner is in a private collection. A grackle effigy vessel pinpoints an owner is a *mam-ajaw,* "elder/grandfather-lord; D. Stuart and P. Stuart, "Bird Vase," fig. 2. An early sign going back into the Preclassic often opens texts; M. Coe, *Maya Scribe,* pl. 1; Schele and Miller, *Blood of Kings,* pl. 32. Its traits, which include a prominent nose and possible hair, recall the *mam* sign, suggesting an equivalent value. Deletaille tripod: Hellmuth, "Early Maya Iconography," fig. 4.2. The tripod is intriguing historically, for it suggests that the Ucanal dynasty descended, by sixteen or so generations, from the founder of the royal family of Tikal; S. Martin, "Line of the Founder," 16.

6. Quote: Stanzione, *Rituals of Sacrifice,* 225. Demographic shifts: Troyansky, *Old Age,* 3.

7. Melanesia: Gottlieb, *Afterlife,* 80–81. Transmission: Cole, *Journey,* 12. On Africa, and providing the quotations here: LaGamma, "Eternal Ancestors," 21, 27. Comparative anthropology: Godelier, *Metamorphoses of Kinship,* 167;

also Parkin, "Alternate Generation," 14, who comments on India and beyond, where generations do not form a "ladder" but a limited, recycled set of generations. According to one theory, underlying systems of marriage helped create these patterns: Hage, "Maya Kinship System," 7. On weak evidence, Hage finds in these the origins of directional symbolism in the Americas and spouse-exchanging groups.

8. Sahlins, *Kinship,* 44. Other resuscitations of kinship as a theme in anthropological research: Franklin and McKinnon, *Relative Values;* McKinnon and Cannell, *Vital Relations.*

9. For trenchant analogies from ancient China: Brashier, *Ancestral Memory,* 1, 39 ("lord-father analogy"), 105 ("structured amnesia systems").

10. Two quotations: Sahagún, *Florentine Codex,* Book 10: 11, 191. On spirit force of the old: López Austin, *Human Body,* I: 285, 290.

11. S. Martin quote: "Old Man," 1. Codex Borbonicus (Codex du Corps Legislatif, Bibliothèque de l'Assemblée Nationale, París, Y 120), c. 1521–1540, fol. 21. Codex Magliabechiano: Boone, *Magliabechiano,* II, 214–15, fols. 77v–78r. Discussion of creator couple: Anders, Jansen, and Reyes García, *Libro del ciuacoatl,* 181–85; Boone, *Cycles,* 24–28; Guilliem Arroyo, "Templo Calendárico," 51; López Austin, "Magia," 25; Robelo, "Origen," 337–50; Sahagún, *Florentine Codex,* Book 4: f.3v. On the Piedra de Coatlan and nearby Cuernavaca as a possible place of first emergence: Rojas, "Casting Maize Seeds," 469, citing Garibay, "Historia," 106. Aztec divination: Olivier, "Word," 216–35. On hands and cords: Ruiz de Alarcón, *Treatise,* 141–61. Ethnography of maize kernel divination, "seeing," and mitigation: Rojas, "Casting Maize Seeds," 463. According to Rojas, the seeds represent individual, often deceased people, and the orientation of the kernel as it falls betokens a malign or a positive augury.

12. Pairs of progenitors, discussion in S. Martin, "Old Man"; see also Guiteras Holmes, *Perils,* 292; Holland, *Medicina maya,* 113; Miles, "Pokom-Maya," 748; Bassie, "Creator Gods." Maya midwife goddess: Taube, "Birth Vase," 657–58; *Major Gods,* 99–105.

13. Reflective surfaces and curing: Ruiz de Alarcón, *Treatise,* 162.

14. Martin, "Old Man"; Stuart, "Old Notes." Old god and emergent humans: K501. Instruction: K1196, Kimbell Art Museum, Fort Worth, Texas; AP

2004.04. Probable *Itzam* and misshapen courtiers: K5093.

15. Watanabe, *Maya Saints*, 107, 111, 117. Santiago Atitlan: Stanzione, *Rituals of Sacrifice*, 184. Tzeltal *lab*: Pitarch, *Jaguar and the Priest*, 120–21.

16. Levy, "Life Expectancies," 17–18.

17. Aged ruler, Bird Jaguar III, on lintel: Mayer, *Maya Monuments*, pls. 253–54. Piedras Negras: Stuart and Graham, *Piedras Negras*, 44, 49, glyphs Y1–Y15. Remains at Copan: Buikstra et al., "Copan Acropolis," 192–201.

18. Senile god: Taube and Taube, "Aesthetics and Morality," 250, fig. 9.9. Chiik Nahb: S. Martin, "Painted Pyramid," 70–71, figs. 23, 25.

19. Los Angeles County Museum of Art, K5113; see also Taube, "Birth Vase." Sun God vase: unpublished rollout, shared by Simon Martin. Old god with herniated belly: K1182, K2794, K8927.

20. Uaxactun pot: Houston, Stuart, and Taube, *Memory of Bones*, 191, fig. 5.16, original in Smith, *Ceramics*, fig. 2g.

21. Comparative comment: Covey, "Perceptions," 93–98; Simons, *Sex of Men*, 179–80; Alison Stewart, *Unequal Lovers*, 13–34; Taube and Taube, "Aesthetics and Morality," 239–42, figs. 9.2–9.4. *Itzam* and ladies: Boston Museum of Fine Arts, #1988.1174.

22. Princeton vase: K511, # y1975–17; also M. Coe, *Maya Scribe*, pl. 42. On Chinese age, virtue, and art: Silbergeld, "Chinese Concepts," 103.

23. Destruction of mural: Gamboni, *Destruction*, 143–44. The Gelman portrait, 1943, is now held by the Vergel Foundation.

24. Karttunen, *Analytical Dictionary*, 8; S. McCafferty and G. McCafferty, "Gender Identities," 198.

25. Sahagún, *Florentine Codex*, Book 10: 12, 13, 55, 89.

26. Sahagún, *Florentine Codex*, Book 9: 93, 98–99, 102, 110; see also Durán, *Book of the Gods*, 435.

27. Dearth of discussion: Joyce, *Gender and Power*; secondary citations: Ardren, "Studies of Gender," 8; Chilam Balam: Sigal, *Moon Goddesses*, 68, 223.

28. Adultery and fornication: Ara, *Vocabulario*, 319, 504. Penetration, scourging, lust, and concubinage: Laughlin, *Santo Domingo Zinacantán*, I: 221, 253, 263–64. Bolles, "Yucatecan Mayan Language": "la muger mala de su cuerpo ora sea publica ora no . . . Ah con tzubul: puta que ella se comvida y vende."

29. Calakmul murals: Carrasco Vargas and Cordeiro Baqueiro, "Murals of Chiik Nahb," fig. 2; Martin, "Painted Pyramid." Standard account of competition between Calakmul and Tikal: Martin and Grube, *Chronicle*, 104–11. Trading ladies, as first noted by Karl Taube: Houston, Stuart, and Taube, *Memory of Bones*, 110, fig. 3.4; also Halperin, *Maya Figurines*, fig. 3.36.

30. Ladies of water: M. Coe, *Lords of the Underworld*, pl. 11; Houston, Stuart, and Taube, *Memory of Bones*, fig. 5.18.

31. Sahagún, *Florentine Codex*, Book 9: 94.

32. On prostitution more generally: Hartnett and Dawdy, "Illegal and Illicit Economies," 43. Japan: Downer, "City Geisha," 223. On the "floating world" of Japan: Screech, *Sex*, 53. At Maya sites, there may be rooms for possible sexual service: Child, "Religious Movements," fig. 4.23; also Houston, Stuart, and Taube, *Memory of Bones*, 117, fig. 3.13. The arts of the courtesan are now seen by some scholars as a fruitful basis for comparison: Feldman and Gordon, *Courtesan's Arts*. Jainas and females: O'Neil, "Whistle," 409.

33. Courtesans may appear in: Princeton Art Museum, #2005–65 a-b, a gaudy serving lady doubling as a container for liquids; Metropolitan Museum of Art, #1993.441; and the lids of tapaderas on Early Classic food bowls (K1550). Drinking and elderly Aztecs: Berdan and Anawalt, *Codex Mendoza*, 146–47, fol. 71r. A vase at the Princeton Art Museum may also show an elaborately dressed woman giving an enema to a trader, #1998–451. On Greece: Kurke, "Inventing the Hetaira"; Glazebrook and Henry, "Why Prostitutes?," 9.

34. Trampled older gods: K1560.

35. Tz'utujil: Stanzione, *Rituals of Sacrifice*, 5, 57, 60 (*mam* as teacher), 180, 261 (*mam* as "pathfinder"), 263 (shaping of new *mam*), 316 (paying debts to the *mam*), 60. Flutes and whistles from Jaina: Ishihara-Brito and Taube, "Whistle," 429–30. Other examples: Yale University Art Gallery, #1973.88.11a; National Museum of the American Indian, #24/451; Cleveland Museum of Art, 1967.155; Gardiner Museum, G83.1.0127; see Ishihara-Brito and Taube, "Whistle," 429, for comparisons.

BIBLIOGRAPHY

Ackerman, Robert. *J. G. Frazer: His Life and World.* Cambridge: Cambridge University Press, 1987.

Adams, Richard E. W. "Comments on the Glyphic Texts of the 'Altar Vase.'" In *Social Process in Maya Prehistory: Studies in Honour of Sir Eric Thompson,* ed. Norman Hammond, 409–20. New York: Academic, 1977.

Adams, Richard E. W., and Robert C. Aldrich. "A Reevaluation of the Bonampak Murals: A Preliminary Statement on the Paintings and Texts." In *Third Palenque Round Table, 1978, Part 2,* ed. M. G. Robertson, 45–59. Austin: University of Texas Press, 1980.

Adams, Richard N. "A Survival of the Meso-American Bachelor House." *American Anthropologist,* n.s. 54 (1952): 589–93.

Alberti, Benjamin. "Archaeology, Men, and Masculinities." In *Handbook of Gender in Archaeology,* ed. Sarah M. Nelson, 401–34. Lanham, Md.: AltaMira, 2006.

Algazi, Gadi. "Introduction: Doing Things with Gifts." In *Negotiating the Gift: Pre-Modern Figurations of Exchange,* ed. Gadi Algazi, Valentin Groebner, and Bernhard Jussen, 9–27. Göttingen: Vandenhoeck and Ruprecht, 2003.

Allen, Nick. "Using Hubert and Mauss to Think About Sacrifice." In *Sacrifice and Modern Thought,* ed. Julia Meszaros and Johannes Zachhuber, 147–62. Oxford: Oxford University Press, 2014.

Amrhein, Laura M. "An Iconographic and Historic Analysis of Terminal Classic Phallic Imagery." Ph.D. diss., Virginia Commonwealth University, 2001.

Anaya Hernández, Armando, Stanley Guenter, and Peter Mathews. "An Inscribed Wooden Box from Tabasco, Mexico." *Mesoweb Report and News* (2001). Accessed Dec. 15, 2014. http://www.mesoweb.com.

Anders, Ferdinand, Maarten Jansen, and Luis Reyes García, eds. *El libro del Ciuacoatl: Homenaje para el año llamado Códice Borbónico.* Mexico City: Fondo de Cultura Económica, 1991.

Andrews, E. Wyllys, IV. *A Group of Related Sculptures from Yucatán.* Contributions to American Anthropology and History 26. Carnegie Institution of Washington Publication 509. Washington, D.C.: Carnegie Institution of Washington, 1939.

Andrews, E. Wyllys, IV. "Pustunich, Campeche, Some Further Related Sculptures." In *Los mayas antiguos: Monografías de arqueología, etnografía y lingüística mayas,* ed. César Lizardi Ramos, 125–35. Mexico City: El Colegio de Mexico, 1941.

Anestis, Stephanie F. "Testosterone in Juvenile and Adolescent Male Chimpanzees (*Pan troglodytes*): Effects of Dominance Rank, Aggression, and Behavioral Style." *American Journal of Physical Anthropology* 130 (2006): 536–45.

Appadurai, Arjun. "Gastro-Politics in Hindu South Asia." *American Ethnologist* 8 (1981): 494–511.

Appadurai, Arjun. "Introduction: Commodities and the Politics of Value." In *The Social Life of Things: Commodities in Cultural Perspective,* ed. Arjun Appadurai, 3–63. Cambridge: Cambridge University Press, 1986.

Appleby, Joanna E. P. "Why We Need an Archaeology of Old Age, and a Suggested Approach." *Norwegian Archaeological Review* 43 (2010): 145–68.

Ara, Domingo de. 1986. *Vocabulario de lengua Tzeldal según el orden de Copanabastla,* ed. Mario Humberto Ruz. Mexico City: Universidad Autónoma de México, 1986.

Archer, John. "Does Sexual Selection Explain Human Sex Differences in Aggression?" *Behavioral and Brain Sciences* 32 (2009): 249–66.

Ardren, Traci. "Studies of Gender in the Prehispanic Americas." *Journal of Archaeological Research* 16 (2008): 1–35.

Ardren, Traci. "Masculinity in Classic Maya Culture." In *Que(e)rying Archaeology: Proceedings of the 37th Annual Chacmool Conference,* ed. Susan Terendy, Natasha Lyons, and Michelle Janse-Smekal, 50–58. Calgary: Chacmool Archaeological Association, University of Calgary, 2009.

Ardren, Traci. "The Phalli Stones of the Classic Maya Northern Lowlands: Masculine Anxiety and Regional Identity." In *Power and Identity in Archaeological Theory and Practice: Case Studies from Ancient Mesoamerica,* ed. Eleanor Harrison-Buck, 53–62. Salt Lake City: University of Utah Press, 2012.

Ardren, Traci, and David Hixson. "The Unusual Sculptures of Telantunich, Yucatán: Phalli and the Concept of Masculinity Among the Ancient Maya." *Cambridge Archaeological Journal* 16 (2006): 7–25.

Ardren, Traci, and Scott H. Hutson, eds. *The Social Experience of Childhood in Ancient Mesoamerica.* Boulder: University Press of Colorado, 2006.

Ariès, Phlippe. *Centuries of Childhood: A Social History of Family Life.* New York: Vintage, 1962.

Ariss, Robert. "Foucault in the Highlands: The Production of Men in Papua New Guinea Societies." *Australian Journal of Anthropology* 3 (1992): 142–49.

Aristotle. *De Partibus Animalium I and De Generatione Animalium I (with passages from II. 1–3).* Trans. David M. Balme. Oxford: Clarendon, 1972.

Arnett, Jeffrey J. "Adolescent Storm and Stress, Reconsidered." *American Psychologist* 54 (1999): 317–26.

Arnett, Jeffrey J. "Stanley Hall's Adolescence: Brilliance and Nonsense." *History of Psychology* 9 (2006): 186–97.

Arnett, Jeffrey J. "Emerging Adulthood: What Is It Good For?" *Child Development Perspectives* 1 (2007): 68–73.

Arnett, Jeffrey J. *Emerging Adulthood: The Winding Road from the Late Teens Through the Twenties.* 2nd ed. Oxford: Oxford University Press, 2015.

Arnett, Jeffrey J., Rita Žukauskienė, and Kazumi Sugimura. "The New Life Stage of Emerging Adulthood at Ages 18–29 Years: Implications for Mental Health." *The Lancet Psychiatry* 1 (2014): 569–76.

Arnold, John H., and Sean Brady. "Introduction." In *What Is Masculinity? Historical Dynamics from Antiquity to the Contemporary World,* ed. John H. Arnold and Sean Brady, 1–14. Basingstoke, England: Palgrave Macmillan, 2011.

Arrellano Hernández, Alfonso. "Diálogo con los abuelos." In *La pintura mural prehispánica en México I, Área maya, Tomo II: Bonampak, Estudios,* ed. Leticia Staines Cicero, 255–98. Mexico City: Instituto de Investigaciones Estéticas, Universidad Nacional Autónoma de México, 1998.

Arvey, Margaret C. "Women of Ill-Repute in the Florentine Codex." *The Role of Gender in Pre-Columbian Art and Architecture,* ed. Virginia Miller, 179–204. Lanham, Md.: University Press of America, 1988.

Aulie, H. Wilbur, Evelyn W. de Aulie, and Emily F. Scharfe de Stairs. "Diccionario Ch'ol-Español de Tumbalá, Chiapas, con variaciones dialectales de Tila y Sabanilla (1999)." Accessed Mar. 6, 2017. http://www.sil.org/americas/mexico/maya/chol-tumbala/S121a-Diccionario-CTU.htm.

Babcock, Barbara A. "Obituary: Victor Turner (1920–1983)." *Journal of American Folklore* 97 (1984): 461.

Balser, Carlos, and Instituto Nacional de Seguros (Costa Rica). *Jade precolombino de Costa Rica.* San José, Costa Rica: Litografía e Imprenta Lil, 1980.

Barrera Rubio, Alfredo, and Karl A. Taube. "Los relieves de San Diego: Una nueva perspectiva." *Boletín de la Escuela de Ciencias Antropológicas de la Universidad de Yucatán* 16 (1987): 3–18.

Barrera Vásquez, Alfredo. *El libro de los Cantares de Dzitbalché.* Mexico City: Instituto Nacional de Antropología e Historia, 1965.

Barrera Vásquez, Alfredo. *Diccionario Maya-Español, Español-Maya.* Mérida, Yucatan: Ediciones Cordemex, 1980.

Barthel, Thomas S. "Regionen des Regengottes." *Ethnos* 18 (1953): 86–105.

Bassett, Molly H. *The Fate of Earthly Things: Aztec Gods and God-Bodies.* Austin: University of Texas Press, 2015.

Bassie, Karen. "Maya Creator Gods." *Mesoweb* (2002). Accessed Aug. 17, 2015. http://www.mesoweb.com.

Bassie, Karen. *Maya Sacred Geography and the Creator Deities.* Norman: University of Oklahoma Press, 2008.

Bassie, Karen, and Marc Zender. "The Wooden Offering Container of Aj K'ax B'ahlam of Tortuguero." In *The Jay I. Kislak Collection at the Library of Congress,* ed. Arthur Dunkelman, 14–15. Washington, D.C.: Library of Congress, 2007.

Bateson, Gregory. *Steps to an Ecology of Mind: Collected Essays in Anthropology, Psychiatry, Evolution, and Epistemology.* Chicago: University of Chicago Press, 1972.

Bateson, Gregory, Donald D. Jackson, Jay Haley,

and John Weakland. "Toward a Theory of Schizophrenia." *Behavioral Science* 1 (1956): 251–64.

Battaglia, Debbora. "Problematizing the Self: A Thematic Introduction." In *Rhetorics of Self-Making*, ed. D. Battaglia, 1–15. Berkeley: University of California Press, 1992.

Baudez, Claude F. "The House of the Bacabs: An Iconographic Analysis." In *The House of the Bacabs, Copan, Honduras*, ed. David Webster, 73–81. Studies in Pre-Columbian Art and Archaeology 29. Washington, D.C.: Dumbarton Oaks Research Library and Collection, 1989.

Bauer, Brian S. *Ancient Cuzco: Heartland of the Inka*. Austin: University of Texas Press, 2004.

Baxter, P. T. W., and Uri Almagor. "Introduction." In *Age, Generation, and Time: Some Features of East African Age Organisations*, ed. P. T. W. Baxter and Uri Almagor, 1–35. New York: St. Martin's, 1978.

Beard, Mary. "Frazer, Leach, and Virgil: The Popularity (and Unpopularity) of the Golden Bough." *Comparative Studies in Society and History* 34 (1992): 203–24.

Beaumont, Lesley A. *Childhood in Ancient Athens: Iconography and Social History*. London: Routledge, 2012.

Becerra Rodríguez, Raúl, and Gabino López Arenas. "Hallazgos en el recinto ceremonial de Tenochtitlan." *Arqueología mexicana* 16 (2008): 18–25.

Becquelin, Pierre, and Eric Taladoire. *Tonina, une cité maya du Chiapas (Mexique)*. Études mésoamericaines VI, Tome IV. Mexico City: Centre d'études mexicaines et centraméricaines, 1990.

Bedaux, Jan B. "Introduction." In *Pride and Joy: Children's Portraits in the Netherlands, 1500–1700*, ed. Jan Baptist Bedaux and Rudi Ekkart, 10–31. Amsterdam: Ludion, 2001.

Bederman, Gail. *Manliness and Civilization: A Cultural History of Gender and Race in the United States, 1880–1917*. Chicago: University of Chicago Press, 1995.

Beetz, Carl P., and Linton Satterthwaite. *The Monuments and Inscriptions of Caracol, Belize*. University Museum Monograph 45. Philadelphia: University Museum, University of Pennsylvania, 1981.

Beidelman, Thomas O. "Secrecy and Society: The Paradox of Knowing and the Knowing of Paradox." In *Secrecy: African Art that Conceals and Reveals*, ed. Mary H. Nooter, 40–47. New York: Museum of Africa Art, 1993.

Beliaev, Dmitri. "*Wayaab'* Title in Maya Hieroglyphic Inscriptions: On the Problem of Religious Specialization in Classic Maya Society." In *Continuity and Change: Maya Religious Practices and Temporal Perspective: 5th European Maya Conference, University of Bonn, December 2000*, ed. Daniel Graña Behrens, Nikolai Grube, Christian M. Prager, Frauke Sachse, Stefanie Teufel, and Elisabeth Wagner, 121–30. Markt Schwaben: Verlag Anton Saurwein, 2004.

Beliaev, Dmitri, Albert Davletshin, and Alexandre Tokovinine. "Sweet Cacao and Sour Atole: Mixed Drinks on Classic Maya Ceramic Vases." In *Pre-Columbian Foodways: Interdisciplinary Approaches to Food, Culture, and Markets in Ancient Mesoamerica*, ed. John E. Staller and Michael D. Carrasco, 257–72. New York: Springer, 2009.

Bellman, Beryl L. "The Paradox of Secrecy." *Human Studies* 4 (1981): 1–24.

Berdan, Frances E., and Patricia F. Anawalt. *The Essential Codex Mendoza*. Berkeley: University of California Press, 1997.

Bergh, Susan E. "Death and Renewal in Moche Phallic-Spouted Vessels." *RES: Anthropology and Aesthetics* 24 (1993): 78–94.

Berjonneau, Gerald, and Jean-Luc Sonnery. *Rediscovered Masterpieces of Mesoamerica: Mexico–Guatemala–Honduras*. Boulogne: Editions Art 135, 1985.

Bernal, Guillermo. "Dignatarios cuatripartitas y cultos direccionales en las inscripciones de Palenque, Copán y Quiriguá." Ms. in possession of author, 2008.

Berthelot, Geoffroy, Stéphane Len, Philippe Hellard, Muriel Tafflet, Marion Guillaume, Jean-Claude Vollmer, Bruno Gager, Laurent Quinquis, Andy Marc, and Jean-François Toussaint. "Exponential Growth Combined with Exponential Decline Explains Lifetime Performance Evolution in Individual and Human Species." *Age* 34 (2012): 1001–9.

Bindman, David. "Text as Design in Gillray's caricature." In *Icons—Texts—Iconotexts: Essays in Ekphrasis and Intermediality*, ed. Peter Wagner, 309–23. Berlin: Walter de Gruyter, 1996.

Blackless, Melanie, Anthony Charuvastra, Amanda Derryck, Anne Fausto-Sterling, Karl Lauzanne, and Ellen Lee. "How Sexually Dimorphic Are We? Review and Synthesis." *American Journal of Human Biology* 12 (2000): 151–60.

Blainey, Marc. "Surfaces and Beyond: The Political, Ideological, and Economic Significance of Ancient Maya Iron-Ore Mirrors." Master's thesis, Trent University, 2007.

Bledsoe, Caroline, and Gilles Pison. "Introduction." In *Nuptiality in Sub-Saharan Africa: Contemporary Anthropological and Demographic Perspectives,* ed. Caroline Bledsoe and Gilles Pison, 1–22. Oxford: Clarendon, 1994.

Bloch, Maurice. *From Blessing to Violence: History and Ideology in the Circumcision Ritual of the Merina of Madagascar.* Cambridge: Cambridge University Press, 1986.

Blom, Frans. "Commerce, Trade, and Monetary Units of the Maya." *Middle American Research Series* 4 (1932): 531–56.

Bodenhorn, Barbara, and Gabriele vom Bruck. " 'Entangled in Histories': An Introduction to the Anthropology of Names and Naming." In *The Anthropology of Names and Naming,* ed. Gabriele vom Bruck and Barbara Bodenhorn, 1–30. Cambridge: Cambridge University Press, 2006.

Bogin, Barry. *Patterns of Human Growth.* Cambridge: Cambridge University Press, 1999.

Bolles, David. "Combined Dictionary–Concordance of the Yucatecan Mayan Language" (2001). Accessed June 2, 2014. http://www.famsi.org.

Bongmba, Elias K. "Ancestor Veneration in Central Africa." In *Eternal Ancestors: The Art of the Central African Reliquary,* ed. Alisa LaGamma, 78–85. New York: Metropolitan Museum of Art, 2007.

Boon, James A. "Circumcision/Uncircumcision: An Essay Amidst the History of a Difficult Description." In *Implicit Understandings: Observing, Reporting, and Reflecting on the Encounters Between Europeans and Other Peoples in the Early Modern Era,* ed. Stuart B. Schwartz, 556–85. Cambridge: Cambridge University Press, 1999.

Boone, Elizabeth H. *The Codex Magliabechiano and the Lost Prototype of the Magliabechiano Group.* Berkeley: University of California Press, 1983.

Boone, Elizabeth H. *Stories in Red and Black: Pictorial Histories of the Aztec and Mixtec.* Austin: University of Texas Press, 2000.

Boone, Elizabeth H. *Cycles of Time and Meaning in the Mexican Books of Fate.* Austin: University of Texas Press, 2007.

Boot, Eric. "Portraits of Four Kings of the Early Classic? An Inscribed Bowl Excavated at Uaxactún and Seven Vessels of Unknown Provenance." *Mesoweb* (2005). Accessed July 11, 2016. http://www.mesoweb.com.

Bordo, Susan. *The Male Body: A New Look at Men in Public and in Private.* New York: Farrar, Straus and Giroux, 1999.

Born, Lester K. "The Perfect Prince: A Study in Thirteenth- and Fourteenth-Century Ordeals." *Speculum* 3 (1928): 470–504.

Bourdieu, Pierre. "The Social Space and the Genesis of Groups." *Theory and Society* 14 (1985): 723–44.

Bourdieu, Pierre. "La domination masculine." *Actes de la recherche en sciences sociales* 84 (1990): 2–31.

Bourdieu, Pierre. *The Logic of Practice.* Trans. Richard Nice. Stanford, Calif.: Stanford University Press, 1990.

Bourdieu, Pierre. *Masculine Domination.* Stanford, Calif.: Stanford University Press, 2001.

Bourke, Joanna. *Dismembering the Male: Men's Bodies, Britain, and the Great War.* London: Reaktion, 1996.

Bourne, John. *Recollections of My Early Travels in Chiapas: Discoveries at Oxlahuntun (el Perro), Miguel Angel Fernandez, Bonampak, and Lacanhá.* Santa Fe, N. Mex.: Privately published, 2001.

Brandes, Stanley. *Metaphors of Masculinity: Sex and Status in Andalusian Folklore.* Philadelphia: University of Pennsylvania Press, 1980.

Brandes, Stanley. "Sex Roles and Anthropological Research in Andalusia." *Women's Studies* 13 (1987): 357–72.

Brashier, Kenneth E. *Ancestral Memory in Early China.* Harvard-Yenching Institute Monograph 72. Cambridge, Mass.: Harvard University Press, 2011.

Breuil, Abbé Henri. *Quatre cents siècles d'art pariétal: Les cavernes ornées de l'âge du renne.* Montignac: Centre d'études et de documentation préhistoriques, 1952.

Bribiescas, Richard G. *Men: Evolutionary and Life History.* Cambridge, Mass.: Harvard University Press, 2006.

Bricker, Victoria R. *Ritual Humor in Highland Chiapas.* Austin: University of Texas Press, 1973.

Brisson, Luc. *Sexual Ambivalence: Androgyny and Hermaphroditism in Graeco-Roman Antiquity.* Berkeley: University of California Press, 2002.

Brooks, Peter. *Reading for the Plot: Design and Intention in Narrative.* Cambridge, Mass.: Harvard University Press, 1992.

Bucholtz, Mary. "Youth and Cultural Practice." *Annual Review of Anthropology* 31 (2002): 525–52.

Buckley, Thomas, and Alma Gottlieb, eds. *Blood Magic: The Anthropology of Menstruation.* Berkeley: University of California Press, 1988.

Buikstra, Jane E., T. Douglas Price, Lori E. Wright, and James A. Burton. "Tombs from the Copan Acropolis: A Life-History Approach." In *Understanding Early Classic Copan,* ed. Ellen E. Bell, Marcello A. Canuto, and Robert J. Sharer, 191–212. Philadelphia: University of Pennsylvania Museum of Archaeology and Ethnology, 2004.

Bunzel, Ruth. *Chichicastenango: A Guatemalan Village.* Seattle: University of Washington Press, 1959.

Burkhart, Louise M. *Before Guadalupe: The Virgin Mary in Early Colonial Nahuatl Literature.* Institute for Mesoamerican Studies Monographs 13. Albany: State University of New York at Albany, 2001.

Burrow, John A. *The Ages of Man: A Study in Medieval Writing and Thought.* Oxford: Clarendon, 1986.

Butler, Judith. *Gender Trouble: Feminism and the Subversion of Identity.* New York: Routledge, 1990.

Butler, Judith. *Bodies That Matter: On the Discursive Limits of "Sex."* New York: Routledge, 1993.

Callaghan, Michael G. "Maya Polychrome Vessels as Inalienable Possessions." In *The Inalienable in the Archaeology of Mesoamerica,* ed. Brigitte Kovacevich and Michael Callaghan, 112–27. Archaeological Papers of the American Anthropological Association 23(1). Washington, D.C.: American Anthropological Association, 2013.

Callaghan, Michael G., and Nina Neivens de Estrada. *The Ceramic Sequence of the Holmul Region, Guatemala.* Anthropological Papers of the University of Arizona 77. Tucson: University of Arizona Press, 2016.

Calvin, Inga E. "Between Text and Image: An Analysis of Pseudo-glyphs on Late Classic Maya Pottery from Guatemala." Ph.D. diss., University of Colorado, Boulder, 2006.

Campbell, Benjamin C. "Andrenarche and Middle Childhood." *Human Nature* 22 (2011): 327–49.

Card, Jeb, and Marc Zender. "A Seventh-Century Inscribed Miniature Flask from Copan Found at Tazumal, El Salvador." *Ancient Mesoamerica* 27 (2016): 279–92.

Carmack, Robert M. *The Quiché Mayas of Utatlán: The Evolution of a Highland Guatemala Kingdom.* Norman: University of Oklahoma Press, 1981.

Carrasco Vargas, Ramón, and María Cordiero Baqueiro. "The Murals of Chiik Nahb Structure 1–4, Calakmul, Mexico." In *Maya Archaeology 2,* ed. Charles Golden, Stephen Houston, and Joel Skidmore, 8–59. San Francisco: Precolumbia Mesoweb, 2013.

Carsten, Janet, ed. *Blood Will Out: Essays on Liquid Transfers and Flows.* Malden, Mass.: Wiley-Blackwell, 2013.

Chankowski, Andrzej S. *L'Éphébie hellénistique: Étude d'une institution civique dans les cités grecques des îles de la Mer Égée et de l'Asie Mineure.* Culture et cité 4. Paris: De Boccard, 2010.

Chapin, Anne P. "Boys Will Be Boys: Youth and Gender Identity in the Theran Frescoes." In *Constructions of Childhood in Ancient Greece and Italy,* ed. Ada Cohen and Jeremy B. Rutter, 229–55. *Hesperia* Suppl. 41. Princeton: American School of Classical Studies at Athens, 2007.

Chase, Arlen F., and Diane Z. Chase. *Investigations at the Classic Maya City of Caracol, Belize, 1985–1987.* Pre-Columbian Art Research Institute Monograph 3. San Francisco: Pre-Columbian Art Research Institute, 1987.

Chase, Arlen F., and Diane Z. Chase. "At Home in the South: Investigations in the Vicinity of Caracol's South Acropolis: 2003 Field Report of the Caracol Archaeological Project." Accessed June 23, 2016. http://www.caracol.org/reports/2003.php.

Chase, Arlen F., and Diane Z. Chase. "'Interpreting the Maya 'Collapse': Continued Investigation of Residential Complexes in and near Caracol's Epicenter: 2009 Field Report of the Caracol Archaeological Project." Accessed June 23, 2016. http://www.caracol.org/reports/2009.php.

Chase, Diane Z., and Arlen F. Chase. *A Postclassic Perspective: Excavations at the Maya Site of Santa Rita Corozal, Belize.* Pre-Columbian Art Research Institute Monograph 4. San Francisco: Pre-Columbian Art Research Institute, 1988.

Chase, Diane Z., and Arlen F. Chase. "The Early Classic Period at Santa Rita Corozal: Issues of Hierarchy, Heterarchy, and Stratification in Northern Belize." *Research Reports in Belizean Archaeology* 2 (2005): 111–29.

Cheal, David. "'Showing Them You Love Them': Gift Giving and the Dialectic of Intimacy." *Sociological Review* 35 (1987): 150–69.

Cheek, Charles D., and Mary L. Spink. "Excavaciones en el Grupo 3, Estructura 223 (Operación VII)." In *Excavaciones en el área urbana de Copán, Tomo 1: Proyecto Arqueológico, segunda fase,* ed. William T. Sanders, 27–154. Tegucigalpa: Instituto Hondureño de Antropología e Historia, 1986.

Chen, Sanping. "Succession Struggle and the Ethnic Identity of the Tang Imperial House." *Journal of the Royal Asiatic Society,* 3rd ser., 6 (1996): 379–405.

Chew, Samuel C. *The Pilgrimage of Life.* New Haven: Yale University Press, 1962.

Child, Mark B. "The Archaeology of Religious Movements: The Maya Sweatbath Cult of Piedras Negras." Ph.D. diss., Yale University, 2006.

Chinchilla Mazariegos, Oswaldo. *Observaciones sobre los nombres personales en las inscripciones mayas del período clásico temprano, con especial referencia a Tikal.* Licenciatura thesis, Universidad de San Carlos de Guatemala, 1990.

Chinchilla Mazariegos, Oswaldo. *Imágenes de la mitología maya.* Guatemala City: Museo Popol Vuh, 2011.

Chodorow, Nancy. *The Reproduction of Mothering: Psychoanalysis and the Sociology of Gender.* Berkeley: University of California Press, 1978.

Chojnacki, Stanley. *Women and Men in Renaissance Venice: Twelve Essays on Patrician Society.* Baltimore: Johns Hopkins University Press, 2000.

Christenson, Allen J. *Popol Vuh: The Sacred Book of the Maya.* Norman: University of Oklahoma Press, 2007.

Christenson, Allen J. "Maize Was Their Flesh: Ritual Feasting in the Maya Highlands." In *Pre-Columbian Foodways: Interdisciplinary Approaches to Food, Culture, and Markets in Ancient Mesoamerica,* ed. John Staller and Michael Carrasco, 577–600. New York: Springer, 2009.

Chroust, Anton H., and Robert J. Affeldt. "The Problem of Private Property According to St. Thomas Aquinas." *Marquette Law Review* 34 (1950–51): 151–82.

Chuchiak, John F. "Secrets Behind the Screen: Solicitantes in the Colonial Discourse of Yucatan and the Yucatec Maya, 1570–1785." In *Religion in New Spain,* ed. Susan Schroeder and Stafford Poole, 83–113. Albuquerque: University of New Mexico Press, 2007.

Ciudad Real, Antonio de. *Calepino Maya de Motul: Edición crítica y anotada por René Acuña.* Mexico City: Plaza y Valdés Editores, 2001.

Clavigero, Francisco. J. *Historia antigua de México.* Mexico City: Porrúa, 1945.

Clendinnen, Inga. *The Cost of Courage in Aztec Society: Essays on Mesoamerican Society and Culture.* Cambridge: Cambridge University Press, 2010.

Clottes, Jean, and David Lewis-Williams. *The Shamans of Prehistory: Trance and Magic in Painted Caves.* New York: Abrams, 1998.

Coe, Michael D. *The Maya Scribe and His World.* New York: Grolier Club, 1973.

Coe, Michael D. "A Carved Wooden Box from the Classic Maya Civilization." In *Primera Mesa Redonda de Palenque Part II,* ed. Merle G. Robertson, 51–58. Pebble Beach: Robert Louis Stevenson School, 1974.

Coe, Michael D. *Lords of the Underworld: Masterpieces of Classic Maya Ceramics.* Princeton: Art Museum, Princeton University, 1978.

Coe, Michael D. "The Hero Twins: Myth and Image." In *The Maya Vase Book: A Corpus of Rollout Photographs of Maya Vases, Volume 1,* ed. Barbara Kerr and Justin Kerr, 161–84. New York: Kerr Associates, 1989.

Coe, Michael D., and Stephen Houston. *The Maya.* 9th ed. London: Thames and Hudson, 2015.

Coe, Sophie D. *America's First Cuisines.* Austin: University of Texas Press, 1994.

Coe, Sophie D., and Michael Coe. *The True History of Chocolate.* 3rd ed. London: Thames and Hudson, 2013.

Coe, William R. *Piedras Negras Archaeology: Artifacts, Caches, and Burials.* Philadelphia: University Museum, University of Pennsylvania, 1959.

Coe, William R. *Tikal Report No. 14, Volume V: Excavations in the Great Plaza, North Terrace, and North Acropolis of Tikal.* University Museum Monograph 61. Philadelphia: University Museum, University of Pennsylvania, 1990.

Colas, Pierre R. *Sinn und Bedeutung klassicher Maya-Personennamen: Typologische Analyse von Anthroponymphrasen in den Hieroglypheninschriften der klassischen Maya-Kultur als Beitrag zur allgemeinen Onomasktik.* Acta Mesoamericana 15. Markt Schwaben, Germany: Anton Saurwein, 2004.

Colby, Benjamin N., and Lore M. Colby. *The Daykeeper: The Life and Discourse of an Ixil Diviner.* Cambridge, Mass.: Harvard University Press, 1981.

Cole, Thomas R. *The Journey of Life: A Cultural History of Aging in America.* Cambridge: Cambridge University Press, 1992.

Coleman, James S. *The Adolescent Society.* Glencoe, Ill.: Free Press, 1961.

Collins, James. "Social Reproduction in Classrooms and Schools." *Annual Review of Anthropology* 38 (2009): 33–48.

Colton, Harold S. *Hopi Kachina Dolls.* Albuquerque: University of New Mexico Press. 1959.

Comaroff, Jean, and John L. Comaroff. "Occult Economies and the Violence of Abstraction: Notes from the South African Postcolony." *American Ethnologist* 26 (1999): 279–303.

Connell, Raewyn W., and James W. Messerschmidt. "Hegemonic Masculinity: Rethinking the Concept." *Gender and Society* 19 (2005): 829–59.

Connell, Raewyn W., Jeff Hearn, and Michael S. Kimmel. "Introduction." In *Handbook of Studies of Men and Masculinities,* ed. Michael S. Kimmel, Jeff Hearn, and R. W. Connell, 1–10. Thousand Oaks, Calif.: Sage, 2005.

Connell, Robert [Raewyn] W. *Masculinities.* Berkeley: University of California Press, 1995.

Connelly, Joan B. *Portrait of a Priestess: Women and Ritual in Ancient Greece.* Princeton: Princeton University Press, 2007.

Cooley, Alison. *Res Gestae divi Augusti: Text, Translation and Commentary.* Cambridge: Cambridge University Press, 2009.

Corbin, Alain, Jean-Jacques Courtine, and Georges Vigarello, eds. *A History of Virility.* New York: Columbia University Press, 2016.

Cortés de Brasdefer, Fernando. "A Maya Vase from 'El Señor del Petén.'" *Mexicon* 18 (1996): 6.

Courtine, Jean-Jacques. "Impossible Virility." In *A History of Virility*, ed. Alain Corbin, Jean-Jacques Courtine, and Georges Vigarello, 399–402. New York: Columbia University Press, 2016.

Covey, Herbert C. "Perceptions and Attitudes Toward Sexuality of the Elderly During the Middle Ages." *Gerontologist* 29: 93–100.

Crocker, Christopher. "Men's House Associates Among the Eastern Bororo." *Southwestern Journal of Anthropology* 25 (1969): 236–60.

Crown, Patricia L. "Life Histories of Pots and Potters: Situating the Individual in Archaeology." *American Antiquity* 72 (2007): 677–90.

Cucina, Andrea, and Vera Tiesler. "The Companions of Janaab' Pakal and the 'Red Queen' from Palenque, Chiapas: Meanings of Human Companion Sacrifice in Classic Maya Society." In *Janaab' Pakal of Palenque: Reconstructing the Life and Death of a Maya Ruler*, ed. Vera Tiesler and Andrea Cucina, 102–25. Tucson: University of Arizona Press, 2006.

Culbert, T. Patrick. *The Ceramics of Tikal.* Philadelphia: University Museum, 1993.

Dal, Erik, with Povl Skårup. *The Ages of Man and the Months of the Year.* Det Kongelige Danske Videnskabernes Selskab Historisk-filosofiske Skrifter 9(3). Copenhagen: Munksgaard, 1980.

D'Altroy, Terence N. *The Incas.* 2nd ed. Somerset: Wiley-Blackwell, 2014.

Dante [Alighieri]. *The Convivio of Dante Alighieri.* London: J. M. Dent, 1903.

Daston, Lorraine, and Katherine Park. "Hermaphrodites in Renaissance France." *Critical Matrix* (1985): 1–19.

Davidson, James N. *The Greeks and Greek Love: A Bold New Exploration of the Ancient World.* New York: Random House, 2007.

Davis, Natalie Z. "The Reasons of Misrule: Youth Groups and Charivaris in Sixteenth-Century France." *Past and Present* 50 (1971): 116–22.

Davis, Natalie Z. *The Gift in Sixteenth-Century France.* Madison: University of Wisconsin Press, 2000.

Davis, Richard H. *Ritual in an Oscillating Universe: Worshipping Śiva in Medieval India.* Princeton: Princeton University Press, 1992.

Davis, Richard H. "The Origin of Liṅga Worship." In *Religions of India in Practice*, ed. Donald S. Lopez, 637–47. Princeton: Princeton University Press, 1995.

Davis, Whitney. *Queer Beauty: Sexuality and Aesthetics from Winckelmann to Freud and Beyond.* New York: Columbia University Press, 2010.

Dean, Carolyn. "Andean Androgyny and the Making of Men." In *Gender in Pre-Hispanic America*, ed. Cecelia F. Klein, 143–82. Washington, D.C.: Dumbarton Oaks Research Library and Collection, 2001.

Deaner, Robert O., David C. Geary, David A. Puts, Sandra A. Ham, Judy Kruger, Elizabeth Fles, Bo Winegard, and Terry Grandis. "A Sex Difference in the Predisposition for Physical Competition: Males Play Sports Much More than Females Even in the Contemporary U.S." *PLoS ONE* 7 (2012): e49168. doi:10.1371/journal.pone.0049168.

De Block, Andreas, and Siegfried Dewitte. "Darwinism and the Cultural Evolution of Sports." *Perspectives in Biology and Medicine* 52 (2009): 1–16.

de Coto, Fray Thómas. *[Thesavrvs Verborvm] Vocabvulario de la lengua cakchiquel v[el] guatemalteca, nueuamente hecho y recopilado con summo estudio, trauajo y erudición.* Ed. René Acuña. Mexico City: Universidad Nacional Autónoma de México, 1983.

de Heusch, Luc. "The Symbolic Mechanisms of Sacred Kingship: Rediscovering Frazer." *Journal of the Royal Anthropological Institute* 3 (1997): 213–32.

De Nie, Giselle. "Seeing and Believing in the Early Middle Ages: A Preliminary Investigation." In *The Pictured Word: Word and Image Interactions 2*, ed. Martin Heusser, Claus Clüver, Leo Hoek, and Lauren Weingarden, 67–76. Amsterdam: Rodopi, 1998.

Derrida, Jacques. *Given Time: 1. Counterfeit Money.* Trans. Peggy Kamuf. Chicago: University of Chicago Press, 1992.

De Vos, Jan. *La paz de Dios y del Rey: La conquista de la Selva Lacandona (1525–1821).* Mexico City: Fondo de Cultura Económica, 1988.

De Vos, Jan. *No queremos ser cristianos.* Mexico City: Dirección General de Publicaciones del Consejo Nacional para la Cultura y las Artes/Instituto Nacional Indigenista, 1990.

Dieseldorff, Erwin P. *Kunst und Religion der Mayavölker im alten und heutigen Mittelamerika.* Berlin: Springer, 1926.

Dietler, Michael. "Theorizing the Feast: Rituals of Consumption, Commensal Politics, and Power in African Contexts." In *Feasts: Archaeological and Ethnographic Perspectives on Food, Politics, and Power,* ed. Michael Dietler and Brian Hayden, 65–114. Washington, D.C.: Smithsonian Institution Press, 2001.

Dobler, Andreas. "Prins Ernst." In *Fürstenkinder: Porträts vom 16. bis 21. Jh. im Hause Hessen,* by Markus Miller, Christine Klössel, Andreas Dobler, and Mikael Bøgh Rasmussen, 48–49. Eichenzell, Germany: Michael Imhof, 2008.

Donnan, Christopher B., and Donna McClelland. *Moche Fineline Painting: Its Evolution and Artists.* Los Angeles: Fowler Museum of Cultural History, University of California Los Angeles, 1999.

Douglas, Mary. *Natural Symbols: Explorations in Cosmology.* London: Barrie and Rockliff, 1970.

Douglas, Mary. "No Free Gifts." Foreword in *The Gift: The Form and Reason for Exchange in Archaic Societies,* by Marcel Mauss, vii–xviii. New York: W. W. Norton, 1990.

Dover, Kenneth. *Greek Homosexuality.* Cambridge, Mass.: Harvard University Press, 1978.

Dowden, Ken. "Fluctuating Meanings: 'Passage Rites' in Ritual, Myth, Odyssey, and the Greek Romance." In *Rites of Passage in Ancient Greece: Literature, Religion, Society,* ed. Mark W. Padilla, 221–43. Lewisburg, Penn.: Bucknell University Press, 1999.

Downer, Lesley. "The City Geisha and Their Role in Modern Japan: Anomaly or Artistes?" In *The Courtesan's Arts: Cross-Cultural Perspectives,* ed. Martha Feldman and Bonnie Gordon, 223–42. New York: Oxford University Press, 2006.

Doyle, James A. "Creation Narratives on Ancient Maya Codex-Style Ceramics in the Metropolitan Museum." *Metropolitan Museum Journal* 51 (2016): 42–63.

Driver, W. David. "An Early Classic Colonnaded Building at the Maya Site of Blue Creek, Belize." *Latin American Antiquity* 13 (2002): 63–84.

Druc, Isabelle. "Ceramic Production in San Marcos, Acteopan, Puebla, Mexico." *Ancient Mesoamerica* 11 (2000): 77–89.

Duby, Georges. *Hommes et structures du moyen age.* Paris: Mouton, 1973.

Dunlop, Fiona S. "Mightier Than the Sword: Reading, Writing, and Noble Masculinity in the Early Sixteenth Century." In *Representing Medieval Genders and Sexualities in Europe: Construction, Transformation, and Subversion, 600–1530,* ed. Elizabeth L'Estrange and Alison More, 161–72. Farnham, England: Ashgate, 2011.

Durán, Diego. *Book of the Gods and Rites and the Ancient Calendar.* Norman: University of Oklahoma Press, 1971.

Durán, Diego. *The History of the Indies of New Spain.* Trans. Doris Heyden. Norman: University of Oklahoma Press, 1994.

Durham, Deborah. "Youth and the Social Imagination in Africa: Introduction to Parts 1 and 2." *Anthropological Quarterly* 73 (2000): 113–20.

Easby, Elizabeth K., and John F. Scott. *Before Cortés: Sculpture of Middle America.* New York: Metropolitan Museum of Art, 1970.

Eberl, Markus. "Community Heterogeneity and Integration: The Maya Sites of Nacimiento, Dos Ceibas, and Cerro de Cheyo (El Peten, Guatemala) During the Late Classic." Ph.D. diss., Tulane University, 2007.

Eggan, Fred, and William H. Scott, 1963. "Ritual Life of the Igorots of Saqada: From Birth to Adolescence." *Ethnology* 2 (1963): 40–54.

Ehmer, Josef. "The 'Life Stairs': Ageing, Generational Relations, and Small Commodity Production." In *Ageing and Intergenerational Relations over the Life Course: A Historical and Cross-Cultural Perspective,* ed. Tamara K. Haraven, 53–74. Berlin: Walter de Gruyter, 1996.

Ehmer, Josef, and P. Gutschner, eds. *Das Alter im Spiel der Generationen.* Vienna: Böhlau, 2000.

Ellis, Bruce J. "Risky Adolescent Behavior: An Evolutionary Perspective." In *Adolescent Identity: Evolutionary, Cultural, and Developmental Perspectives,* ed. Bonnie L. Hewlett, 40–72. New York: Routledge, 2013.

Enel, Catherine, Gilles Pison, and Monique Lefebvre. "Migration and Marriage Chance: A Case Study of Mlomp, a Joola Village in Southern Senegal." In *Nuptiality in Sub-Saharan Africa: Contemporary Anthropological and Demographic Perspectives,* ed. Caroline Bledsoe and Gilles Pison, 92–113. Oxford: Clarendon, 1994.

Erasmus, Desiderius. *The Education of a Christian Prince.* Ed. Lisa Jardine. Cambridge: Cambridge University Press, 1997.

Erikson, Erik H. *Identity: Youth and Crisis.* New York: W. W. Norton, 1968.

Estrada-Belli, Francisco, and Alexandre Tokovinine. "A King's Apotheosis: Iconography, Text, and Politics from a Classic Maya Temple at Holmul." *Latin American Antiquity* 27 (2016): 149–68.

Estrada Monroy, Agustín. *El mundo K'ekchi' de la Vera-Paz.* Guatemala City: Editorial del Ejercito, 1979.

Eyben, Emiel. *Restless Youth in Ancient Rome.* London: Routledge, 1993.

Fares, Jean, Varun Gauri, Emmanuel Y. Jimenez, Mattias K. A. Lundberg, David McKenzie, Mamta Murthi, Cristobal Ridao-Cano, and Nistha Sinha. *World Development Report 2007: Development and the Next Generation.* Washington, D.C.: World Bank, 2006.

Farr, James R. *Artisans in Europe, 1300–1914.* Cambridge: Cambridge University Press, 2000.

Fash, William L., Richard V. Williamson, Carlos Rudy Larios, and Joel Palka. "The Hieroglyphic Stairway and Its Ancestors: Investigations of Copan Structure 10L-26." *Ancient Mesoamerica* 3 (1992): 105–15.

Fastlicht, Samuel. "Dental Inlays and Filings Among the Ancient Mayas." *Journal of the History of Medicine and Allied Sciences* 17 (1962): 393–401.

Fausto-Sterling, Anne. *Sexing the Body: Gender Politics and the Construction of Sexuality.* New York: Basic, 2000.

Feldman, Lawrence H. *A Dictionary of Poqom Maya in the Colonial Era.* Lancaster, Calif.: Labyrinthos, 2004.

Feldman, Martha, and Bonnie Gordon, eds. *The Courtesan's Arts: Cross-Cultural Perspectives.* New York: Oxford University Press, 2006.

Fields, Virginia M., and Dorie Reents-Budet. *Lords of Creation: The Origins of Sacred Maya Kingship.* Los Angeles: Los Angeles County Museum of Art, 2005.

Fields, Virginia M., and Alexandre Tokovinine. "Carved Bowl." In *Ancient Maya Art at Dumbarton Oaks,* ed. Joanne Pillsbury, Miriam Doutriaux, Reiko Ishihara-Brito, and Alexandre Tokovinine, 104–7. Pre-Columbian Art at Dumbarton Oaks 4. Washington, D.C.: Dumbarton Oaks Research Library and Collection, 2012.

Finamore, Dan, and Stephen Houston. *Fiery Pool: The Maya and the Mythic Sea.* New Haven: Yale University Press, 2010.

Fischer, Clare B., and Luh Estiti Andarawati. "Tooth-Filing in Bali: One Woman's Experience." *Journal of Ritual Studies* 12 (1998): 39–46.

Fitzsimmons, James L., Andrew Scherer, Stephen D. Houston, and Héctor L. Escobedo. "Guardian of the Acropolis: The Sacred Space of a Royal Burial at Piedras Negras, Guatemala." *Latin American Antiquity* 14 (2003): 449–68.

Flannery, Kent V., and Joyce Marcus. *Excavations at San José Mogote 1: Household Archaeology.* Memoir 40. Ann Arbor: Museum of Anthropology, University of Michigan, 2005.

Fletcher, Joseph. "Turco-Mongolian Monarchic Traditions in the Ottoman Empire." *Harvard Ukrainian Studies* 3 (1979): 236–51.

Forge, Anthony. "Tooth and Fang in Bali." *Canberra Anthropology* 3 (1980): 1–16.

Fortes, Meyer. "Ritual and Office in Tribal Society." In *Essays on the Ritual of Social Relations,* ed. Max Gluckman, 53–88. Manchester: Manchester University Press, 1962.

Foucault, Michel. *Discipline and Punish: The Birth of the Prison.* New York: Vintage, 1995

Franklin, Sarah, and Susan McKinnon. *Relative Values: Reconfiguring Kinship Studies.* Durham, N.C.: Duke University Press, 2002.

Fraschetti, Augusto. "Roman Youth." In *A History of Young People in the West, Volume 1: Ancient and Medieval Rites of Passage,* ed. Giovanni Levi and Jean-Claude Schmitt, 51–82. Cambridge: Belknap, 1997.

Freeman, Derek. *Margaret Mead and Samoa: The Making and Unmaking of an Anthropological Myth.* Cambridge, Mass.: Harvard University Press, 1983.

Friedman, David M. *A Mind of Its Own: A Cultural History of the Penis.* New York: Free Press, 2001.

Fuentes y Guzmán, Francisco. *Recordación Florida, Tomo 2.* Guatemala City: Tipografía Nacional, 1933.

Furth, Charlotte. "From Birth to Birth: The Growing Body in Chinese Medicine." In *Chinese Views of Childhood,* ed. Anne B. Kinnery, 157–91. Honolulu: University of Hawai'i Press, 1995.

Gamboni, Dario. *The Destruction of Art: Iconoclasm and Vandalism Since the French Revolution.* London: Reaktion, 1997.

García Campillo, José M. "Informe epigráfico sobre Oxkintok y la cerámica Chocholá." In *Oxkintok 4: Misión Arqueológica de España en México, Proyecto Oxkintok Año 1990,* ed. Miguel R. Dorado, 185–200. Madrid: Ministerio de Cultura, 1992.

Garibay, Ángel M. "Historia de México." In *Teogonía e historia de los mexicanos: Tres opúsculos del siglo XVI,* ed. Ángel M. Garibay, 91–121. Mexico City: Porrúa, 1979.

Garrison, Thomas G., and David Stuart. "Un análisis preliminar de las inscripciones que se relacionan con Xultun, Petén, Guatemala." In *XVII Simposio de Investigaciones Arqueológicas en Guatemala, 2003,* ed. Juan Pedro Laporte, Barbara Arroyo, Héctor Escobedo, and Héctor Mejía, 829–42. Guatemala

City: Museo Nacional de Arqueología y Etnología, 2004.

Geary, Patrick J. "Gift Exchange and Social Science Modeling: The Limitations of a Construct." In *Negotiating the Gift: Pre-Modern Figurations of Exchange*, ed. Gadi Algazi, Valentin Groebner, and Bernhard Jussen, 129–40. Göttingen: Vandenhoeck and Ruprecht, 2003.

Geller, Pamela L. "Altering Identities: Body Modification and the Pre-Columbian Maya." In *Social Archaeology of Funerary Remains*, ed. Rebecca Gowland and Christopher J. Knüsel, 279–91. Oxford: Oxbow, 2006.

Gillespie, Susan D. "Beyond Kinship: An Introduction." In *Beyond Kingship: Social and Material Reproduction in House Societies*, ed. Rosemary A. Joyce and Susan D. Gillespie, 1–21. Philadelphia: University of Pennsylvania Press, 2000.

Gillis, John. *Youth and History: Tradition and Change in European Age Relations, 1750–Present.* New York: Academic, 1975.

Gilmore, David D. *Manhood in the Making: Cultural Concepts of Masculinity.* New Haven: Yale University Press, 1990.

Glazebrook, Allison, and Madeleine M. Henry. "Introduction: Why Prostitutes? Why Greece? Why Now?" In *Greek Prostitutes in the Mediterranean, 800 BCE–200 CE*, ed. Allison Glazebrook and Madeline M. Henry, 3–13. Madison: University of Wisconsin Press, 2011.

Gluckman, Max. *Essays on the Ritual of Social Relations.* Manchester: Manchester University Press, 1962.

Godelier, Maurice. *The Making of Great Men: Male Domination and Power Among the New Guinea Baruya.* Paris: Éditions de la Maison des Sciences de l'Homme; Cambridge: Cambridge University Press, 1986.

Godelier, Maurice. *The Enigma of the Gift.* Trans. Nora Scott. Chicago: University of Chicago Press, 1999.

Godelier, Maurice. *The Metamorphoses of Kinship.* London: Verso, 2011.

Golden, Charles W., Andrew K. Scherer, and Arturo R. Muñoz. "Exploring the Piedras Negras-Yaxchilán Border Zone: Archaeological Investigations in the Sierra del Lacandón, 2004." *Mexicon* 27 (2005): 11–16.

Gombrich, Ernst H. "Image and Word in Twentieth-Century Art." *Word and Image* 1 (1985): 213–41.

González Cruz, Arnoldo. *La reina roja: Una tumba real de Palenque.* Mexico City: Turner, 2011.

Goody, Jack. "Introduction." In *Succession to High Office*, ed. Jack Goody, 1–56. Cambridge: Cambridge University Press, 1966.

Gottlieb, Alma. *The Afterlife Is Where We Come From: The Culture of Infancy in West Africa.* Chicago: University of Chicago Press, 2004.

Graff, Harvey J. *Conflicting Paths: Growing Up in America.* Cambridge, Mass.: Harvard University Press, 1995.

Graham, Ian. *Corpus of Maya Hieroglyphic Inscriptions, Volume 3, Part 1: Yaxchilan.* Cambridge, Mass.: Peabody Museum of Archaeology and Ethnology, Harvard University, 1979.

Graham, Ian. *Corpus of Maya Hieroglyphic Inscriptions, Volume 3, Part 2: Yaxchilan.* Cambridge, Mass.: Peabody Museum of Archaeology and Ethnology, Harvard University, 1982.

Graham, Ian, and Peter Mathews. *Corpus of Maya Hieroglyphic Inscriptions, Volume 6, Part 2: Tonina.* Cambridge, Mass.: Peabody Museum of Archaeology and Ethnology, Harvard University, 1996.

Graham, Ian, and Eric von Euw. *Corpus of Maya Hieroglyphic Inscriptions, Volume 2, Part 1: Naranjo.* Cambridge, Mass.: Peabody Museum of Archaeology and Ethnology, Harvard University, 1975.

Graham, Ian, and Eric von Euw. *Corpus of Maya Hieroglyphic Inscriptions, Volume 4, Part 3: Uxmal, Xcalumkin.* Cambridge, Mass.: Peabody Museum of Archaeology and Ethnology, Harvard University, 1992.

Graham, Ian, Lucia R. Henderson, Peter Mathews, and David Stuart. *Corpus of Maya Hieroglyphic Inscriptions, Volume 9, Part 2: Tonina.* Cambridge, Mass.: Peabody Museum of Archaeology and Ethnology, Harvard University, 2006.

Green, Judith S. "First Blood: A Childhood Rite Commemorated on Classic Maya Ceramics." In *Climates of Change: The Shifting Environment of Archaeology*, ed. Sheila Kulyk, Cara G. Tremaine, and Madeleine Sawyer, 163–176. Alberta, Canada: Department of Anthropology and Archaeology, University of Calgary, 2014.

Greenfield, Patricia M. *Weaving Generations Together: Evolving Creativity in the Maya of Chiapas.* Santa Fe, N. Mex.: School of American Research Press, 2004.

Gregor, Thomas. "The Men's House: Touching and Wrestling Among Mehinaku Men." In *The Book of Touch*, ed. Constance Classen, 162–65. Oxford: Berg, 2005.

Groark, Kevin P. "Pathogenic Emotions: Sentiment, Sociality, and Sickness Among the Tzotzil Maya of San Juan Chamula, Chiapas, Mexico." Ph.D. diss., University of California Los Angeles, 2005.

Groark, Kevin P. "The Angel in the Gourd: Ritual, Therapeutic, and Protective Uses of Tobacco (*Nicotiana tabacum*) Among the Tzeltal and Tzotzil Maya of Chiapas, Mexico." *Journal of Ethnobiology* 30 (2010): 5–30.

Grube, Nikolai. "Classic Maya Dance: Evidence from Hieroglyphs and Iconography." *Ancient Mesoamerica* 3 (1992): 201–18.

Grube, Nikolai. "Speaking Through Stones: A Quotative Particle in Maya Hieroglyphic Inscriptions." In *50 años de estudios americanistas en la Universidad de Bonn*, ed. Sabine Dedenbach-Salazar Sáenz, Carmen Arellano Hoffmann, Eva Konig, and Heiko Prumers, 543–58. Markt Schwaben, Germany: Anton Sauerwein, 1998.

Grube, Nikolai. "Monumentos esculpidos e inscripciones jeroglíficas en el triángulo Yaxhá-Nakum-Naranjo." In *El sitio maya de Topoxté: Investigaciones en una isla del lago Yaxhá, Petén, Guatemala*, ed. Wolfgang W. Wurster, 249–68. Mainz: Philipp von Zabern, 2000.

Grube, Nikolai. "Die Hieroglyphentexte auf den Keramiken." In *Die Maya: Schrift und Kunst im Ethnologischen Museum Berlin*, by Nikolai Grube and Mari Gaida, 58–81. Berlin: SMB DuMont, 2006.

Grube, Nikolai, and Maria Gaida. "Katalog Ethnologisches Museum Berlin." In *Die Maya: Schrift und Kunst im Ethnologischen Museum Berlin*, by Nikolai Grube and Maria Gaida, 82–225. Berlin: SMB DuMont, 2006.

Grube, Nikolai, and Camilo Alejandro Luín. "A Drum Altar from the Vicinity of Yaxchilan." *Mexicon* 36 (2014): 40–48.

Grube, Nikolai, and David Stuart. *Observations on T110 as the Syllable Ko.* Research Reports on Ancient Maya Writing 8. Washington, D.C.: Center for Maya Research, 1987.

Guilliem Arroyo, Salvador. "El Templo Calendárico de México-Tlatelolco." *Arqueología mexicana* 34 (1998): 46–53.

Guiteras-Holmes, Calixta. *Perils of the Soul: The World View of a Tzotzil Indian.* Glencoe, Ill.: Free Press, 1961.

Guthe, Carl E. *Pueblo Pottery Making: A Study at the Village of San Ildefonso.* Papers of the Southwestern Expedition 2. New Haven: Yale University Press, 1925.

Guthrie, R. Dale. *The Nature of Paleolithic Art.* Chicago: University of Chicago Press, 2005.

Gutmann, Mathew C. "Trafficking in Men: The Anthropology of Masculinity." *Annual Review of Anthropology* 26 (1997): 385–409.

Gutmann, Mathew C. "Do We Need 'Masculinist' (Manly?) Defenses of Feminist Archaeology?" *Archaeological Dialogues* 5 (1998): 112–15.

Gwinnett, A. J., and L. Gorelick. "Inlayed Teeth of the Ancient Mayans: A Tribological Study using the SEM." *Scanning Electron Microscopy* 3 (1979): 575–80.

Hage, Per. "The Ancient Maya Kinship System." *Journal of Anthropological Research* 59 (2003): 5–21.

Hall, G. Stanley. *Adolescence: Its Psychology and Its Relations to Physiology, Anthropology, Sociology, Sex, Crime, Religion and Education.* 2 vols. New York: D. Appelton, 1904.

Halperin, Christina A. *Maya Figurines: Intersections Between State and Household.* Austin: University of Texas Press, 2014.

Hamann, Byron. "The Social Life of Pre-sunrise Things: Indigenous Mesoamerican Archaeology." *Current Anthropology* 43 (2002): 351–82.

Hamann, Byron. "Child Martyrs and Murderous Children: Age and Agency in Sixteenth-Century Transatlantic Religious Conflicts." In *The Social Experience of Childhood in Ancient Mesoamerica*, ed. Traci Ardren and Scott H. Hutson, 203–31. Boulder: University Press of Colorado, 2006.

Hamilton, William. *An Account of the Remains of the Worship of Priapus, Lately Existing at Isernia, in the Kingdom of Naples.* London: T. Spillsbury, 1786.

Hanks, William F. *Referential Practice: Language and Lived Space Among the Maya.* Chicago: University of Chicago Press, 1990.

Hann, Chris H. "Introduction: The Embeddedness of Property." In *Property Relations: Renewing the Anthropological Tradition*, ed. Chris H. Hann, 1–47. Cambridge: Cambridge University Press, 1998.

Hann, Chris H. "Moral Dispossession." *InterDisciplines* 2 (2011): 11–37.

Harrison, Peter D. "The Central Acropolis, Tikal, Guatemala: A Preliminary Study of Its Structural Components During the Late Classic Period." Ph.D. diss., University of Pennsylvania, 1970.

Hart, Jason. "Introduction." In *Years of Conflict: Adolescence, Political Violence, and Displacement*, ed. Jason Hart, 1–20. New York: Berghahn, 2008.

Hartnett, Alexandra, and Shannon L. Dawdy. 2013. "The Archaeology of Illegal and Illicit Economies." *Annual Review of Anthropology* 42 (2013): 37–51.

Haviland, William, and Anita de L. Haviland. "Glimpses of the Supernatural: Altered States of Consciousness and the Graffiti of Tikal, Guatemala." *Latin American Antiquity* 6 (1995): 295–309.

Havill, Lorena M., Diane M. Warren, Keith P. Jacobi, Karen D. Gettelman, Della Collins Cook, and K. Anne Pyburn. "Late Postclassic Tooth Filing at Chau Hiix and Tipu, Belize." In *Bones of the Maya: Studies of Maya Skeletons*, ed. Stephen L. Whittington and David M. Reed, 89–104. Washington, D.C.: Smithsonian Institution Press, 1997.

Headland, Thomas N. "Teeth Mutilation Among the Casiguran Dumagat." *Philippine Quarterly of Culture and Society* 5 (1977): 54–64.

Heidenreich, Conrad E. "Huron." In *Handbook of North American Indians, Volume 15: Northeast*, ed. Bruce C. Trigger, 368–88. Washington, D.C.: Smithsonian Institution Press, 1978.

Hellmuth, Nicholas M. "Early Maya Iconography on an Incised Cylindrical Tripod." In *Maya Iconography*, ed. Elizabeth P. Benson and Gillett G. Griffin, 152–74. Princeton: Princeton University Press, 1988.

Hennessy, Cecily. *Images of Children in Byzantium.* Farnham, England: Ashgate, 2008.

Herdt, Gilbert H. *Guardian of the Flutes: Idioms of Masculinity.* New York: McGraw Hill, 1981.

Herdt, Gilbert, and Stephen C. Leavitt. "Introduction: Studying Adolescence in Contemporary Pacific Island Communities." In *Adolescence in Pacific Island Societies*, ed. Gilbert Herdt and Stephen C. Leavitt, 1–43. Pittsburgh: University of Pittsburgh Press, 1998.

Hermes, Bernard. "La secuencia de ocupación prehispánica en el área de la laguna Yaxha, Petén: Una síntesis." In *Simposio de Investigaciones Arqueológicas en Guatemala, 2000*, ed. Juan Pedro Laporte, A. C. Suasnávar, and Barbara Arroyo, 151–77. Guatemala City: Museo Nacional de Arqueología y Etnología, 2001.

Herring, Adam. "A Royal Artist at Naranjo: Notes on a Late Classic Maya Cylinder Vessel." *Yale University Art Gallery Bulletin* (1995/1996): 34–47.

Herrmann, John J., Jr., and Christine Kondoleon. *Games for the Gods: The Greek Athlete and the Olympic Spirit.* Boston: Museum of Fine Arts, 2004.

Herzfeld, Michael. *The Poetics of Manhood: Contest and Identity in a Cretan Mountain Village.* Princeton: Princeton University Press, 1985.

Hewlett, Bonnie L. "Introduction: Adolescent Identity, Risk, and Change." In *Adolescent Identity: Evolutionary, Cultural, and Developmental Perspectives*, ed. Bonnie L. Hewlett, 1–22. New York: Routledge, 2013.

Hewlett, Bonnie L., and Barry S. Hewlett. "Hunter-Gatherer Adolescence." In *Adolescent Identity: Evolutionary, Cultural, and Developmental Perspectives*, ed. Bonnie L. Hewlett, 73–101. New York: Routledge, 2013.

Hogan, LaMicha, Katherine Rinard, Cathy Young, Alden E. Roberts, Myrna L. Armstrong, and Thomas Nelius. "A Cross-Sectional Study of Men with Genital Piercings." *British Journal of Medical Practitioners* 3 (2010): 315–22.

Holland, William R. *Medicina maya en los altos de Chiapas: Un estudio del cambio socio-cultural.* Colección de antropología social 2. Mexico City: Instituto Nacional Indigenista, 1963.

Houston, Stephen D. "An Example of Homophony in Mayan Script." *American Antiquity* 49 (1984): 790–805.

Houston, Stephen D. "A Feather Dance at Bonampak, Chiapas, Mexico." *Journal du Société des Américanistes* 70 (1985): 127–38.

Houston, Stephen D. *Problematic Emblem Glyphs: Examples from Altar de Sacrificios, El Chorro, Río Azul, and Xultun.* Research Reports on Ancient Maya Writing 3. Washington, D.C.: Center for Maya Research, 1986.

Houston, Stephen D. "The Phonetic Decipherment of Mayan Glyphs." *Antiquity* 62 (1988): 126–35.

Houston, Stephen D. "Archaeology and Maya Writing." *Journal of World Prehistory* 3 (1989): 1–32.

Houston, Stephen D. *Hieroglyphs and History at Dos Pilas: Dynastic Politics of the Classic Maya.* Austin: University of Texas Press, 1993.

Houston, Stephen D. "Literacy Among the Precolumbian Maya: A Comparative Perspective." In *Writing Without Words: Alternative Literacies in Mesoamerica and the Andes*, ed. E. Boone and W. Mignolo, 27–49. Durham, N.C.: Duke University Press, 1994.

Houston, Stephen D. "A King Worth a Hill of Beans." *Archaeology* May/June (1997): 40.

Houston, Stephen D. "Classic Maya Depictions of the Built Environment." In *Form and Function in Classic Maya Architecture*, ed. Stephen Houston, 333–72. Washington, D.C.: Dumbarton Oaks Research Library and Collection, 1998.

Houston, Stephen D. "Maya Multilinguals." *Maya Decipherment: A Weblog on the Ancient Maya Script* (2008). Accessed Mar. 6, 2017. https://decipherment.wordpress.com/2009/01/19/maya-multilinguals/.

Houston, Stephen D. "A Splendid Predicament: Young Men in Classic Maya Society." *Cambridge Archaeological Journal* 19 (2009): 149–78.

Houston, Stephen D. "Carved Panel." In *Ancient Maya*

Art at Dumbarton Oaks, ed. Joanne Pillsbury, Miriam Doutriaux, Reiko Ishihara-Brito, and Alexandre Tokovinine, 48–57. Pre-Columbian Art at Dumbarton Oaks 4. Washington, D.C.: Dumbarton Oaks Research Library and Collection, 2012.

Houston, Stephen D. "The Good Prince: Transition, Texting, and Moral Narrative in the Murals of Bonampak, Chiapas, Mexico." *Cambridge Archaeological Journal* 22 (2012): 153–75.

Houston, Stephen D. "Heavenly Bodies." *Maya Decipherment: A Weblog on the Ancient Maya Script* (2012). Accessed Oct. 9, 2016. https://decipherment.wordpress.com/2012/07/16/heavenly-bodies/.

Houston, Stephen D. "Routine, Mass-Made, Pseudo: Thoughts on the Farther Reaches of Literacy." Paper presented at the Maya Meetings at Texas, University of Texas at Austin, 2012.

Houston, Stephen D. "Courtesans and Carnal Commerce." *Maya Decipherment: A Weblog on the Ancient Maya Script* (2014). Accessed Aug. 7, 2015. https://decipherment.wordpress.com/2014/06/08/courtesans-and-carnal-commerce/.

Houston, Stephen D. "A Game with a Throne." *Maya Decipherment: A Weblog on the Ancient Maya Script* (2014). Accessed Feb. 2, 2015. https://decipherment.wordpress.com/2014/01/24/a-game-with-a-throne/.

Houston, Stephen D. *The Life Within: Classic Maya and the Matter of Permanence.* New Haven: Yale University Press, 2014.

Houston, Stephen D. "*Pehk* and 'Parliaments.' " *Maya Decipherment: A Weblog on the Ancient Maya Script* (2014). Accessed Jan. 31, 2014. https://decipherment.wordpress.com/2014/10/07/pehk-and-parliaments/.

Houston, Stephen D. "Crafting Credit: Authorship Among Classic Maya Painters and Sculptors." In *Making Value, Making Meaning: Techné in the Pre-Columbian World,* ed. Cathy L. Costin, 391–431. Washington, D.C.: Dumbarton Oaks Research Library and Collection, 2016.

Houston, Stephen D. "Gladiatrix." *Maya Decipherment: A Weblog on the Ancient Maya Script* (2016). Accessed June 12, 2016. https://decipherment.wordpress.com/2016/06/08/gladiatrix/.

Houston, Stephen D., and Takeshi Inomata. *The Classic Maya.* Cambridge: Cambridge University Press, 2009.

Houston, Stephen D., and Simon Martin. "Let Thy Glyphs Be Few: Abbreviations in Maya Writing." *Maya Decipherment: A Weblog on the Ancient Maya Script* (2011). Accessed Mar. 6, 2017. http://decipherment.wordpress.com/2011/01/16/let-thy-glyphs-be-few-abbreviations-in-maya-writing/.

Houston, Stephen D., and Patricia McAnany. "Bodies and Blood: Critiquing Social Construction in Maya Archaeology." *Journal of Anthropological Archaeology* 22 (2003): 26–41.

Houston, Stephen D., and Andrew Scherer. "La ofrenda máxima: El sacrificio humano en la parte central del área maya." In *Nuevas perspectivas sobre el sacrificio humano entre los Mexicas,* ed. Leonardo López Luján and Guilhem Olivier, 167–91. Mexico City: Universidad Nacional Autónoma de México, 2010.

Houston, Stephen D., and David Stuart. "Of Gods, Glyphs, and Kings: Divinity and Rulership Among the Classic Maya." *Antiquity* 70 (1996): 289–312.

Houston, Stephen D., and David Stuart. " 'Hastily but Carelessly Torn': Maya Glyphs from Palenque in Montrose, Scotland." In *Decorum and Experience: Essays in Ancient Culture for John Baines,* ed. Elizabeth Frood and Angela McDonald, 226–31. Oxford: Griffith Institute, 2013.

Houston, Stephen D., and Alexandre Tokovinine. "Caracol at Cambridge." *Maya Decipherment: A Weblog on the Ancient Maya Script* (2016). Accessed Mar. 5, 2017. https://decipherment.wordpress.com/2016/09/12/caracol-at-cambridge/.

Houston, Stephen D., John Robertson, and David Stuart. *Quality and Quantity in Glyphic Nouns and Adjectives.* Research Reports on Ancient Maya Writing 47. Washington, D.C.: Center for Maya Research, 2001.

Houston, Stephen D., David Stuart, and Karl Taube. "Folk Classification from Classic Maya Pottery Texts." *American Anthropologist* 91 (1989): 720–26.

Houston, Stephen D., David Stuart, and Karl Taube. *The Memory of Bones: Body, Being, and Experience Among the Classic Maya.* Austin: University of Texas Press, 2006.

Houston, Stephen D., David Stuart, Claudia Woolley, and Lori Wright. "A Death Monument: Dos Pilas Throne 1." Ms. in possession of author, 1991.

Hubert, Henri, and Marcel Mauss. *Sacrifice: Its Nature and Function.* Chicago: University of Chicago Press, 1964.

Hull, Kerry M. "An Abbreviated Dictionary of Ch'orti' Maya." Final report, Foundation for the Advancement of Mesoamerican Studies, 2005.

Hull, Kerry M. "Poetic Tenacity: A Diachronic Study of Kennings in Maya Languages." In *Parallel Worlds: Genre, Discourse, and Poetics in Contemporary, Colonial, and Classic Maya Literature,* ed. Kerry M.

Hull and Michael D. Carrasco, 73–122. Boulder: University Press of Colorado, 2011.

Hurwit, Jeffrey M. "The Words in the Image: Orality, Literacy, and Early Greek Art." *Word and Image* 6 (1990): 180–97.

Hutton, Patrick H. *Philippe Ariès and the Politics of French Cultural History.* Amherst: University of Massachusetts Press, 2004.

Inomata, Takeshi. "The Last Day of a Fortified Classic Maya Center: Archaeological Investigations at Aguateca, Guatemala." *Ancient Mesoamerica* 8 (1997): 337–51.

Inomata, Takeshi, and Markus Eberl. "Stone Ornaments and Other Stone Artifacts." In *Life and Politics at the Royal Court of Aguateca: Artifacts, Analytical Data, and Synthesis,* ed. Takeshi Inomata and Daniela Triadan, 84–117. Salt Lake City: University of Utah Press, 2014.

Ishihara-Brito, Reiko, and Karl A. Taube. "Anthropomorphic Whistle." In *Ancient Maya Art at Dumbarton Oaks,* ed. Joanne Pillsbury, Miriam Doutriaux, Reiko Ishihara-Brito, and Alexandre Tokovinine, 426–30. Pre-Columbian Art at Dumbarton Oaks 4. Washington, D.C.: Dumbarton Oaks Research Library and Collection, 2012.

Jenkins, Ian, and Victoria Turner. *The Greek Body.* Los Angeles: J. Paul Getty Museum, 2009.

Jensen, Frances, and Amy E. Nutt. *The Teenage Brain: A Neuroscientist's Survival Guide to Raising Adolescents and Young Adults.* New York: Harper, 2015.

Jones, Alan. "Dental Transfigurements in Borneo." *British Dental Journal* 191 (2001): 98–102.

Jones, Christopher, and Linton Satterthwaite. *Tikal Report No. 33, Part A: The Monuments and Inscriptions of Tikal: The Carved Monuments.* University Museum Monograph 44. Philadelphia: University Museum, University of Pennsylvania, 1982.

Jones, Grant D. *The Conquest of the Last Maya Kingdom.* Stanford, Calif.: Stanford University Press, 1998.

Joyce, Rosemary A. *Gender and Power in Prehispanic Mesoamerica.* Austin: University of Texas Press, 2000.

Joyce, Rosemary A. "Girling the Girl and Boying the Boy: The Production of Adulthood in Ancient Mesoamerica." *World Archaeology* 31 (2000): 473–83.

Joyce, Rosemary A. "A Precolumbian Gaze: Male Sexuality Among the Ancient Maya." In *Archaeologies of Sexuality,* ed. Robert A. Schmidt and Barbara L. Voss, 263–86. London: Routledge, 2000.

Joyce, Rosemary A. *Ancient Bodies, Ancient Lives: Sex, Gender, and Archaeology.* London: Thames and Hudson, 2009.

Joyce, Rosemary A. "Archaeology of Gender in Mesoamerican Societies." In *The Oxford Handbook of Mesoamerican Archaeology,* ed. Deborah L. Nichols and Christopher A. Pool, 663–72. Oxford: Oxford University Press, 2012.

Just, Bryan R. *Dancing into Dreams: Maya Vase Painting of the Ik' Kingdom.* Princeton: Princeton University Art Museum, 2012.

Kammen, Michael. "Changing Perceptions of the Life Cycle in American Thought and Culture." *Proceedings of the Massachusetts Historical Society* 91 (1979): 35–66.

Kan, Sergei. *Symbolic Immortality: The Tlingit Potlatch of the Nineteenth Century.* 2nd ed. Seattle: University of Washington Press, 2016.

Karttunen, Frances. *An Analytical Dictionary of Nahuatl.* Norman: University of Oklahoma Press, 1992.

Kaufman, Terrence. *El proto-Tzeltal-Tzotzil: Fonología comparada y diccionario reconstruido.* Centro de Estudios Mayas Cuaderno 5. Mexico City: Universidad Nacional Autónoma de México, 1998.

Kaufman, Terrence S. "A Preliminary Mayan Etymological Dictionary." (2003). Accessed Mar. 6, 2017. http://www.famsi.org/reports/01051/pmed.pdf.

Kaufman, Terrence S., and W. Norman. "An Outline of Proto-Cholan Phonology, Morphology, and Vocabulary." In *Phoneticism in Mayan Hieroglyphic Writing,* ed. John S. Justeson and Lyle Campbell, 77–166. Institute for Mesoamerican Studies Monographs 9. Albany: State University of New York at Albany, 1984.

Keesing, Roger M. "Prologue: Toward a Multidimensional Understanding of Male Initiation." In *Rituals of Manhood: Male Initiation in Papua New Guinea,* ed. Gilbert Herdt, 1–43. New Brunswick, N.J.: Transaction, 1998.

Keller, Kathryn C., and Plácido Luciano Gerónimo. *Diccionario Chontal de Tabasco.* Tucson: Summer Institute of Linguistics, 1997.

Kelley, David H. *Deciphering the Maya Script.* Austin: University of Texas Press, 1976.

Kellogg, Susan. "The Woman's Room: Some Aspects of Gender Relations in Tenochtitlan in the Late

Pre-Hispanic Period." *Ethnohistory* 42 (1995): 563–76.

Kennell, Nigel M. *Ephebeia: A Register of Greek Cities with Citizen Training Systems in the Hellenistic and Roman Periods.* Nikephoros-Beihefte 12. Hildesheim, Germany: Olms-Weidmann, 2006.

Kett, Joseph F. *Rites of Passage: Adolescence in America 1790 to the Present.* New York: Basic, 1977.

Keuls, Eva. C. *The Reign of the Phallus: Sexual Politics in Ancient Athens.* New York: Harper and Row, 1985.

Kidder, Alfred V. *The Artifacts of Uaxactun, Guatemala.* Carnegie Institution of Washington 576. Washington, D.C.: Carnegie Institution of Washington, 1947.

Kimball, Geoffrey. "Aztec Homosexuality: The Textual Evidence." *Journal of Homosexuality* 26 (1993): 7–24.

Kimmel, Michael. *Guyland: The Perilous World Where Boys Become Men.* New York: Harper, 2008.

Kindlon, Dan, and Michael Thompson. *Raising Cain: Protecting the Emotional Life of Boys.* New York: Ballantine, 2000.

Kirkpatrick, John. "Taure'are'a: A Liminal Category and Passage to Marquesan Adulthood." *Ethos* 15 (1987): 382–405.

Kleijwegt, Marc. *Ancient Youth: The Ambiguity of Youth and the Absence of Adolescence in Greco-Roman Society.* Amsterdam: J. C. Gieben, 1991.

Klein, Cecelia F. "None of the Above: Gender Ambiguity in Nahua Ideology." In *Gender in Pre-Hispanic America,* ed. Cecelia F. Klein, 183–253. Washington, D.C.: Dumbarton Oaks Research Library and Collection, 2001.

Klein, Cecelia F. "Archaeology of Androgyny." *The International Encyclopedia of Human Sexuality,* 1–111. Malden, Mass.: Wiley-Blackwell, 2015.

Knapp, Bernard. "Who's Come a Long Way Baby? Masculinist Approaches to a Gendered Archaeology." *Archaeological Dialogues* 5 (1998): 91–106.

Knowles, Susan M. "A Descriptive Grammar of Chontal Maya (San Carlos Dialect)." Ph.D. diss., Tulane University, 1984.

Knowlton, Timothy. "Diphrastic Kennings in Mayan Hieroglyphic Literature." *Mexicon* 24 (2002): 9–13.

Knub, Julie N., Simone Thun, and Christophe Helmke. "The Divine Rite of Kings: An Analysis of Classic Maya Impersonation Statements." In *The Maya and Their Sacred Narratives: Text and Context in Maya Mythologies,* ed. Geneviève Le Fort, Raphaël Gardiol, Sebastian Matteo, and Christophe Helmke, 177–95. Acta Mesoamericana 20. Markt Schwaben, Germany: Anton Saurwein, 2009.

Koch-Harnack, Gundel. *Knabenliebe und Tiergeschenke: Ihre Bedeutung im päderastischen Erziehungssystem Athens.* Berlin: Gebrüder Mann, 1983.

Kockelman, Paul. "Inalienable Possession as Grammatical Category and Discourse Pattern." *Studies in Language* 33 (2009): 25–68.

Kohlberg, Lawrence. *Essays on Moral Development, Volume I: The Philosophy of Moral Development.* San Francisco: Harper and Row, 1981.

Kolbert, Elizabeth. "The Terrible Teens: What's Wrong with Them?" *New Yorker* Aug. 31 (2015): 83–86.

Komter, Aafke E. "Introduction." In *The Gift: An Interdisciplinary Perspective,* ed. Aafke Komter, 3–12. Amsterdam: Amsterdam University Press, 1996.

Komter, Aafke E., ed. *Social Solidarity and the Gift.* Cambridge: Cambridge University Press, 2005.

Konstan, David. *Beauty: The Fortunes of an Ancient Greek Idea.* Oxford: Oxford University Press, 2014.

Korbin, Jill E. "Children, Childhoods, Violence." *Annual Review of Anthropology* 32 (2003): 431–46.

Kozak, Leslie. "Greek Government and Education: Re-Examining the Ephēbeia and Education." In *A Companion to Greek Government,* ed. Hans Beck, 302–16. Malden, Mass.: Wiley, 2013.

Kraemer, Helena C., Janice R. Horvat, Charles Doering, and Patrick R. McGinnis. "Male Chimpanzee Development Focusing on Adolescence: Integration of Behavioral with Physiological Changes." *Primates* 23 (1982): 393–405.

Kramer, Karen L. *Maya Children: Helpers at the Farm.* Cambridge, Mass.: Harvard University Press, 2005.

Kratz, Corrine A. *Affecting Performance: Meaning, Movement, and Experience in Okiek Women's Initiation.* Washington, D.C.: Smithsonian Institution Press, 1993.

Kurke, Leslie. *The Traffic in Praise: Pindar and the Poetics of Social Economy.* Ithaca, N.Y.: Cornell University Press, 1991.

Kurke, Leslie. "Inventing the Hetaira: Sex, Politics, and Discursive Conflict in Archaic Greece." *Classical Antiquity* 16 (1997): 106–50.

Lacadena García-Gallo, Alfonso. "El anillo jeroglífico del juego de pelota de Oxkintok." In *Oxkintok 4: Misión Arqueológica de España en México, Proyecto Oxkintok Año 1990,* ed. Miguel Rivera Dorado, 177–84. Madrid: Ministerio de Cultura, 1992.

Lacadena García-Gallo, Alfonso. "Passive Voice in Classic Mayan Texts: CV-*h*-C-*aj* and -*n*-*aj* Constructions." In *The Linguistics of Maya Writing,* ed. Søren Wichmann, 165–94. Salt Lake City: University of Utah Press, 2004.

Lacadena García-Gallo, Alfonso, and Søren Wichmann. "On the Representation of the Glottal Stop in Maya Writing." In *The Linguistics of Maya Writing*, ed. Søren Wichmann, 100–162. Salt Lake City: University of Utah Press, 2004.

Laes, Christian, and Johan Strubbe. *Youth in the Roman Empire: The Young and the Restless Years?* Cambridge: Cambridge University Press, 2014.

La Fontaine, J. S. *Initiation.* Manchester: Manchester University Press, 1986.

LaGamma, Alisa. "Eternal Ancestors: The Art of the Central African Reliquary." In *Eternal Ancestors: The Art of the Central African Reliquary*, ed. Alisa LaGamma, 2–31. New York: Metropolitan Museum of Art, 2007.

Langdon, Susan. "The Awkward Age: Art and Maturation in Early Greece." In *Constructions of Childhood in Ancient Greece and Italy*, ed. Ada Cohen and Jeremy B. Rutter, 173–91. *Hesperia* Suppl. 41. Athens: American School of Classical Studies at Athens, 2007.

Laporte, Juan Pedro, and Vilma Fialko. "Un reencuentro con Mundo Perdido, Tikal, Guatemala." *Ancient Mesoamerica* 6 (1995): 41–94.

Las Casas, Bartolomé de. *Apologética historia sumaria cuanto a las cualidades, disposición, descripción, cielo y suelo destas tierras, y condiciones naturales, policías, repúblicas, manera de vivir e costumbres de las gentes destas Indias Occidentales, cuyo imperio soberano pertenece a los Reyes de Castilla*, ed. Edmundo O'Gorman. 2 vols. Mexico City: Universidad Nacional Autónoma de México, 1967.

Lattas, Andrew. "Poetics of Space and Sexual Economies of Power: Gender and the Politics of Male Identity in West New Britain." *Ethos* 18 (1990): 71–102.

Laughlin, Robert M. *The Great Tzotzil Dictionary of San Lorenzo Zinacantán.* Smithsonian Contributions to Anthropology 19. Washington, D.C.: Smithsonian Institution Press, 1975.

Laughlin, Robert M. *The Great Tzotzil Dictionary of Santa Domingo Zinacantán.* 3 vols. Smithsonian Contributions to Anthropology 31. Washington, D.C.: Smithsonian Institution Press, 1988.

Lave, Jean, and Étienne Wenger. *Situated Learning: Legitimate Peripheral Participation.* Cambridge: Cambridge University Press, 1991.

Law, Danny. *Language Contact, Inherited Similarity, and Social Difference: The Story of Linguistic Interaction in the Maya Lowlands.* Current Issues in Linguistic Theory 328. Amsterdam: John Benjamins, 2014.

Le Breton, David. "The Anthropology of Adolescent Risk-Taking Behaviours." *Body and Society* 10 (2004): 1–15.

León-Portilla, Miguel. *La filosofía náhuatl estudiada en sus fuentes.* Mexico City: Universidad Nacional Autónoma de México, 1979.

Levy, Daniel S. "The Life Expectancies of Colonial Maryland Legislators." *Historical Methods: A Journal of Quantitative and Interdisciplinary History* 20 (1987): 17–27.

Lewis-Williams, David. *The Mind in the Cave: Consciousness and the Origins of Art.* London: Thames and Hudson, 2004.

Lincoln, Charles E. "Ethnicity and Social Organization at Chichen Itza, Yucatan, Mexico." Ph.D. diss., Harvard University, 1990.

Lissarrague, François. *The Aesthetics of the Greek Banquet: Images of Wine and Ritual.* Princeton: Princeton University Press, 1990.

Lombard, Anne S. *Making Manhood: Growing Up Male in Colonial New England.* Cambridge, Mass.: Harvard University Press, 2003.

Lombardo, Michael P. "On the Evolution of Sport." *Evolutionary Psychology* 10 (2012): 1–28.

Long, Kathleen P. *Hermaphrodites in Renaissance Europe.* Aldershot, England: Ashgate, 2006.

Longyear, John, III. *Archaeological Investigations in El Salvador.* Memoirs of the Peabody Museum of Archaeology and Ethnology 9, no. 2, Harvard University. Cambridge, Mass.: Harvard University, 1944.

Longyear, John, III. *Copan Ceramics: A Study of Southeastern Maya Pottery.* Washington, D.C.: Carnegie Institution of Washington, 1952.

Looper, Matthew. "Women-Men (and Men-Women): Classic Maya Rulers and the Third Gender." In *Ancient Maya Women*, ed. Traci Ardren, 171–202. Walnut Creek, Calif.: Altamira, 2002.

López Austin, Alfredo. *The Human Body and Ideology: Concepts of the Ancient Nahuas.* 2 vols. Salt Lake City: University of Utah Press, 1988.

López Austin, Alfredo. "La magia y la advinación en la tradición Mesoamericana." *Arqueología mexicana* 69 (2004): 20–29.

Loughmiller-Cardinal, Jennifer A., and Dmitri Zagorevski. "Maya Flasks: The 'Home' of Tobacco and Godly Substances." *Ancient Mesoamerica* 27 (2016): 1–11.

Loughmiller-Newman, Jennifer A. "The Analytic Reconciliation of Classic Mayan Elite Pottery: Squaring Pottery Function with Form, Adornment, and Residual Contents." Ph.D. diss., State University of New York at Albany, 2012.

Lounsbury, Floyd G. "Astronomical Knowledge and Its Uses at Bonampak, Mexico." In *Archaeoastronomy in the New World,* ed. A. F. Aveni, 143–68. Cambridge: Cambridge University Press, 1982.

Love, Bruce. *Maya Shamanism Today: Connecting with the Cosmos in Rural Yucatan.* San Francisco: Precolumbia Mesoweb, 2012.

Love, Bruce. "Rezar and K'ex, San Silverio, Quintana Roo, 2012." *Mesoweb* (2012). Accessed Jan. 31, 2015. http://www.mesoweb.com.

Lowie, Robert H. *Primitive Society.* New York: Liverwright, 1947.

Machiavelli, Niccolò. *The Prince.* Trans. T. Parks. London: Penguin, 2009.

MacLeod, Barbara. "Deciphering the Primary Standard Sequence." Ph.D. diss., University of Texas, Austin, 1990.

MacLeod, Barbara, and Yuriy Polyukhovich. "Deciphering the Initial Sign." In *Sourcebook for the XXIXth Maya Meetings,* ed. David Stuart, 166–74. Austin: University of Texas, 2005.

MacLeod, Barbara, and Dorie Reents-Budet. "The Art of Calligraphy: Image and Meaning." In *Painting the Maya Universe: Royal Ceramics of the Classic Period,* by Dorie Reents-Budet, 106–63. Durham, N.C.: Duke University Press, 1994.

Maler, Teobert. *Researches in the Central Portion of the Usumatsintla Valley: Reports of Explorations for the Museum. Part 2.* Memoirs of the Peabody Museum of American Archaeology and Ethnology 2, no. 2, Harvard University. Cambridge, Mass.: Harvard University, 1903.

Marcus, Joyce, and Kent V. Flannery. *Zapotec Civilization: How Urban Society Evolved in Mexico's Oaxaca Valley.* London: Thames and Hudson, 1996.

Martin, Richard P. "Hesiod, Odysseus, and the Instruction of Princes." *Transactions of the American Philological Association* 114 (1984): 29–48.

Martin, Simon. "Tikal's 'Star War' Against Naranjo." In *Eighth Palenque Mesa Redonda, 1993,* ed. Martha Macri and Jan MacHargue, 223–35. San Francisco: Pre-Columbian Art Research Institute, 1996.

Martin, Simon. "The Queen of Middle Classic Tikal." *Pre-Columbian Art Research Newsletter* 27 (1999): 4–5.

Martin, Simon. "Court and Realm: Architectural Signatures in the Classic Maya Southern Lowlands." In *Royal Courts of the Ancient Maya, Volume 1,* ed. Takeshi Inomata and Stephen Houston, 168–94. Boulder, Colo.: Westview, 2001.

Martin, Simon. "The Baby Jaguar: An Exploration of Its Identity and Origins in Maya Art and Writing." In *La organización social entre los mayas prehispánicos, coloniales y modernos: Memoria de la Tercera Mesa Redonda de Palenque I,* ed. Vera Tiesler Blos, Rach Cobos, and Merle Greene Robertson, 49–78. Mexico City: Instituto Nacional de Antropología e Historia, 2002.

Martin, Simon. "In Line of the Founder: A View of Dynastic Politics at Tikal." In *Tikal: Dynasties, Foreigners, and Affairs of State,* ed. Jeremy A. Sabloff, 3–45. Santa Fe, N. Mex.: School of American Research, 2003.

Martin, Simon. "Moral-Reforma y la cotienda por el oriente de Tabasco." *Arqueología mexicana* (2003): 44–47.

Martin, Simon. "A Broken Sky: The Ancient Name of Yaxchilan as *Pa' Chan.*" *PARI Journal* 5 (2004): 1–7.

Martin, Simon. "Carved Bowl." In *Ancient Maya Art at Dumbarton Oaks,* ed. Joanne Pillsbury, Miriam Doutriaux, Reiko Ishihara-Brito, and Alexandre Tokovinine, 408–19. Pre-Columbian Art at Dumbarton Oaks 4. Washington, D.C.: Dumbarton Oaks Research Library and Collection, 2012.

Martin, Simon. "Hieroglyphs from the Painted Pyramid: The Epigraphy of Chiik Nahb Structure Sub 1–4, Calakmul, Mexico." *Maya Archaeology 2,* ed. Charles Golden, Stephen Houston, and Joel Skidmore, 60–81. San Francisco: Precolumbia Mesoweb, 2013.

Martin, Simon. "The Classic Maya Polity: An Epigraphic Approach to a Pre-Hispanic Political System." Ph.D. diss., University College London, 2014.

Martin, Simon. "Early Classic Co-Rulers on Tikal Temple VI." *Maya Decipherment: A Weblog on the Ancient Maya Script* (2014). Accessed Dec. 3, 2014. http://decipherment.wordpress.com/2014/11/22/early-classic-co-rulers-on-tikal-temple-vi/.

Martin, Simon. "The Old Man of the Maya Universe: A Unitary Dimension Within Ancient Maya Religion." In *Maya Archaeology 3,* ed. Charles Golden, Stephen Houston, and Joel Skidmore, 186–227. San Francisco: Precolumbia Mesoweb, 2015.

Martin, Simon, and Nikolai Grube. *Chronicle of the Maya Kings and Queens: Deciphering the Dynasties of the Classic Maya.* London: Thames and Hudson, 2008.

Martos López, A. "The Discovery of Plan de Ayutla, Mexico." In *Maya Archaeology 1,* ed. Charles Golden, Stephen Houston, and Joel Skidmore, 60–75. San Francisco: Precolumbia Mesoweb, 2009.

Mathews, Peter. "Notes on the Dynastic Sequence of Bonampak, Part 1." In *Third Palenque Round Table, 1978, Part 2*, ed. Merle Greene Robertson, 60–73. Austin: University of Texas Press, 1980.

Mathews, Peter. *Corpus of Maya Hieroglyphic Inscriptions, Volume 6, Part 1: Tonina.* Cambridge, Mass.: Peabody Museum of Archaeology and Ethnology, Harvard University, 1983.

Matlock, James G. "Alternate-Generation Equivalence and the Recycling of Souls: Amerindian Rebirth in Global Perspective." In *Amerindian Rebirth: Reincarnation Belief Among North American Indians and Inuit*, ed. Antonia Mills and Richard Slobodin, 263–83. Toronto: University of Toronto Press, 1994.

Matos Moctezuma, Eduardo, and Leonardo López Luján. *Escultura monumental mexica.* Mexico City: Fondo de Cultura Económica, 2012.

Maudslay, Alfred P. *Archaeology: Biologia Centrali Americana, or, Contributions to the Knowledge of the Fauna and Flora of Mexico and Central America.* London: R. H. Porter and Dulau, 1889–1902.

Mauss, Marcel. *The Gift: The Form and Reason for Exchange in Archaic Societies.* Trans. Wilfred D. Halls. New York: W. W. Norton, 1990.

Maxwell, Judith M., and Robert M. Hill, II. *Kaqchikel Chronicles: The Definitive Edition.* Austin: University of Texas Press, 2006.

Mayer, Karl H. *Maya Monuments: Sculptures of Unknown Provenance, Supplement 4.* Graz: Academic, 1995.

McCafferty, Geoffrey G., and Sharisse D. McCafferty. "Crafting the Body Beautiful: Performing Social Identity at Santa Isabel, Nicaragua." In *Mesoamerican Figurines: Small-Scale Indices of Large-Scale Social Phenomena*, ed. Christina T. Halperin, Katherine A. Faust, Rhonda Taube, and Aurore Giguet, 183–204. Gainesville: University Press of Florida, 2009.

McCafferty, Sharisse D., and Geoffrey G. McCafferty. "Alternative and Ambiguous Gender Identities in Postclassic Central Mexico." In *Que(er)ying Archaeology: Proceedings of the 30th Annual Chacmool Conference*, ed. Susan Terendy, Natasha Lyons, and Michelle Janse-Smekal, 196–206. Calgary: Archaeological Association, University of Calgary Press, 2009.

McGinn, Thomas A. J. *The Economy of Prostitution in the Roman World: A Study of Social History and the Brothel.* Ann Arbor: University of Michigan Press, 2004.

McKinnon, Susan, and Fenella Cannell, eds. *Vital Relations: Modernity and the Persistent Life of Kinship.* Santa Fe, N. Mex.: SAR Press, 2013.

McNiven, Timothy J. "Behaving Like a Child: Immature Gestures in Athenian Vase Painting." In *Constructions of Childhood in Ancient Greece and Italy*, ed. Ada Cohen and Jeremy B. Rutter, 85–99. *Hesperia* Suppl. 41. Athens: American School of Classical Studies at Athens, 2007.

Mead, Margaret. *Coming of Age in Samoa: A Psychological Study of Primitive Youth for Western Civilisation.* New York: William Morrow, 1928.

Meehan, Courtney L., and Alyssa N. Crittenden, eds. *Childhood: Origins, Evolution, and Implications.* Santa Fe, N. Mex.: SAR Press, 2016.

Mena, Ramón. *Catálogo del salón secreto: culto al falo.* Mexico City: Museo Nacional de Arqueología, Historia y Etnografía, 1926.

Merwin, Raymond E., and George C. Vaillant. *The Ruins of Holmul, Guatemala.* Memoirs of the Peabody Museum of Archaeology and Ethnology 3, no. 2, Harvard University. Cambridge, Mass.: Harvard University, 1932.

Mesquida, Christian G., and Neil I. Wiener. "Male Age Composition and the Severity of Conflicts." *Politics in the Life Sciences* 18 (1999): 181–89.

Metcalf, Peter, and Richard Huntington. *Celebrations of Death: The Anthropology of Mortuary Ritual.* 2nd ed. Cambridge: Cambridge University Press, 1991.

Miles, Susanna W. "The Sixteenth Century Pokom-Maya: A Documentary Analysis of Social Structure and Archaeological Setting." *Transactions of the American Philosophical Society*, n.s. 47 (1957): 735–81.

Miles, Susanna W. "Summary of Preconquest Ethnology of the Guatemala-Chiapas Highlands and Pacific Slopes." In *Handbook of Middle American Indians, Volume 2*, ed. Robert Wauchope and Gordon R. Willey, 276–87. Austin: University of Texas Press, 1965.

Miller, Lucien. "Children of the Dream: The Adolescent World in Cao Xueqin's *Honglou Men*." In *Chinese Views of Childhood*, ed. Anne B. Kinnery, 219–47. Honolulu: University of Hawai'i Press, 1995.

Miller, Mary E. *The Murals of Bonampak.* Princeton: Princeton University Press, 1986.

Miller, Mary E., and Claudia Brittenham. *The Spectacle of the Late Maya Court: Reflections on the Murals of Bonampak.* Austin: University of Texas Press, 2013.

Miller, Mary E., and Stephen D. Houston. "Algunos comentarios sobre las inscripciones jeroglíficas en las pinturas de la estructura 1 de Bonampak." In *La pintura mural prehispánica en México II, Área maya, Tomo II(2): Bonampak, Estudios*, ed. Leticia Staines Cicero, 245–54. Mexico City: Instituto de

Investigaciones Estéticas, Universidad Nacional Autónoma de México, 1998.

Miller, Mary, and Simon Martin. *Courtly Art of the Ancient Maya.* San Francisco: Fine Arts Museums of San Francisco, 2004.

Miller, William I. *Humiliation.* Ithaca, N.Y.: Cornell University Press, 1993.

Mills, Barbara J. "The Establishment and Defeat of Hierarchy: Inalienable Possessions and the History of Collective Prestige Structures in the Pueblo Southwest." *American Anthropologist* 106 (2004): 238–51.

Mitchell, Alexandre G. *Greek Vase-Painting and the Origins of Visual Humour.* Cambridge: Cambridge University Press, 2009.

Mitchell-Boyask, Robin. "Euripedes' *Hippolytus* and the Trials of Manhood (The Epehebia?)." In *Rites of Passage in Ancient Greece: Literature, Religion, Society,* ed. Mark W. Padilla, 42–66. Lewisburg, Penn.: Bucknell University Press, 1999.

Moffitt, Terrie E. "Adolescence-Limited and Life-Course Persistent Antisocial Behavior: A Developmental Taxonomy." *Psychological Review* 100 (1993): 674–701.

Moffitt, Terrie E. "The New Look of Behavioral Genetics in Developmental Psychopathology: Gene–Environment Interplay in Antisocial Behaviors." *Psychological Bulletin* 131 (2005): 533–54.

Moholy-Nagy, Hattula. *Tikal Report No. 27, Part B: The Artifacts of Tikal: Utilitarian Artifacts and Unworked Material.* University Museum Monograph 118. Philadelphia: University of Pennsylvania Museum of Archaeology and Anthropology, 2003.

Moholy-Nagy, Hattula. *Tikal Report No. 27, Part A: The Artifacts of Tikal: Ornamental and Ceremonial Artifacts and Unworked Material.* University Museum Monograph 127. Philadelphia: University of Pennsylvania Museum of Archaeology and Anthropology, 2008.

Monod Becquelin, Aurore, Valentia Vapnarsky, Cédric Becquey, and Alain Breton. "Paralelismo, varientes y variaciones: Decir, contar y rezar la diversidad maya." In *Figuras mayas de la diversidad,* ed. Aurore Monod Becquelin, Alain Breton, and Mario Humberto Ruz Sosa, 101–56. Mexico City: Universidad Nacional Autónoma de México, Instituto de Investigaciones Filológicas, 2010.

Moore, Alexander. "Initiation Rites in a Mesoamerican Cargo System: Men and Boys, Judas and the Bull." *Journal of Latin American Lore* 5 (1979): 55–81.

Moorrees, Coenraad F. A., Elizabeth A. Fanning, and Edward E. Hunt, Jr. "Age Variation of Formation Stages in Permanent Teeth." *Journal of Dental Research* 42 (1963): 1490–502.

Munafò, Marcus R., Binnaz Yalcin, Safron A. Willis-Owen, and Jonathan Flint. "Association of the Dopamine D4 Receptor (DRD4) Gene and Approach-Related Personality Traits: Meta-analysis and New Data." *Biological Psychiatry* 63 (2008): 197–206.

Murphy, William P. "Secret Knowledge as Property and Power in Kpelle Society." *Africa* 50 (1980): 193–207.

Murray, Gail S. "Children and Culture." In *Jacksonian and Antebellum Age: People and Perspectives,* ed. Mark R. Cheathem, 35–54. Santa Barbara, Calif.: ABC-CLIO, 2008.

Nasrullah, Muazzam, Sana Muazzam, Zulfiqar A. Bhutta, and Anita Raj. "Girl Child Marriage and Its Effect on Fertility in Pakistan: Findings from Pakistan Demographic and Health Survey, 2006–2007." *Maternal and Child Health Journal* 18 (2014): 534–43.

Nederman, Cary J. "The Mirror Crack'd: The Speculum Principum as Political and Social Criticism in the Late Middle Ages." *The European Legacy* 3 (1998): 18–38.

Neer, Richard T. *Style and Politics in Athenian Vase-Painting: The Craft of Democracy, ca. 530–460 B.C.E.* Cambridge: Cambridge University Press, 2002.

Neer, Richard T. *The Emergence of the Classical Style in Greek Sculpture.* Chicago: University of Chicago Press, 2010.

Neer, Richard T. *Greek Art and Archaeology, c. 2500–c. 150 B.C.E.: A New History.* London: Thames and Hudson, 2012.

Neubauer, John. *The Fin-de-Siècle Culture of Adolescence.* New Haven: Yale University Press, 1992.

Newton-Fisher, Nicholas E. "Female Coalitions Against Male Aggression in Wild Chimpanzees of the Budongo Forest." *International Journal of Primatology* 27 (2006): 1589–99.

Nicholson, Henry B. "Religion in Pre-Hispanic Central Mexico." In *Handbook of Middle American Indians, Volume 10, Part 1: Archaeology of Northern Mesoamerica,* ed. Robert Wauchope, Gordon Ekholm, and Ignacio Bernal, 395–446. Austin: University of Texas Press, 1971.

Norbeck, Edward. "Age-Grading in Japan." *American Anthropologist* 52 (1953): 373–84.

Olivier, Guilhem. *Mockeries and Metamorphoses of an Aztec God: Tezcatlipoca, "Lord of the Smoking Mirror."* Boulder: University Press of Colorado, 2003.

Olivier, Guilhem. "Homosexualidad y prostitución entre los nahuas y otros pueblos del Pósclasico." In *Historia de la vida cotidiana en Mexico, Volume 1: Mésoamerica y los ámbitos indígenas de la Nueva España,* ed. Pablo Escalante Gonzalbo, 301–38. Mexico City: Colegio de México/Fondo de Cultura Económica, 2004.

Olivier, Guilhem. "The Word, Sacrifice, and Divination: Aztec Man in the Realm of the Gods." In *The Adventure of the Human Intellect: Self, Society, and the Divine in Ancient World Cultures,* ed. Kurt A. Raaflaub, 216–38. Malden, Mass.: Wiley-Blackwell, 2016.

O'Neil, Megan E. "Anthropomorphic Whistle." In *Ancient Maya Art at Dumbarton Oaks,* ed. Joanne Pillsbury, Miriam Doutriaux, Reiko Ishihara-Brito, and Alexandre Tokovinine, 404–9. Pre-Columbian Art at Dumbarton Oaks 4. Washington, D.C.: Dumbarton Oaks Research Library and Collection, 2012.

Orea Magaña, Haydée, Gilberto Buitrago Sandoval, and Olga L. González Correa. "Recientes intervenciones en Bonampak: Hacia una nueva lectura de los murales en el Templo de las Pinturas." *Intervención* 2 (2011): 58–65.

Orellana, Sandra L. *The Tzutujil Mayas: Continuity and Change, 1250–1630.* Norman: University of Oklahoma Press, 1984.

Osteen, Mark. "Introduction: Questions of the Gift." In *The Question of the Gift: Essays Across Disciplines,* ed. Mark Osteen, 1–41. London: Routledge, 2002.

Pannock, Caroline D. *Bonds of Blood: Gender, Lifecycle, and Sacrifice in Aztec Culture.* Basingstoke, England: Palgrave Macmillan, 2008.

Papalexandrou, Nassos. *The Visual Poetics of Power: Warriors, Youths, and Tripods in Early Greece.* Lanham, Md.: Lexington, 2005.

Paredes Maury, Sophia. "Surviving in the Rainforest: The Realities of Looting in the Rural Villages of El Petén, Guatemala." Report to the Foundation for Mesoamerican Research. Accessed Dec. 10, 2014. http://www.famsi.org/reports/95096/.

Parker, Geoffrey. *Philip II.* 3rd ed. Chicago: Open Court, 1995.

Parkin, Robert. "Reincarnation and Alternate Generation Equivalence in Middle India." *Journal of Anthropological Research* 44 (1988): 1–20.

Parsons, Elsie C. "Some Aztec and Pueblo Comparisons." *American Anthropologist* 35 (1933): 611–31.

Paul, Benjamin, and Lois Paul. "The Life Cycle." In *Heritage of Conquest: The Ethnology of Middle America,* ed. Sol Tax, 174–92. Glencoe, Ill.: Free Press, 1952.

Pendergast, David. *Excavations at Actun Polbiche, Belize.* Archaeology Monograph 1. Toronto: Royal Ontario Museum, 1974.

Pérez, Vitalino, Federico García, Felipe Martínez, and Jeremías López. *Diccionario Ch'orti, Jocotán, Chiquimula: Ch'orti'–Español.* Antigua, Guatemala: Proyecto Lingüístico Marroquin, 1996.

Pfeiffer, John E. *The Creative Explosion: An Inquiry into the Origins of Art and Religion.* New York: Harper and Row, 1982.

Piaget, Jean, and Bärbel Inhelder. *The Psychology of the Child.* New York: Basic, 1969.

Piña Chán, Román. *Jaina, la casa en el agua.* Mexico City: Instituto Nacional de Antropología e Historia, 1966.

Pindborg, J. J., I. J. Möller, and I. Effendi. "Dental Mutilations Among Villagers in Central Java and Bali." *Community Dentistry and Oral Epidemiology* 3 (1975): 190–93.

Pipher, Mary. *Reviving Ophelia: Saving the Selves of Adolescent Girls.* New York: Riverhead, 2005.

Pitarch, Pedro. *The Jaguar and the Priest: An Ethnography of Tzeltal Souls.* Austin: University of Texas Press, 2010.

Plummer, Ken. "Male Sexualities." In *Handbook of Studies on Men and Masculinities,* ed. Michael S. Kimmel, Jeff Hearn, and R. W. Connell, 178–95. Thousand Oaks, Calif.: Sage, 2005.

Pollock, Harry E. D. *The Puuc: An Architectural Survey of the Hill Country of Yucatan and Northern Campeche, Mexico.* Memoirs of the Peabody Museum of Archaeology and Ethnology 19, Harvard University. Cambridge, Mass.: Peabody Museum of Archaeology and Ethnology, Harvard University, 1980.

Potts, Alex. *Flesh and the Ideal: Winckelmann and the Origins of Art History.* New Haven: Yale University Press, 2000.

Powers, Karen Vieira. *Women in the Crucible of Conquest: The Gendered Genesis of Spanish American Society, 1500–1600.* Albuquerque: University of New Mexico Press, 2005.

Prager, Christian M. "Die Inschriften von Pusilha: Epigraphische Analyse und Rekonstruktion der Geschichte einer klassischen Maya-Stätte."

Master's thesis, Rheinischen Friedrich-Wilhelms-Universität zu Bonn, 2002.

Proskouriakoff, Tatiana. "Historical Data in the Inscriptions of Yaxchilan, Part I: The Reign of Shield Jaguar." *Estudios de Cultura Maya* 3 (1963): 149–69.

Proskouriakoff, Tatiana. *Maya History.* Austin: University of Texas Press, 1993.

Prufer, Keith M., and James E. Brady, eds. *Stone Houses and Earth Lords: Maya Religion in the Cave Context.* Boulder: University Press of Colorado, 2005.

Pugh, Timothy W., Prudence M. Rice, Evelyn Chan Nieto, and Don S. Rice. "A Chak'an Itza Center at Nixtun-Ch'ich', Petén, Guatemala." *Journal of Field Archaeology* 41 (2016): 1–16.

Quilter, Jeffrey. *The Moche of Ancient Peru: Media and Messages.* Cambridge, Mass.: Peabody Museum Press, 2011.

Radcliffe-Brown, Alfred R. "Age Organization—Terminology." *Man* 29 (1929): 21.

Reents-Budet, Dorie. *Painting the Maya Universe: Royal Ceramics of the Classic Period.* Durham, N.C.: Duke University Press, 1994.

Reents-Budet, Dorie, Ronald L. Bishop, Jennifer T. Taschek, and Joseph W. Ball. "Out of the Palace Dumps: Ceramic Production and Use at Buenavista del Cayo." *Ancient Mesoamerica* 11 (2000): 99–121.

Reina, Ruben E., and Robert M. Hill, II. *The Traditional Pottery of Guatemala.* Austin: University of Texas Press, 1978.

Remesal, Antonio de. *Historia general de las Indias Occidentales, y particular de la gobernación de Chiapa y Guatemala.* Biblioteca "Goathemala" de la Sociedad de Geografía e Historia, 4–5. Guatemala City: Tipografía Nacional, 1932.

Resić, Sanimir. "From Gilgamesh to Terminator: The Warrior as Masculine Ideal—Historical and Contemporary Perspective." In *Warfare and Society: Archaeological and Social Anthropological Perspectives,* ed. Ton Otto, Henrik Thrane, and Helle Veldkinde, 423–32. Aarhus: Aarhus University Press, 2006.

Ringle, William M. *Of Mice and Monkeys: The Value and Meaning of T1016, the God C Hieroglyph.* Research Reports on Ancient Maya Writing 18. Washington, D.C.: Center for Maya Research, 1988.

Ringle, William M. "Concordance of the Morán Dictionary of Ch'olti'." Digital file in possession of author, n.d.

Ripley, Amanda. "How America Outlawed Adolescence." *Atlantic,* November 2016. Accessed Oct. 12, 2016. http://www.theatlantic.com/magazine.

Robelo, Cecilio A. "Origen del calendario Náhuatl." *Anales del Museo Nacional de Arqueología, Historia y Etnología* 3 (1911): 337–50.

Robertson, John S., Danny Law, and Robbie Haertel. *Colonial Ch'olti': The Seventeenth-Century Morán Manuscript.* Norman: University of Oklahoma Press, 2010.

Robertson, Merle Greene. "The Giles G. Healey 1946 Bonampak Photographs." In *Third Palenque Round Table, 1978, Part 2,* ed. Merle G. Robertson, 3–44. Austin: University of Texas Press, 1980.

Robicsek, Francis, and Donald M. Hales. *The Maya Book of the Dead: The Ceramic Codex.* Charlottesville: University of Virginia Art Museum, 1981.

Rocke, Michael. *Forbidden Friendships: Homosexuality and Male Culture in Renaissance Florence.* New York: Oxford University Press, 1996.

Rodman, Margaret C. "Moving Houses: Residential Mobility and the Nobility of Residences in Longana, Vanuatu." *American Anthropologist* 87 (1985): 56–72.

Rogoff, Barbara. "Adults and Peers as Agents of Socialization: A Highland Guatemalan Profile." *Ethos* 9 (1981): 18–36.

Rojas, Araceli. "Casting Maize Seeds in an Ayöök Community: An Approach to the Study of Divination in Mesoamerica." *Ancient Mesoamerica* 27 (2016): 461–78.

Romero, Javier. "Dental Mutilation, Trephination and Cranial Deformation." In *Handbook of Middle American Indians, Volume 9: Physical Anthropology,* ed. Thomas D. Stewart, 50–67. Austin: University of Texas Press, 1970.

Roscoe, Will. *Changing Ones: Third and Fourth Genders in Native North America.* New York: St. Martin's, 1998.

Rosenwein, Barbara H. "Francia and Polynesia: Rethinking Anthropological Approaches." In *Negotiating the Gift: Pre-Modern Figurations of Exchange,* ed. Gadi Algazi, Valentin Groebner, and Bernhard Jussen, 361–79. Göttingen: Vandenhoeck and Ruprecht, 2003.

Rossi, Franco D. "The Brothers Taaj: Civil-Religious Orders and the Politics of Expertise in Late Maya Statecraft." Ph.D. diss., Boston University, 2015.

Roth, Christopher F. "Goods, Names, and Selves: Rethinking the Tsimshian Potlatch." *American Ethnologist* 29 (2002): 123–50.

Rousseau, Jean-Jacques. *Rousseau's Émile, or Treatise*

on Education. Ed. William H. Payne. New York: D. Appleton, 1918.

Rowe, Richard, Barbara Maughan, Carol M. Worthman, E. Jane Costello, and Adrian Angold. "Testosterone, Antisocial Behavior, and Social Dominance in Boys: Pubertal Development and Biosocial Interaction." *Biological Psychiatry* 55 (2004): 546–52.

Roys, Ralph L. *The Book of Chilam Balam of Chumayel.* Norman: University of Oklahoma Press, 1967.

Ruiz de Alarcón, Hernando. *Treatise on the Heathen Superstitions That Today Live Among the Indians Native to This New Spain, 1629.* Trans. and ed. J. Richard Andrews and Ross Hassig. Norman: University of Oklahoma Press, 1984.

Ruppert, Karl, J. Eric S. Thompson, and Tatiana Proskouriakoff. *Bonampak, Chiapas, Mexico.* Publication 602. Washington, D.C.: Carnegie Institution of Washington, 1955.

Rutgers WPF Pakistan and Adolescent Girls Empowerment Project. *The Puppets and the Puppeteers: An Account of Consultative Process on Child Marriages* (n.d.) Accessed Jan. 14, 2015. http://www.rutgerswpfpak.org/content/pdfs/IEC/AGE/AGE-CP-Report.pdf.

Rutter, Jeremy B. "Children in Aegean Prehistory." In *Coming of Age in Ancient Greece: Images of Childood from the Classical Past,* ed. Jenifer Neils and John H. Oakley, 30–57. New Haven: Yale University Press, 2003.

Ruz, Mario H. "Ecosistema y tradición: Notas sobre algunos procesos de cambio en la organizació." In *Los legítimos hombres: Aproximación antropológica al grupo tojolabal, Volumen III,* ed. Mario H. Ruz, 45–113. Mexico City: Centro de Estudios Mayas, Universidad Nacional Autónoma de México, 1982.

Ruz, Mario H. *Los legítimos hombres: Aproximación antropológica al grupo tojolabal, Volumen II.* Mexico City: Centro de Estudios Mayas, Universidad Nacional Autónoma de México, 1982.

Ruz Lhuillier, Alberto. *El Templo de las Inscripciones, Palenque.* Colección Científica Arqueología 7. Mexico City: Instituto de Antropología e Historia, 1973.

Sabloff, Jeremy A. *Excavations at Seibal, Department of Peten, Guatemala, Number 2: Ceramics.* Memoirs of the Peabody Museum of Archaeology and Ethnology 12, no. 2, Harvard University. Cambridge, Mass.: Harvard University, 1975.

Safronov, Alexander. "Yaxchilan Wars in the Reign of 'Itsamnaaj B'alam IV (771–ca. 800)." In *Wars and Conflicts in Prehispanic Mesoamerica and Andes,* ed. Peter Eeckhout and Geneviève Le Fort, 50–57. British Archaeological Report International Series 1385. Oxford: Archaeopress, 2005.

Sahagún, Bernardino de. *The Florentine Codex: General History of the Things of New Spain.* Trans. Arthur J. O. Anderson and Charles E. Dibble. Salt Lake City: University of Utah Press, 1950–1982.

Sahlins, Marshall D. *What Kinship Is… and Is Not.* Chicago: University of Chicago Press, 2013.

Sandstrom, Alan R. "The Weeping Baby and the Nahua Corn Spirit: The Human Body as Key Symbol in the Huasteca Veracruzana, Mexico." In *Mesoamerican Figurines: Small-Scale Indices of Large-Scale Social Phenomena,* ed. Christina T. Halperin, Katherine A. Faust, Rhonda Taube, and Aurore Giguet, 261–96. Gainesville: University Press of Florida, 2009.

Satterthwaite, Linton, Jr. "Maya Practice Stone-Carving at Piedras Negras." *Expedition* 7 (1965): 9–18.

Saturno, William A., Karl A. Taube, and David Stuart. *The Murals of San Bartolo, El Petén, Guatemala, Part 1: The North Wall.* Ancient America 7. Barnardsville, N.C.: Center for Ancient American Studies, 2005.

Saul, Frank P., and Julie M. Saul. "The Preclassic Population of Cuello." In *Cuello: An Early Maya Community in Belize,* ed. Norman Hammond, 134–58. Cambridge, Mass.: Cambridge University Press, 1991.

Schele, Linda. "Some Suggested Readings for the Event and Office of Heir-Designate at Palenque." In *Phoneticism in Mayan Hieroglyphic Writing,* ed. John S. Justeson and Lyle Campbell, 287–305. Institute for Mesoamerican Studies Monographs 9. Albany: State University of New York at Albany, 1984.

Schele, Linda. "The Hauberg Stela: Bloodletting and the Mythos of Maya Rulership." In *Fifth Palenque Round Table, 1983,* ed. M. G. Robertson and V. Fields, 135–50. San Francisco: Pre-Columbian Art Research Institute, 1985.

Schele, Linda. "Founders of Lineages at Copán and Other Maya Sites." *Ancient Mesoamerica* 3 (1992): 135–44.

Schele, Linda, and Mary E. Miller. *The Blood of Kings: Dynasty and Ritual in Maya Art.* Fort Worth, Tex.: Kimbell Art Museum, 1986.

Scherer, Andrew K. *Mortuary Landscapes of the Classic Maya: Rituals of Body and Soul.* Austin: University of Texas Press, 2015.

Scherer, Andrew K. "Osteology of the El Diablo Complex: Burial 9 and Associated Caches." In *Temple of the Night Sun: A Royal Tomb at El Diablo, Guatemala,* by Stephen Houston, Sarah Newman, Edwin Román, and Thomas Garrison, 180–207. San Francisco: Precolumbia Mesoweb, 2015.

Scherer, Andrew K., Charles Golden, Ana Lucía Arroyave, and Griselda Pérez Robles. "Danse Macabre: Death, Community, and Kingdom at El Kinel, Guatemala." In *The Bioarchaeology of Space and Place: Ideology, Power, and Meaning in Maya Mortuary Contexts,* ed. Gabriel Wrobel, 193–224. New York: Springer, 2014.

Schlegel, Alice, and Herbert Barry III. "The Evolutionary Significance of Adolescent Initiation Ceremonies." *American Ethnologist* 7 (1980): 696–715.

Schlegel, Alice, and Herbert Barry III. *Adolescence: An Anthropological Inquiry.* New York: Free Press, 1991.

Schlegel, Susanne. "Figuras en estuco en un chultún en Xkipché." *Mexicon* 19 (1997): 117–19.

Schmidt, Peter, Mercedes de la Garza, and Enrique Nalda. *Maya.* New York: Rizzoli, 1998.

Scholes, France V., and Ralph L. Roys. *The Maya Chontal Indians of Acalan-Tixchel: A Contribution to the History and Ethnography of the Yucatan Peninsula.* Norman: University of Oklahoma Press, 1968.

Schumann, Otto. *La lengua Chol, de Tila (Chiapas).* Centro de Estudios Mayas Cuaderno 8. Mexico City: Universidad Nacional Autónoma de México, 1973.

Schwartz, Barry. "The Social Psychology of the Gift." *American Journal of Sociology* 73 (1967): 1–11.

Schweizer, Paul D. *Thomas Cole's Voyage of Life.* Utica, N.Y.: Munson-Williams-Proctor Arts Institute, 2014.

Screech, Timon. *Sex and the Floating World: Erotic Images in Japan 1700–1820.* London: Reaktion, 1999.

Seaford, Richard. *Reciprocity and Ritual: Homer and Tragedy in the Developing City-State.* Oxford: Oxford University Press, 1994.

Sears, Elizabeth. *The Ages of Man: Medieval Interpretations of the Life Cycle.* Princeton: Princeton University Press, 1986.

Sedgwick, Eve. *Between Men: English Literature and Male Homosocial Desire.* New York: Columbia University Press, 1985.

Shankman, Paul. *The Trashing of Margaret Mead: Anatomy of an Anthropological Controversy.* Madison: University of Wisconsin Press, 2009.

Shankman, Paul. "The 'Fateful Hoaxing' of Margaret Mead: A Cautionary Tale." *Current Anthropology* 54 (2013): 51–70.

Shapiro, H. Allen. "Fathers and Sons, Men and Boys." In *Coming of Age in Ancient Greece: Images of Childhood from the Classical Past,* ed. Jenifer Neils and John H. Oakley, 84–111. Hanover, N.H.: Hood Museum of Art, 2003.

Sigal, Pete. *From Moon Goddesses to Virgins: The Colonization of Yucatecan Maya Sexual Desire.* Austin: University of Texas Press, 2000.

Sigal, Pete. "The Cuiloni, the Patlache, and the Abominable Sin: Homosexualities in Early Colonial Nahua Society." *Hispanic American Historical Review* 85 (2005): 555–94.

Sigal, Pete. "Queer Nahuatl: Sahagún's Faggots and Sodomites, Lesbians and Hermaphrodites." *Ethnohistory* 54 (2007): 9–34.

Sigal, Pete. *The Flower and the Scorpion: Sexuality and Ritual in Early Nahua Culture.* Durham, N.C.: Duke University Press, 2011.

Silber, Ilana. "Bourdieu's Gift to Gift Theory: An Unacknowledged Trajectory." *Sociological Theory* 27 (2009): 173–90.

Silbergeld, Jerome. "Chinese Concepts of Old Age and Their Role in Chinese Painting, Painting Theory, and Criticism." *Art Journal* 46 (1987): 103–14.

Simmel, Georg. *The Sociology of Georg Simmel.* Glencoe, Ill.: Free Press, 1950.

Simmel, Georg. "Faithfulness and Gratitude." In *The Gift: An Interdisciplinary Perspective,* ed. E. Komter Aafke, 39–48. Amsterdam: Amsterdam University Press, 1996.

Simons, Patricia. *The Sex of Men in Premodern Europe: A Cultural History.* Cambridge: Cambridge University Press, 2011.

Skardhamar, Torbjørn. "Reconsidering the Theory on Adolescent-Limited and Life-Course-Persistent Antisocial Behaviour." *British Journal of Criminology* 49 (2009): 863–78.

Skidmore, Joel. "Two Stelae from Dos Caobas." *Mesoweb Resources* (2013). Accessed Aug. 6, 2015. http://www.mesoweb.com.

Smailus, Ortwin. *El Maya-Chontal de Acalan: Análisis lingüístico de un documento de los años 1610–1612.* Centro de Estudios Mayas Cuaderno 9. Mexico City: Instituto de Investigaciones Estéticas, Universidad Nacional Autónoma de México, 1975.

Smith, A. Ledyard. *Uaxactun, Guatemala: Excavations of 1931–1937.* Publication 588. Washington, D.C.: Carnegie Institution of Washington, 1950.

Smith, A. Ledyard, and Alfred V. Kidder. *Explorations

in the Motagua Valley, Guatemala. Contributions to American Anthropology and History 41. Washington, D.C.: Carnegie Institution of Washington, 1943.

Smith, B. Holly. "Standards of Human Tooth Formation and Dental Age Assessment." *Advances in Dental Anthropology,* ed. Marc A. Kelley and Clark Spencer Larsen, 143–68. New York: Wiley-Liss, 1991.

Smith, Robert E. *Ceramic Sequence at Uaxactun, Guatemala, Volume 2.* Middle American Research Institute Publication 20. New Orleans: Tulane University, 1955.

Snow, Dean R. "Sexual Dimorphism in European Upper Paleolithic Cave Art." *American Antiquity* 78 (2014): 746–61.

Sousa, Lisa. "Tying the Knot: Nahua Nuptials in Colonial Central Mexico." In *Religion in New Spain,* ed. Susan Schroeder and Stafford Poole, 33–65. Albuquerque: University of New Mexico Press, 2007.

Sparrow, John. *Visible Words: A Study of Inscriptions in and as Books and Works of Art.* Cambridge: Cambridge University Press, 1969.

Spencer, Robert F., and Samuel A. Barrett. "Notes on a Bachelor House in the South China Area." *American Anthropologist,* n.s. 50 (1948): 463–78.

Spickard, James V. "A Guide to Mary Douglas's Three Versions of Grid/Group Theory." *Sociological Analysis* 50 (1989): 151–71.

Staines Cicero, Leticia. "Bonampak a través de las copias de Augustín Villagra." In *La pintura mural prehispánica en México I, Área maya, Tomo II: Bonampak, Estudios,* ed. Leticia Staines Cicero, 255–98. Mexico City: Instituto de Investigaciones Estéticas, Universidad Nacional Autónoma de México, 1998.

Staines Cicero, Leticia., ed. *La pintura mural pre-hispánica en México II, Área maya, Tomo II (1 and 2): Bonampak.* Mexico City: Instituto de Investigaciones Estéticas, Universidad Nacional Autónoma de México, 1998.

Stanzione, Vincent. *Rituals of Sacrifice: Walking the Face of the Earth on the Sacred Path of the Sun.* Albuquerque: University of New Mexico Press, 2003.

Steinberg, Laurence. *The Age of Opportunity: Lessons from the New Science of Adolescence.* New York: Houghton Mifflin Harcourt, 2014.

Steinberg, Laurence, and Richard M. Lerner. "The Scientific Study of Adolescence: A Brief History." *Journal of Early Adolescence* 24 (2004): 45–54.

Stewart, Alison G. *Unequal Lovers: A Study of Unequal Couples.* New York: Abaris, 1977.

Stewart, Andrew. *Art, Desire, and the Body in Ancient Greece.* Cambridge: Cambridge University Press, 1997.

Stewart, Andrew, and Celina Gray. "Confronting the Other: Childbirth, Aging, and Death on an Attic Tombstone at Harvard." In *Not the Classical Ideal: Athens and the Construction of the Other in Greek Art,* ed. Beth Cohen, 248–74. Leiden: Brill, 2000.

Stewart, Frank H. *Fundamentals of Age-Group Systems.* New York: Academic Press, 1977.

Stierlin, Henri. *Mexique, Terre des Dieux, trésors de l'art précolumbien.* Geneva: Musées d'Art et d'Histoire, 1998.

St. John, Graham, ed. *Victor Turner and Contemporary Cultural Performance.* New York: Berghahn, 2008.

Stone, Andrea J. "Commentary." *Mexicon* 9 (1987): 37.

Stone, Andrea J. "Disconnection, Foreign Insignia and Political Expansion: Teotihuacan and the Warrior Stelae of Piedras Negras." In *Mesoamerica After the Decline of Teotihuacan AD 700–900,* ed. Richard A. Diehl and Janet Catherine Berlo, 153–72. Washington, D.C.: Dumbarton Oaks Research Library and Collection, 1989.

Stone, Andrea J. "Aspects of Impersonation in Classic Maya Art." In *Sixth Palenque Round Table, 1986,* ed. Virginia M. Fields, 194–202. Norman: University of Oklahoma Press, 1991.

Stone, Andrea J. *Images from the Underworld: Naj Tunich and the Tradition of Maya Cave Painting.* Austin: University of Texas Press, 1995.

Stone, Andrea J., and Marc U. Zender. *Reading Maya Art: A Hieroglyphic Guide to Ancient Maya Painting and Sculpture.* London: Thames and Hudson, 2011.

Stone, Rachel. "Masculinity Without Conflict: Noblemen in Eighth- and Ninth-Century Francia." In *What Is Masculinity? Historical Dynamics from Antiquity to the Contemporary World,* ed. John H. Arnold and Sean Brady, 76–93. Basingstoke, England: Palgrave Macmillan, 2011.

Strathern, Andrew. "Men's House, Women's House: The Efficacy of Opposition, Reversal, and Pairing in the Melpa *Amb Kor* Cult." *Journal of the Polynesian Society* 88 (1979): 37–51.

Stross, Brian. "Tzeltal Marriage by Capture." *Anthropology Quarterly* 47 (1974): 328–46.

Stuart, David. "The Inscription on Four Shell Plaques from Piedras Negras, Guatemala." In *Fourth Palenque Round Table, 1980,* ed. Elizabeth P. Benson, 175–83. San Francisco: Pre-Columbian Art Research Institute, San Francisco, 1985.

Stuart, David. *Ten Phonetic Syllables.* Research Reports on Ancient Maya Writing 14. Washington, D.C.: Center for Maya Research, 1987.

Stuart, David. "Hieroglyphs on Maya Vessels." In *The Maya Vase Book: A Corpus of Rollout Photographs of Maya Vases, Volume 1,* ed. Justin Kerr, 213–14. New York: Kerr Associates, 1989.

Stuart, David. "The Maya Artist: An Iconographic and Epigraphic Analysis." Bachelor's thesis, Princeton University, 1989.

Stuart, David. "Kings of Stone: A Consideration of Stelae in Ancient Maya Ritual and Representation." *RES: Anthropology and Aesthetics* 29/30 (1996): 148–71.

Stuart, David. "Kinship Terms in Maya Inscriptions." In *The Language of Maya Hieroglyphs,* ed. Martha Macri, 1–11. San Francisco: Pre-Columbian Art Research Institute, San Francisco, 1997.

Stuart, David. " 'The Fire Enters His House': Architecture and Ritual in Classic Maya Texts." In *Function and Meaning in Classic Maya Architecture,* ed. Stephen Houston, 373–425. Washington, D.C.: Dumbarton Oaks Research Library and Collection, Washington, 1998.

Stuart, David. " 'The Arrival of Strangers': Teotihuacan and Tollan in Classic Maya History." In *Mesoamerica's Classic Heritage: From Teotihuacan to the Aztecs,* ed. Davíd Carrasco, Lindsay Jones, and Scott Sessions, 465–514. Boulder: University Press of Colorado, 2000.

Stuart, David. "The Royal Child: Notes on Youths in Classic Maya History and Ritual." Notes in possession of author, 2002.

Stuart, David. "On the Paired Variants of TZ'AK. *Mesoweb* (2003): 1–5. Accessed Aug. 2, 2015. http://www.mesoweb.com.

Stuart, David. "New Year Records in Classic Maya Inscriptions." *PARI Journal* 5 (2004): 1–6.

Stuart, David. *Glyphs on Pots: Decoding Classic Maya Ceramics.* Sourcebook for the 29th Maya Meetings at Texas, The University of Texas at Austin, 2005. Accessed Mar. 6, 2017. http://decipherment.files.wordpress.com/2013/09/stuartceramictexts.pdf.

Stuart, David. "Ideology and Classic Maya Kingship." In *A Catalyst for Ideas: Anthropological Archaeology and the Legacy of Douglas Schwartz,* ed. Vernon L. Scarborough, 257–85. Santa Fe, N. Mex.: School of American Research, 2005.

Stuart, David. *The Inscriptions from Temple XIX at Palenque: A Commentary.* San Francisco: Pre-Columbian Art Research Institute, 2005.

Stuart, David. "The Great Bird's Descent: Tracing the Legacy and Meaning of a Foundational Myth in Maya and Mesoamerican Religion." Paper presented at Ecology, Power, and Religion in Maya Landscapes, 11th European Maya Conference, Malmö University, December 2006.

Stuart, David. "Jade and Chocolate: Bundles of Wealth in Classic Maya Economics and Ritual." In *Sacred Bundles: Ritual Acts of Wrapping and Binding in Mesoamerica,* ed. Julia Guernsey and F. Kent Reilly III, 127–44. Barnardsville, N.C.: Boundary End Archaeology Research Center, 2006.

Stuart, David. "A Brief Introduction to Maya Writing." In *Sourcebook, the XXXI Maya Meetings: Inscriptions of the River Cities, Yaxchilan, Piedras Negras, and Pomona, March 9–14, 2007,* by David Stuart, 67–158. Austin: Mesoamerica Center, Department of Art and Art History, University of Texas at Austin, 2007.

Stuart, David. "The Maya Hieroglyphs for *Mam,* 'Grandfather, Grandson, Ancestor.' " *Maya Decipherment: A Weblog on the Ancient Maya Script* (2007). Accessed Oct. 1, 2014. http://decipherment.wordpress.com/2007/09/29/the-mam-glyph/.

Stuart, David. "Old Notes on the Possible ITZAM Sign." *Maya Decipherment: A Weblog on the Ancient Maya Script* (2007). Accessed Aug. 17, 2015. https://decipherment.wordpress.com/2007/09/29/old-notes-on-the-possible-itzam-sign/.

Stuart, David. "Bonampak's Place Name." *Maya Decipherment: A Weblog on the Ancient Maya Script* (2008). Accessed Oct. 7, 2011. https://decipherment.wordpress.com/2008/03/16/bonampaks-place-name/.

Stuart, David. "A Childhood Ritual on the Hauberg Stela." *Maya Decipherment: A Weblog on the Ancient Maya Script* (2008). Accessed Jan. 14, 2015. https://decipherment.wordpress.com/2008/03/27/a-childhood-ritual-on-the-hauberg-stela/.

Stuart, David. "The Chocolatier's Dog." *Maya Decipherment: A Weblog on the Ancient Maya Script* (2014). Accessed June 24, 2016. https://decipherment.wordpress.com/2014/03/26/the-chocolatiers-dog/.

Stuart, David. "Four Interesting Logograms." Paper presented at the Word in Context: Perspectives and Strategies for the Lexicography of Classic Mayan, Nordrhein-Westfälische Akademie der Wissenschaften und der Künste, Düsseldorf, October 2014.

Stuart, David, and Ian Graham. *Corpus of Maya Hieroglyphic Inscriptions, Volume 9, Part 1: Piedras Negras.* Cambridge, Mass.: Peabody Museum of

Archaeology and Ethnology, Harvard University, 2003.

Stuart, David, and George Stuart. *Palenque: Eternal City of the Maya.* London: Thames and Hudson, 2008.

Stuart, David, and Peter Stuart. "An Early Classic Bird Vase." *Maya Decipherment: A Weblog on the Ancient Maya Script* (2015). Accessed July 15, 2016. https://decipherment.wordpress.com/2015/02/09/an-early-classic-bird-vase/.

Sutton, Robert F., Jr. "The Good, the Base, and the Ugly: The Drunken Orgy in Attic Vase Painting and the Athenian Self." In *Not the Classical Ideal: Athens and the Construction of the Other in Greek Art,* ed. Beth Cohen, 180–202. Leiden: Brill, 2000.

Taddei, Ilaria. *Fanciulli e giovani: Crescere a Firenze nel Rinascimento.* Florence: Leo S. Olschki, 2001.

Tarn, Nathaniel, and Martin Prechtel. "Constant Inconstancy: The Feminine Principle in Atiteco Mythology." In *Symbol and Meaning Beyond the Closed Community: Essays in Mesoamerican Ideas,* ed. Gary H. Gossen, 173–84. Studies on Culture and Society 1. Albany: Institute for Mesoamerican Studies, State University of New York at Albany, 1986.

Tarr, Roger P. " 'Visible Parlare': The Spoken Word in Fourteenth-Century Central Italian Painting." *Word and Image* 13 (1997): 223–44.

Tate, Carolyn E. *Yaxchilan: The Design of a Maya Ceremonial City.* Austin: University of Texas Press, 1992.

Taube, Karl A. "The Classic Maya Maize God: A Reappraisal." In *Fifth Palenque Round Table, 1983,* ed. Virginia M. Fields, 171–81. San Francisco: Pre-Columbian Art Research Institute, 1985.

Taube, Karl A. "Ritual Humor in Classic Maya Religion." In *Word and Image in Maya Culture: Explorations in Language, Writing, and Representation,* ed. William F. Hanks and Don S. Rice, 351–82. Salt Lake City: University of Utah Press, 1989.

Taube, Karl A. *The Major Gods of Ancient Yucatan.* Studies in Pre-Columbian Art and Archaeology 32. Washington, D.C.: Dumbarton Oaks Research Library and Collection, 1992.

Taube, Karl A. "The Temple of Quetzalcoatl and the Cult of Sacred War at Teotihuacan." *RES: Anthropology and Aesthetics* 21 (1992): 53–87.

Taube, Karl A. "The Birth Vase: Natal Imagery in Ancient Maya Myth and Ritual." In *The Maya Vase Book, Volume 4: A Corpus of Rollout Photographs of Maya Vases,* ed. Justin Kerr, 652–85. New York: Kerr Associates, 1994.

Taube, Karl A. "Ancient and Contemporary Maya Conceptions About the Field and Forest." In *The Lowland Maya Area: Three Millennia at the Human Wildland Interface,* ed. Arturo Gómez-Pompa, Michael F. Allen, Scott L. Fedick, and Juan J. Jiménez-Osorino, 461–92. Binghamton, N.Y.: Haworth, 2003.

Taube, Karl A. "Structure 10L-16 and Its Early Classic Antecedents: Fire and the Evocation and Resurrection of K'inich Yax K'uk' Mo'." In *Understanding Early Classic Copan,* ed. Ellen Bell, Marcello Canuto, and Robert Sharer, 265–95. Philadelphia: University of Pennsylvania Museum, 2003.

Taube, Karl A. "Tetitla and the Maya Presence at Teotihuacan." In *The Maya and Teotihuacan: Reinterpreting Early Classic Interaction,* ed. Geoffrey E. Braswell, 273–314. Austin: University of Texas Press, 2003.

Taube, Karl., and Marc Zender. "American Gladiators: Ritual Boxing in Ancient Mesoamerica." In *Blood and Beauty: Organized Violence in the Art and Archaeology of Mesoamerica and Central America,* ed. Heather Orr and Rex Koontz, 161–220. Los Angeles: Cotsen Institute of Archaeology Press, 2009.

Taube, Karl A., William A. Saturno, David Stuart, and Heather Hurst. *The Murals of San Bartolo, El Petén, Guatemala, Part 2: The West Wall.* Ancient America 10. Bernardsville, N.C.: Boundary End Archaeology Research Center, 2010.

Taube, Rhonda, and Karl Taube. "The Beautiful, the Bad, and the Ugly: Aesthetics and Morality in Maya Figurines." In *Mesoamerican Figurines: Small-Scale Indices of Large-Scale Social Phenomena,* ed. Christina T. Halperin, Katherine A. Faust, Rhonda Taube, and Aurora Giuget, 236–58. Gainesville: University Press of Florida, 2009.

Teiwes, Helga. *Kachina Dolls: The Art of Hopi Carvers.* Tucson: University of Arizona Press, 1991.

Thoen, Irma. *Strategic Affection? Gift Exchange in Seventeenth-Century Holland.* Amsterdam: Amsterdam University Press, 2007.

Thomas, Nicholas. *Entangled Objects: Exchange, Material Culture, and Colonialism in the Pacific.* Cambridge, Mass.: Harvard University Press, 1991.

Thompson, Edward P. "Folklore, Anthropology, and Social History." *Indian Historical Review* 3 (1977): 252–72.

Thompson, J. Eric S. *Ethnology of the Mayas of Southern and Central British Honduras.* Field Museum Anthropological Series 17. Chicago: Field Museum, 1930.

Thompson, J. Eric S. "Sixteenth and Seventeenth Century Reports on the Chol Mayas." *American Anthropologist* 40 (1938): 584–604.

Thompson, J. Eric S. *Thomas Gage's Travels in the New World.* Norman: University of Oklahoma Press, 1958.

Thompson, J. Eric S. *The Rise and Fall of Maya Civilization.* 2nd ed. Norman: University of Oklahoma Press, 1966.

Thompson, J. Eric S. "Bacabs: Their Portraits and Their Glyphs." In *Monographs and Papers in Archaeology*, ed. William R. Bullard, 459–65. Papers of the Peabody Museum of Archaeology and Ethnology 61. Cambridge, Mass.: Harvard University, 1970.

Thompson, J. Eric S. *Maya History and Religion.* Norman: University of Oklahoma Press, 1970.

Thompson, J. Eric S. *Maya Hieroglyphic Writing: An Introduction.* 3rd ed. Norman: University of Oklahoma Press, 1971.

Tiesler, Vera. "Studying Cranial Vault Modifications in Ancient Mesoamerica." *Journal of Anthropological Sciences* 90 (2012): 1–26.

Tokovinine, Alexandre. "Painted Vessel: Plate 62." In *Ancient Maya Art at Dumbarton Oaks*, ed. Joanne Pillsbury, Miriam Doutriaux, Reiko Ishihara-Brito, and Alexandre Tokovinine, 344–53. Pre-Columbian Art at Dumbarton Oaks 4. Washington, D.C.: Dumbarton Oaks Research Library and Collection, 2012.

Tokovinine, Alexandre. "Two Vessels in the Tucson Museum of Art." In *Pre-Columbian Art: Selections from the Tucson Museum of Art Permanent Collection*, ed. Katie E. Perry, 14–22. Tucson, Ariz.: Tucson Museum of Art, 2014.

Topper, Kathryn. *The Imagery of the Athenian Symposium.* Cambridge: Cambridge University Press, 2012.

Tovalín Ahumada, A., and V. M. Ortiz Villareal. "Avances en la historia constructive de la acropolis de Bonampak o ¿qué hubo antes de Chan Muan II?" In *Estudios del patrimonio cultural de Chiapas*, ed. Alejandro Sheseña, Sophia Pincemin, and Carlos Uriel del Carpio, 85–107. Tuxtla Gutiérrez, Mexico: Universidad de Ciencias y Artes de Chiapas, 2008.

Tozzer, Alfred M. *Landa's Relación de las cosas de Yucatan.* Papers of the Peabody Museum of Archaeology and Ethnology 18. Cambridge, Mass.: Harvard University, 1941.

Trexler, Richard C. "Ritual in Florence: Adolescence and Salvation in the Renaissance." In *The Pursuit of Holiness in Late Medieval and Renaissance Religion*, ed. Charles Trinkhaus and Heiko Oberman, 200–264. Leiden: Brill, 1974.

Trexler, Richard C. "Making the American Berdache: Choice or Constraint?" *Journal of Social History* 35 (2002): 613–33.

Trexler, Richard C. "Gender Subordination and Political Hierarchy in Pre-Hispanic America." In *Infamous Desire: Male Homosexuality in Colonial Latin America*, ed. Pete Sigal, 70–101. Chicago: University of Chicago Press, 2003.

Troyansky, David G. *Old Age in the Old Regime: Image and Experience in Eighteenth-Century France.* Ithaca, N.Y.: Cornell University Press, 1989.

Turner, James W. "Kinship Matters: Structures of Alliance, Indigenous Foragers, and the Austronesian Diaspora." *Human Biology* 85 (2013): 359–81.

Turner, Jeffrey S. "To Tell a Good Tale: Kierkegaardian Reflections on Moral Narrative and Moral Truth." In *Kierkegaard After MacIntyre Essays on Freedom, Narrative, and Virtue*, ed. John J. Davenport, and Anthony Rudd, 39–57. Peru, Ill.: Open Court, 2001.

Turner, Victor. *The Ritual Process: Structure and Anti-Structure.* New York: Aldine de Gruyter, 1969.

Turner, Victor. *Dramas, Fields, and Metaphors: Symbolic Action in Human Society.* Ithaca, N.Y.: Cornell University Press, 1975.

Turton, David. "Territorial Organisation and Age Among the Mursi." In *Age, Generation, and Time: Some Features of East African Age Organisations*, ed. P. T. W. Baxter and Uri Almagor, 95–131. New York: St. Martin's, 1978.

Udry, J. Richard, and John O. G. Billy. "Initiation of Coitus in Early Adolescence." *American Sociological Review* 52 (1987): 841–55.

Uglow, Jenny. *Hogarth: A Life and a World.* New York: Farrar, Straus and Giroux, 1997.

Urdal, Henrik. "A Clash of Generations? Youth Bulges and Political Violence." *International Studies Quarterly* 50 (2006): 607–29.

Urton, Gary. "Animal Metaphors and the Life Cycle in an Andean Community." In *Animal Myths and Metaphors in South America*, ed. Gary Urton, 251–84. Salt Lake City: University of Utah Press, 1985.

Vale de Almeida, Miguel. "Gender, Masculinity and Power in Southern Portugal." *Social Anthropology* 5 (1996): 141–58.

van Bokhoven, Irene, Stephanie H. M. van Goozen, Herman van Engeland, Benoist Schaal, Louise Arseneault, J. R. Séguine, Jean-Marc Assaad, Daniel S. Nagin, Frank Vitaro, and Richard E. Tremblay. "Salivary Testosterone and

Aggression, Delinquency, and Social Dominance in a Population-Based Longitudinal Study of Adolescent Males." *Hormones and Behavior* 50 (2006): 118–25.

van Gennep, Arnold. *The Rites of Passage.* Trans. Manika B. Vizedom and Gabrielle L. Caffee. Chicago: University of Chicago Press, 1960.

Vautravers, Alexandre J. "Why Child Soldiers Are Such a Complex Issue." *Refugee Survey Quarterly* 27 (2008): 96–107.

Vidal-Naquet, Pierre. *The Black Hunter: Forms of Thought and Forms of Society in the Greek World.* Trans. Andrew Szegedy-Maszak. Baltimore: Johns Hopkins University, 1986.

Villagutierre, Juan de. *Historia de la conquista de Itzá.* Madrid: Historia 16, 1985.

Villela, Khristaan. *Ancient Civilizations of the Americas: Man, Nature and Spirit in Pre-Columbian Art.* Kōka, Japan: Miho Museum, 2011.

Vogt, Evon Z. *Zinacantan: A Maya Community in the Highlands of Chiapas.* Cambridge, Mass.: Belknap Press, Harvard University Press, 1969.

Vogt, Evon Z. *Tortillas for the Gods: A Symbolic Analysis of Zinacanteco Rituals.* Cambridge, Mass.: Harvard University Press, 1976.

Wagner, Roy. "Ritual as Communication: Order, Meaning, and Secrecy in Melanesian Initiation Rites." *Annual Review of Anthropology* 13 (1984): 143–55.

Wagner-Hasel, Beate. "Egoistic Exchange and Altruistic Gift: On the Roots of Marcel Mauss's Theory of the Gift." In *Negotiating the Gift: Pre-Modern Figurations of Exchange,* ed. Gadi Algazi, Valentin Groebner, and Bernhard Jussen, 141–71. Göttingen: Vandenhoeck and Ruprecht, 2003.

Wallach, Alan. "The Voyage of Life as Popular Art." *Art Bulletin* 59 (1977): 234–41.

Walpole, Horace. *Memoirs of King George II.* Ed. John Brooke. 3 vols. New Haven: Yale University Press, 1985.

Walsh, David. *Distorted Ideals in Greek Vase-Painting: The World of Mythological Burlesque.* Cambridge: Cambridge University Press, 2009.

Ware, Gene, Stephen Houston, Mary Miller, Karl Taube, and Beatriz de la Fuente. "Infrared Imaging of Precolumbian Murals at Bonampak, Chiapas, Mexico." *Antiquity* 76 (2002): 325–26.

Watanabe, John M. *Maya Saints and Souls in a Changing World.* Austin: University of Texas Press, 1992.

Waterson, Roxana. "Houses and Hierarchies in Island Southeast Asia." In *About the House: Lévi-Strauss and Beyond,* ed. Janet Carsten and Stephen Hugh-Jones, 47–68. Cambridge: Cambridge University Press, 1995.

Webster, David. "The House of the Bacabs: Its Social Context." In *The House of the Bacabs, Copan, Honduras,* ed. David Webster, 5–40. Studies in Pre-Columbian Art and Archaeology 29. Washington, D.C.: Dumbarton Oaks Research Library and Collection, 1989.

Weiner, Annette B. *Inalienable Possessions: The Paradox of Keeping-While-Giving.* Berkeley: University of California Press, 1992.

Weismantel, Mary. "Moche Sex Pots: Reproduction and Temporality in Ancient South America." *American Anthropologist* 106 (2004): 495–505.

Weitlaner, Roberto J., and Searle Hoogshagen. "Grados de edad en Oaxaca." *Revista mexicana de estudios antropológicos* 16 (1960): 183–209.

Wendrich, Willeke. "Archaeology and Apprenticeship: Body Knowledge, Identity, and Communities of Practice." In *Archaeology and Apprenticeship: Body Knowledge, Identity, and Communities of Practice,* ed. Willeke Wendrich, 1–19. Tucson: University of Arizona Press, 2013.

White, Randall. *Dark Caves, Bright Visions: Life in Ice Age Europe.* New York: American Museum of Natural History, 1986.

White, Randall. "Looking for Biological Meaning in Cave Art." *American Scientist* 94 (2006): 361.

Whitehouse, Harvey. *Arguments and Icons: Divergent Modes of Religiosity.* Oxford: Oxford University Press, 2000.

Whiting Beatrice B., and Carolyn P. Edwards, 1988. *Children of Different Worlds: The Social Formation of Social Behavior.* Cambridge, Mass.: Harvard University Press, 1988.

Wichmann, Søren. "Mayan Historical Linguistics and Epigraphy: A New Synthesis." *Annual Review of Anthropology* 35 (2006): 279–94.

Williams, Craig A. *Roman Homosexuality.* 2nd ed. Oxford: Oxford University Press, 2010.

Williams, Jocelyn S., and Christine D. White. "Dental Modification in the Postclassic Population from Lamanai, Belize." *Ancient Mesoamerica* 17 (2006): 139–51.

Wilson, Adrian. "The Infancy of the History of Childhood: An Appraisal of Philippe Ariès." *History and Theory: Studies in the Philosophy of History* 19 (1980): 132–52.

Wilson, Richard. *Maya Resurgence in Guatemala: Q'eqchi' Experiences.* Norman: University of Oklahoma Press, 1995.

Wisdom, Charles. *The Chorti Indians of Guatemala.* Chicago: University of Chicago Press, 1940.

Wisdom, Charles. Materials on the Chorti Language. University of Chicago Microfilm Collection of Manuscripts of Cultural Anthropology 28. Chicago: Joseph Regenstein Library, University of Chicago, 1950.

Worthman, Carol M. "Adolescence in the Pacific: A Biosocial View." In *Adolescence in Pacific Island Societies,* ed. Gilbert Herdt and S. C. Leavitt, 27–52. Pittsburgh: University of Pittsburgh Press, 1998.

Wright, Lori E. "Immigration to Tikal, Guatemala: Evidence from Stable Strontium and Oxygen Isotopes." *Journal of Anthropological Archaeology* 31 (2012): 334–52.

Wright, Lori E., Henry Schwarcz, and Renaldo Acevedo. "La dieta de los habitantes de Topoxté, una reconstrucción isotópica." In *El sitio maya de Topoxté: Investigaciones en una isla del Lago Yaxhá, Petén, Guatemala,* ed. Wolfgang Wurster, 158–64. Mainz: Verlag Philipp von Zabern, 2000.

Ximénez, Francisco de. *Historia de la provincia de San Vicente de Chiapas y Guatemala de la orden de predicadores.* 3 vols. Guatemala City: Tipografía Nacional, 1929–31.

Xiu, Gaspar Antonio. *Usos y costumbres de los indios de Yucatán.* Mérida, Yucatan: Maldonado Editores, 1986.

Yarborough, Alison. "Apprentices as Adolescents in Sixteenth-Century Bristol." *Journal of Social History* 13 (1979): 67–81.

Yarrow, Simon. "Masculinity as a World Historical Category of Analysis." In *What Is Masculinity? Historical Dynamics from Antiquity to the Contemporary World,* ed. John H. Arnold and Sean Brady, 114–38. Basingstoke, England: Palgrave Macmillan, 2011.

Yoffee, Norman. *Myths of the Archaic State: Evolution of the Earliest Cities, States, and Civilizations.* Cambridge: Cambridge University Press, 2005.

Zagorevski, Dmitri V., and Jennifer A. Loughmiller-Newman. "The Detection of Nicotine in a Late Mayan Period Flask by Gas Chromatography and Liquid Chromatography Mass Spectrometry Methods." *Rapid Communications in Mass Spectrometry* 26 (2012): 403–11.

Zender, Marc U. "The Morphology of Intimate Possession in Mayan Languages and Classic Maya Glyphic Nouns." In *The Linguistics of Maya Writing,* ed. Søren Wichmann, 195–209. Salt Lake City: University of Utah Press, 2004.

Zender, Marc U. "A Study of Classic Maya Priesthood." Ph.D. diss., University of Calgary, 2004.

Zender, Marc U. "Teasing the Turtle from Its Shell: AHK and MAHK in Maya Writing." *PARI Journal* 6 (2005): 1–14.

Zender, Marc U. "On the Reading of Three Classic Maya Portrait Glyphs." *PARI Journal* 15 (2014): 1–14.

Zender, Marc U., Ricardo Armijo, and Judith M. Gallegos. "Vida y obra de Aj Pakal Tahn, un sacerdote del siglo VIII en Comalcalco, Tabasco, México." *Los investigadores de la Cultura Maya* 9 (2001): 387–98.

(fig. 68); reconstruction, Yale University Art Gallery,
Gift of Bonampak Documentation Project, illustrated
by Heather Hurst and Leonard Ashby (figs. 70, 71,
73, 74, 76); images by Stephen Houston and Gene
Ware, courtesy of the Bonampak Documentation
Project (fig. 75); photograph by David Stuart (fig. 78);
photograph by Claudia Obrocki, © Ethnologisches
Museum, Staatliche Museen zu Berlin (fig. 79);
© Bibliothèque de l'Assemblée Nationale (fig. 80);
© Biblioteca Medicea-Laurenziana, photography
by Donato Pineider (figs. 82, 89); photograph by
Rick Frehsee, courtesy of Barbara Fash (fig. 85);
© Dumbarton Oaks, Pre-Columbian Collection,
Washington, D.C. (fig. 87); © ImageBROKER/Alamy
Stock Photo (fig. 88); © The Cleveland Museum of
Art (fig. 91).